0043281

DATE DUE

APR 20 1994	
APR 26 1995	
APR 21 1997	
MAY 12 1997	

TT
507
C92
1988

Cunningham,
Rebecca.

The magic garment

$23.77

THE MAGIC GARMENT

*I don't want realism. I want magic! Yes, yes, magic!
I try to give that to people.*

A STREETCAR NAMED DESIRE   Tennessee Williams

THE MAGIC GARMENT

Principles of Costume Design

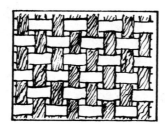

REBECCA CUNNINGHAM

Brooklyn College

Longman

New York & London

The Magic Garment: Principles of Costume Design

Longman Inc., 95 Church Street, White Plains, N.Y. 10601

Associated companies:
Longman Group Ltd., London
Longman Cheshire Pty., Melbourne
Longman Paul Pty., Auckland
Copp. Clark Pitman, Toronto
Pitman Publishing Inc., New York

Executive editor: Gordon T.R. Anderson
Production editor: Elsa van Bergen
Text and cover design: Jill Francis Wood
Costume Design by Judith Dolan,
    The Barber of Seville,
    New York City Opera, 1984
Production supervisor: Judith Stern

Library of Congress Cataloging-in-Publication Data

Cunningham, Rebecca.
    Principles of costume design.

    Bibliography: p.
    1. Costume design. 2. Costume. 3. Theater—Production and direction. I. Title.
TT507.C92 1988   792'.026   88-640

ISBN 0-8013-0062-3

89 90 91 92   9 8 7 6 5 4 3 2 1

Acknowledgments

Frontis: Tennessee Williams, *A Streetcar Named Desire*. Copyright 1947 by Tennessee Williams. Reprinted by permission of New Directions Publishing Corporation.

p. 17: From *The Glass Menagerie*, by Tennessee Williams, © 1945 by Tennessee Williams and Edwina Williams. Renewed © 1973 Tennessee Williams. Reprinted with permission of Random House Inc.

pp. 29, 192: From *Remembrance of Things Past* by Marcel Proust. Translated by C.K. Scott Moncrieff & Frederick A. Blossom. © 1932 renewed 1960 by Random House Inc. Reprinted with permission of Random House Inc.

p. 36: From *The Bald Soprano* by Eugene Ionesco. Reprinted with permission of Grove Press.

p. 40: From *Pygmalion* by Bernard Shaw. Reprinted with permission of The Society of Authors on behalf of the Bernard Shaw Estate.

pp. 46, 55, 85: From *Cyrano de Bergerac* by Brian Hooker. Translated by Edmond Rostand. © 1923 Holt, Rinehart, and Winston. © 1951 by Doris C. Hooker. Reprinted with permission of Holt, Rinehart and Winston.

p. 78: From *The Fantasticks* by Tom Jones and Harvey Schmidt. Drama Book Specialist Publishers. New York, 1968. Reprinted with permission.

p. 97: From *Of Mice and Men* by John Steinbeck. © 1937 John Steinbeck. Renewed by John Steinbeck. Reprinted with permission of Viking Penguin Inc.

p. 105: From *Sonia Debuney: Rhythmes et Couleurs*, Hermann, editeurs de sciences et des arts. Paris, 1971.

pp. 183, 229: From "The Weavers" by Gerhart Hauptmann. Translated by Mary Morison. Taken for *Dramatic Works, Vol. One: Social Dramas* by Gerhart Hauptmann, edited by Ludwig Lewisohn. © 1913 by B.W. Huebsch, Inc. Renewed © 1940 by Ludwig Lewisohn. Reprinted with permission of Viking Penguin Inc.

p. 262: From "The Misanthrope" by Moliere from MOLIERE: *The Misanthrope and Other Plays*. Translated by John Wood (Penguin Classics 1959), p. 48. © 1948 John Wood, 1959.

Illustration credits appear with the captions.

To my daughter, husband, friends, and students

Contents

Foreword

Beckie Cunningham entered my life some eighteen years ago. By some incredible stroke of good fortune, I had received a scholarship to study costumes at Brooklyn College. Beckie was one of the faculty members.

For two years she laid down a foundation of knowledge which has stood me well to this day. She taught me primarily refinement of line . . . then the overriding importance of color . . . then an attention to detail. She taught me approaches to a problem, not solutions to a specific. She gave me the tools with which to ply my art and craft.

In the years since I was a student, I have seen Beckie work and grow with her foundations of design. Her exquisitely refined line can become rags. Her breathtaking colors can become garish with a hard black line around them. Her details can be stripped to nothing. It is this adaptability to a show that makes a costume designer exactly that.

In this book Beckie has laid out those design foundations to be shared with the other members of this community we call theater. It is a book to go back to year after year to glean yet another understanding of an approach. It is Beckie's innate understanding that we deal in art and because it is art, everyone's interpretation will be different and personal. It is that very understanding that makes these foundations valid.

Hilary A. Sherred

Preface

I offer this book as a source of basic information for all those interested in costume design for theater. The costume designer's art lies in effective interpretation, collaboration, and execution. It requires an understanding of the artistic principles that apply to all art forms, plus specific knowledge of dramatic literature, theater techniques, history of costume, styles of visual presentation, and fabric and materials, as well as skills in research, drawing, painting, conceptualizing, interpretation, communication, and collaboration — all topped with great dollops of imagination. The fundamentals of relevant areas of study are presented here to provide the beginning designer with a foundation upon which to build advanced costume skills. I hope this book will help the reader to understand the relationship of these skills to one another. I also hope an understanding of the process of costuming a production will lead to an increased respect for those who design and produce costumes.

While I emphasize that a variety of approaches to costume design are possible, I focus mainly on development through character and script because most costume designers usually work this way. After developing the skills to address projects in this way, a more advanced student may be prepared to attempt more conceptual approaches to design.

I would like to thank the following designers for their generous advice and gracious permission to reproduce their work from which this book so greatly benefits: Eldon Elder, Patton Campbell, Michael J. Cesario, Judith Dolan, Eduardo Sicongco, Carol Oditz, Carol Helen Beule, William Ivey Long, Tony Straiges, Natalie Garfinkle,

Susan Hum, David Murin, Patricia McGourty, and Rouben Ter-Arutunian.

I would also like to acknowledge the kind assistance, encouragement, and generosity of the following people in the preparation of this book: Hilary Sherred, Jack Cunningham, Kim Konikow, Julie Yarrow, Melissa Wentworth, Glen Loney, Howard Becknell, Blaine Reid, Gordon T.R. Anderson, Elsa van Bergen, Dee Josephson, Jill Francis Wood, and Fran Gonzalez.

Rebecca Cunningham

THE
MAGIC GARMENT

Chapter 1
Understanding Stage Costumes

Lend me thy hand,
And pluck my magic garment from me.

THE TEMPEST   William Shakespeare

A costume is a "magic" garment — a garment that enables an actor to become, for a time, someone else. Like Prospero's cape, which concentrated his supernatural powers over the winds and sea, an actor's costume helps concentrate the powers of imagination, expression, emotion, and movement into the creation and projection of a character to an audience.

This magic has a long history. Theatrical costume is one of the oldest art forms known to humanity. Prehistoric cultures used animal heads and skins as masks and costumes for ritual dances. These dances were created to relive and retell experiences. They were used to invoke the spirit world and were thought to favorably influence the hunt, the weather, and fertility. Long before plays were written or paintings were painted, costumes and makeup were used to magically transform the dancer/actor. Modern costumes still have this aura of magic.

Costumes have come a long way from animal heads and skins, yet each time an actor dons a costume, some vestige of that ancient magic is called upon to transform the actor into the character portrayed. Sometimes this magic works subtly by affecting the posture, walk, and presence of the actor, and by touching the store of cultural information in the collective memory of audience. Other costume images are so well-known within a culture that the appearance of an actor in that costume immediately identifies that character and evokes a suitable attitude or frame of mind in the audience. Costumes of this type may be based on traditional theatrical characters like Harlequin (Figure 2.4), or they may draw on familiar associations from outside the theater. The costume in Figure 1.1 is based on the dress Annie wears in the comic strip, "Little Orphan Annie"; drawing on broad-based cultural experience, it projects an instantly recognizable character to the audience.

FIGURE 1.1 *Annie.* Designed by Theoni V. Aldredge. Photo © Martha Swope.

BASIC FUNCTIONS

What is a stage costume? A stage costume may be defined as any-thing worn on stage. The real question is, "What is an *effective* stage costume?" An effective costume is one that engages the audience's attention and enhances the production and the actor's performance. It performs these two basic functions: (1) it *visually* defines the character portrayed by the actor, and (2) it helps establish the over-all theme (idea) and mood (atmosphere) of the production as inter-preted by the director. An effective costume speaks to the audience's subconscious store of knowledge and experience, helping them to identify the individual characters even before they speak and even if they are silent.

Defining Character

Differences between characters must be clearly visible, enabling all members of the audience to distinguish them and to understand the action. Even when other characters in the play are confused about the identity of certain characters, the audience should usually have no doubts. In Shakespeare's *Comedy of Errors* the plot involves two sets of twins and depends on the confusion of one twin brother for another. Costumes for these characters must be similar enough for the confusion to be logical, but different enough for the audience to understand which character is on stage. (See Color plate 1.)

How does the costume visually define a character? What does the audience need to know? The costume must (1) set the character in time (historical period) and space (geographical or imaginary place), (2) establish the approximate age and gender of a character, (3) establish the rank or social status of the character, (4) establish the personality of the character, and (5) reflect any changes in time, space, age, status, and personality that the character goes through during the play.

Setting a Character in Time and Space

When and where did this character live? Often the playwright specifies the date and locale of the play either by a statement at the beginning of the script or by specific reference to a person or his-torical event. When a period or date is specified, the playwright usually has a reason for setting the play in that time. Perhaps the ambience or mystique of the period or place enhances his theme. Shakespeare's setting of *Macbeth* on the misty moors of Scotland in a time distant even to his own day added mystery and magic to his

FIGURE 1.2 Hypolita, *A Midsummer Night's Dream*. Designed by Carol Oditz for The Acting Company.

comment on the violent nature of man (and woman). Perhaps a historical incident allows safe comment on a current, parallel situation. *The Crucible*, by Arthur Miller, is set in seventeenth-century Salem, Massachusetts. This play about the witch trials in early America reflects Miller's views on the McCarthy hearings taking place in his own time. If no reference to date can be found, the designer may assume the play was set in the time in which it was written. Sometimes, however, the style, theme, and mood of the play may suggest a historical period different from that in which it was written or set by the playwright.

A director may choose to move the play into a different time period. A new emphasis or fresh point of view on a classic play may be gained by changing its traditional period and locale or by establishing a fantasy world in which to place the production. Shakespeare's *A Midsummer Night's Dream* has been produced in ancient Greek costume, Elizabethan costume, Empire costume, modern dress, and many other styles, each contributing a slightly different point of view. In Figure 1.2 a design for Hypolita in *A Midsummer Night's Dream* uses nonperiod cut, snakeskin, feathers, and animal motifs to evoke a strange, exotic, and imaginary world.

Establishing Age

An audience needs a clear idea of the age of each character. A major part of the responsibility for projecting age falls on the actor, but the costume must support that characterization. Age can be suggested in a costume by the length of the garment, the length or type of sleeve, the shape of the neckline, and many other design considerations. Wig or hair style and makeup may also be designed by the costume designer. In Figure 1.3 the youth and innocence of Olivia and Sebastian in *Twelfth Night* are emphasized by the use of white and pastel colors, lightweight fabrics, the cut of the garments, and the type of accessories.

Appropriate age projection in the costume is especially important when the actor and the character being portrayed are far apart in age. Few thirteen-year-old actresses would have the understanding and skill to portray the thirteen-year-old Juliet. In almost every production of *Romeo and Juliet* the young lovers are played by actors older than Shakespeare's characters. Careful handling of the costumes will help the actors project the youth and immaturity so essential to these characters.

Establishing the Rank or Social Status

In most period (historical) plays a hierarchy of characters is established and is basic to the action. The primary action often

FIGURE 1.3 Olivia and Sebastian, *Twelfth Night*. Designed by the author for Brooklyn College. Photo: Richard Grossberg.

centers on conflict between characters or groups of *different* rank or social status — rich versus poor, ruler versus subject(s), church versus secular government, servant versus master. For example, the cast of characters for *The Marriage of Figaro* by Jean-Pierre de Beaumarchais includes a count, a countess (nobility), a doctor, music master (middle class), household servants, and various peasants. The plot matches the wit of the servants against the power of the nobility.

Even in plays that do not feature kings, queens, counts, or bishops, some element of class, ethnic or regional origin, lifestyle, occupation, or income level is necessary to define all characters. These elements are intended to create variety and to make us draw on our own experiences to help us understand the characters. George S. Kaufman and Moss Hart's *You Can't Take It With You* features an odd assortment of characters including the Vanderhof-Sycamore family: Grandpa, a philosopher; Penny, a middle-aged mother, painter, and playwright; Penny's husband, Paul, a part-time fireworks manufacturer; Mr. De Pinna, a boarder, formerly the iceman; Penny and Paul's daughter Essie, an amateur ballet dancer and candy maker; Essie's husband, Ed, a printer and xylophone player; Alice, Penny and Paul's second daughter, a secretary; two black household servants; and the Kirbys: Tony, Alice's beau; Mr. Kirby, Tony's millionaire businessman father; Mrs. Kirby, Tony's mother and uptight socialite; plus a Russian countess working as a waitress; a Russian dance instructor; an inebriated actress; and a pair of FBI agents. The social or economic status (real or imagined) of each character contributes something to the understanding of the play's meaning. The conflict between the free lifestyle of the Sycamores and the luxurious but staid existence of the Kirbys must be supported by the contrast in the styles of dress worn by them.

The costumes in Figure 1.4 reflect the differing social positions of the characters in *Woyzeck*. The low status of the young Woyzeck (center) is expressed in his simple costume, contrasted to the more exaggerated and elaborate costumes of the other characters.

Modern plays tend to focus on inner conflicts, conflicts between a character and his or her own social or economic group, or between closely associated groups. Regardless of the nature of the conflict, correct establishment of the social milieu in which the play takes place is an important part of the designer's job.

Establishing Personality

The costume designer must assist the actor in projecting the character's personality. In television and films the camera can move in for close-ups to catch facial reactions which reveal character; on stage, however, broad gestures and large-scale visual clues are needed to make the point. From the moment of Nora's entrance in *A Doll's House* the audience must know that she is the doll about whom Henrik Ibsen is writing. Her costume should suggest the pampered innocence in which she is living. The cut of a garment, the color, the fit, the type of trim, the accessories, *all* aspects of the costume can express something about the character's personality.

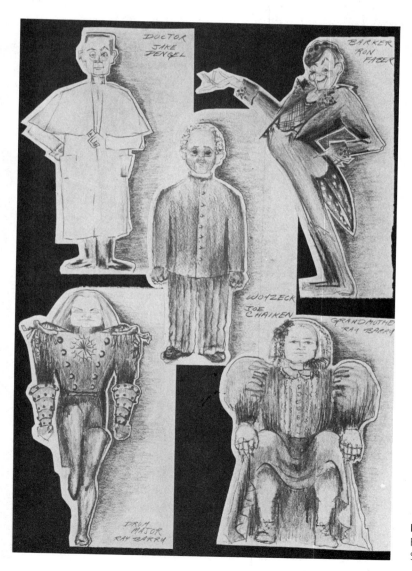

FIGURE 1.4   *Woyzeck.* Designed by Patricia McGourty for the New York Shakespeare Festival.

Sometimes the costume must belie the character to contrast what that character pretends to be and what he or she really is. In Figure 1.5 the costume design for Mrs. Candor in *A School for Scandal* shows her as lovely and charming as she believes she is, not as her actions reveal her to be.

Reflecting Changes

One of the easiest ways to reflect a change in a character is to change costumes. A new costume clearly and dramatically demonstrates that something has occurred. However, not all changes of character condition are dramatic or obvious. Some take place

FIGURE 1.5 *School for Scandal.* Designed by Michael J. Cesario for Centre Theatre Group, Toronto, Canada.

gradually and subtly. These changes must be reflected by slight variations in the appearance: opening a blouse, loosening the tie, changing shoes. Not all characters in a play go through a change of condition, but major characters almost always progress or regress as a result of the conflicts in the plot. The changes in Eliza Doolittle are the major focus of George Bernard Shaw's *Pygmalion* and her costumes would obviously parallel the improvements in her speech and behavior. The changes in Higgins, barely perceptible, are not acknowledged by him and would scarcely be reflected in his dress.

The two costumes for *Comedy of Errors* illustrated in Figure 1.6 show a character in two conditions. First Dr. Pinch appears in arrogant splendor. Later he reappears in tatters after being beaten, set on fire, and thrown down a well.

FIGURE 1.6 *Comedy of Errors.* Designed by the author for Brooklyn College.

Supporting Theme, Concept, and Mood

A play exists because a playwright has one or more ideas to express. A play may be based on an existing story, but the playwright has some comment or point of view on that story that forms the *theme*. He or she consciously or unconsciously transmits that theme to the audience through what is included or omitted from the story, the way the incidents are presented, and the language that is used to tell the story. The director of each production is responsible for interpreting the playwright's theme anew. The costumes of a given production collectively express the director's interpretation of the theme for that production. This is referred to as the *director's concept*. Concepts which evolve from the study of the script and are based on either the action or the language of the play are said to be *organic*. These interpretations are triggered by ideas found in the play itself, not found elsewhere and applied to the surface of the play. Setting *Julius Caesar* in Nazi Germany may sound like a great idea, but what elements in the play support this change and will the play work well in its new setting? The concept should enhance the play not smother it.

Many plays lend themselves to a variety of valid interpretations. *Hamlet* has been interpreted in many ways, some stressing the political aspects of the play and some stressing the psychological aspects.

The *mood* of a play is the emotional feeling which pervades the experience. Mood may be part of the playwright's theme or imposed by the director's concept. Melancholy, joy, terror, anger, humor, and disorientation are all moods which can be found in plays. In some plays the mood varies between different feelings; in other plays one prevailing mood gradually builds throughout the play.

The theme, concept, and mood of a production are supported by the costumes through (1) style, (2) color, (3) scale, and (4) texture.

Style

Style is the manner or mode in which a designer creates the costumes in order best to interpret the mood and concept. It is the result of decisions and choices made by the designer. The two basic styles are *realism* and *stylization*. Costumes done in a realistic style are as close to actual dress as the demands of the play and theatrical values will allow. Stylized costumes are those that depart from real clothes in some obvious way. The designer may choose to exaggerate shape, silhouette, color, trim, or other aspects of the costume. The more realistic a production is, the more subtle the coordination of the costumes can be; the more stylized the production is, the more obviously coordinated the costumes can be. Within these two approaches, hundreds of variations are possible.

Color

After choosing colors appropriate to each individual character, the designer must consider how all the costumes will look together and what the overall effect will be when all the costumes in a given scene are on stage together. Do the major characters stand out against the crowd or blend into the group? Do the colors project the mood or feeling desired? Do the colors express comedy or tragedy?

Scale

The scale of an object is its size relative to a norm or to other related objects. Realistic productions call for realistic or slightly exaggerated scale (depending on the size of the theater). More stylized productions may exaggerate the scale (larger or smaller) for humor, horror, or other effects. Costumes for the show girls in *My One and Only* (Figure 1.7) incorporate enormous tobacco leaves, bananas, and pineapple slices. Exaggerating the scale of ordinary objects introduces humor into these costumes.

Texture

All materials have texture, smooth to rough. While contrast between textures is desirable, the proportion of one to the other affects one's

FIGURE 1.7   *My One and Only*. Designed by Rita Ryack. Photo © Kenn Duncan.

perception of the whole group. A costume of predominantly rough materials suggests a primitive or earthy character. If all the costumes are constructed of rough materials, then these characteristics are shared by the whole group. The designer uses textures to tell the audience something about the character and relationships between the characters in the play. The overall textural feeling of costumes and scenery helps project the feeling or mood of the play.

HOW DOES THE DESIGNER WORK?

> . . . What are these
> So withered and so wild in their attire,
> That look not like the inhabitants o' the earth,
> And yet are on 't. . .
> You should be women,
> And yet your beards forbid me to interpret
> That you are so.
>
> MACBETH   William Shakespeare

The costume designer's art lies in effective interpretation, collaboration, and execution. The designer must be able to interpret visually and verbally the action, style, and characters of the play, the costumes and manners of the historical period, and the elements of the style of presentation. Collaboration involves the ability to communicate and compromise with the director, the actors, and the other designers. Critical to real success is the costume designer's ability to effect not just the execution of a sketch, but the translation of the sketch to a final costume which serves both the actor and the production in visual and practical terms.

Designing costumes for a play then is a very complex project. How does the designer begin? What steps need to be taken and in what order? Each designer develops an individual approach to attacking the myriad tasks of designing, but most follow the same basic outline.

Reading and Studying the Play

The script usually indicates directly or indirectly most of the basic information needed by the designer: historical period, character information, special problems (quick changes, broad action, disguises), and mood or style. Several careful readings may be needed to find this information. The stage directions give some insight into the action and personality of each character. Even more valuable, however, will be the character's dialogue and what others say about that character. Banquo's comment on the witches in *Macbeth* is very revealing. Bearded, withered, and wildly dressed, they appear unearthly to him. His observations as well as other lines suggest the eerie mood and pervading sense of evil on the moor. If the script does not give enough information, the designer, director, and/or actor will need to decide on the points in question. Notes on all pertinent information are then organized into various lists known as ''plots,'' which express visually the information needed to design the show.

Collaboration between Designers and Director

Collaboration is a key word in the success of most theatrical productions. Careful discussion of ideas, effects, images, concepts, schedules, and other pertinent information helps to keep all participants working toward the same goals. While the director is the guiding force behind the production, a good director knows how to give the design team an indication of the style desired without squelching their creativity. To be an effective participant in this collaboration, the costume designer must know enough about the tasks of the director, the scenic designer, and the lighting designer to discuss the overall production intelligently and to understand how a decision in one area might affect another area of the production. Attendance at rehearsals and discussions with the actors about the characters they play give the designer insights into the total production.

The designer must also have sufficient understanding of construction and cost factors to design within budget limitations. He or she must be prepared to adjust, make changes, and even start completely over in some situations. Communication, coordination, and cooperation are essential to good collaboration.

Doing Research

The designer needs a basic knowledge of costume history even to begin researching a period play. The type and amount of research required for a show vary considerably from play to play. Modern plays may require visits to places where people similar to the characters can be found. Plays set in historical periods may require extensive study of the painting, literature, and existing artifacts of that period. Some research material is readily available; some must be ferreted out with great diligence. After collecting stacks of research, the designer sorts, evaluates, and develops the materials for effective use.

Developing the Costumes

Using the ideas expressed in designer/director discussions and the collected research, the designer develops a series of quick sketches called *roughs*. In these sketches the designer begins to work out the overall look of the show as well as individual character approaches. These sketches then serve as the basis for further discussions with the director.

Analysis of the costume roughs should indicate if major characters stand out from subordinate characters, if character delineation is clear, and if relationships between characters are indicated. Many roughs may be necessary before the various problems of a specific costume are solved.

Unifying the Whole

The designer constantly works to unify the production, to establish the feeling that all parts belong to the whole. Collaboration with the director and other designers should bring a clear concept and approach into focus. Comparison of the costumes designs with the set designs and the plans of the lighting designer should determine if all approaches agree. Adjustments in all areas of the design may be needed.

Rendering the Costume Sketches

When most of the decisions have been made concerning each costume's design, the designer does a series of color illustrations for the costumes. These *renderings* may be done in watercolor, ink, pastel, pencil, gouache, tempera, or any combination of suitable media. The drawing should be carefully done so that a pattern can be made for the costume. As in Figure 1.8, additional working sketches and notes may be needed to indicate fully the problems to be solved. *Swatches*, small samples of selected fabrics, should be attached and the rendering should clearly indicate where each is used. Swatches may come from the designer's collection or from the shopper's research, or they may be attached after the fabric is purchased.

Choosing Fabrics for Costumes

The painter's medium is paint; the sculptor's medium may be metal, wood, or clay: the costume designer's medium is fabric. The choice

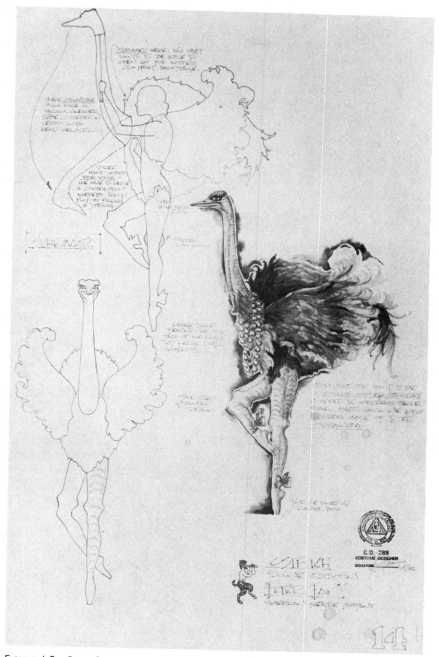

FIGURE 1.8 *Peter Pan*. Included on this costume sketch by Eduardo Sicongco are the details of the construction and mechanism of this design for the Ostrich. Designed for American Theatre Company.

of fabric is a major influence on the final look of each costume and the overall look of the production. The same garment, cut of different fabrics, can suggest characters of very different ages, personalities, or economic levels. A group of costumes designed in a variety of fabrics has an interesting, and usually realistic, feeling. A set of costumes that uses only a few fabrics, on the other hand, tends to be very strongly unified and stylized. Fabric choice must be suitable for the garment, period style, character's personality, concept of production, budget allotments, and maintenance requirements of the production.

Getting the Show Together

The designer's responsibility to the show does not end with the completion of the sketches. Different situations require different types of involvement. For some productions the designer must also locate, rent, buy, or build the costumes. In other situations the costume shop manager is responsible for the delegation of portions of the work to the various staff members, leaving the designer to supervise details. The designer must attend rehearsals, supervise dress rehearsals and previews, and instruct wardrobe crews regarding special problems of quick changes and maintenance. The designer is also responsible for keeping the show costs within the budget. Some of the designer's work may be delegated to design assistants.

These stages of the design process often overlap or reverse order depending on the design problems of a given production or the approach of a particular designer.

While a successful costume design effort should substantially contribute to the total effect of the production, the scenery, lights, and costumes should usually complement and balance each other and provide support for the acting and direction of the play. The importance of the costumes in a given play is relative and subjective. Some plays make strong visual statements; others stress verbal or psychological meanings. Some directors are interested in strong visual effects; others stress emotion and movement. While many lavish and spectacular productions are remembered for their beauty or extravagance, the visual and technical trappings of a production should enhance, not overshadow, the audience's understanding of the theme of the play.

The art of the costume designer lies in the ability to weave all aspects of costuming into a seamless, unified production. The following chapters examine the basic skills and information the designer needs in order to approach and coordinate these aspects of costume design.

Chapter 2
Understanding the Play

Yes, I have tricks in my pocket, I have things up my sleeve. But I am the opposite of a stage magician. He gives you illusion that has the appearance of truth. I give you truth in the pleasant disguise of illusion.

THE GLASS MENAGERIE   Tennessee Williams

WHAT IS A PLAY?

A play is a playwright's version of some truth, an illusion often more real or penetrating than reality. A play is a live representation of selected actions. Plays "happen" in the present no matter what time they represent. The stage is a magic time machine on which we view events from other eras and from the minds and imaginations of other men and women. The script for a play is but a blueprint for these events, not a finished product. It contains dialogue, character information, and directions for action. The script is the playwright's attempt to reveal a personal vision to the audience.

Before the task of designing a play can begin, a thorough study of the script is necessary. The designers must seek the playwright's vision and combine with it their own and that of the director in order to reveal that vision to the audience.

In order to understand the play, to discuss it intelligently with the director, and to design suitable and effective costumes, a designer must understand the various types of drama and their characteristics.

WHAT KIND OF PLAY IS IT?
FORMS OF DRAMA

The actors are come hither, my lord ... the best actors in the world, either for tragedy, comedy, history, pastoral, pastoral– comical, historical–pastoral, tragical–historical, tragical– comical–historical–pastoral, scene individable, or poem un- limited.... These are the only men.

HAMLET   William Shakespeare

A list of forms of drama creates not a series of specific types, but a spectrum of forms, some shades broader than others, some with undefined edges, and some tones flecked with contrasting hues. To understand the classification of various plays takes study and ex- perience in reading scripts. Many plays can easily be interpreted in more than one way, leaving the final classification to be determined by the director's contribution.

Tragedy

A dramatic form centering on themes of great philosophical impor- tance, *tragedy* explores the individual's purpose and destiny, one's relationship to forces greater than oneself, and the nature of good and evil. Usually tales of kings, queens, and gods, tragedy has a scope and scale beyond the daily experience of the average human being. The playwright seeks to arouse pity and fear in the audience and to provide catharsis and moral enlightenment. Despite stag- gering adversity, the humanity, spirit, and integrity of the human race (in the person of the protagonist) remain intact. The most formal theatrical form, *classical tragedy* dates from the Greek Golden Age. Tightly structured and written in verse, Greek tra- gedy explored profound questions regarding humanity's existence through the retelling of Greek myths of men, women, and the gods. Examples of the Greek tragedies are *Medea* by Euripides and *Oedi- pus Rex* by Sophocles.

In the seventeenth century, French playwrights turned to the Greek tragedies as models for inspiration and style. *French classical tragedies* include *Polyeucte* by Pierre Corneille and *Phaedra* by Jean Racine.

Although written in blank verse and with a less formal con- struction than Greek tragedy, *Elizabethan tragedies* also explore questions of power, good and evil, purpose, and destiny. However, these plays tend to focus on extraordinary human beings and their failings rather than on the influence of fate or the interference of the gods. Shakespeare's *Othello* and *Hamlet* are among a long list of great Elizabethan tragedies.

Modern tragedies explore the dilemmas of ordinary persons caught in situations that test their morals, strength of character, and sanity. Arthur Miller's *Death of a Salesman* is usually accepted as an example of modern tragedy.

Serious modern plays, *dramas*, share many aspects of tragedy but lack the profundity and universality of traditional tragedy. Usually featuring ordinary people, these plays explore ideas, sociological and philosophical issues, and behavior under the stresses of modern life. Dramas look for meaning in a rapidly changing world, often with tragic results. Henrik Ibsen's *A Doll's House*, Clifford Odets' *The Country Girl*, and Tennessee Williams' *Summer and Smoke* are fine examples of this form.

Costumes for tragedy have traditionally been elaborate and designed in grand scale. The Greeks and Romans used masks and thick soled boots to make the actors "larger-than-life." (See Figure 2.1.) Costumes for classical tragedy may stress universality over the specifics of historical time and place. Modern tragedies and dramas are usually costumed in realistic or near-realistic, historically accurate dress.

Melodrama

This popular form of escapist drama got its name in the late eighteenth century when music was used to heighten the effect of stage action. Often exaggerated, this form of play emphasizes suspense, action, and the contrast between good and evil. Usually ending happily, melodrama is the form of detective stories, soap operas, and adventure plays in the theater, on film, and on television. Perhaps the most well-known melodrama of the nineteenth century is *Uncle Tom's Cabin* based on the novel by Harriet Beecher Stowe. (See Figure 2.2.) Robert Sherwood's *Petrified Forest* is a twentieth-century example of this genre.

Melodrama may depend rather heavily on stereotypes. These characters are often recognized by their costumes: Heroine in sweet white dress, Villain in black, Hero in white. The closer to drama the melodrama is, the more realistic the costumes tend to be.

Comedy

On the lighter side of the spectrum is found a broad selection of comic plays. Primarily entertaining, comedies are usually funny and end happily. Most comedies do not question values, but explore

FIGURE 2.1   Tragedy Mask.   From Pompeii, this fine marble sculpture represents a theater mask of the type found in Greek and Roman Tragedy. Photo: Westair Surveys.

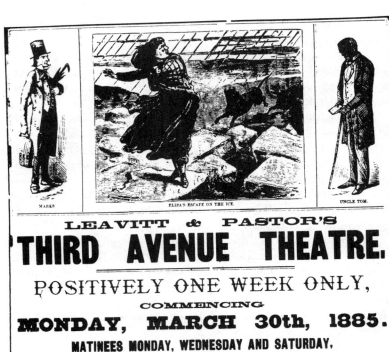

FIGURE 2.2 *Uncle Tom's Cabin.* This extremely popular nineteenth-century melodrama was often lavishly produced. The Theater Collection; Museum of the City of New York.

behavior. The characters of comedy may be fairly realistic, but they are caught in compromising circumstances that reveal their humanity.

High comedy is a form of comedy based on subtle, intellectual observation and wit. Usually dealing with characters in polite society, these plays deal primarily with language, not action. *Private Lives* by Noel Coward is an example of this type of comedy.

A sophisticated comedy set in court circles or upper-class

society is sometimes called a *comedy of manners*. This dramatic form displays the contrast between parlor etiquette and the real nature of people. These comedies reveal and ridicule pretentious and hypocritical behavior. Examples of this type of play are *She Stoops to Conquer* by Oliver Goldsmith, *Lady Windermere's Fan* by Oscar Wilde, the *The Misanthrope* by Molière. *Restoration comedies* are comedies of manners written in England in the latter half of the seventeenth century (after the restoration of the monarchy). *The Country Wife* by William Wycherly is from this period.

When action and situation are of primary importance and language is unimportant, except for the use of vulgarities, the play is said to be an example of *low comedy*. The emphasis is placed on physical deformities, malfunctions, and mishaps sometimes called "comic bits." Characters tend to be personifications of one or two characteristics. The comedians of early films were particularly adept at physical forms of comedy. Laurel and Hardy, Buster Keaton, and Bud Abbott and Lou Costello were all masters of this genre.

Low comic scenes may be included in other types of drama for *comic relief*. The "gatekeeper's scene" in *Macbeth* and the "grave-digger's scene" in *Hamlet* are scenes of comic relief.

By coloring the tragic aspects of human life with irony and humor, *black comedy* enables us to look at situations that might otherwise be too painful to contemplate. Plays such as *A Day in the Death of Joe Egg* by Peter Nichols help us consider the plight of those in circumstances we may never personally know.

Tragicomedy also blends elements of tragedy with humor, irony, and pathos. More bittersweet than black comedy, tragicomedy is about characters that are more recognizable and approachable. Tragicomedy can touch an audience deeply. Lanford Wilson's *Fifth of July* is such a play.

Originally *burlesque* was a kind of satire or "mockery" of a well-known figure or type of person. In the twentieth century burlesque came to mean bawdy humor. In vaudeville, for example, a series of comic skits was combined with dance acts featuring female dancers in provocative costumes. In Figure 2.3, a scene from *Sugar Babies*, "the schoolteacher" and the "bad boy" engage in a comic bit based on a traditional vaudeville skit.

Based on ridiculous and improbable situations, *farce* has laughter as its sole purpose. An extremely active form of theater, farce builds at a frantic pace, piling one outrageous action on top of another until everything collapses in a hysterical heap. Plays in the farcical form include Shakespeare's *Comedy of Errors* and Michael Frayn's *Noises Off*.

Costumes for comedy span a very wide range. High comedies

FIGURE 2.3 *Sugar Babies.* Designed by Raoul Pene du Bois. Photo © Martha Swope.

and comedies of manners are usually done in appropriate period dress, elegant and beautiful, although exaggeration of dress or decoration is frequent. Low comedy, farce, and burlesque costumes often feature distortion of body shapes, bold colors, and large size decoration. Comic costumes are developed through the same comic devices used by writers.

Comic Devices

Comic writers work with four basic "comic devices" when creating funny situations. These devices should be understood by the costume designer.

Derision is a form of criticism aimed at pomposity, hypocrisy, and sanctimoniousness. Derision must be leveled at symbols of authority to be funny; deriding the weak or pathetic becomes cruel and humorless.

Physical deformity is a very old comic device. Many comic characters are intentionally distorted and exaggerated in appearance through the use of masks, padded costumes, phallic symbols, or makeup. The spirit in which this is done and how far the device is taken determine the humor of the device.

Incongruity, the juxtaposing of two contrasting objects, situations, people, or other elements of a scene, creates a humorous effect. A large woman wearing a very small hat, speech inappropriate to the speaker or occasion, a character in unfamiliar surroundings, and action contrary to expectations of a character all produce laughter.

When a character loses his or her human flexibility and behaves in a mechanical way, when situations repeat themselves as if a machine is at work, when dialogue becomes repeated for comic effect, the playwright is making use of the device of *automatism*.

Many scenes illustrate more than one comic device. Identifying the comic devices used by the playwright gives the costume designer clues to costuming the characters.

Many playwrights have felt free to mix elements of several dramatic forms in the same play. This freedom provides a broad variety of plays for us to enjoy. Still, the predominant form should be identified to guide the director and designers in making artistic decisions about the production. The choice of color, texture, and scale as well as the relative importance of the visual elements in the total production will vary according to the form of the play.

HOW IS THE PLAY STRUCTURED?
ELEMENTS OF DRAMA

Plays are composed of certain elements, and the proportion of these differs in each play, providing endless variations. These elements are *plot*, *character*, *theme*, *audio elements*, and *visual elements*.

Plot

The plot is the skeleton or armature on which the playwright molds the play. The plot is not the story, but the arrangement in which the events of the story are told, the form of its actions, dialogue, and characters.

Most plays are organized into "acts," which may be divided into "scenes." The action takes place in a series of interchanges between characters that are grouped together for a purpose: to give the audience background information, to establish the circumstances, to demonstrate a challenge or problem, to find a solution, or to resolve the situation. Act divisions may indicate a passage of time, change of scene, or a turning point in the action. Blackouts, intermissions, or scene breaks provide the opportunity to change scenery and costumes. Scenes can be organized in two basic ways: *climactic* and *episodic*.

A play with *climactic* structure follows a linear sequence of events, in chronological order, leading to a specific result. The plot begins late in the story, near the climax, and is shown in only one or two locales. Past incidents affecting the action are revealed by the dialogue. The number of characters is limited and the action is compressed into a brief time period. Some tightly constructed climactic plays are referred to as "well-made" plays. *Antigone* by Sophocles and *Of Mice and Men* by John Steinbeck are two examples of plays with climactic structure.

Plays written with an *episodic* structure exhibit many opposite characteristics, such as short, fragmented scenes, many threads of action, various locales, and numerous characters. The plot may begin early in the story and skip large segments of time or may be told in flashback or simultaneous scenes. Examples of episodic plays are *Peer Gynt* by Henrik Ibsen and the *Caucasian Chalk Circle* by Bertolt Brecht.

The structure of a play influences the design concept. Plays with climactic structures take place within a specific time frame. Logic, unity, and realism within the costumes may be indicated by this type of structure. Episodic plays usually give the designer more freedom because of their looser structure.

Character

The beings that inhabit the play are the characters through which the playwright presents a point of view and then challenges that view. Characters can be humans, animals, spirits, even concepts and normally inanimate objects. Characters in a play differ from characters in a novel because the audience rarely hears what the former are thinking. Occasionally a playwright uses a special device, such as a *soliloquy* or *monologue*, to give the audience insight into the character's mind. However, that knowledge is more commonly gained from a character's dialogue, actions, and reactions. Much must be read "between the lines." Actors and directors refer to such information as the *subtext*.

Play characters tend to fall into certain categories which are useful for designer/director discussions.

Those roles through and around which the primary action in a play is built are called *main characters* or *major characters*. They provide the focus of the plot and either precipitate the action or find themselves the recipients of it.

Supporting characters are smaller parts intended to support the action of the main characters. The playwright uses these characters — often very interesting roles — to provide balance and counterpoint to the main characters. Just as a composer repeats a theme on different instruments, or introduces contrasting rhythms to a piece of music, a playwright may use supporting characters to emphasize a theme either by subtle variation, strong harmony, or sharp contrast.

The additional characters needed to complete the picture and populate the world of the play are called the *extras*. Many playwrights specify who these people are — policemen, waiters, peasants; other playwrights leave the decision up to the director. A designer should be prepared to assist in designating the individuals in a crowd.

The *chorus* is a special group of extras. The original chorus in Greek drama spoke in unison to set the scene, comment on the action, and express the moral of the play. The Greek chorus was an anonymous group (townspeople, old men), not a group of individuals. The use of a chorus in contemporary drama is primarily found in opera and musical theater. Here the singing chorus may represent large groups of similar people (sailors, schoolgirls, nuns), or may be represented as individuals within a large group (a street scene including peddlers, newsboys, a taxi driver, rich "swells," a baby nurse with carriage, sailors on leave, schools girls, business men and women, and so on). In some modern plays the chorus has been reduced to one actor; now a narrator, the chorus becomes a supporting role or major character.

Many modern plays are constructed for *ensemble* acting, where almost equal importance is given to all characters. The focus shifts from one character to another and back again throughout the play.

Certain types of characters have long traditions in the theater, some dating back to Greek and Roman theater. *Stock characters* symbolize a particular type of person or an outstanding characteristic of human behavior to the exclusion of almost everything else. Found particularly in comedy, these characters developed sure-fire combinations of physical attributes, idiosyncrasies, and "comic bits" that have become linked to them for hundreds of years. Often known by the name given them during the development of the *commedia dell'arte*, these characters can be traced from Greek and Roman drama through Molière and Shakespeare and up to modern

TV situation comedies. Two of the most familiar of these characters, Harlequin and Pantalon, are found in Figure 2.4 in their traditional attire.

Similar to stock characters, *stereotypical characters* are recognizable types and express only two or three characteristics, often based on ethnic models. Lacking depth as written, these characters depend on the actor and director to provide the human dimension neglected by the playwright.

Ideas/Vision

As works of art, plays express the artist's vision or concept of the world. The playwright's vision includes not only the story to be told, but the point of view from which it is told and the style (mode) in which it is told. Some playwrights support the prevailing philosophy of their age; some challenge the mores and morals of their time. Some plays have as their purpose to enlighten us, some to entertain us.

The director searches for the theme of a play and for ways to transmit the essence of the work to the audience. The designer needs to understand this essence when conceptualizing the cos-

FIGURE 2.4 Commedia dell'arte, sixteenth century. Wearing their traditional costumes, the patched and torn Harlequin and the bearded Pantalon in his robe sing to the accompaniment of the Zany Corneto. Drottningsholms Teatremuseum, Stockholm, Sweden.

tumes, so the visual messages do not conflict with the underlying themes. Themes are rarely stated directly by the playwright. Careful reading and discussion with all members of the design/directing staff may be needed to determine the playwright's point of view.

Sometimes a shift in emphasis by the director can alter the overall concept of a play. The designer needs to be aware of the director's concept as well as the playwright's intent. A designer should ask for a clear statement of theme from the director. What aspects of the play does the director wish to stress? When directing George Bernard Shaw's *Major Barbara*, for example, a director might choose to emphasize the domestic situation (father–daughter conflict), the boy–girl relationships of the younger characters, the moral–political questions raised by the manufacture of munitions, or the religious questions of charity and salvation.

Audio Elements

Communication through sound is fundamental to drama. Except for mime or pantomime, all plays are composed of audio elements. Character, ideas, and emotions are expressed through *dialogue*, from great poetic verse forms to common street language and even meaningless sounds. Verbal communication between characters reveals to us their situation, social standing, and education or intelligence, as well as information about other characters. Not only the lines as written, but the shades of meaning given them by the actor, reveal to us the nature of the character speaking. Is this a great man or a charlatan? Is this a prince or a pauper? Is this a warm or cold person? Does this character speak in down-to-earth language or elevated rhetoric?

The rhythms of the dialogue create a subtle feeling of music and movement which add to the understanding of the characters and the situations the playwright presents to us. Short, clipped speech moves us along rapidly with the action, whereas fluid, undulating speech creates a languid, romantic aura and touches us emotionally. The playwright uses the choice of words, the metaphors, and the rhythms of speech as the designer will use fabric, color, and line. The designer should study the language of the play to find its appropriate visual expressions.

Many plays are enhanced with background *music* even though the script may not actually specify its use. Music can underscore the action or ease transitions; it can express the mood of the scene or provide clues to the characters or situations. Music can range from simple sound effects to complete musical scores for musicals, operettas, or operas. The more important the music becomes in a production, the more the costume designer must take it into consideration. In musical theater and opera the style of the music becomes the main consideration in one's visualization of the style of the production. Figure 2.5 shows how the decadent qualities expressed in the music for *Threepenny Opera* can be reflected in the style of the costumes.

Visual Elements/Spectacle

The scenery, costumes, and lights produce the physical environment for the play. The set suggests the place, time, and atmosphere which combine to create the world of the play. The set provides the areas for action, the arenas for the conflict required for the play. Stage lighting illuminates the action and intensifies the atmosphere. Like music, lighting can create strong emotional reactions in an audience. The costumes define the characters and relate to the other visual elements. The total impression conveyed by these visual elements must support the theme and concept of the play and set the mood intended by the playwright.

Movement and dance introduced into a play create interest, express moods and feelings, and help set the atmosphere for scenes and events. Many plays call for crowd scenes, parades, battle

FIGURE 2.5 *The Threepenny Opera.* The decadent qualities of Kurt Weill's music are expressed in use of fabric and trim in these costumes by Michael J. Cesario. Photo: Carl Davis, Nina Vance Alley Theatre.

scenes, and other large gatherings on stage to provide contrast to the more intimate scenes and to show the relationship of a character to the surrounding community.

Modern productions often introduce slides, film, and other special effects to advance the play rapidly and effectively by providing information visually.

The proportions of these elements in each production depend on the purpose of the playwright, the concept of the director, the budget, and the audience for which the production is intended.

Most plays are written with stress on one or two of these elements. Some plays, like *The Italian Straw Hat* by Eugène Labiche and Marc-Michel, stress plot and action, leaving the characters two-dimensional and underdeveloped. Other plays, like Arthur Miller's *Death of a Salesman*, are deep character studies with little action or spectacle. Most plays are open to numerous interpretations and variations. One production might stress the philosophical or political ideas inherent in a script by stripping away the audio and visual elements. Another production of the same play may use the visual and audio elements to stress the poetry and romance also embodied within the text. The question to be answered is *not* "Is this right or wrong?" but "Does this work for *this* production?"

The balance of the elements can shift and change, but no element should be overemphasized to the detriment of the meaning of the play or the playwright's intention.

IN WHAT MODE (STYLE) IS THE PLAY WRITTEN?

> . . . for style is for the writer, as for the painter, a question, not of technique but of vision. It is the revelation — impossible by direct and conscious means — of the qualitative differences in the way the world appears to us, differences which, but for art, would remain the eternal secret of each of us.
>
> REMEMBRANCE OF THINGS PAST   Marcel Proust

The style and manner of expression chosen by the playwright to convey the play's meaning is referred to as the *mode of drama*. Effective costumes may depend on the designer's understanding of the play's mode or style. Plays written within a historical period and cultural milieu usually share many characteristics reflecting the prevailing philosophy and morals of that age. Playwrights have often been among the vanguard of artistic movements which have included visual artists, philosophers, architects, and writers of other literary forms. To fully understand a given play, the designer may need to examine the historical context and the prevailing philosophies of its period, and to study the visual arts and other literary works of its time.

All theatrical styles have certain *conventions* which have developed to assist in their presentation. A stage whisper is accepted by the audience as an intimate comment, unheard by the other characters on stage, even though hundreds of audience members heard it quite clearly. The conventions of musical theater allow the characters to burst into song whenever the mood strikes them. Spotlights, masks, voice projection, and many other "tricks of the trade" can be accepted by the audience once the style of the play is established.

Broadly speaking, plays can be divided into two styles, *representational* and *presentational*. Representational plays propose to show events from life as they happen and allow the audience to "overhear" the action. The goal of a representational production is to have the audience forget it is in the theater and, to that end, the actors never acknowledge their presence. A presentational performance seeks to challenge the audience directly, to heighten the experience by making the audience participate in the event. The conventions of a presentational play allow the actors to step out of character and address the audience, leave the stage and mingle with the audience, and otherwise break the audience/stage barrier. Plays of both styles can be found among the plays in the following modes.

Classicism

The word "classic" has many shades of meaning. The mode of "classic" drama is derived from the style of Greek plays. Usually describing tragedies, classicism stresses order, clean line, and a formal structure. Written in verse, classical plays emphasize dialogue, emotion, and ideas, and minimize action. Violence is rarely seen: only the result of violence is displayed or discussed. Classical tragedies stress universal concepts and deal with humanity's relationship to the gods or the forces of fate. The main characters of classical tragedies are extraordinary people — kings, queens, children of the gods — who are caught in some kind of monumental struggle. Classical comedies are those based on Greek and Roman models.

Sometimes a play may be referred to as a "classic." This use of the word does not refer to its style, but to the fact that it is an outstanding example of its type, whatever style or form that may be, and that it deserves to be produced for and enjoyed by audiences of all times.

Later playwrights, admiring the great Greek classical plays, attempted to write new plays in the same style. These *neoclassic* plays were written in verse and followed the same general construction as their precursors.

Costumes designed for plays in the "classic or neoclassic mode" usually stress clean, flowing lines, simple shapes, and formal grace.

Romanticism

Plays in the romantic style glorify love, exaggerate emotion, and tend to suffer from an excess of "prettiness" and a lack of depth. The various meanings of the word "romantic" can be misleading to a designer. "Romantic" can describe any play that is about tender feelings and sweet emotions and that has a basically optimistic, happy ending. The term "romantic" is also used to designate a style of literature from the early nineteenth century. This entire period is sometimes called the Romantic Period and some costume history authors designate clothing from this period as Romantic Costume. When a designer or director uses this term, the meaning should be made absolutely clear.

Romantic costumes tend to be in pastel or floral tones, to make excessive use of ribbons, lace, and trim, and to have a generally frothy and youthful effect.

Sentimentalism

An unembarrassed appeal for pity or sympathy and an unquenchable optimism may signal an excessive dose of sentimentalism in a play. An intensely good or innocent character, like a child or animal (whose sole or primary claim to the attention of the audience is being intensely pathetic), may be the central character, seen struggling against seemingly insurmountable odds. A style associated with melodrama, sentimentalism has broad appeal but little depth. *The Streets of New York* by Dion Boucicault is typical of the nineteenth-century sentimental melodrama.

Realism

The predominant mode of modern drama is realism. Realism seeks to show life as it is. Influenced by the philosophies of Darwin, Marx, and Freud, playwrights began in the late 1800's to write plays about ordinary men and women caught in familiar dilemmas. While still carefully constructed, the plays of the realists minimized the histri-onics and artifice of the prevalent nineteenth-century styles and eventually influenced acting and directing profoundly. Using every-day language, playwrights built plays stressing ideas rather than action, and revealing the emotions and motivations of the charac-ters. The audience was allowed to look "through the keyhole" at the everyday lives of the characters. For the realistic style, every attempt is made to reproduce correctly the details of dress and ac-cessories, allowing for the requirements of the theater. Examples of realistic drama are *The Little Foxes* by Lillian Hellman and *Cat on a Hot Tin Roof* by Tennessee Williams. In the scene from *The Little*

FIGURE 2.6   *The Little Foxes.* Realistic details give great depth and texture to a production. Designed by Florence Klotz for The Elizabeth Company. Photo © Martha Swope.

Foxes (Figure 2.6), the integration of scenery and costume effects and the wealth of realistic detail are evident.

Selective realism is an approach that chooses or "selects" certain aspects of a play (usually the costumes and props) and represents them realistically while treating other aspects of the production (the set and lights) in a fragmentary, abstract, or stylized manner.

Naturalism

An extreme form of realism, naturalism was an effort to present in the most direct and immediate way, through the language and the physical aspects of the play, the utmost in reality. Also emerging in the late 1800's, naturalism gave way to other forms, in part because of the difficulties of production. Stage representations of a tenement, for example, were no longer adequate for the naturalist; a *real* tenement would be reassembled on stage. Plots emphasized the predestination of man as shaped by his heredity and environment. The form produced some notable works such as Maxim Gorky's *Lower Depths* before its proponents began to drift away into other styles.

Stylization

In the twentieth century many movements sought effective modes of theatrical expression. The term *stylization* has come to mean some departure from realistic presentation. The key to stylized presentation is to find a visual expression of the spirit and meaning of a play. These modes of presentation are often related to movements in the visual arts and are also important in opera and dance presentation.

Symbolism

Plays in this style deal not with intellect and logic, but with the spiritual aspects of life. The significance of silence and the duality of objects, personality, actions, and situations are explored. Whereas the realist holds up a mirror to reflect the reality of life for the audience, the symbolist offers the audience a window through which to view the spirituality of life. One such play is *The Blue Bird* by Maurice Maeterlinck.

The word "symbolism" in common usage has come to mean any partial representation of objects or actions, or an action, object, or decorative motif that represents an idea, person, or other action. Since all literary works contain some metaphors or symbols, the director or designer may decide to stress one of these literary devices to conceptualize the playwright's theme for the audience.

Symbolic costumes take many forms. Some may represent an inanimate object like a ''rose'' or a concept like ''love.'' In fact all costumes are symbolic in some way since their function is to help the actors represent someone or something other than themselves.

Constructivism

Not a style of play, but an approach to visual interpretation, constructivism was developed by Vsevolod Meyerhold. He rejected pictorial realism and naturalism and laid bare the machinery of the stage for the audience to see. Ramps, stairs, platforms, and other structural elements were combined, with the primary purpose of providing for maximum mobility for the actor through various kinds and levels of acting space. Illusions were banned, and decorations were eliminated or minimized. The resulting skeletal assemblage emphasized an individual's position in the mechanized world in a bold and dynamic way. Many plays that are written in other styles have been produced in this mode.

Expressionism

A very subjective style, expressionism forces the audience to view the action through the eyes of the central character. Distortion and

FIGURE 2.7 The Expressionistic mode (style) is more evident in scenery than in costumes, as in this scene from the 1923 production of *The Adding Machine*. Billy Rose Theater Collection, The New York Public Library at Lincoln Center; Astor, Lenox and Tilden Foundations.

repetition are substituted for character development. An expressionistic play presents a mental landscape.

Emerging from the turmoil of World War I and the Russian Revolution, expressionistic plays were a reaction to the mechanization and dehumanization of humanity. These plays are harsh and provocative, pointing out the limits of human morality and sanity. Some plays in this genre are *The Adding Machine* by Elmer Rice and *The Skin of Our Teeth* by Thornton Wilder. A scene from *The Adding Machine* (Figure 2.7) shows the machine as an enormous apparatus almost beyond human control.

Related to the works of constructivism and expressionism are the theater works of the Dada art movement and the dance designs by the painters of Cubism and the Bauhaus school. These works often emphasize the concept of "man as machine." Figure 2.8 shows costumes done by the artist Sonia Delaunay in the Cubist style.

Epic Theater

A very presentational style, epic theater was developed by Bertoldt Brecht. Generally episodic in structure, Brecht's plays make no effort to disguise the fact that an actor is "playing a role." Often the actors sit on the stage until called upon to present themselves in a scene. The audience is to be aware of being in a theater at all times. Visual elements are very theatrical, not necessarily realistic. *Mother Courage* and *The Caucasian Chalk Circle* are two of Brecht's best-known plays.

FIGURE 2.8 An emphasis on geometric shape marks these costumes by Sonia Delaunay (*Rythmes et couleurs*, Hermann, editeurs des sciences et des arts, Paris, 1971)

Documentary

The documentary is a dramatization in a "news format." Declaring itself objective, a documentary basically has an educational purpose. This mode was used by the Federal Theater Project for *The Living Newspaper* during the Depression.

Absurdism

Believing the modern world to be absurd, playwrights in this genre stress a sense of alienation in an illogical, unjust, ridiculous world. Representing an existentialist point of view, these plays are peopled with characters devoid of personal motivation and past history. Absurdist plays defy logic, traditional beliefs, and common understandings. They challenge the audience with nonsense, non sequiturs, and contradictory statements, as in the excerpt from *The Bald Soprano* in Box 2.A. Many of these plays are written with a climactic structure, but the result of the series of actions is illogical. Absurdists are fond of using comic devices for ironic effects and poking fun at sacred ideas. Samuel Beckett's *Waiting for Godot* and Eugene Ionesco's *The Bald Soprano* are two celebrated absurdist plays.

Costumes for constructivist, expressionist, and absurdist plays range from rather realistic to exaggerated and distorted variations of dress.

Box 2.A   Absurdist dialogue: *The Bald Soprano* by Eugene Ionesco

Mrs. Smith: Poor Bobby.

Mr. Smith: Which Bobby do you mean?

Mrs. Smith: It is his wife that I mean. She is called Bobby too, Bobby Watson. Since they both had the same name, you could never tell one from the other when you saw them together. It was only after his death that you could really tell which was which. And there are still people today who confuse her with the deceased and offer their condolences to him. Do you know her?

Mr. Smith: I only met her once, by chance, at Bobby's burial.

Mrs. Smith: I've never seen her. Is she pretty?

Mr. Smith: She has regular features and yet one cannot say that she is pretty. She is too big and stout. Her features are not regular but still one can say that she is very pretty. She is a little too small and too thin. She's a voice teacher.

(*The clock strikes five times. A long silence.*)

Establishing the Mode

When producing plays from other periods, the director and the designers are faced with the question, "Should this play be produced in its original style or be reinterpreted?" Some plays can be successfully interpreted in many ways, while others depend so heavily on their mode for substance that they cannot be successfully reinterpreted in any major way. Many plays originally presented in the realistic style can be reinterpreted in a selective realism or other stylized concept. A play written in the expressionistic style, however, depends heavily on that mode for its meaning and loses its impact in too realistic a production.

One of the first important functions of collaboration between designers and directors is the discussion of the style or mode of the play. However, the director is the final authority on style for any given production and makes the decision either to follow the playwright's intention, to give a historically accurate interpretation, or to reinterpret the script from a new point of view. Establishing the mode or style of a play gives the designer a point from which to conceptualize and visualize the play.

READING THE PLAY

> . . . 'Tis not alone my inky cloak, good mother,
> Nor customary suits of solemn black,
> Nor windy suspiration of forced breath,
> No, nor the fruitful river in the eye,
> Nor the dejected 'havior of the visage,
> Together with all forms, moods, shapes of grief,
> That can denote me truly. These indeed seem,
> For they are actions that a man might play.
> But I have that within which passeth show;
> These but the trappings and the suits of woe.
> HAMLET   William Shakespeare

The *first reading* of the script should be done for an overall sense of the story and characters. Reading the play in one sitting should provide a good sense of its flow and movement. The designer should try to find pleasure in this first reading and should resist the temptation to take extensive notes. *After* the first reading, the designer might make notes on the structure, form, and mode of the play. What themes were apparent from the first reading? The designer should try not to prejudge and impose personal taste on the play.

During the *second reading* the designer's attention should

focus on the language and imagery of the play. What kind of language does the playwright use? Poetry? Street talk? Dialect? Witty repartee? Does it vary with the characters? What rhythms are established? What words or phrases are repeated often? How do they relate to the central theme? What are the most meaningful phrases in each scene and who says them? Does one image represent the central theme or the soul of the play?

While these questions should be considered, the designer must remember that the primary responsibility for the interpretation of the script and development of the production concept belongs to the director. The designer must be prepared, however, to participate intelligently in discussions with the director. The director's concept may be stated in nonvisual terms, and the designer may need to translate the concept into a visual idea. A central part of the collaboration process is the exchange of ideas about the visual and conceptual needs of the play.

Some ideas come to the designer spontaneously while he or she is reading the script. The designer should be open to impressions, ideas, and flashes of inspiration that come during the first and second reading, without stopping to analyze or work them out.

After a designer has a clear understanding of the general outlines of the script, a meticulous *third reading* should provide answers to specific questions. All possibilities and all limitations should be sought. Many designers mark references to costumes, entrances, exits, and pertinent action in the script with a pen or yellow marker.

Determining the historical period of the play is a necessity for the costume designer. Some plays indicate clearly the time in which the play is set, either in a foreword or by reference to historical characters or events. What purpose did the playwright have for setting the play in a specific period? In what way does the essence of the time affect the characters or the action? If the playwright has not specified a date, the style of the play may suggest a time period. A strongly romantic play may suggest to a designer a period in which the costumes are particularly soft and flowing or light in hue. Some plays take place in a fantasy time, either the past or the future. The designer and the director must carefully discuss the aspects of the "time" in which these plays take place.

Careful study of a play may suggest relationships to other periods which the designer may wish to suggest for consideration. Some directors want to move plays out of the time in which they are written in order to point out these relationships or the universality of the theme of the play. Color plate 2 shows a production of *Mother Courage* set not in seventeenth-century Europe, as written, but in nineteenth-century America during the Civil War, a period of history more accessible to a modern American audience.

Many plays are thus transferred to modern dress or "no period." An unspecific time, "no period" usually is a combination of long dresses (of no particular period) for women; long pants, shirts, and coats for men.

If no reference to the date can be found, the designer may assume the play was set in the time in which it was written. Even with a historical play, the date it was *written* may be as important to a designer as the period in which it is set. The influence of the playwright's world will be reflected in any play, even if set in another period. Many plays have been set in a historical period either to disguise or to reveal the playwright's view of a contemporary situation. For example, *The Resistible Rise of Arturo Ui* by Bertolt Brecht draws a frightening parallel between Hitler and the crime lords of Chicago.

From the third and successive readings of the play, the costume designer makes detailed notes on each character. How many characters are there? Are they male or female? What kind of characters are they? Main characters? Chorus members? Stock characters? How are they used? To present information? To focus attention? To state the playwright's point of view? What specifics are known about each one? Some playwrights give detailed descriptions of each character in the stage directions; others give no specific description. The designer ferrets out the needed information from what the character says or from what is said about the character. Specific facts and adjectives are sought. A character's actions reveal important information, but what he or she fails to do may be equally revealing. All other conditions suggested by the playwright must be considered as well — occasion, time of day, climate or weather conditions, specific action requiring costume accessories.

In Box 2.B, an excerpt from *Pygmalion*, Shaw gives us a complete description of Liza. While the designer is not in all cases bound by the playwright's description, careful consideration should be given to the playwright's intent. More binding to the designer is information about a character which is found in the dialogue. In Box 2.C, an excerpt from *Twelfth Night*, Maria describes Malvolio as wearing yellow, cross-gartered stockings, information that the costume designer should not overlook.

The designer should try to visualize the action in each scene as if sitting in the middle of the theater. Is the same actor who was the last character on stage in one scene also the first one on stage in the next scene? Is there a time lapse? Is a costume change indicated? Will that costume need to be rigged for a "quick change"? What

---

Box 2.B Costume description in stage directions: *Pygmalion* by Bernard Shaw

The Flower Girl (picking up her scattered flowers and replacing them in the basket) Theres menners f' yer! Te-oo banches o voylets trod into the mad. *(She sits down on the plinth of the column, sorting her flowers, on the lady's right. She is not at all a romantic figure. She is perhaps eighteen, perhaps twenty, hardly older. She wears a little sailor hat of black straw that has long been exposed to the dust and soot of London and has seldom if ever been brushed. Her hair needs washing rather badly: its mousy color can hardly be natural. She wears a shoddy black coat that reaches nearly to her knees and is shaped to her waist. She has a brown skirt with a coarse apron. Her boots are much the worse for wear. She is no doubt as clean as she can afford to be; but compared to the ladies she is very dirty. Her features are no worse than theirs; but their condition leaves something to be desired; and she needs the services of a dentist).*

Act I

Box 2.C Costume description in dialogue: *Twelfth Night* by William Shakespeare

Maria: If you will see the fruits of the sport, mark his first approach before my lady: he will come to her in yellow stockings, and 'tis a color she abhors, and cross-gartered, a fashion she detests; and he will smile upon her, which will now be so unsuitable to her disposition, being addicted to a melancholy as she is, that it cannot but turn him into a notable contempt. If you will see it, follow me.

Act II, Scene V

---

physical activities are required of the actors? Dancing? Acrobatics? Bike riding? Tricks? Is anyone in disguise? Does the audience know about the disguise? Are the other characters fooled?

Boxes 2.D and 2.E are sample Designer Checklists for play analysis and character information. Answering these questions will help the designer focus on the information needed to design the show.

Arranging this information in a *Costume Plot* (Figure 2.9) pro-

---

Box 2.D   Designer Checklist I: Play Analysis

1. What form of drama is this play? Could it be interpreted any other way?
2. What type of structure does it have? What is the basic story?
3. In what style (mode) is it written? Could it be interpreted in other ways?
4. Where and when does this play take place? What are the climatic conditions? Are there other possibilities?
5. What is the mood of the play? Does this vary with scenes or characters? What are the pivotal scenes (turning points in the course of events)?
6. What colors and textures are suggested by the mood, style, and form of drama of this play?
7. What images are evoked throughout the play? Do they reoccur? To whom are these images related? Which images are central to or represent the soul or spirit of the play? List words that evoke visual images. Do images change from scene to scene?
8. What is the time sequence of the play? In what season(s) do the scenes take place?
9. Can the images in the play be visualized? Do they relate to characters specifically?
10. How are the various characters in the play used by the playwright? To which other characters does each character relate? With which other characters is he or she in conflict?
11. What comic devices does the playwright use?
12. Outline the action of each scene.
13. Combine information in a chart and/or costume plot which graphically illustrates the action and costume needs of the play.

---

vides a visual reference that helps set the play in the designer's mind and facilitates quick retrieval of information. The Costume Plot is a chart that provides a box for each character and each division of the script — act, scene, musical number. In each box are listed the costume items needed and pertinent information about entrances, exits, costume business, and quick changes in that scene. Brief descriptions of time-of-day, scene action, or setting are also helpful. The plot should be updated as needed throughout the design process. The Costume Plot helps focus designer/director discussions and simplify the designer's research and planning.

Box 2.E   Designer Checklist II: Character Information

1. What kind of character is this — major, minor, stock, abstract, allegorical?
2. What are the character's physical characteristics?
   a. Age?
   b. Physical appearance?
   c. Carriage and bearing? Vitality?
   d. Ethnic background?
   e. Mannerisms or affectations?
   f. Speech patterns or dialect?
3. What are the character's mental characteristics?
   a. Education? IQ?
   b. Artistic accomplishments or tendencies?
   c. Ability to relate to reality?
4. What personality traits does this character exhibit? What is the character's emotional state? Does it change as the play progresses?
5. What is the character's social status or rank?
   a. Economic status?
   b. Moral viewpoint?
   c. Religion?
   d. Profession?
   e. Political viewpoint?
   f. Social standing with peers?
   g. Introvert or extrovert?
6. What is the character's objective? Does this character represent the playwright's point of view?
7. How should the dress of this character reflect this analysis?
8. What events in the life of this character have had lasting effects on his on her character?
9. What specific references are made in the script to this character's clothing? What actions are performed by this character which affect the clothing? For what occasions is this character present in the play? In what scenes does this character appear; is he or she the focal point or supporting character?
10. Will the actor cast in this role need special padding, shoes, or other items to "look the part"?
11. Do the characters dress in agreement with all aspects of their personalities and roles or do they attempt to hide, disguise, or deny the reality of their personalities from the other characters and/or the audience?

COSTUME PLOT

BLITHE SPIRIT — NOEL COWARD

ONE SET – RUTH & CHARLES LIVING ROOM

ACT	I			II			III	
SCENE	1	2		1	2	3		1	2
SCENE NOTES → / CHARACTER / PLATE #	Before dinner	after dinner		The next morning	Following afternoon	Evening– a few days later		after dinner– a few days later	Several hours later
EDITH – the maid	#1	#1		#1 new apron	#1 new apron	#1			#23
RUTH – wife #2	#2	#2	INTERMISSION	#8	30 SECONDS #11 ★	5 minutes #16 ★	INTERMISSION	#22	#22
CHARLES – the husband	#3	#3		#9	#13	10 minutes #18 ★		#20	#20 IN DISARRAY
DR. BRADMAN	#4 REMOVE COAT & GLOVES	#4				#17			
MRS. BRADMAN	#5 REMOVE WRAP & GLOVES	#5				#15			
MADAME ARCATI – the medium	#6 REMOVE. CLOAK & GLOVES	#6			#12 REMOVES COAT			#6	#6 IN DISARRAY
ELVIRA – the ghost of wife #1		#7		#10	#14	10 minutes #19 ★		#21	#21

★'s QUICK CHANGES !!!

FIGURE 2.9 Costume Plot. Analyzing and arranging information about the play in the plot helps the designer to visualize the whole play and its costume needs at a glance.

COLLABORATION: DIRECTOR/DESIGNER DISCUSSIONS

At some point during this process of reading and studying the play, the designer will have a first conference with the director. Each director has an individual approach to directing a play. Some directors present the designers with a complete plan and specific requirements at the first meeting; others speak in very abstract terms at first and more specifically later. Some never give a designer specifics. Some directors are nonvisual; they do not have or cannot express visual ideas. The designer must learn to interpret and translate the director's verbal concepts into visual ideas.

Ideally, a designer and director develop a working relationship which stimulates the best ideas and work from both of them. This type of relationship occurs more easily if an atmosphere of mutual respect and a spirit of cooperation are generated.

Because the amount of pre-production time varies with each producing organization, the length and scope of these meetings will also vary. The more "homework" a designer has done, the more productive the director/designer conferences should be.

The designer may return many times to the script for further information and inspiration. Any unanswered questions the designer has from reading the play should be addressed to the director. If the director cannot answer the question, the final clue may come from the actor's interpretation of the character. Because the rehearsal period is an exploratory time, many discoveries are made and new ideas are continually being tried out. The designer must be prepared for some revisions in concepts as the actors and the director explore the script together. The director and/or stage manager should inform the designer of innovations that affect the costumes, but the wise designer makes time to attend rehearsals periodically to evaluate the situation personally. On the other hand, the wise director realizes that major changes in concept are extremely costly and time-consuming once construction of costumes has begun and prepares thoroughly in advance to minimize the necessity for major changes.

Other questions for the director include the following: Will any roles be double cast (two actors in one role) or doubled (same actor playing two roles)? How many extras are planned and how are they to be used? What budget has been allotted to costumes? What are the director's priorities? How will the costumes be used? Are the pockets, closures, or other costume features practical (do they need to be real or can they be faked)?

The costume designer may at this time meet the scenic and lighting designers. Their plans may affect the final approach to the costumes. Often the scenic designer is hired before the costume designer. The style of the scenery may already be established and the costume designer may need to work within that framework. Usually the lighting designer will wait until certain work on the scenery has been completed before making a lot of decisions, but he or she may have ideas about what color light would establish the correct mood in each scene. Questions of the scenic designer include the following: How high and wide are the doors? Are there stairs? Ramps? Rough textures? Will the stage floor be flat or raked? Will there be adequate room for backstage changes? What kind of furniture will be used? Will there be tables on stage on which characters may place accessories, or will the actors have to carry them throughout the scene?

Not all of this information may be available at the first designer/ director conference, but the sooner these questions are answered, the better the planning and the fewer problems there will be as the production progresses.

Good collaboration among director, designers, and actors takes patience, experience, and skill. The designer must understand that the production of a unified whole is the goal. Some personalities work better together than others, but all members of the team must learn to cooperate and make concessions to accomplish the goal. Box 2.F is a Designer Checklist to assist the designer in conferences with the director.

The Production Schedule

At the first or second meeting the designer and director will want to establish a set of deadlines for the production. Starting from the opening night and working backward, dates are set for dress rehearsals, measuring actors, discussing finished sketches and roughs for the costumes, and all other meetings between the director and designer, and the designer and actors. As the work proceeds, more deadlines are added to the production schedule. The schedule varies according to the length of time available for a specific production. Some productions have 6 to 9 months to develop; others are pulled together in days. The essential meetings and deadlines are spread out or compressed as allotted time requires. (See sample production schedule, Figure 2.10.)

Box 2.F   Designer Checklist III:
Director/Designer Conference

1. What does the director see as the mode (style) and form of the drama of the play?
2. What theme or concept has the director developed for the play? Is the concept clearly stated?
3. Can the play be described in one word? Innocent? Decadent? Frivolous? Does that word express the *essence* of the play?
4. How does the director see the characters? How many male and how many female? What physical types are they? What psychological types? What image does the director wish projected by each character?
5. Will any roles be doubled or double cast? How many costumes will need to be duplicated for additional cast, for stress, or for other practical considerations?
6. How many extras are planned? How are they to be used?
7. How many changes of costume for each character does the director envision?
8. How elaborate is the production to be? What is the budget?
9. What are the director's priorities?
10. When is casting to be completed?
11. When do dress rehearsals begin? Are any pieces needed before dress rehearsals (rehearsal props)?
12. What deadlines need to be set?
13. Set up production calendar. Include dates for dress rehearsals, dress parade, fittings, measurements, final sketch approval, preliminary sketch conference, and first blocking rehearsals.

DEVELOPING AND STATING A CONCEPT

Fair ladies — shine upon us like the sun,
Blossom like flowers around us....
CYRANO DE BERGERAC   Edmond Rostand

A major goal of the director/designer conferences is to state a specific approach to, or concept for, the entire production. Doing this may take several discussions, with time for research and thought in between. Not *every* production of *every* play can have a new and exciting concept. However, *every* production of *every* play should make a *clear statement*. Usually, a concept emerges naturally and organically from studying the script and conferring with the director.

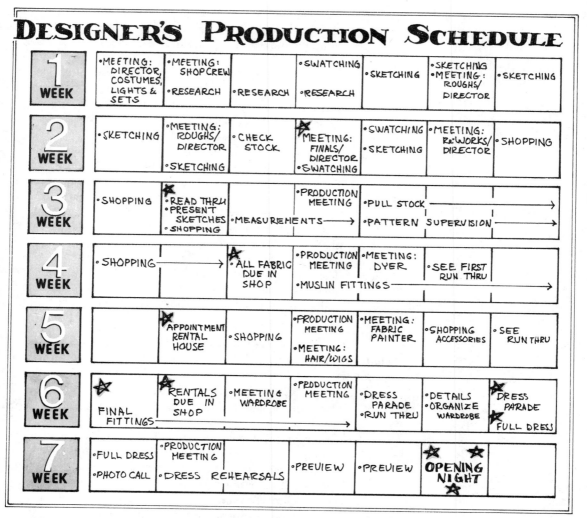

DESIGNER'S PRODUCTION SCHEDULE

WEEK 1	•MEETING: DIRECTOR, COSTUMES, LIGHTS & SETS	•MEETING: SHOP CREW •RESEARCH	•RESEARCH	•SWATCHING •RESEARCH	•SKETCHING	•SKETCHING •MEETING: ROUGHS/ DIRECTOR	•SKETCHING
WEEK 2	•SKETCHING	•MEETING: ROUGHS/ DIRECTOR •SKETCHING	•CHECK STOCK	✿MEETING: FINALS/ DIRECTOR •SWATCHING	•SWATCHING •SKETCHING	•MEETING: Re-WORKS/ DIRECTOR	•SHOPPING
WEEK 3	•SHOPPING	✿•READ THRU •PRESENT SKETCHES •SHOPPING	•MEASUREMENTS→	•PRODUCTION MEETING	•PULL STOCK ————→ •PATTERN SUPERVISION ———→		
WEEK 4	•SHOPPING ————————→	✿•ALL FABRIC DUE IN SHOP	•PRODUCTION MEETING •MUSLIN FITTINGS ———	•MEETING: DYER	•SEE FIRST RUN THRU ———————————→		
WEEK 5		✿APPOINTMENT RENTAL HOUSE	•SHOPPING	•PRODUCTION MEETING •MEETING: HAIR/WIGS	•MEETING: FABRIC PAINTER	•SHOPPING ACCESSORIES	•SEE RUN THRU
WEEK 6	✿ FINAL FITTINGS ———	✿RENTALS DUE IN SHOP ———	•MEETING WARDROBE	•PRODUCTION MEETING ————→	•DRESS PARADE •RUN THRU	•DETAILS •ORGANIZE WARDROBE	✿DRESS PARADE FULL DRESS
WEEK 7	•FULL DRESS •PHOTO CALL	•PRODUCTION MEETING •DRESS REHEARSALS	•PREVIEW	•PREVIEW	✿ ✿ OPENING NIGHT ✿		

Here are some suggestions for developing concepts:

1. Study notes made from the script. What visual images are expressed? Are they related? Play word games with the recurring adjectives. For examples: airy — light — angel — wings — feathers. Can these words be translated into a visual concept?

2. Catchwords and phrases from the script may lead off in many directions. Free associate. Drift with the images. Exercise no restrictions or judgments. Do seemingly unrelated images emerge? Does the quote from *Cyrano* bring up images of ladies in flower-toned gowns? Are there supporting phrases for the idea?

FIGURE 2.10 Production Schedule. This varies, depending on the length of time available. The example is based on a six- to seven-week production period.

3. What will the set look like? Imagine the play as it might be played on stage.
4. What feelings and emotions are evoked by the play? Express the emotion of the play in a collage or doodle. Does this exercise suggest the kind of color, line, texture, or rhythm that is appropriate for the play?
5. Can the play be described in one word? Is it innocent? Decadent? Intellectual? Flamboyant? Poetic? Does that word capture the *essence* of the play?
6. Research may take the designer down many streets, looking for the connections between the play and other elements of the period or milieu of the play. What painters, musicians, sculptors, philosophers, scientists, authors, and famous figures were contemporary with the period of the play? What other work expresses the same ideas as the play?
7. Discovery of interesting materials may stimulate the designer's thinking in new directions. Costume designers have found ways to use foam, mylar, latex, Plexiglas, and various materials never intended for clothing or costumes.

The design concept should be stated briefly and concisely. Here are some examples of concepts for productions represented in this text.

Comedy of Errors. An Elizabethan circus inspired by Miró. A fast-moving farce. Stylized period costumes. (See Color plate 1.)

The Marriage of Figaro. An unfinished painting viewed by candlelight. A work in progress. An earthy, romantic comedy inspired by Goya tapestry cartoons. Not rigidly period. (See Color plate 8.)

Room for One Woman. A drama in realistic, modern, non-specific, time. Space also represents time. The set is not only a room, but time or period of life. Images of plant life: mature, blooming; aging, autumnal; dying, barren. The costumes reflect the life cycles of the plants referred to in the script: green and blooming for the younger woman, brown, orange, and autumnal for the aging woman, and gray, beige, and barren for the old woman.

The designer must have a clear approach to the project, stated in meaningful terms, against which to evaluate the costume decisions for each character.

Chapter 3
Doing Research

. . . There's my pretty darling Kate! The fashions of the times have almost infected her, too. By living a year or two in town, she's as fond of gauze and French frippery as the best of them. Blessing on my pretty innocence! drest out as usual, my Kate. Goodness! What a quantity of superfluous silk has thou got about thee, girl! I could never teach the fools of this age, that the indigent world could be clothed out of the trimmings of the vain.
SHE STOOPS TO CONQUER   Oliver Goldsmith

Extensive research is absolutely necessary to the successful designing of almost every play. For the professional designer, research is a way of life. A background in literature, world history, art, architecture, costume, and theater history are all needed by the costume designer. Seeing plays, visiting museums, nosing around antique shops, searching out both new and old books with information about costumes, manners, and etiquette of different periods, and reading biographies and period novels are all activities that become part of a designer's lifestyle and help provide a rich background of information from which to draw.

GOALS: FOR WHAT ARE WE SEARCHING?

A costume designer seeks two types of research: *factual* for information and *evocative* for inspiration. Factual research is studying sources of history, current events, science, and craft for a range of

facts. Evocative research involves seeking stimuli for creative interpretation. These stimuli may come from many sources: music,
fabrics, art, travel, literature, the language of the play. Some sources
may be suggested during the course of factual research. Factual
research involves diligent effort; evocative research requires being
open and receptive to all experiences and seeing connections to
design problems.

Factual research for each production should provide a general
understanding of the period and culture in which the play takes
place and specific information on the types of garments suitable for
each character in the play. Evocative research seeks sources that
share, illuminate, and project the essence of the play, characters,
and theme.

Understanding the period and culture is extremely important
and too often overlooked by the novice designer. What social
mores of the time or place affected dress and manners? What were
the views on courtship and marriage and the roles of men and
women? What were the erogenous zones (areas of the body considered sexually provocative)? What colors were used and why?
What materials and dyes were available? What kinds of work were
performed? What leisure activities were enjoyed? Permitted? Were
special garments worn for work or play? What differences were
established between age groups, married and unmarried, rich and
poor? What was the political system under which the characters
lived? What religious beliefs were held? How did these beliefs affect
dress and manners? What assumptions were made about people
based on their dress? How did they view themselves in relationship
to the world? The answers to these and other questions give the
designer a context in which to consider the design choices.

SOURCES: WHERE TO LOOK?

Research material falls into two basic categories. *Primary sources*
(the first) are original materials or copies and translations of original
materials. Paintings (or reproductions of paintings) representing the
time in which they were painted, novels representing the author's
contemporaries, and original artifacts from a period or place are all
primary source materials. *Secondary sources* are materials that
represent or discuss a subject in more general terms, are based on
primary sources, and draw broad concepts and conclusions. En-
cyclopedias, textbooks, and general reference books are very valuable as distilled sources of information.

Secondary Sources: Where to Begin?

Beginning with the secondary sources will give the designer an overall view of the costumes needed. For the novice designer a good costume history textbook will provide basic information. Several general texts might be consulted for a broad understanding against which to evaluate other material uncovered by more extensive research. (One such basic outline of fashion history is in Appendix II.) The designer should find several areas of further research suggested by these texts. Because costume texts usually concentrate on the fashionable dress of the period, characters requiring ethnic, peasant, or occupational costumes may not be represented. A list of special topics of research should be started as the needs for specific information are noted.

Since many costume texts present composite or redrawn examples of period dress, care should be taken to check these drawings against primary source materials. Secondary sources may vary from the original as a result of the artist's drawing style, or the conscious or unconscious taste and editing of the artist or author. The original artist may also have flattered the subject or stylized the presentation, further complicating the designer's task.

Distinguishing primary research from secondary research may be difficult. In Figure 3.1 a number of similar garments are analyzed.

The closer one gets to modern times, the more important careful dating of research material can be. Changes may occur in the basic look of garments within a relatively short period of time. In Figure 3.2 a series of nineteenth-century fashion plates illustrate some of the differences in silhouettes during that century.

Understanding the basic look of the period is essential when the designer is approaching such primary source material. Much of this material carries no date. In some cases only the birth and death dates of the artist or the century in which the painting was created may be given. Transition garments, "fancy dress," fashion aberrations, and even flights of artistic fantasy are often represented in the art of a period. While these garments may be far more interesting and exciting to the costume designer, they would be inappropriate in many plays.

Primary Sources: Where to Go from Here?

After the designer has studied the play, developed the costume plot, and reviewed the costume textbooks, a list of specific areas of research should emerge. (See Chapter 2.) These areas should be investigated in primary sources.

A

B

FIGURE 3.1   Primary and Secondary Research. (a) and (b) are modern photos of eighteenth-century gowns. They are considered primary research because the gowns are period originals. At first glance, (c) appears to be an eighteenth century gown but is a 1920's design for "fancy dress" that echoes the bodice and sleeves of (a) and the skirt of (b); fabric and fit are influenced by 1920's fashion. Compare it with (d), a fashionable tea dress of the 1920's. Both (c) and (d) are primary sources for the 1920's, but (c) is a secondary source for the eighteenth century. (e) is a nineteenth-century gown by the famous designer Worth which also looks like an eighteenth-century gown (embroidered underskirt, the lace collar) but is in reality an evening gown of the 1880's. (f) is also an 1880's evening gown with eighteenth-century influence. These gowns are primary research for the 1880's, not the eighteenth century.

(a) and (b) The Metropolitan Museum of Art, (a) Irene Lewisohn Bequest, 1961 (CI 61.13.lab), (b) Anonymous Loan, 1939 (139.29.lab). All rights reserved, The Metropolitan Museum of Art. (c) Vogue Publishing Co. (d) Courtesy of the Picture Collection, Cooper-Hewitt Museum Library: Smithsonian Institution, New York. (e) by courtesy of Trustees Victoria and Albert Museum. (f) The Corcoran Gallery of Art.

C

D

E

F

A B C

D E

FIGURE 3.2 Fashion Silhouette. The 1807 silhouette (a) is high-waisted, soft, narrow, and vertical. The 1833 silhouette (b) has a natural, tight-fitted waist, broad sloping shoulders with large sleeves, and a short, very wide skirt. The 1850 silhouette (c) retains the horizontal effect with sloping shoulders, modest sleeves, and a long, very full skirt. The 1870 silhouette (d) shows the movement away from the broad shoulder line; it has a narrower shoulder and the skirt now has a bustle. The 1891 silhouette (e) has a long, pointed bodice, narrow shoulders, and trumpet-shaped skirt that create a strong, vertical feeling.
(a) from the collection of the author. (b) Courtesy of the Picture Collection, Cooper-Hewitt Museum Library: Smithsonian Institution, New York. (c) Picture Collection, The Branch Libraries, The New York Public Library. (d) Courtesy of the Picture Collection, Cooper-Hewitt Museum Library: Smithsonian Institution, New York. (e) Picture Collection, The Branch Libraries, The New York Public Library.)

. . . He might have been a model for Callot —
One of those wild swashbucklers in a masque —
Hat with three plumes, and doublet with six points —
His cloak behind him over his long sword
Cocked, like the tail of strutting Chanticleer —
Prouder than all the swaggering Tamburlaines
Hatched out of Gascony. And to complete
This Punchinello figure — such a nose! —
You cannot look upon it without crying: "Oh, no,
Impossible! Exaggerated!" Then
You smile, and say: "Of course — I might have known;
Presently he will take it off" But that
Monsieur de Bergerac will never do.

CYRANO DE BERGERAC   Edmond Rostand

**Box 3.A   Sample Research List
for *Cyrano de Bergerac***

FRENCH COSTUMES 1640–1655

FRENCH HISTORY

Louis XIII, r. 1610–1643
Louis XIV, r. 1643–1715
Richelieu, Cardinal, 1624–1642

MENTIONED IN SCRIPT

Actors/costumes 1640's	Pastry cooks
Paris street life	Cardinals
Swashbucklers	Nuns
Theater performances 1640's	Plumed hats
Doublets (with six points)	Masques
Chanticleer	Capuchin monk
Spanish officers	Tamburlaine
Cadets of Gascoyne	Punchinello
Spanish ruffs	

ARTISTS

Peter Paul Rubens	Jacques Callot
Phillippe de Champaigne	Diego Rodriguez de Silva y
Pierre Mignard	Velasquez
Charles le Brun	Francisco de Zurbaran
Rembrandt van Rijn	Franz Hals
David Teniers, Elder	Cornelius de Vos
David Teniers, Younger	Cornelius Johnson
Adriaen Bouwer	Abraham Bosse
Wenceslaus Hollar, engraver	

FIGURE 3.3 Ads in period magazines are excellent sources for sports attire and unusual accessories. *The Theatre,* January and June, 1910.

FIGURE 3.4 "Homemaker" magazines are brimming with suitable styles for the housewife, adolescents, and young adults. "The Modern Priscilla," May 1914.

Box 3.A is a list of areas of research identified for *Cyrano de Bergerac* from information about the play and from the quote above. Careful study of the entire script would certainly add many other topics to the list.

Primary source material may be found in museums and museum libraries and in art sections and picture collections in libraries. An examination of the art of the period in an art history text or general art reference book (secondary source) should provide the names of painters, engravers, illustrators, and other visual artists to add to the research topic list. (See Bibliography and Appendix I.) The designer then investigates volumes that treat the period in depth, and books or folios of reproductions of the pertinent artists.

As useful garments are found in the research, sketches or photocopies are made for the designer's use. Being well organized at this point is essential to the effective use of the research. A tracing paper pad is a handy way to record details quickly. To protect the volumes or folios, the designer should place a sheet of acetate over the page before tracing the garment from an illustration. Notations on the tracing should include the name of the book or folio, artist's name, page number, date, library, and character for which the garment or detail might be useful. While this approach may seem unnecessarily time-consuming, it will make relocating the source much easier should additional information be needed later. Abbreviations can be used for noting information, but a key should be included in the sketchbook. Some research may be interesting even though its use may not be immediately clear. Sorting and eliminating should be done later. It is better to have more than can be used than to make several trips to the same source.

Most libraries will permit photocopies to be made of source material. These work extremely well for line drawings and lithographs, but photocopies of paintings and photos are often not clear enough to be useful. Experience will indicate when to try photocopying. The cost of this type of reproduction adds up quickly and may limit its use for many designers. Again, labeling is important.

Some libraries and museums will also permit the designer to take snapshots or instant photos of research material. A flash is necessary for clear pictures. However, photos of source material from books may not be clear and the color may be distorted. Permission to photograph must be obtained from the librarian or curator.

Permission to photograph original garments in costume collections may be difficult to obtain. The heat and light required for photography are damaging to delicate fabrics. Some museums will photograph items in their collections for a fee. Photographing museum garments is often impractical for the beginning designer because of the expense, the difficulty in obtaining permission, and the level of photography skill required. Sometimes the garment has already been photographed for exhibit catalogs or other museum purposes, and slides or prints may be available through the museum archives.

The designer must be able to sketch elements of the research in the sketchbook freehand. For some sources, this may be the only way to record information. This approach also provides excellent practice in drawing garments. Most libraries and museums require researchers to use pencils for all sketching and notations, since ink can cause serious damage to books and other research materials.

Museum book stores are valuable sources of art books, reproductions, postcards, posters, and slides. Old magazines and photos can be found in used book shops and thrift markets. (See Figures 3.3, 3.4, and 3.5.)

Care should be taken to identify each research item properly with as much information as can be determined. Accurate identification may be very difficult with some items of research. Portraits were often painted in "fancy dress," garments with details from other

A   B   C

FIGURE 3.5   Photos (first appearing in the mid-nineteenth century) are very useful research material for the designer. Photos reveal the way clothes were actually worn, not just the fashion ideal. (a) shows a couple in wedding finery, complete with boutonniere. (b) is a lovely woman in a simple print frock and brooch. (c) shows a middle-class or working-class woman in her best suit, obviously bought "off the rack," with sleeves too long and less-than-subtle fit. From the collections of Hilary Sherred and John Scheffler.

A

B

FIGURE 3.6 (a) *The Honorable Frances Duncombe*, painted by Gainesborough in the eighteenth century. (b) an authentic seventeenth-century portrait by Rubens. (a) Copyright, The Frick Collection: New York. (b) Courtesy of Calouste Gulbenkian Foundation Museum, Lisbon, Portugal.

periods, or costumes assembled by the artist. Information on the artist's approach to the work may indicate if this is the case, and comparison with other sources is helpful. The correct title of the painting may offer a clue.

Figure 3.6a is an example of an eighteenth-century portrait painted in "fancy dress." In this painting by Gainsborough, the designer might be confused by the seventeenth-century details of the costume, if the lady had not retained her fashionable eighteenth-century wig. A comparison with Figure 3.6b, a *seventeenth-century* portrait by Rubens, painted in the dress of the day, reveals a marked difference in certain details, such as the hair style, bodice length, collar, and weight of the fabrics. Further research would confirm the eighteenth century popularity of dress styled after the paintings of Rubens or Van Dyke.

Special Problems

Research into special groups like Amish communities, early American settlements, Native American tribes, various ethnic groups, and Oriental cultures should follow the same approach. Secondary sources will give some answers and may indicate other questions and other places to look. Some possibilities are *National Geographic* and *Smithsonian* magazines, restoration villages such as Williamsburg, Virginia, museums such as the Museum of the American Indian, and the embassies or consulates of foreign countries in Washington, D.C., or at the United Nations in New York City.

The designer must be prepared to request specific information from such sources, however, and not expect to be sent volumes of general material. Obviously, this type of research is very time-consuming and must be undertaken well in advance of a production.

When a play includes characters based on stock characters, such as *commedia dell'arte* characters, the designer should be familiar with their traditional costumes, even if a decision is made to approach these characters from some other point of view. (See Figure 2.4.) Research into the theater conventions of a period, including costuming practices, can only enrich the designer's work.

Research for contemporary plays can sometimes be difficult. Even in this age of mass media and rapid, continual movement of people from place to place, marked differences can be noted in the dress of persons from different Western European cultures and even different areas of the same country. In large cities, different socio-economic/ethnic groups gravitate to specific areas of the city and influence the type of clothes worn in that area. This situation is particularly pronounced in cities that are ports or points of entry for immigrants.

Research for modern plays may involve visiting areas where persons similar to the play's characters live. Magazines, newspapers, and documentary studies of the area or lifestyle under research are all useful. Mail order catalogs are available that are designed to appeal to particular social, regional, or occupational groups. Ads for these catalogs often appear in the backs of other current magazines. Trade and special interest magazines (sports, crafts) usually have ads from clothing manufacturers whose products are believed to appeal to the group targeted by the magazine. These ads and catalogs might clue the designer to a "look" for certain characters. These magazines can be found in the periodicals sections of large libraries.

Authenticity

How much research is enough? How authentic must designs for a play be? These questions have no fixed answers. The solution of each design problem is different. In general, the more realistic the production, the more precise and exact the research should be. Decisions should be based on information, not ignorance. The kind of hat, purse, or glasses should be chosen from the range of correct possibilities, not from contemporary experience or the lone historical source found. The more options available, the more interesting the final choices will be. Even in productions that are simplified or stylized, a thorough understanding of the appropriate period allows the designer to make the most meaningful choices. One perfect detail may make the complete statement. Research does not limit creativity, but stimulates it. Designers who limit their research also limit their flexibility, scope, and creativity.

ORGANIZATION: WHAT TO DO WITH THE RESEARCH?

By this point in the designer's work some ideas should begin to fall into place. The next step is to organize the research into categories based on the notations or other responses to the assembled research. Categories for this stage of organization might be: character names, chorus, extras, mood, concept, details, style, construction notes. Some garments may be perfect as found in the research. Sometimes the cut is good but the fabric wrong. Perhaps the colors of a painting suggest the feeling or mood of the play even though there are no costumes represented. Different details from several garments may be combined in one costume, provided they are compatible in period and style and appropriate to the character.

Each designer develops a personal approach to dealing with the tons of research collected for a large project. Folders, brown envelopes, or accordion files make it easier to organize the material. Nothing is so distressing as not being able to locate that perfect piece of research in all the clutter. As the project progresses, new research may be needed to supplement the original information.

ANALYSIS: WHAT DOES IT MEAN?

Several problems may arise when the designer is interpreting research material. With primary source material, the artist's style may affect the interpretation of the garments represented. Often the great masters created illusions to flatter the subjects of their paintings. Less gifted and less well-known artists often lacked the skill for these illusions and represented more precisely the details of dress. These artists were more apt to distort the proportions of the figure, however, and so comparison of many sources is important. Personal style, the fashion of the day, and contemporary ideas of beauty influence each artist in the presentation of a subject. Figure 3.7 shows two paintings of approximately the same date. The unknown artist who painted *Dr. Hezekiah Beardsley* (3.7a) carefully reproduced great detail and precise costume information, while in the Gilbert Stuart painting of *The Skater* (3.7b) less importance is

A

FIGURE **3.7** Variety of Sources. Often the less sophisticated painter will show more costume information. (a) unknown artist, *Dr. Hezekiah Beardsley*, Yale University Art Gallery, gift of Gwendolen Jones Giddings. (b) *The Skater (Portrait of William Grant)*; Gilbert Stuart; National Gallery of Art, Washington; Andrew W. Mellon Collection 1950.

B

A

FIGURE **3.8** Foundation Garments. (a) *The Theatre*, January, 1910. (b) *Ladies Field*, 1911. (c) The Metropolitan Museum of Art, The Cloisters Collection, 1947. (47.101.12ab) All rights reserved, The Metropolitan Museum of Art.

B

given to the costume and more emphasis is placed on the body and presence of the model.

To further complicate the task, the modern designer brings a current view of fashion and beauty as well as a personal taste and style to the evaluation and interpretation of period research. Beauty truly *is* in the eye of the beholder. The current ideals of beauty and sex appeal, the fashionable figure type and fashion silhouette, and the designer's personal taste all influence the choice, use, and interpretation of period research.

The influence of contemporary fashion on the interpretation of period costumes can be seen by comparing primary source material with costume interpretations from a later period (secondary sources) and with fashion plates of that later period. (See again Figure 3.1.) Several things happen to a garment when it is interpreted in a later period. Almost always it is worn over the currently fashionable undergarments. These undergarments produce the currently fashionable figure which may or may not relate to the silhouette of the earlier style. In many fashion periods a corset was used to alter the natural body shape. In Figure 3.8a Geraldine Farrar wears the fashionable 1910 corset (Figure 3.8b) under her medieval costume. Figure 3.8c is a statue of a medieval saint in a similar garment, but without a structured undergarment. The effect of the foundation garment on the silhouette is clearly visible. Without the corset the garment is a medieval gown; with the corset it becomes a nineteenth-century stage costume.

Figure 3.9 is a costume sketch for Sarah Bernhardt. The features of the Elizabethan doublet have been interpreted to resemble the fashionable sleeve and bodice shapes of 1907. This garment was clearly to be worn over a corset even though Miss Bernhardt was playing a man!

Reproducing a garment in the currently fashionable fabrics may also substantially alter its period look. (See Figure 7.5a.) A stiff period silhouette reproduced in a soft fabric has a different feeling from that of the original. Often subtle changes in the shape or depth of the neckline, length of the sleeve, and fullness of the skirt are sufficient to distort the period essence of a costume. Trim, color, and decorative design may be strongly influenced by contemporary styles as well. Almost always, shoes, makeup, and hair styles are strongly influenced by current trends. These interpretations are not necessarily inappropriate for their original use, but the designer addressing the research must be aware of the influences upon it.

Concurrent research into the cut of period garments is important even if the designer is not responsible for making the garment. The designer should understand the way patterns, tailoring, under-

c

FIGURE 3.9 Contemporary Influence. Sara Bernhardt wore this Elizabethan doublet over a 1907 corset as "Jacasse" in *Les Bouffons* by Zamacoïs. From the collection of Hilary Sherred.

garments, and padding affect the costume. In Figure 3.10 precision cutting, extra padding in the chest area of the vest and coat, and the tight lacing of the vest combine to produce the small waist and large chest of the 1860's fashionable male silhouette. The costumer will be better able to reproduce the desired effect if the designer can give detailed construction information.

As each project is completed, research should be filed for future used.

DEVELOPING PERSONAL RESEARCH SOURCES

A serious designer develops a personal collection of research material. A library of basic books on costumes, art, history, decorative styles, pattern making, costume construction, and crafts would be essential. (The Bibliography might serve as a guide.) Additional

FIGURE 3.10 Artificial Silhouette. Women's fashion is not alone in altering the natural shape of the body. From the author's collection.

volumes collected for work on specific shows can be added as needed.

A file of magazine clippings, postcards, posters and art reproductions, period patterns — anything that might prove useful — should be developed. Clippings from magazines or newspapers should be mounted on heavy paper or index cards to prevent deterioration. Each research piece should be identified as clearly as possible: period or date, subject, and, if a clipping, the original source. File folders, envelopes, or file boxes properly identified should be used to keep the information in order by play, period, or subject.

When the show is finished, research material should be sorted and filed for future use. Some designers store their research according to the play for which it was done; others find filing material by date or period is more useful. Good research may be reused and redeveloped many times; research should never be discarded. The unused detail may be perfect for the next show in the same period.

Much time can be saved on future productions if the designer has a head start on the research.

In addition to research sources, many designers keep files of fabrics, patterns, and sources. A swatch of fabric is attached to a card labeled with the fiber content, use, source, and price. Patterns should be filed with a line drawing of the garment and a description on the outside of the envelope. A source file should contain information on how to locate needed items. (See Figure 7.6.)

A personal research library saves the designer time in the early stages of the design process but should not be relied on exclusively.

Chapter 4
The Designer's Tools:
The Elements and Principles of Design

. . . O that I were a fool!
I am ambitious for a motley coat.

AS YOU LIKE IT   William Shakespeare

All visual artists work with the same elements of design whether they are working on a painting, a sculpture, an advertisement, or a costume. These elements are combined according to certain principles of design. Each element has both physical and psychological effects on the observer. The particular choices made by a designer in a given situation produce a design with specific characteristics and effects. All elements can be manipulated to the designer's purpose. Knowledge of these elements and principles of design is necessary for one to design costumes effectively and to discuss design concepts with the director and the scenic and lighting designers.

ELEMENTS OF DESIGN

The basic elements of design are space, line, shape, form, light, color, and texture.

Space

Space is defined as the area between or within shapes. The painter works on a canvas; the sculptor works in abstract space; the costume designer works with two specific spaces: (1) the area of the actor's body and costume, and (2) the total area of the stage or screen space.

The Silhouette

The space of the actor's body and/or the outline of the garment is called the *silhouette*. The costume designer establishes the shape of the silhouette and subdivides that space to accomplish the desired effect for each character. Manipulation of space by division results in both physical and psychological effects. Physically, these divisions affect the perception of weight, height, and size. Psychologically, these divisions can affect the emotional response of the audience.

The "Stage Picture"

Almost all theaters can be divided into one of three basic types: proscenium theater, thrust theater, or arena theater. (See Figure 4.1.) These designations are based on the relationship between the audience and the stage.

The *proscenium theater* is an arrangement in which the audience faces the stage, most of which is behind a "picture frame" structure. The actors are seen in a shadow box effect. A curtain can be raised and lowered or pulled from the sides to close off the stage and hide the set and actors. Because of the distance (physical and psychological) and the relationship between the audience and the stage, the "stage picture" can be more precisely controlled in the proscenium theater than in other theaters. By manipulating the areas of light and shadow on stage, controlling the colors of sets and costumes, and using the scenery in various ways, the director and de-

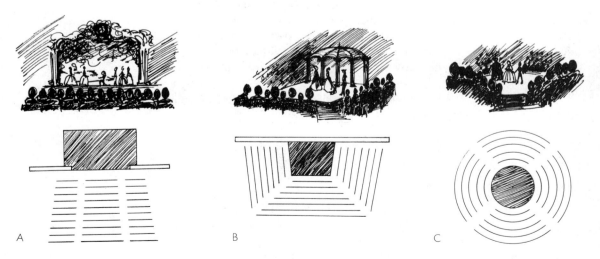

A   B   C

FIGURE 4.1 Types of Theater Arrangements. (a) proscenium, (b) thrust, and (c) arena or theater-in-the-round.

signers can very carefully control the division of space and the image the audience sees.

In the *thrust theater* (also called three-quarters round) the stage is built out into the audience area. In some thrust theaters the fourth side does provide a proscenium area where some effects and scenery can be played. These areas, however, are not generally used for acting. The thrust section of the stage is the main acting area. The actors and the audience may be extremely close and have a sense of sharing the space.

Arena or theater-in-the-round is presented with the audience surrounding the acting space on all sides and with entrance aisles dividing the audience.

In the proscenium style production the acting space is flattened in the audience's perception to an almost two-dimensional picture; in a thrust or theater-in-the round presentation, the costume designer works like a sculptor in a three-dimensional space. The arrangement of actors on stage is the responsibility of the director, and the spatial relationships between them is a result of the action. However, in plays with crowd scenes the costume designer should be aware of the spatial relationships between the various groups of actors on stage. The division of space which results from costuming the group either differently or alike alters the total effect of the "stage picture." In plays like *Oedipus Rex*, the chorus may be seen as a unified, moving mass. In other plays the chorus may be seen as a group of individuals. In Act II of Giacomo Puccini's opera *La Bohème* the chorus is seen as participants in a great Christmas Eve crowd in the Paris Latin Quarter. Various chorus members are depicted as vendors, entertainers, street urchins — individuals, rich and poor.

In films or television the image is controlled within specific shapes (the screens). The figure and the costume on the screen may be seen only in a close-up or as a fragment of the total. When the designer knows how scenes are to be shot, he or she should consider how the divisions of the garment relate to the screen shape.

Pleasing Divisions of Space

Uneven divisions of space are generally the most pleasing. Equal divisions or extremely unequal divisions are generally less pleasing. (See Figure 4.2.) However, an unpleasing effect may be exactly what the designer is obliged to produce for certain characters or scenes, particularly comic or evil ones. Also, the uninteresting division may gain interest if it is unusual in the context in which it is seen. Characters like the trolls in *Peer Gynt* may require a design based on unusual divisions of space.

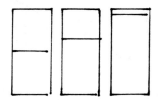

FIGURE 4.2 Divisions of Space.

Line

I don't like that underslung line. It cuts her across the fanny. Makes her look positively duck-bottomed.
THE WOMEN   Clare Booth Luce

An elongated mark connecting two points or defining the edge of a shape is called a *line*. The line of a costume may be expressed by the cut of the garment, the seaming, the application of trim, and the overall silhouette of the period.

Aspects of Line

There are eight aspects to a line: (1) path, (2) thickness, (3) continuity, (4) sharpness, (5) contour, (6) consistency, (7) length, and (8) direction. Within each aspect are numerous variations, each conveying its own psychological and physical effects. These effects of line are based on associations with objects from our experience or from nature.

The costume designer uses line to accent psychological traits of a character and to emphasize or minimize the actor's physical characteristics. Figure 4.3 and Box 4.A show examples of the aspects of line, the basic effects of using each aspect, the psychological characteristics that each stresses, and the way to incorporate each in a garment. The effect of each type of line can be modified by the effect of other elements used with it. The designer would choose those aspects of line that would most clearly reflect the character's traits (Figure 4.3). The basic line of most costumes is vertical since the actor is seen primarily standing or sitting. The effect of the various aspects of line can reinforce or modify the verticality of the actor.

FIGURE 4.3 Aspects of Line. (a) straight; (b) thick; (c) broken; (d) thin, sharp; (e) fuzzy; (f) curved; (g) long, unbroken, smooth; (h) solid; (i) shaped; (j) short; (k) diagonal; (l) porous; (m) vertical; (n) horizontal

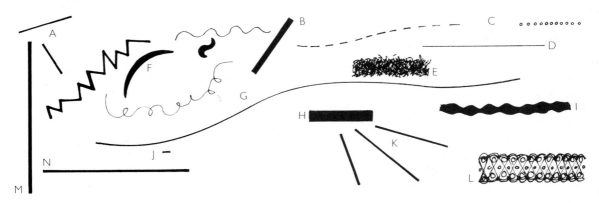

Shape and Form

Your lord does know my mind; I cannot love him.
Yet I suppose him virtuous, know him noble,
Of great estate, of fresh and stainless youth;
In voices well divulged, free, learned, and valiant,
And in dimension and the shape of nature
A gracious person. . . .

TWELFTH NIGHT   William Shakespeare

Shape is flat space enclosed by a line; *form* is a three-dimensional area enclosed by surfaces. Hollow forms are perceived as volume, and solid forms are perceived as mass. Shapes and forms are *defined* space. They assume the effects of the lines surrounding them and the space separating those lines. For example, rectangles and squares, constructed of vertical and horizontal lines, suggest stability, confidence, and assertiveness. Triangles, pentagons, and other shapes with diagonal sides suggest drama and action, but less stability. Shapes with curved sides project the attributes of curved lines with vertical or horizontal effects, but more subtly expressed. The way in which the designer subdivides a shape can alter the audience's perception of that shape (Figure 4.4). Lines inside a shape, subdividing it into smaller shapes, can help the designer create a variety of moods and illusions.

Most shapes have corresponding forms. The human body, and garments designed for it, can be translated into simple two-dimensional forms and yet are understood to be three-dimensional. Basic shapes and forms have names that are useful when one is discussing designs. (See Figure 4.5.)

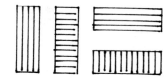

FIGURE 4.4   Dividing Shape.

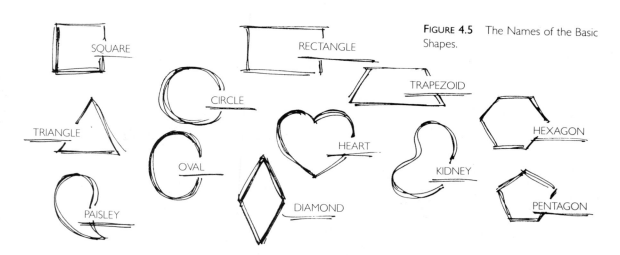

FIGURE 4.5   The Names of the Basic Shapes.

SQUARE

RECTANGLE

TRAPEZOID

CIRCLE

HEXAGON

TRIANGLE

HEART

OVAL

KIDNEY

PAISLEY

DIAMOND

PENTAGON

Box 4.A   Aspects of Line

ASPECT	PHYSICAL EFFECTS	PSYCHOLOGICAL EFFECTS	WAYS TO USE
Path			
Straight	Emphasizes angularity, tends to conceal body contours	Stiffness, directness, tension, stubbornness, masculinity, self-assurance, austerity	Seams, darts, hems, pleats, belts, stripes, geometrics, tucks, ribbons
Straight variations (zigzag)		Sharpness, abruptness, instability, nervousness, excitement	Garment edges, trim
Curved	Emphasizes roundness	Flexibility, grace, femininity, fluidity, ease, subtlety, youth	Seams, garment edges, scallops, patterns, draping
Width			
Thick	Adds weight	Forcefulness, self-assurance, aggressiveness, masculinity	Borders, trims, cuffs, fabric patterns, belts
Thin	Minimizes weight	Delicateness, daintiness, gentleness, serenity, passivity, subtlety	Seams, darts, pattern, trim
Continuity			
Unbroken	Smoothness, emphasizes bumps and curves	Constancy, elegance, smoothness, grace	Seams, pleats, gathers, trim, draping
Broken	Emphasizes irregularities	Less rigidity, playfulness, informality, casualness, busyness	Trims, buttons, edgings, pattern
Sharpness			
Sharp	Emphasizes contours it follows	Assertiveness, boldness, precision, hardness	Seams, darts, edges, trims, stripes
Fuzzy	Softens contour, gently increases area, reduces definition of edge or shape	Softness, indecisiveness, femininity, gentleness, ease	Fringe, fur, feathers, patterns, translucent fabrics, trims

ASPECT	PHYSICAL EFFECTS	PSYCHOLOGICAL EFFECTS	WAYS TO USE
Contour			
Smooth	Reinforces smoothness or accents shapes	Straightforwardness, simplicity, boldness, assertiveness, hardness, definitive precision	Seams, darts, edges, trims, stripes
Shaped	Effect varies depending on elements of shape	Complexity, informality, deviousness	Lace, trim, pattern
Consistency			
Solid	Advances boldly	Smoothness, self-assurance, strength	Stripes, binding, piping, braid, belt, borders
Porous	Does not advance, may recede	Openness, delicacy, weakness, refinement, uncertainty	Lace, crochet, fringe, eyelet trim
Length			
Long	Emphasizes its direction, smooths and elongates	Evaluation relative to figure, stress on continuity, grace	Seams, darts, trims, other
Short	Breaks up spaces	Possibly busyness, agitation	Any of the above
Direction			
Vertical	Lengthens, narrows	Dignity, strength, poise, elegance, superiority, grandness, alertness, austerity	Any of the above
Horizontal	Shortens, widens	Tranquility, repose, calmness, serenity, passiveness	Any of the above
Diagonal	Near vertical — lengthens Near horizontal — widens 45 effect — influenced by other factors	Dramatic, vivacious, unsettled, active, unstable, dynamic	Any of the above

Structural Shape and Form

The units that make up an object contribute to and are inherent in its structural shape or form.

The Human Body

The first form the costume designer must deal with is that of the human body. The separate shapes and forms of the body (head, arms, torso, legs) combine to create the individual's body structure. The structural shape of a specific actor is a given part of the design formula that the designer must use, and the costume must ultimately work on that actor. In addition to taking measurements, the designer should analyze the effect of the actor's figure: well-proportioned? tall, thin, and angular? short, round, and stout? broad-shouldered, narrow-hipped? stooped? The designer must answer the question, "Does the actor's body correspond to the character type required or should physical or visual alterations in the figure be attempted?" Figure 4.6 and Box 4.B demonstrate the visual effects of shape in costume. In the design for Tiger Brown (Figure 4.7) line and shape (structural and decorative) combine to express character. The animal-spot pattern on the vest reflects his name, and the horizontal lines on the pants emphasize his physical girth.

Box 4.B   Visual Effects of Shape in Costume

1. A silhouette (shape) emphasizes the direction of its dominant lines.
2. Subdividing a shape vertically, visually lengthens and narrows it. Subdividing a shape horizontally, shortens and widens it.
3. Shapes standing away from the body add apparent weight and bulk to the figure.
4. Body-skimming shapes may seem to add weight and bulk, but they may also disguise the exact shape and size of the body, making it easier to visually modify the too heavy or too thin figure.
5. Tightly fitted costumes emphasize body contours and may increase the apparent size of the figure.
6. A shape tends to emphasize the part of the body at its edge.
7. A shape conveys the psychological effect of the line enclosing it and the space within it.
8. Impressions of size and shape are initially established by the overall silhouette and its relationship to the surroundings, then internal subdivisions are related to the silhouette.

FIGURE 4.6   The visual effects of shape.

FIGURE **4.7**   Tiger Brown, *The Three-penny Opera*. Designed by Patton Campbell for The Empire State Institute of Performing Arts.

The Costume Silhouette

Throughout history people have been extremely inventive about the shape and division of the space surrounding and including the human body. The silhouette of the historical period in which the costumes are to be designed is also a given part of most design projects. Historical silhouettes and modern clothes can be analyzed in their structural shapes. Analyzing silhouettes in this way (Figure 4.8) helps the designer to determine the effects of the finished costume. Seeing basic shapes and forms is the key to translating research to sketch, sketch to pattern, and pattern to costume.

A careful look at a costume resource reveals the basic shapes and forms. The total effect suggested by the combination of these shapes is either horizontal or vertical. Although the combination of shapes may vary, in most periods the majority of garments give a similar effect. Between the extremes of vertical and horizontal periods are transitional periods which show some characteristics of both the earlier costume styles and the later styles. The designer needs to keep in mind the effects the shapes will suggest on the bodies of the actors and the desirablity of these effects in projecting character traits for each role. Adjustment of the silhouette shapes may be necessary to counter undesirable effects.

Decorative Shape

Once the basic silhouette and the structural shapes of a garment are determined, and designer begins to deal with decorative shapes and forms within the silhouette. Dividing the silhouette into smaller shapes with trim, patterns, seams, and other design devices produces variety and subtlety of effect.

Smaller areas within a silhouette are usually perceived as shape, and larger areas as space. A design is generally more pleasing if there is enough contrast between the size of decorative shape and the size of surrounding space to clearly define each. When seen on stage, costumes that lack sufficient difference between space and shape within the silhouette may be perceived as

FIGURE 4.8 Analyzing Garment Shapes.

merely textured or may create a busy, fussy effect. A motif (decorative shape) that must be recognized as a symbol by the audience will need to be large with much surrounding space to compensate for the distance from stage to audience. A cross or fleur-de-lis on a tunic for St. Joan, for example, has strong character significance and must be readily recognized by the audience. The need to clarify the symbol may lead the designer to simplify other aspects of the garment.

Light

Don't look at us like we are, sir. Please. Remove ten pounds of road dust from these aged wrinkled cheeks. See make-up caked, in glowing powder pink! Imagine a beard, full blown and blowing, like the whiskers of a bear! And hair! Imagine hair. In a box I've got all colors, so I beg you — imagine hair! And not these clothes. Oh no, no, no. Dear God, not rags like any beggar has. But see me in a doublet! Mortimer, fetch the doublet. There — Imagine! It's torn: I know — forget it. It vanishes under light. That's it! That's the whole trick; try to see me under light! . . .
THE FANTASTICKS   Tom Jones and Harvey Schmidt

The portion of the electromagnetic or radiant spectrum that is visible to the human eye is called *light*. This radiant energy results from the vibration of electrons and includes x-ray, ultraviolet, infrared and radio waves. The source of the energy is called the *stimulus* and the visual perception or sensation is termed the *response*. Visible rays are only a tiny part of the electromagnetic spectrum.

Light waves vary from other radiant energy only in wavelength and frequency. *Wavelength* is the distance between the highest point of one wave and the highest point of the next. *Frequency* refers to the speed of the wave vibrations. *Brightness*, or *level of illumination* depends on the amount of energy radiating from the stimulus.

Light makes possible the visual perception of all other design elements. It provides illumination, defines lines and forms and locates their position in space, and identifies the texture and colors of surfaces. Light is perceived in two ways: *direct light* (from the source, i.e., sun, candle) or *reflected light* (reflected from the surfaces of objects).

As in almost no other situation, light on stage can be controlled and manipulated for an esthetic purpose. While the responsibility for the direct light belongs to the lighting designer, the manipulation of reflected light is affected by the choice of materials, fabrics, and trims made by the costume and set designers. The figure on stage may appear different from moment to moment as it moves from one area of light to another. The costume designer must be aware of the lighting possibilities of any given moment in a play and choose fabric and trims that reflect light in suitable ways.

Physical Effects of Light

If our visual perception of an object depends on the reflection of light off its surface, then a designer must understand the effects produced by the manipulation of the aspects of light. The visual effects produced on costumes or scenery vary depending on the direction of the light, angle of light incidence, level of illumination, quality of light, and texture of reflecting surface.

The *direction* of light can generally be controlled by the lighting designer. Light can be focused on the stage from the front, sides, top, back, and sometimes the floor. Lighting for the thrust stage and for arena theater is generally balanced to produce a similar image to the audience on all sides of the stage. Lighting from the different areas of the proscenium stage produces specific effects: front light provides the basic illumination, side light gives the actors and the scenery dimension, and back light separates the actor from the scenery and provides depth. Side lighting and back lighting also help eliminate or control shadows on the actors and the scenery.

The *angle of incidence* refers to the angle at which the light hits an object. A low angle of incidence produces low angle reflection off the surface of the object and long shadows behind the object. A high angle of incidence produces high angle reflection off the surface of the object and short shadows behind it.

The *level of illumination* refers to the degree of brightness of the light. The lighting designer uses the brightness and dimness of the light in a given area of the stage to create focus (helping the audience know where to look), to establish the time of day or climate, and to create a mood.

The *quality of light* on stage may be soft and diffused or sharp and focused, depending on the lighting instruments used and the effects desired. Diffused light is atmospheric; it reduces the contrast between surfaces and softens the contours of objects. Sharp light emphasizes surface quality, accents differences in textures, and stresses dimension. The use of sharp focused light heightens drama by creating strong highlights and dark shadows. (See Box 4.C.)

Surfaces react to light by *reflecting* (bouncing off), *absorbing* (intercepting light rays), or *transmitting* the light rays (passing light through a medium). Using fabrics and trims that react to light in all

---

Box 4.C   Aspects of Stage Light and Their Effects

ASPECT	EFFECT
Direction	Produces highlights and shadows, creates or eliminates distortion, varies importance of objects or actors
Front	Gives general illumination, puts emphasis on areas or specific actors
Side	Defines figures and scenery, mood, atmosphere, and time
Back	Separates figures from scenery, sets mood, creates environment
Down	Reduces shadows on scenery, creates distorted effects on figures
Up	Creates dramatic effects on scenery and figures, is used for lighting drops and cycloramas
Angle of Incidence	
Low angle	Produces low angle reflection, long shadows
Sharp angle	Produces sharp angle reflection, less visible shadows
Level of Illumination	
Higher (brighter)	Reflects more light from the surface, offers higher temperature of radiant energy, directs audience's attention
Lower (dimmer)	Gives less light and less heat, creates atmosphere, draws less attention
Quality of Light	
Sharp	Emphasizes surface quality, accents differences in textures, stresses 3-D quality, heightens drama, creates brighter highlights; produces sharper, harder, darker shadows
Diffused	Reduces contrast, softens contours, creates mood

three ways helps create variety, depth, and interest in both individual and groups of costumes. Although the lighting designer is responsible for the type and placement of the stage lighting, the costume designer can create many special effects by controlling the surfaces on which the light falls. Box 4.D lists some commonly used costume materials and their responses to light.

Box 4.D   Material Responses to Light

HIGH REFLECTION	MEDIUM REFLECTION	HIGH ABSORPTION	TRANSMISSION
Mirror	Raw silk	Velveteen	Organza
Sequins	Brocade	Velvet	Chiffon
Lamé	Taffeta	Wool	Organdy
Vinyl	Crepe	Cotton	Scrim
Satin	Chintz	Velour	Net
Mylar		Knits	Tulle
Polyester			Lace
Lurex			
Glitter cloth			

Hard smooth surfaces are highly reflective materials. Fabrics with fuzzy or irregular surfaces absorb most of the light rays. Fabrics that transmit light have spaces between fibers that permit some light rays to penetrate, or they are made of materials that are translucent or transparent. Highly reflective materials applied in small shapes, such as sequins, reflect the light differently than similar materials used in large flat surfaces because of the size of the surface and different angles of incidence provided by the movement of the wearer. Figure 4.9 shows the glittering and beautiful effect produced by the combination of highly reflective (rhinestones) and transmissive (chiffon and nylon knit) materials chosen for this costume for *My One and Only*.

Psychological Effects of Light

The more light in a space, the more springlike, cheerful, happy, and youthful the perception of that space or shape will be. The less light in a space, the sadder, more melancholy, older, more winterlike the perception of that space or shape will be. Sharp, bright, crisp, warm light in a space gives the feeling of joy, glory, or hope. Soft, diffused, cool light gives the feeling of grief, melancholy, or romance. Harsh, strong light may suggest anger, violence, or power. The color of the light may suggest the time of day, the weather or climatic conditions, and the mood of the scene.

Color Perception

Strictly speaking, objects do not *have* color. They have pigmentation. A *pigment* is a material with the ability to reflect certain light waves. The perception of color in an object is the result of the light

FIGURE 4.9 *My One and Only*. Designed by Rita Ryack. Photo © Kenn Duncan.

reflected from the pigmentation of that object to the eye of the viewer. The color observed in an object depends upon the color pigmentation of that object *and* the color of the light rays illuminating the object.

So called "white light" appears white because it contains all colors of the visible spectrum in balanced proportions. When this light strikes a surface, two effects may result. One, the light may be reflected unchanged as sharp white highlights (such as are reflected off satins, vinyls, and water) or the white light may slightly penetrate the surface of the object, where the pigment in that surface absorbs all the wavelengths but one. That unabsorbed wavelength is reflected to the viewer's eye and the object is perceived as the color of *that wavelength*. The color we perceive is the color *not* absorbed by the surface pigment of the object. If balanced white light is focused on an object with no pigmentation, all the wavelengths are reflected and the object is perceived as white. If a surface contains pigments to absorb all the wavelengths, few are reflected and we perceive the object as black. The perception of black costumes on stage often depends on the color of the area surrounding the actor. The reflection of light from surrounding areas defines the black costume against those areas and compensates for the absorption of light by the black of the costume.

In practice, however, pure white light is seldom used for stage. The lighting designer develops a plan using various colors of light to create a mood or environment for each of the hundreds of moments in a play. The use of dozens of lighting instruments focused on the acting area enable the lighting designer to subtly (or dramatically) direct the audience's attention to the important points of action, and to reflect or enhance the mood of the moment.

Color Theory for Light

Isaac Newton used a prism to separate white light into a spectrum and thereby made visible the magic of light and color. He devised the first color wheel by bending his spectrum into a circle. Other color theorists have since developed the color wheel and theory more completely. Physicists agree that the primary (basic) colors of light are red, green, and blue. These basic colors cannot be mixed by combining any other colors of light, but among them they can create all other light colors. Overlapping red and green light produces yellow; overlapping red and blue light produces magenta; overlapping blue and green light produces blue-green or cyan. Therefore the secondaries in light are yellow, magenta, and cyan. (Pigment colors behave differently from light colors. Color theory for pigments is discussed under *Color*.)

Combining all three primaries produces white light; thus, adding colors of light together is called the *additive theory*. White is the presence of all light and color; black is the absence of all light and color.

Colored lights for stage are produced by inserting a sheet of color medium into a frame which is placed in front of the lighting instrument. This plastic medium (sometimes called *gel*) screens out all wavelengths except that of the medium. Because a pigmented surface can reflect *only* the colors that are in the light that strikes it, colored light can seriously alter the perception of the color of objects on stage. Box 4.E indicates the *probable* effects of colored light

---

Box 4.E   Probable Effects of Colors of Light on Colors of Fabric

FABRIC COLOR	COLORS OF LIGHT						
	Amber (Yellow)	Orange	Red	Violet	Blue	Blue-green (Cyan)	Green
Yellow	Bright yellow	Yellow-orange	Red	Scarlet	Yellow-green	Yellow-green	Yellow-green
Orange	Orange	Bright orange	Bright red-orange	Scarlet	Light brown	Light brown	Light brown
Red	Bright red	Red-orange	Bright red	Scarlet	Purple-black	Dark maroon	Maroon
Violet	Dark brown	Dark brown	Dark gray	Deep violet	Dark violet	Dark violet	Violet
Blue	Dark blue-gray	Black	Gray	Light blue	Dark blue	Light blue-gray	Light blue
Blue-green	Green-blue	Dark green-blue	Black	Dark blue	Very dark blue	Dark blue-gray	Dark green
Green	Bright green	Dark green	Dark gray	Bluish brown	Light olive-green	Light green-gray	Strong green

NOTE: The effect of colored lights on fabric is difficult to anticipate. This chart suggests the probable effects of various colors of light on fabric colors. The exact shade, tint, or intensity of each color, however, may react in an unexpected way. For example, a dark red that has been lowered in intensity because its complement, green, has been added may turn black under red light as the green pigment *absorbs* the red light.

on costume colors. To further complicate matters, stage light usually combines several colors, with the dominant color changing as the play progresses. Variations in the colors of light on stage are designed to give objects and figures dimension, create mood, and stimulate emotional responses from the audience.

Not only is the color of stage light controlled, but the levels of illumination are constantly varied. The level of illumination affects the perception of the object, and some colors may darken more quickly than others as the light dims. Colors with longer wavelengths (reds and oranges) lose their reflecting ability faster and therefore look darker sooner as the lights dim. Colors with shorter wavelengths (blues and violets) retain their reflecting ability longer and darken more slowly. This phenomenon might be an important consideration when scenes overlap and one area of the stage dims as lights go up in another area. Actors in costumes in the darker area should disappear quickly as the lights dim so as not to be "ghosts" moving offstage — unless, of course, this is the desired effect.

In bright, white light, colors seem warmer and tend toward yellow; at low light levels, the same colors seem cooler and tend toward blue. The costume designer may need to compensate for low levels of illumination in certain scenes. For example, if a red fabric is chosen for a dimly lit scene, a red-orange will appear warmer and richer than a pure red or a red with blue undertones. Greens might need to be more yellow to keep from looking too cool in lower illuminations. A moonlight scene such as the balcony scene in *Cyrano de Bergerac* requires some careful thought. Cyrano's black costume will make it easy for him almost to disappear under the balcony as he coaches Christian in the art of wooing, but will he disappear completely? What colors should Roxanne and Christian wear? What light will they be seen in? The usual colors of moonlight (blues) will make blue costumes more intense. Orange-based tones will gray out. Reds with too much blue will appear to vibrate. The costume will appear darker in the lower light levels than it actually is. What effect is desired?

Color

> Beautiful ribbons, Count! That color, now,
> What is it — Kiss-me-Dear
> or Startled-Fawn?
> I call that shade The Dying Spaniard.
> Ha.
> And no false colors either. . . .
> CYRANO DE BERGERAC Edmond Rostand

The most exciting, powerful, and provocative element of design is color. As a purely physical phenomenon, we have seen that color is the result of the reflection of specific wavelengths of light from an object and the perception of those wavelengths by the observer. The physical understanding of this element, however, is only a small part of the story. The emotional or psychological response elicited by color is the result of (1) a vast store of cultural associations shared by a society, and (2) associations unique to each individual. The costume designer must learn to manipulate both the physical and psychological aspects of color in order to produce the desired audience response.

Color Theory for Pigments

The planning of pleasing color schemes for sets of costumes, the mixing of paint for rendering sketches, and the mixing of dyes and paints to be used on fabrics for the costumes all require that the designer understand basic color theory for pigments.

Many color theories have been developed for working with pigments. Pigments do not behave in the same way that light waves do. The color wheel (a device for showing relationships between hues) identifies red, yellow, and blue as pigment *primaries*, that is, as basic colors which cannot be mixed from any other colors but, when combined, produce other hues. Red and yellow combine to make orange, blue and yellow combine to make green, and blue and red combine to make violet. Thus orange, green, and violet are identified as the *secondary colors*. *Tertiary* colors are those produced when a secondary and a primary color are combined. These colors are named red-orange, yellow-orange, blue-green, red-violet, and blue-violet, expressing the influence of the primary color first. (See Color plate 3.)

Colorless objects, such as glass and surfaces with no identifiable hue (white, black, or gray), are called *achromatic*. Objects with identifiable hue are called *chromatic*. Substances that produce color are called *colorants*. For light, the colorant might be a colored filter or "gel." For surfaces, the colorant might be paint, dye, or ink.

Dimensions of Color

To discuss color properly, one needs to understand its different aspects or dimensions. *Hue* is the general term or family name applied to a color, the location of the wavelength on the light spectrum. A pure hue is a color as it appears in the spectrum or on the color wheel. *Value* is the lightness or darkness of a hue. Colors with white added to them are called *tints* and are said to have *high values*. Colors with black added to them are called *shades* and are said to have *low values*. The values of colors can be compared to a gray scale shading from white to black. Every pure hue has its own *home value*. Yellow, the lightest hue, would have the highest home value. The next color in descending value is orange, then red and green at similar home values, then blue, and at the lowest and darkest home value is violet. Changing the value of a hue can alter the psychological effect it produces. Lighter values tend to be purer, clearer, more youthful colors; darker values appear more serious, rich, and meaningful. However, the addition of white or black to some colors tends to alter the hue of that color. Black added to yellow, for example, pushes yellow toward a green hue. Some violets begin to appear pink when white is added. Black, white, and grays are *neutrals* because they express no hue.

Intensity is the brightness or dullness of a hue. Intensity is also referred to as saturation, chroma, purity, or vividness. Colors of high intensity are bright, clear hues; colors of low intensity are dull, slightly grayed hues. A hue is its brightest, therefore at its full intensity, only at its home value. To reduce the intensity of a hue with the least alteration in its value, a small amount of its complement can be added. Equal strengths of complementary colors combine to form a neutral gray. Because pigments are not all of the same concentration, and because different hues are of differing intensities, adjustments in the *amount* of pigment may be needed in order to mix equal *strengths* of two complementary hues. To produce a true neutral, complements must be of equal *strength*.

Physical Effects of Color

Single colors produce certain physical effects, but colors are rarely seen alone. Most are seen in relationships to other colors. Colors next to one another or superimposed on one another are said to be "juxtaposed." Colors in costumes are juxtaposed within the costume, with the hair and skin tone of the actor, with other actors' costumes, and with the scenic elements against which they play.

Each dimension of a color makes a contribution to the physical effects produced by that color.

Physical Effects of Hue

The effects produced by a color on stage may be altered by the color of stage light. The effects described here assume the use of balanced or white stage light. Juxtaposing colors creates many effects. The following effects are most pertinent to the problems of the costume designer.

1. *The same color will look different against two contrasting background colors.* Two costumes of the same color may appear to be different hues if played in front of set areas of greatly differing colors.

2. *Two juxtaposed complements intensify one another.* A green costume on a red-haired actress has the effect of intensifying the hair color.

3. *Two closely related (but not adjacent) juxtaposed hues tend to repel each other.* When the "middle" color is added, a link is provided to draw the colors together by emphasizing their similarities. A character in a red costume and one in a violet costume might appear quite independent of each other until a third character in red-violet completes the color group.

4. *A color gives the effect of its complement to colors juxtaposed with it.* A neutral, tint, or shade will tend to take on the character of the complement of the juxtaposed color. An orange costume may cause a neutral gray back-drop to have a cold blue feeling. The exception: Bright colors may reflect onto juxtaposed colors.

5. *Reds, oranges, and white tend to spread and merge with each other and with other colors; greens, blues, violets, and black tend to separate and delineate colors.* Shapes outlined in white look lighter and merge with one another and surrounding space. Shapes outlined in black are sharp and distinct. A costume with skirt ruffles outlined in white will look lighter and more delicate; a costume with skirt ruffles outlined in black will look heavier, crisper, and more distinct.

6. *Edges between adjacent hues of like value and intensity tend to fade.* Groups of chorus or crowd members who need to be nonspecific will be less distinct if costumed in adjacent colors of similar value and intensity — for example, medium-value, low-intensity blues; medium-value, low-intensity greens; and medium-value, low-intensity blue-greens.

Visual mixtures are blendings of color that occur in the eye and brain rather than on the surface of objects. Dots of color placed next to one another are blended by the eye and brain. Visual mixtures are particularly interesting for stage use because the distance from stage to audience is a necessary ingredient in the process. With the addition of multicolored stage light, the richness of visual mixtures is enhanced. Visual mixing is achieved through choice of fabrics with small flecks, dots, or patterns of color or by spattering or spraying the garment with paint or dye. The colors produced by visual mixing have more depth, richness, and vibrancy than colors achieved through pigment mixing.

7. *Visual mixtures of points or dots of two primary colors produce vibrant secondary or tertiary colors.*

8. *Visual mixtures of all three primaries and/or black and white tend to mix more quickly and are muted.* These visual mixtures provide rich neutrals for background or chorus colors.

9. *Color points of similar value and intensity mix more easily than those of extremely contrasting values or intensities.*

10. *Smaller dots of color blend visually at shorter distances than larger dots of color.* The closer the audience is to the acting area, the smaller the points of color need to be for complete visual mixing.

Physical Effects of Value

Contrast in value is one of the most powerful principles of visual design. The stronger the value contrast, the bolder and more severe the effect; the softer the value contrast, the gentler and more subtle the effect.

1. *Light values advance and enlarge; dark values recede and reduce.* Lighter values tend to pick out individuals from large groups on stage. The main character dressed in a lighter value should be clearly visible standing in front of the chorus.

2. *Value affects apparent density.* If two shapes are the same size and are seen against a neutral background, the dark one will appear to weigh more. This effect explains the top-heavy feeling given by some garments when the upper portion is dark and the lower portion is light.

3. *Light and dark values juxtaposed push each other apart, stressing their differences.* Light values make dark values seem darker; dark values make light colors seem lighter. The stronger the contrast in value between costumes, the less the characters will seem to be related. This effect can be overcome by the use of different values of the same hue.

4. *When value contrast is extreme, the hues involved are less noticeable; when values are closer together, the hues are*

more apparent. The audience is more aware of the strong contrast in hue than in the colors involved. When costumes are closer in value, the variety of hue becomes more important.

Physical Effects of Intensity

The careful manipulation of color intensities provides an infinite variety of color effects for the costume designer's use.

1. *Brighter intensities demand more attention.* In general, the brighter the intensity of a hue, the less of the color is needed for effect. A strong accent of bright red will draw attention on a black dress, even if rather small.

2. *Bright intensities advance and enlarge; dull intensities recede.* Bright intensities worn by important characters make them stand out from low-intensity group colors. With stage lighting, however, a group of similar intensities can be lowered by reducing the amount of light or altering the color of the light on them. Spotlighting one member of a group makes that character's costume color a brighter intensity than the rest of the group in a lower light level.

3. *Large areas of unrelieved, bright-intensity color can become tiring to the observer.* This effect, too, can be altered with stage lighting; variations in light color and level of illumination create different intensities of color on large areas of the same hue.

4. *Different intensities intensify each other regardless of hue.* Any differences in color will be emphasized when there is contrast in intensity. A high-intensity red and a low-intensity blue used together will visually separate and delineate each other. Medium intensities of these colors used together will tend to be less distinct and the edges between the two may blur at a distance.

5. *Small areas of bright intensity balance larger areas of dull intensity.* Conversely, large areas of bright intensity tend to overpower smaller areas of low-intensity color (face, hair). Scenes with many characters in low-intensity colors can easily be accented with small areas of bright-intensity color (scarves, flowers, hats, ties). More difficult may be very colorful scenes (musical numbers, dance, crowd scenes) where focus may wander from the actors' faces. Careful variation of hue and intensity and introduction of neutrals are approaches to the problem.

Psychological Effects of Color

Our emotional response to a color is the result of a triggering of some subconscious association we have with that color. These associations begin to accumulate when, as very small children, we first perceive and respond to colors. Researchers have shown that red, yellow, green, and blue at bright intensities and normal values are the first colors to attract the attention of young children. As a child grows and develops, colors become associated with the objects of everyday experience. Blue sky, brown earth, and green trees are almost universal associations. Colors of the changing seasons become associated with the concepts of time passage, age, temperature, and climate. Groups of people with similar experiences of the world will share the same color associations. Religious concepts have for centuries been expressed in symbolic colors. (See Box 4.F.) Citizens of most countries have such strong associations with the colors of their country's flag that the colors themselves will elicit patriotic feelings even when the flag is not present. Colors are powerful symbols and can communicate to large groups of people in a common language.

Some color associations come from experiences unique to the individual. These experiences can be either negative or positive and may alter the expected viewer response. The costume designer cannot anticipate these associations in the individual audience members. Some thought should be given to those personal associations that may affect the designer's *own* color responses, however. Such associations may lead to the use of personal color preferences that are unrelated to the mood or character. Personal color prejudices limit the designer's ability to succeed in a broad range of theater work.

The various dimensions of color all contribute to the emotional responses and associations of the observer.

Psychological Effects of Hue

In human experience certain colors have become associated with sources of light and heat. The red glow of burning coals, the yellow flicker of a candle flame, and the orange of molten metal are subconsciously related by the observer to those colors in other forms. Because of these associations, these colors are referred to as *warm colors*. Colors from the opposite side of the color wheel — blue, green, and violet — are associated with the sky, mountains, and water in various forms, all of which have cool, refreshing connotations, and so these are called *cool colors*. Yellow-green and red-violet have warm effects juxtaposed to cool colors, but they will

Box 4.F Historical Color Symbolism

WEST AND MIDDLE EAST

	Red	Yellow and Gold	Green	Blue	Purple	White	Black	Other
Egypt	Mortals	Sun, universal power	Nature	Heaven, sacred	Earth			
Greece	Love and sacrifice		Learning	Truth, integrity, altruism		Divinity, purity		
Druids			Wisdom	Truth		Supremeness, purity		
Judaism	Sacrifice, love, glory, salvation, sin	Of heaven	Of earth	Glory of the Lord	Divine condescension, splendor	Purity, victory		
Cabalism	Strength	Beauty	Victory	Mercy	"The Foundation"	"The Crown"	Understanding	Orange: glory Gray: wisdom
Christianity	Holy Ghost, human body, blood of Christ, suffering, Hell,	Glory, power, God the Son, the human mind, earth	Immortality, faith, contemplation	Hope, diety, serenity, heaven, God the Father, the human	Penance, suffering, repentance, self-sacrifice, faith, endurance, affliction,	Purity, innocence, chastity, joy, glory	Death	

Heraldry	martyrdom, charity, sacrifice	Courage, zeal	Loyalty	Youth, hope	spirit, sincerity, love of divine works, assigned to Virgin Mary	Sacrifice, patriotism, royalty; melancholy	Faith, purity	Grief, penitence	Orange: strength, endurance
Academics	Theology	Science	Medicine	Philosophy	Piety, sincerity	Law	Arts and letters		Orange: engineering; Pink: music
FAR EAST									
Brahmanism	Sacred	Universal understanding			True hue of sun			Evil	
Confucianism		Sacred to Confucius			Sacred, the Ultimate			Sacred	
Buddhism	Love, sin	Sun, universal power, sacred to Buddha							
Shintoism	Blood of life		Wisdom				Eternity		
Persia		Glory	Immorality				Infinite joy	Mystery	
Mohammedanism	Sacred		World mother, sacred to Mohammed				Salvation	Sin	

behave like cool colors when combined with warm colors. On the color wheel warm colors have cool colors as complements.

Warm colors appear to advance and cool colors appear to recede. Because we associate distance with size of objects, shapes in advancing warm colors seem larger and shapes in receding cool colors seem smaller.

The perception of colors as "warm" and "cool" has a great deal to do with the associations attached to those colors. Box 4.G shows the major color associations of Western European and American cultures. Some colors have opposing connotations depending on the context in which the color is seen. Green, for example, has associations with summer, growth, and naturalness when seen in a costume, but might suggest disease or terror if used for skin tones. The designer should not ignore the prevalent associations with specific colors, nor be restricted by them. The designer should be aware, however, that these associations operate in the audience primarily on a subconscious level.

Psychological Effects of Value

The effects of value can alter the effect of hue. A lighter value (tint) of a color dilutes the associations made with the pure color. A darker value (shade) deepens or controls the emotional response to the pure color. For example, a light pink (a *tint* of red), while still warm, is not considered passionate or loud but may still express love or quiet sacrifice. A dark garnet red (a *shade* of red) might still express passion or danger, but with control and sophistication.

Because light colors *reflect* more light, light-colored surfaces *absorb less* light and therefore *less heat*. For centuries, societies in warm climates have preferred light-colored garments for their comfort. Because dark colors *absorb more* light, therefore *more heat* from the radiant source, people in cold climates have leaned toward darker colors. These associations have been transferred to seasonal clothing and, in spite of air conditioning and central heating, persist today in psychological associations.

Lighter values of naturally low-value colors (tints of blue or violet) appear less dense than the pure hues, and light values of cool colors begin to advance. Low values of naturally high-value colors (shades of red, yellow) appear denser than the pure hues, and low values of warm colors begin to recede.

Psychological Effects of Intensity

Since a color appears in its full intensity on the color wheel, its intensity can only be lowered from that level. The effect of lowering the intensity of a color is to subdue the effects of its hue. Lowering the intensity of orange, for example, quiets and stabilizes its effects.

Box 4.G   Major Color Associations of Western European and American Cultures

COLOR	GENERAL APPEARANCE	ASSOCIATIONS
Red	Brilliant, intense, enlarging, masculine, active, opaque, dry	Fire, heat, strength, love, passion, power, danger, primitiveness, excitement, patriotism, sin, fierceness, sacrifice, vitality, loudness, impulsiveness, blood
Red-orange	Intense, bright, dry, enlarging, masculine	Autumn, energy, gaiety, impetuousness, strength, spirit, boldness, action, warmth, loudness
Orange	Bright, luminous, dry, enlarging, masculine, glowing	Autumn, warmth, cheer, youthfulness, vigor, exuberance, excitement, extremism, earthiness, satiety, loudness, charm
Yellow-orange	Bright, radiant, dry, enlarging, masculine	Autumn, happiness, prosperity, hospitality, gaiety, optimism, openness
Yellow	Sunny, incandescent, radiant, feminine, enlarging, dry	Spring, brightness, wisdom, enlightenment, happiness, kindness, cowardice, treachery, ill health, warmth, sunlight
Yellow-green	Tender, bright, enlarging	Spring, friendship, youth, sparkle, warmth, restlessness, newness
Green	Clean, moist, reducing	Summer, youth, inexperience, growth, envy, restlessness, newness, quiet, naturalness, wealth, coolness, water, refreshing, ghastliness, disease, terror, guilt
Blue-green	Quiet, clean, moist	Summer, quietness, reserve, relaxation, faithfulness, smoothness, discriminating, rational
Blue	Transparent, wet, deep, reducing	Winter, peace, restraint, loyalty, sincerity, youth, conservativism, passivity, honor, purity, depression, melancholy, sobriety, serenity, gentleness, innocence
Blue-violet	Deep, soft, reducing, moist	Tranquility, spiritualism, modesty, reflection, somberness, maturity, aloofness, dignity, fatigue
Violet	Deep, soft, dark, misty, atmospheric, reducing	Stateliness, royalty, drama, dominance, mystery, dignity, pomposity, supremacy, formality, melancholy, quietness, mourning, loneliness, desperation, profundity, artistic, philosophical
Red-violet	Deep, soft, dark, warm	Drama, enigma, intrigue, tension, remoteness, intensity
Brown	Warm, dark, deep	Autumn, casualness, friendliness, naturalness, earthiness, tranquility, honesty, security, substance, stability, humility
White	Spatial, light, deep	Winter, snow, youthfulness, virginity, joy, purity, cleanliness, honesty, hope, innocence, spiritualism, enlightenment, forgiveness, worthiness, delicacy, love, day
Black	Spatial, dark, deep	Night, mourning, ominous, deadly, death, formality, sophistication, gloom, uncertainty, evil, mystery, dignity, sorrow
Gray	Neutral, misty	Calmness, dignity, serenity, versatility, resignation, death, ghastliness, obscurity, penitence

MONOCHROMATIC

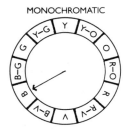

ADJACENT

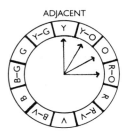

COMPLEMENTARY

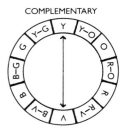

DOUBLE COMPLEMENTARY

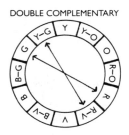

ADJACENT COMPLEMENTARY

As a color is neutralized, its effects become more neutral.

High-intensity colors are simple, youthful, and dynamic; low-intensity colors are mature, sophisticated, and complex, hinting at associations instead of shouting them.

Some color effects have been overused and run the risk of being trite or stereotyped. The designer must look for a variety of color choices to express the range of associations desired.

Color Schemes

Some basic formulas for combining colors have been developed through the use of the color wheel. These color schemes are guides for the designer who is choosing colors for costumes, but they should not be viewed as rules. The basic color scheme can be further developed by the use of a wide range of values and intensities of each color and by the addition of neutral colors. (Some popular schemes such as red, white, and blue do not fall under these formulas.) The following schemes are based on the color wheel. (See Figure 4.10.)

A *monochromatic* color scheme is based on one hue and is developed with a range of tints, values, and intensities of that hue. An example of a monochromatic scheme would be light blue, royal blue, and navy blue.

Analogous or *adjacent* color schemes are based on two to four hues that are next to each other on the color wheel. Yellow, yellow-orange, orange, and red-orange would represent an adjacent color scheme.

Complementary color schemes are based on two hues opposite one another on the color wheel. Violet and yellow are complementary colors.

A *double complementary* scheme would include two adjacent hues and their complements. Yellow-orange and orange with blue and blue-violet would make a four-hue base for a double complementary scheme.

An *adjacent complementary* scheme is made up of two complements and a color next to one of them. Green, red, and red-orange would combine for an adjacent complementary scheme.

Single split complementary schemes start with a pair of complements, take the hues on each side of one of the complements, then omit *that* complement. Yellow, red-violet, and blue-violet (omitting violet) would be a single split complementary scheme.

A *double split complementary* scheme starts with a pair of complements, takes the hues on each side of the complements, then omits *both* complements. The resulting four-hue base includes two sets of complements that are not adjacent to one another.

Yellow, orange (omitting yellow-orange), violet, and blue (omitting blue-violet) would combine for a double split complementary color scheme.

Triad color schemes are based on three hues equally spaced on the color wheel. The primaries, red, yellow, and blue, are an example of such a color scheme.

Tetrad color schemes are based on four hues equally spaced on the color wheel. Yellow-orange, red, blue-violet, and green would form a tetrad color scheme.

A *neutral* color scheme would make use of black, white, and gray. Sometimes low intensities and very high or very low values of other colors are called neutral because their hue is difficult to determine. A color like navy blue, tan, or cream can vary a neutral color scheme or contribute beautifully to a scheme including its home value.

These formulas offer only a guide for developing pleasing combinations of color. To find suitable combinations the chosen hues might be lightened, darkened, or dulled. A carefully balanced contrast in both value and intensity is needed in order for a color scheme to be harmonious and for the desired physical and psychological effects to be produced. The emotional quality of a given color will differ as its forms differ. The greater the contrast in values and intensities in a scheme, the stronger, more dramatic the physical effect and the bolder or more severe the psychological effect. Subtle combinations are more difficult to achieve, but they offer intricate variations in meaning. Harmony is generally perceived in color combinations that either are closely related or are opposites. Color experiments indicate that more pleasing results are achieved with either very small differences in color or very large differences. The distinction between colors that are very close in value or intensity is easily lost on stage, however. Stage lighting tends to blend similar values and intensities together.

Texture

> *I think you're nuts.*
>
> *No, I ain't. George says I ain't. I like to pet nice things with my fingers. Soft things.*
>
> *Well, who don't? Everybody likes that. I like to feel silk and velvet. You like to feel velvet?*
>
> OF MICE AND MEN   John Steinbeck

The *texture* of an object is its tactile surface characteristics or a visual representation of a tactile surface. There is a tendency to associate texture with "rough," but the word "texture" applies to a

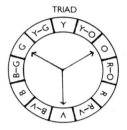

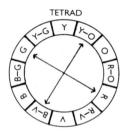

FIGURE **4.10** The most common color schemes (see text for definitions).

quality of all surfaces. Tactile sensations tell us a fabric is smooth, rough, fuzzy, or nubby. By the time we are adults, we have vast experience with textures. We no longer need to touch a surface to understand and relate a sensation to a given texture. Just as we relate colors to experiences of the world around us, so we may relate textures to objects we have experienced: "smooth as glass," "rough as gravel," "soft as fur." We experience these textures vicariously when we see them visually represented.

Fortunately for the costume designer, fabric (the basic medium of costumes) comes in an almost endless variety of textures. In Figure 4.11 textural materials are deftly used to create the costume for Old Deuteronomy in *Cats*. In addition, the designer can add textural interest to costumes with trims, paint, and such design detail as tucking, pleating, shirring, ruching, ruffles, smocking, embroidery, appliqué, or quilting.

Aspects of Texture

Structural texture is the result of the elements of a substance and the method of its construction. Each medium used by an artist has unique textural qualities. The basic ingredients in paint produce certain textural effects. The method of application produces additional effects. The surface to which the paint is applied may add another textural element. Fabrics, like other media, have unique properties which need to be understood for effective manipulation.

The basic structural elements of fabric are *fiber, yarn, construction*, and *finish*. Varying these elements produces fabrics each with a different "hang" (draping quality), "hand" (the way a fabric feels when handled), and surface effect. Further discussion of fabric can be found in Chapter 7.

Visual texture refers to the visual and mental response to structural texture, or the impression of a tactile surface created by visual representations of actual textures or by decorative pattern. The use of textures (fabrics) by the costume designer creates variety in the individual costume and relates or contrasts the whole group of costumes. By varying the type of textures employed, the designer can produce totally different design concepts. Similar structural textures (similar fabrics) with varying decorative textures (motifs or trims) provide one approach. Varying structural textures (different fabrics) can be unified with related decorative textures.

In addition to fabric and trim in the costume, the designer must consider the relationship of textures in the actor's hair and skin, in the costume accessories, and in the scenery as components of a total composition.

Fabrics span the range of textures from smooth/hard to rough/

FIGURE 4.11 *Cats*. Old Deuteronomy, designed by John Napier, is a marvel of textures and bulk used to suggest his great age and status among the other cats. Photo © Martha Swope.

soft. Some other descriptive terms for both structural and visual texture are:

scratchy	heavy	crisp	fuzzy
satiny	pebbly	papery	bristly
velvety	sandy	furry	

Physical Effects of Texture

Textures can either alter or support the physical perception of the effects of light, color, line, and form. Rough textures soften the edges of forms and create irregular outlines. They break up light and diffuse it. Rough textures tend to enlarge shape, but small, even textures do not necessarily reduce shape. Smooth, hard textures present forms distinctly and reflect light in sharp highlights. Rough textures soften the effect of strong line; smooth textures strengthen the effects of line. Rough textures soften or dull the effects of color; smooth, hard textures emphasize color. Medium-textured fabrics provide neutral background spaces for textural effects in decorative trim. Extreme contrasts in texture may have harsh or severe effects, whereas lack of contrast in textures becomes uninteresting unless contrast is provided by some other design element. The costume designer uses texture to modify or strengthen effects of other design elements in the costume and to assist in creating variety and interest.

Psychological Effects of Texture

Textures express moods or associations which modify or support the psychological effects of color, line, and form. Texture is a strong tool for the designer. The use of various textures can suggest character, status, personality, sophistication, age, occasion or season, fragility or strength. We associate fragile-looking fabrics with occasions that put no stress on garments and with characters that do no hard physical labor. A costume for Laura in *The Glass Menagerie* might make good use of a soft, smooth, almost sheer fabric to express her delicate, fragile quality. Sturdy textures are associated with more vigorous occasions and characters. Box 4.H describes the physical and psychological effects of some basic textures.

When planning textures for the stage, the designer must take into consideration the distance between the audience and the stage. More delicate textures tend to disappear over long distances and their effects are lost on the audience. The effect of visual mixing (Color, p. 88) may eliminate the texture but enhances the color and the three-dimensionality of the costume.

Pattern

A special form of visual texture is *pattern*. Made up of other elements (line, form, color, and space), pattern creates a special kind of texture from the stage. Smaller patterns are indistinguishable at a distance and behave like medium or small textures. Medium to large patterns, however, have stronger effects than their counterparts

---

Box 4.H   Effects of Texture

TEXTURE	PHYSICAL EFFECT	PSYCHOLOGICAL EFFECT (MOOD)
Smooth, crisp	Sharp silhouette, much reflected light	Refined, hard, cheerful, perky, sophisticated
Smooth, soft	Sharp silhouette, much reflected light	Sensuous, relaxed, luxurious
Velvety soft	Enlarging, but less defined, dense, less reflected light	Rich, luxurious
Fuzzy	Enlarging, but less defined, dense, less reflected light	Luxurious, cuddly, primitive, untamed
Rough	Softer silhouette, less reflected light	Sporty, natural, uncouth, coarse, primitive, casual
Coarse	Enlarging, less reflected light	Uncouth, earthy, uncivilized
Medium (regular)	Neutralizing, medium reflected light	Businesslike, mature, stable, conservative
Medium (irregular)	Neutralizing, medium reflected light	Stable, active, warm

---

in structural texture. Identifiable pattern creates psychological responses in the viewer and sends messages about the character which are stronger than those sent by any other element except color.

Patterns are derived from four sources: *nature, made objects, imagination,* and *symbolism* (see Figure 4.12). Patterns derived from nature are pleasing and calming and, unless severely distorted, suggest positive associations. Patterns based on made objects have strong associations to time, place, gender, and events. Patterns derived from imagination fall into two categories: geometric and free-form. Few perfectly geometrical forms appear in nature (visible to the naked eye), but artisans for centuries have decorated clothing, everyday objects, and ritual accoutrements with geometric designs. Many of these motifs may have originated in the weaving of baskets or cloth and later been applied to other objects with paint. Free-form pattern can be inspired by nonvisual sources and may suggest feelings or moods rather than objects. Symbolism uses pattern based on any source and gives that motif a specific and widely accepted meaning. Symbols identify large, complex ideas in quick immediate ways. They are very useful to the costume design-

FIGURE 4.12 Types of Pattern. (a) Natural sources, (b) made objects, (c) geometrical designs, (d) free-form pattern, and (e) symbolic pattern (stars and stripes seem to symbolize the flag of the United States and the associated patriotic feelings regardless of color). Photos by Hilary Sherred.

A

B

C

D

E

A

B

C

D

E

F

er, making possible quick identification of characters and the ideas with which they are associated. The problem for the designer is to use symbols in ways that are not simplistic, cliché, or anachronistic.

No matter what the source of pattern inspiration, it must be interpreted in some way. The choice of presentation form is determined by the effect desired. Patterns may be presented in realistic, stylized, and abstract forms. The costume designer's choice depends on character interpretation, period, and production style and concept.

The arrangement of pattern on a costume is an important consideration for the costume designer. The distance between audience and actor may alter the perception of pattern. Small spaces between pattern repeats may merge and reduce definition. Detail between repeats may be lost and cause central motifs to advance, creating a spotty effect.

Pattern repeats can be arranged in any of six ways (see Figure 4.13):

1. *All-over*: Patterns that have the same effect from any direction.
2. *One way*: Patterns that have the same effect from one direction only.
3. *Two way*: Patterns that have the same effect from top to bottom and bottom to top.
4. *Four way*: Patterns that have the same effect from top to bottom, bottom to top, left to right, and right to left.
5. *Border*: Patterns arranged to place main motifs along one or both selvages of fabric.
6. *Panel*: Self-contained motif which may repeat only once within the garment and is designed for specific usage; for example, a scarf or a decorative neckline.

Physical Effects of Pattern

Since a pattern combines the elements of space, shape, line, and color, it is subject to all the physical effects of the design elements used to develop it. In addition, the following effects seem prominent:

1. Pattern accents the area in which it is used.
2. Pattern complements simple structural design.
3. Pattern adds visual interest.
4. Pattern attracts attention away from silhouette, distracting the eye from less pleasing body contours.
5. Larger patterns are enlarging, but smaller patterns do not necessarily reduce.

6. Sharply outlined motifs are more emphatic, dramatic, and enlarging than fuzzy-edged motifs.
7. Patterns that create optical illusions quickly become distracting and visually tiring.

Psychological Effects of Pattern

Pattern is also subject to all the psychological effects of the design elements used to develop it. In addition, the following effects of pattern seem prominent in westernized cultures:

1. Closely spaced motifs may create a crowded, pressured feeling. Widely spaced motifs may create a spotty impression.
2. Flattened motifs (those without shading or dimension) suggest youth, simplicity, casualness, or humor.
3. Plant, floral, and flowing motifs are viewed as feminine; animal and geometric motifs are considered more masculine.
4. Large motifs are viewed as dynamic and bold; small motifs are viewed as dainty.

Generally, the patterns used in a production should be related in scale and style. The use of multiple patterns in one costume can suggest carelessness, naiveté, or in some cases extreme sophistication, depending on the context of the costume. In Figure 4.14 the use of several patterns gives Ed from *You Can't Take It with You* an air of innocence and points up his lack of worldly goods. Effective use of pattern makes a set of costumes interesting and varied.

PRINCIPLES OF DESIGN

The theatre . . . should be a perfectly pure juxtaposition, a series of precise concatenations, each element gauged to its exact value. Beauty resides in the power of suggestion inciting the spectator's participation. Creation is incomplete without his contribution and spirit. Beauty refuses to bow to the limitations of meaning or description.

Sonia Delaunay

If the elements of design are the components with which designers work, the principles of design are the techniques or guidelines for using those components. A principle of design is both the *method* of manipulating the elements and the *effect* of successfully applying that method. The sixteen principles discussed

FIGURE 4.14 *You Can't Take It With You*. Designed by Hilary Sherred for Center Stage. Photo © Richard Anderson.

here fall into three groups: (1) *directional*, (2) *highlighting*, and (3) *synthesizing* principles (see Figure 4.15). All principles can be used either structurally or decoratively. Each principle is intricately related to the other principles and an example of one may also involve the use of others.

Directional Principles

Generally the simplest, the directional principles lead the eye from one place to another, build to a climax, and emphasize a direction.

• *Repetition* is the use of a design unit more than once. A color repeated in two areas of a costume, rows of trim on the skirt and cuff of a garment, a series of buttons on the front of a vest, are

FIGURE 4.15   Principles of Design. (a) repetition; (b) transition; (c) parallelism; (d) concentricity; (e) gradation; (f) radiation; (g) sequence; (h) alternation; (i) rhythm

all examples of repetition. *Regular* repetition repeats identical elements; *irregular* repetition repeats related but slightly different elements. Irregular repetition weakens direction but increases interest. Repetition causes the eye to follow the repeated elements, thus strengthening the direction of the line between them or of the space they occupy. Repetition is a strong tool for creating unity in a costume or group of costumes.

• *Parallelism* is the use of equidistant units on the same plane. Parallelism applies to line, shape, and space. Effective use of parallelism creates interest and emphasis. Like repetition, which it closely resembles, parallelism causes the eye to follow the direction of the parallel elements. In Figure 4.16 parallel divisions of space (stripes, tucks, trim) emphasize the height of the actor.

• *Sequence* is one unit following after another in a particular order and in regular succession. Sequences build to a climax, relax, then build up to a climax again. They are less flowing than other directional effects, but they can be versatile and playful while establishing a sense of order.

• *Alternation* is the sequence of two units changing back and forth. The alternation of two things causes the eye to follow the direction of the sequence. Primarily decorative in its application, alternation is usually calming but may become boring.

• *Gradation* is the sequence of adjacent units, identical in all respects but one, which changes in specific steps from one unit to the next. Gradation may reverse at the climax and return to step one of unit one, or it may repeat as in a sequence, or it may end at a climax. Gradation has powerful potential for costume development because its use heightens and intensifies the psychological effects of the element gradated.

● *Transition* is the smooth, continuous movement from one position or condition to another. Lines, shapes, colors, spaces, and textures can make smooth transitions within a costume design. These transitions sweep the eye along in the direction of the movement with graceful, gentle, but powerful force.

FIGURE 4.16 *Romeo and Juliet*. Designed by Tony Straiges for Yale University.

- *Radiation* is a sense of movement outward from a central point (visible or implied). It produces strong directional effects of outward movement; see Figure 4.17, a costume for *La Belle Hélène*.
- *Rhythm* is the perception of organized movement. Design

FIGURE 4.17 *La Belle Hélène.* This sketch by Patton Campbell illustrates several principles of design. The pleats of the cape *radiate* from neck to hem. The stars on the belt-ends are *gradated*, with the smallest at the waist and the larger ones at the bottom. The motifs above the hem *alternate* for interest. Designed for The New York City Opera Company.

FIGURE 4.18 Contrast between aspects of elements.

units organized to create the feeling of movement can have either calm, soothing beats or sharp, staccato beats. The psychological responses to rhythm can be casual, playful, sensuous, stately, or militant. Some types of rhythm are:

flowing	looping	sweeping	syncopated
jerky	marching	swinging	undulating
lilting	stately	swirling	vibrating

Highlighting Principles

Highlighting principles focus our attention on the differences between one unit and another.

• *Concentricism* is the layering of shapes, each progressively larger and each having the same center. Concentric shapes lead the eye inward to the next smaller shape and finally to a visual climax in the center.

• *Contrast* is the juxtaposition of unlike units. The more unlike the units, the sharper the contrast. The sharper the contrast, the stronger the pull on the eye to the spot where the contrast occurs. Strong contrast is invigorating and dramatic, whereas subtle contrasts are desirable for delicate effects. Contrast is required in each costume and between different costumes that will be grouped together on stage. Box 4.1 shows ways to create contrast between various aspects of the design elements.

Contrast creates interest and emphasis. The eye is drawn to the different element in a costume and to the different costume in a group. Figure 4.18 shows how contrast is used in a series of

---

Box 4.1   Ways to Contrast Design Elements

ELEMENTS	CONTRAST
Space	
Filled	Unfilled
Large	Small
Line	
Thick	Thin
Smooth	Rough
Solid	Broken
Vertical	Horizontal
Straight	Curved
Shape	
Straight-edged	Curved-edged
Large	Small
Light	
Harsh	Diffused
Bright	Low (dim)
Reflected	Absorbed
Color	
Pure (saturated)	Low intensity
Hue	Complement
High value	Low value
Hue	Neutral
Texture	
Smooth	Rough
Soft	Hard
Patterned	Plain
Shiny	Dull

costumes. In (a) the costume contrasts the curved line of the collar with the straight line of the gown. In (b) the patterned body of the gown is contrasted with the solid undergown. In (c) a tucker of a high-value color (light tone) contrasts with a gown of low-value color (dark tone). In (d) the small shapes of the hood and shoulder cape contrast with the larger shape of the cape. Color plate 4 also illustrates the use of color for contrast. The colored aprons contrast with the black uniforms and differentiate individuals among the group of maids. In Color plate 5 bold areas of color and dramatic

FIGURE 4.19 Emphasis.

bands of pattern are contrasted with areas of black in a costume for Kitty in *The Royal Family*.

● *Emphasis* is the placement of focus on a point or area of the design — the center of interest to which all other areas are subordinated. Emphasis implies organization and complementary relationships of dominant and supporting elements.

In costume design the area of the garment emphasized also draws attention to that part of the body. By controlling emphasis, the designer can focus attention to the appropriate areas of the character's body. In theater, focusing on face and neck facilitates communication between audience and actor. In dance, however, the emphasis might be preferred on the feet or line of the body, not on the expression of the face or voice.

Figure 4.19 demonstrates how each element of design can be manipulated to create emphasis in a costume and bring attention to a specific part of the body. *Space*: in (a) an area of filled space (the patterned bodice) emphasizes an area of open space (the neck and chest). *Line*: in (b) a strong line (the baldric) emphasizes the areas of the costume adjacent to it. *Shape*: in (c) a prominent shape (the triangular stomacher) focuses the viewer's eye on the areas around it (the waist). *Color*: in (d) a bright splash of color, like this bandana, focuses the attention on the face. *Light*: in (e) reflective materials used on a costume draw attention to the area of "glitz." *Texture*: in (f) the texture created by a mass of curly hair successfully focuses attention on the face.

Emphasis can diminish undesirable physical attributes by drawing attention to more desirable ones. The natural tendency of the eye is to seek out and differentiate between similarities and differences. The advancing, assertive effects of an element usually provide the best means of creating emphasis: warm colors; sharp, bold lines; shiny, reflective surfaces; contrast in elements — all create emphasis. Basically, the odd element attracts the eye and creates emphasis at that point.

The edges of a garment emphasize neighboring parts of the body. Structural lines leading to a point create emphasis, and so do unusual closings, seaming, and draping. When carefully manipulated, garment decoration can provide emphasis, but, if overdone, it merely creates confusion and fussiness. In Figure 4.20 primary emphasis is clearly placed at the neck of this design for *Black Elk Lives*. The stars and half moon draw the eye to the face of the actor, but a spot of color on the sleeves provides secondary emphasis on the hands.

A major problem for the production team is controlling the focus on stage at all times. In films and television it is the camera that focuses our attention on the important action, reaction, or character in a scene. We see only what the camera sees and can take the point of view only of the camera. With stage productions the attention of the audience must be subtly directed to the important characters and action. On stage the director may move an actor to a more prominent stage position. The lighting designer may spotlight important characters or dim the light on less important ones. The costume designer works with line, shape, color, and texture to create emphasis (focus) on a character. In the musical *Little Mary Sunshine*, Mary is not much different in age and general appearance from the young ladies of the chorus, but she must not be lost among them.

Synthesizing Principles

Synthesizing principles guide the total combination of elements in a design to relate and integrate the parts.

● *Proportion* is the result of the comparative relationships of distances, sizes, amounts, degrees, or parts to the whole. These relationships work in four ways:

FIGURE **4.20** *Black Elk Lives.* Designed by David Murin.

1. *Within each part*, as in comparing the length with the width of a rectangle or silhouette.
2. *Between parts*, as in comparing the area of one shape with that of a neighboring one, such as the sleeve to the bodice.
3. *Part to whole*, as in comparing the area of the whole garment with that of the bodice.
4. *Whole to environment*, as in comparing the area occupied by the figure with that of the full stage.

The proportions of the elements appropriate in a given costume are relative to the effects of all the design elements in that costume. Figure 4.21 shows shapes divided in various proportions. The strength and number of the colors, patterns, textures, spaces, lines, and reflective surfaces (light) must be balanced for suitable effects (c–f). A designer must experiment and learn to evaluate the visual impact of the proportions of elements chosen.

Evaluation of pleasing proportion is culturally influenced. Many cultures have developed guides for pleasing proportions, usually expressed in mathematical formulas. However, the most pleasing proportions are often slightly off the mathematical formulas and related to a personal esthetic sense. Application of proportion follows the same general guideline as do all principles and elements of design: enough variety for interest, but not so much as to create confusion or conflict. Basic relationships of two-thirds to one-third, or two-fifths to three-fifths, are generally viewed as pleasing. There are, however, always those artists with the sensitivity and skill to push proportion to extremes and still present pleasing relationships in a design.

Functionally, the proportions of a costume must agree with the proportions of the actor's body to allow for movement and comfort. Arms, legs, heads, waists, and feet must be able to function as the action requires. A mermaid doesn't need to walk, but most characters do!

When considering proportion, we think first of the division of space. However, the consideration of proportions applies also to color, texture, and pattern. Smaller proportions of more advancing elements work well against larger proportions of receding elements.

• *Scale* is the relative size of shapes to the whole and to each other, or comparative proportional size relationships. The scale of theatrical designs is necessarily exaggerated to make the costumes visible to the audience throughout the theater. The less "real" the style of presentation, the more exaggerated the scale can be. In Figure 4.22 the same style garment has been interpreted in three different scales for realistic, theatrical, and humorous effect.

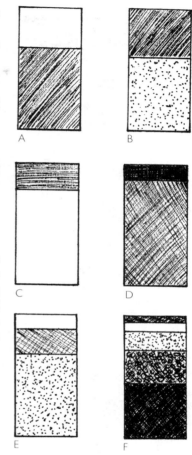

A   B
C   D
E   F

FIGURE 4.21 Proportion. Proportions of one-third to two-thirds (a) or two-fifths to three-fifths (b) are generally considered pleasing.

Larger scale shapes are more aggressive and advancing than smaller scale shapes. The sizes of decorative shapes, motifs, patterns, or accessories must be adjusted to relate to the part of the garment to which it is applied or to the body as a whole. "Outscaled" (very large) or "underscaled" (very small) shapes or accessories are often used for comic costumes. The circus clown with the too-small hat and too-large shoes is a well-known example.

• *Balance* is the sense of evenly distributed weight, size, density, or tension which results in stability. Balance in a design is achieved when each part interacts with all others and with the whole to achieve stability. When the right side balances the left side, designs are said to have *horizontal balance.* When the top balances the bottom, designs are said to have *vertical balance.* When the whole is balanced around a central point, designs are said to have *radial balance.* Horizontal balance is necessary if the figure is to appear sober, stable, and upright. Vertical balance is necessary if the figure is to appear to rest firmly on the ground without looking top-heavy or weighed down. This type of balance is generally desirable. An exception might be dance costumes, particularly ballet costumes, where every effort is made to buoy the figure to enhance the feeling of weightlessness and flight.

There are two types of horizontal balance: *symmetrical* and *asymmetrical.* Designs balanced symmetrically have identical right and left sides. The determination of one side automatically is mirrored on the other side. Asymmetrical designs are different on each side of the central dividing line but still have a feeling of equally distributed weight. A skillful combination of elements is required to create a design that is balanced asymmetrically. Balance is crucial to a psychological feeling of security and stability. Symmetrical balance is stately and dignified, but obvious, static, and unassuming. Characters with formal, stable, or dignified traits would be well defined by costumes with symmetrical balance. Asymmetrical balance is casual, dramatic, complex, lively, and rhythmic. Characters with erratic, flamboyant, eccentric, or comic traits might be well defined with asymmetrically balanced costumes. In Figure 4.23 a series of costumes illustrate the effect of the different approaches to balancing a garment. A symmetrical garment (a) tends to give a conservative or formal look to the figure, whereas an asymmetrical garment (b) tends to be less formal and suggests youth and vitality and sometimes sophistication. When one considers vertical balance, large areas of *dark color* at the bottom of a figure (c) give it a solid, feet-on-the-ground feeling. Large areas of *light color* at the bottom of the figure (d) will balance a smaller area of

FIGURE 4.22   Scale. (a) Realistic scale. (b) The same style garment is reinterpreted in a theatrical scale for a medium-size theater. (c) The costume is exaggerated in scale for a humorous effect.

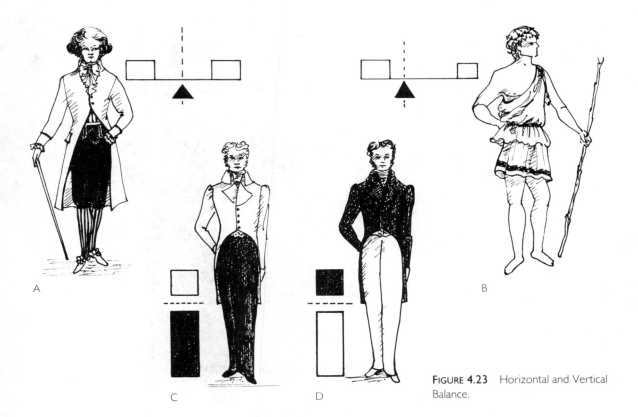

A

B

C

D

FIGURE 4.23   Horizontal and Vertical Balance.

dark color at the top of the figure but will suggest a character with a streak of dandyism or happy-go-lucky traits.

Symmetrically balanced garments emphasize irregularities of the figure, while asymmetrically balanced garments disguise irregularities. Figure 4.24 shows a design for a full-figured woman which takes advantage of the dynamic movement of an asymmetrically balanced garment to focus on the head and shoulders.

Garments and figure must also balance in profile. The size and shape of the hat or hair are an essential element in balancing both front and profile views of the figure.

• *Harmony* is a pleasing combination of elements, a consistency of feeling, mood, and function. Harmony demands an agreement among the functional, structural, and decorative aspects of the design. Harmony is strongly influenced by culture, fashion, and time. Some ideas of harmony pass quickly and others become classic. The determining factors in this process are (1) how broadly recognized and accepted a mood or idea is, (2) how well that idea or

FIGURE 4.24 *Broadway Rhythm.* The asymmetrical design of this dress by Michael J. Cesario sweeps the eye up to the face of the singer. The jeweled focal point at the shoulder also emphasizes the face and completes the visual effect.

mood is interpreted by the design elements and the principles used, and (3) how well the functional, structural, and decorative aspects of the design agree.

Advancing qualities agree with other advancing qualities, and receding qualities agree with other receding qualities, but skillful combining of receding and advancing qualities provide complex and engaging costume designs which reflect the complexities of the characters portrayed. (See Box 4.J.)

The perception of harmony in individual costumes and costumes as a group is not exclusively a visual perception. Harmony

Box 4.J   Advancing and Receding Effects of the Design Elements and Principles

	RECEDING	ADVANCING
Space	Small, closed, broken	Large, open, unbroken
Line	Curved, broken, thin, fuzzy, horizontal, short, porous	Straight, continuous, thick, sharp, solid, diagonal, vertical, long
Shape	Small, concave, porous	Large, solid, straight-edged, convex
Light	Dim, cool, diffused	Warm, brilliant, focused
Color	Cool hues, dark values, dull intensities	Warm hues, light values, bright intensities
Texture	Smooth, supple, porous, sheer, fine, delicate	Rough, bulky, stiff, thick
Pattern	Dainty motifs, soft edges, subtle shading, muted colors, small all-over or directional patterns	Bold motifs, sharp edges, flat and bright colors, geometric shapes, borders, spaced motifs, figure and ground distinct
Direction	Transition	Gradation, concentricism, emphasis
Rhythm	Smooth, flowing, gentle	Staccato, dynamic, dramatic
Contrast	Subtle, close	Bold, extreme
Balance	Formal, simple	Informal, complex
Scale	Small, dainty	Large, bold

must be established between the visual aspects of the costumes themselves *and* between costumes and the concept of the play. Beautifully designed costumes and sets that do not support the concept of the play are not in harmony with the production.

 • *Unity* is the feeling of wholeness, of all parts complete and necessary to the totality. Harmony and unity are closely related; unity without harmony is impossible, but harmony without unity is possible. Unity integrates all aspects of the design but cannot truly be separated from them. Unity is subtle. It is the result of design elements well used, design principles well applied. Structural, functional, and decorative elements must all work toward a unified result.

In the theater, unity and harmony must be evaluated by a different set of functional standards from those used for other art forms. As one develops costume design skills, one must also develop the standards by which to judge harmony and unity on stage.

These principles of design provide basic guidelines for the use of design elements, but the designer must decide what effects are *desired* and must choose the elements and principles accordingly. The final question asked about any costume design is, "Does it work?"

Chapter 5
Developing the Costume

. . . Costly thy habit as thy purse can buy,
But not expressed in fancy; rich, not gaudy;
For the apparel oft proclaimes the man . . .
HAMLET   William Shakespeare

For the purpose of discussion, the different steps of the costume design process have been separated here, but one should understand that these steps are intricately interwoven and cannot in fact be separated completely. Nor is their order rigidly set. No two designers work exactly alike and the same designer may work in different ways on different productions. In one situation a strong overall concept may evolve from reading the play and individual characters are based on aspects of the concept. In other cases strong characters provide the starting point for the design approach and the overall concept develops outward from the decisions made about those characters. In some cases the design concept is developed before research is done; in others, the research leads to the unifying element. In some productions the historical period is part of the unifying element; in other productions the theme may be a deliberate confusion of time. Consistency is the key — even if it means being consistently inconsistent!

Some theatrical forms (dance, performance art, avant-garde, nonverbal theater) approach costumes from a purely thematic or conceptual point of view. These costumes are based not on period or character, but on ideas. Designers seek to create the "essence," not the "reality" of the character, play, or period.

In producing organizations that provide long developmental periods (workshops) for new scripts or experimental approaches to established works, the costume designer may be asked to participate in the process. After attending rehearsals, the designer helps develop the costumes through collaboration with the actors and director. The actors may bring in garments and objects to incorporate, and the designer assists in refining the look and locating desired pieces. The emphasis is placed on the process of discovery rather than on the finished project. Sketches may not be involved. The production may be presented to the public as a "work-in-progress," may be remounted as a full production incorporating ideas from the workshop, or may not be presented at all.

In a majority of productions, however, once the overall concept is agreed upon, the designer proceeds to develop ideas about the individual characters, gradually refining both theme and character projection.

DEVELOPING CHARACTER CONCEPTS

Many inexperienced designers are at a loss to know how to begin when they sit down to sketch. They may know what ideas are to be expressed, but not how to express them. Using the information provided by the script and the director, the designer should be able to describe each character in specific terms. (After the show is cast, adjustments in character concept may be necessary if the director has cast against type, or if exaggeration or deemphasis of physical attributes is desirable.) A written statement about each character helps to focus the designer's thoughts on the desired effect of the costume, the ideas to be projected to the audience. What elements or principles of design could assist in projecting these ideas? (Refer again to the boxes in Chapter 4.)

Sorting out the accumulated research according to the characters for whom it seems appropriate helps the designer get started. Which examples seem to suit each character? What elements or principles of design are demonstrated by these examples? Do they project appropriate concepts for the character? What modifications are needed? Just as lines, colors, and textures have associations, costume features such as accessories, fit, and cut have cultural associations which the designer can tap for character definition. A costume need not be consistent in all aspects, but the majority of design features should agree with each other if a clear message is to be sent to the audience.

Boxes 5.A, 5.B, 5.C, and 5.D offer broad outlines for suggesting age, social status, personality, and character traits. The notes in

Box 5.A   Expressing Age in Costume Features
(Subject to Period and Personality)

FEATURE	OLD AGE	MATURITY	YOUTH	CHILDHOOD
Cut				
Skirt/pant length	Long	Long	Short	Shortest
Sleeve	Long	Medium to long	Long or short	Long or short
Neckline	High or medium	Low or high	Low or medium	Medium or high
Hair				
Female	Coiffed (outdated) or frazzled	Coiffed, specific	Loose	Long, loose or braided
Male	Balding, frazzled	Tightly controlled	Freer style	Loose, longer
Colors	Low intensities, low values	Secondaries, lower intensities	Stronger pastels, primaries, secondaries, high intensities, high values	Pastel or primaries
Fit	Body fitting or sagging	Body fitting, relative to period	Neat, but may be loose	Loose, not figure fitting
Silhouette	Complex or simple	Most complex	Simple to medium complex	Simplest

Box 5.B   Expressing Rank or Social Status in Costume Features
(Subject to Period and Personality)

FEATURE	RICH	MIDDLE CLASS	POOR
Cut			
Skirt length	Longest	Long	Shortest
Style	Most complex	Simple to complex	Simple
Color	Vibrant, intense	Lower intensity, Lower value	Low intensities, Low values
Fit	Proper fit	Neat, proper fit	Poorly fitted
Silhouette	Fashion silhouette	Not latest silhouette	Outdated silhouette
Texture	Smooth, shiny, napped	Medium textures, low shine	Rough, bold textures
Condition	New, clean	Worn, clean	Worn, ragged, dirty

Box 5.C   Expressing Personality in Costume Features
(Subject to Period)

FEATURE	EXTROVERT	INTROVERT
Cut	Lavish, low neckline, shorter skirt, bare arms or short sleeves	Modest, high neckline, longer skirt, long sleeves
Fit	Body revealing	Body concealing
Texture	Hard, shiny	Medium to fine
Hair	Loose, bold style	Tight, close to the head
Colors	Warm colors, high intensities, high values	Cool colors, low intensities, low values
(See also Chapter 1, Color)		
Silhouette	Simple and dramatic, or complex	Simple
Line	Exaggerated curves, zigzags, diagonals	Gentle curves, straight lines

these charts are *not* rules, but general associations which the designer can use or adjust to specific needs. These associations may change with current fashion or taste. Obviously, the requirements of a given historical period will affect the choices made by a designer. The more complex the character, the more subtle and complicated the costume may become. There will be dozens of reasons for going against these associations in specific situations, but they serve as a guide for evaluating research and for developing the rough sketch. As an example, Figure 5.1 shows how simple differences in a garment cut can affect the projection of age in four female characters. Variations in the skirt length and fullness, depth of neckline, length of sleeve, and waistline treatment alter a simple costume style to suggest childhood, youth, maturity, and age.

Design features are judged in relation to the fashion ideal of the historical period. If straight skirts were in fashion, then fuller skirts might be desirable for less fashionable characters (more room for activity of peasant or working class). If very full skirts were considered chic, skirts with less fullness would be worn by peasants and the working class because less fabric, therefore less money, would be required to make them. In any fashion period, the working and

Box 5.D   Expressing Character Traits in Costume Features (Subject to Period)

FEATURE	LOVING	SENSUOUS	INNOCENT	EVIL	MISERLY	SEVERE
Cut	Open, flowing, modest	Full cut, open, lavish	Full cut, modest	Tight, straight cut	Tight, straight cut	Tight, straight cut
Fit	Body revealing	Body revealing	Body concealing	Body revealing	Body revealing	Body revealing
Texture	Soft, fuzzy	Soft, shiny, smooth	Soft, fine	Harsh, rough, hard, shiny	Hard, rough or medium	Hard, rough
Hair	Soft, generous volume	Elegant, generous volume, or severe, sexy	Soft, loose	Severe or frazzled	Severe or frazzled	Severe, tight style
Colors	Warm, medium intensity, high or low values	Warm, medium intensity, high or low values	Cool, medium intensity, high value	Warm, high or low intensity, low value	Cool, medium or low intensity, medium to low values	Medium or low intensity, medium to low values

(See also Chapter 1, Color)

FEATURE	LOVING	SENSUOUS	INNOCENT	EVIL	MISERLY	SEVERE
Silhouette	Round or oval shapes	Round or oval shapes	Round or oval	Straight shapes	Straight shapes	Straight shapes
Line	Wide curves, soft edged	Undulating lines	Gently curved lines	Hard, straight or zigzag lines	Hard, straight lines	Hard, straight or zigzag lines

middle classes and the elderly are the last to give up the older fashions. Furthermore, these groups will usually choose the more conservative elements of the newer styles when they do adopt them.

Adjustments may be made for periods that do not offer all the alternatives, but research should be sought for all the characters. Keep in mind that persons with different personalities, rank, and age

FIGURE 5.1 Variations on a simple costume style project different ages.

have existed in all periods and have found ways of expressing themselves in dress. Modern associations sometimes interfere with an accurate projection of period information. Ordinarily, the costumes should not require program notes for clarification. The designer must decide if certain information will be understood by the audience or if modifications are necessary. One aspect of costume that often deviates from the specified period is the neckline. To help a modern audience understand the sensuality of a character, for example, a deep décolletage may be developed in a period of basically modest necklines.

Few plays are meant to be exact historical recreations. *Theatrical license* is the term used for liberties taken with historical accuracy. These liberties are usually taken to clarify the spirit or essence of the theme and to make it work esthetically in the theatrical setting. Elaboration, exaggeration, and even fantastication may be necessary for theatrical dress. The objective is effective interpretation, not simply precise representation.

No two designers are likely to solve a design problem in exactly the same way. Because of different production concepts, different actors playing the role, and the different ways designers approach the work, designs could vary considerably. Figure 5.2a shows a costume design by Judith Dolan for Lady Fidget in *The Country Wife*; Figure 5.2b, a costume by Michael Cesario, is for the same character. The interpretations differ, but many similarities remain.

Historical research must be adapted in some way for all productions. Rarely can a period garment be used without some modifications. The pattern or trim may need to be in a larger scale in order to be seen in the theater. The construction may be too confining for the action, or the color may be inappropriate.

A

B

FIGURE 5.2 Lady Fidget, *The Country Wife*. Different production concepts, different actors in the role, and different designer approaches to a work will produce two different design solutions. (a) Sketch by Judith Dolan for The Acting Company; (b) by Michael Cesario for The Krannert Center for the Performing Arts.

Modern clothing places few restrictions on movement. Authentically cut period garments may seriously limit a character's movement, however. The importance of recreating period movement in a given production is determined by the director and is of fundamental importance to the costume designer. The designer should point out to the director the advantages and restrictions that the use of authentic garments would create. If authentic costumes severely restrict the projected movement, is that movement appropriate to the play? Would characters of the period move in that way, or have too many modern ideas been applied to the script and not enough research? The more accurate the movement must be, the more accurate the costume should be. Bodice construction, skirt length, corset, and shoes *all* affect movement. Modifications should be made to permit the projection of character, theme, mode, and form of drama, and to allow for required or desired action.

ROUGH SKETCHES

Roughs are quick sketches, usually in pencil or pastel, which suggest the main ideas of the costume for each character. Some roughs indicate color. Some designers work in "thumbnail" size (2 to 3 inches); others use larger size figures (6 to 18 inches). (The novice designer will find that sketching in a larger size is good practice for the rendering process to come.) Using the costume plot, research, and character statements as guides, the designer sketches one or more roughs for each required costume. By determining the shape of the silhouette, the division of the silhouette space, and finally, the accessories and trim, the designer works to create the desired effect.

A simple approach to roughs is to use tracing paper over a basic figure. Until a designer is comfortable and fast at figure drawing, this approach saves time in the early design stages. Meanwhile, the basic figure proportions are becoming set in the designer's subconscious mind.

Some designers develop rough sketches by observing rehearsals and sketching the actors as they develop the posture and physicality of the character. Unfortunately, not all production schedules

FIGURE 5.3   Adele, *Die Fledermaus*. A series of "roughs" by Eduardo Sicongco show preliminary thinking and final design (opposite page) of the costume for Glimmerglass Opera.

allow for this approach. However, a sense of the type of character, overall silhouette, posture, and presence should be considered in the rough sketch stage no matter how these sketches are derived. The overall feeling is more important than the detail at the early stages. Once this basic look of the character is established, the designer proceeds to develop and refine the costume.

A designer may develop a series of sketches before the final choice is made. Figure 5.3 shows a series of sketches by Eduardo Sicongco illustrating preliminary thinking and the final design of a costume for Adele in *Die Fledermaus*.

FIGURE 5.4 Agatha Posket, *The Magistrate*. Emphasis is not always on the face. Designed by David Murin for The Hartman Theater.

Individual Focus (Emphasis)

Each costume design should have a focal point. For most characters the head and face are emphasized. There are times, however, when other areas of the figure are more important; legs or feet for dancers, hands for magical characters, or stomachs for fat, jolly characters. One trick for checking focus is to view the color sketch turned upside down. What area commands attention? Is this area relative to the character's action or personality? More than one area of emphasis may be developed in a costume. In Figure 5.4 the jeweled neck of this costume for Agatha Posket in *The Magistrate* creates emphasis at the neck and face when the character is facing forward, but as she turns to the side and back, the sweep of the drape and the profusion of pleats provide an amusing bustle interest. (See also Figure 4.20 for primary interest at the neck.)

Focus can be created in many ways. Strong lines pointing to the same point or strong shapes relating to an area provide emphasis on that area. An advancing color carefully placed on an area is one of the most effective focus devices. A large white collar on a costume usually focuses our attention on the face of the actor. However, in Color plate 6 the white collar and hat blend with the white-face makeup, and the exuberant patch pattern of this Harlequin draws attention to the body of the dancer. (See also Figure 4.19.)

Considering the Actor's Physicality

When the actor for a character is cast, consideration must be given to that actor's physical proportions in relation to the character ideal. When the physical characteristics are important to the role, a designer may wish visually to underscore those characteristics. In Figure 5.5 the character's bulk has been emphasized by the use of large patch pockets, a wide belt, and jodhpur-style pants for this costume for the Bey of Deraa in *Ross*. Not infrequently, a director chooses to ignore obvious physical differences between the actor and the character and to cast for a desired voice quality or superior acting ability. Particularly in operas and musicals, the voice requirements are always considered first and the visual requirements second. The designer is then called on to create a costume that brings the actor as close to the desired visual interpretation of the character as possible. The designer must make a careful study of the period garments and all the effects of the elements and principles of design to create a garment with the most appropriate visual effect. Even if historical accuracy must be nearly abandoned, certain characters must be costumed in becoming garments.

Conversations with the cast members will give the designer insight into the physical problems, preferences, and character interpretations of each actor. A designer may not be able to meet all the requests of the cast members and still serve the whole production, but if an actor's strong point of view (hated colors, styles) is ignored by the designer, trouble could develop later. Fitting prob-

FIGURE 5.5 Bey of Derea, *Ross.* Designed by Tony Straiges for Yale University.

lems are best dealt with in the planning stage as well. An actor with unusual proportions cannot be ignored! Dealing with figure problems and special sizes requires tact and diplomacy. If special effort will be needed to meet special needs, extra time must be allowed for handling the problem. Remember that the actor must feel self-assured and confident to perform well and the ultimate goal is a unified, quality production.

Accessories

Careful consideration should be given to shoes, hats, gloves, handbags, canes, and other accessories. These small items add visual interest and character detail and provide possibilities for stage business. Some items may be required in the script; others may be requested by the actors; still others may be suggested by the designer or director for visual or practical purposes.

Shoes are extremely important to the character's walk and posture and contribute to the sense of period. The heel height, general weight, and type of shoe should be indicated in the rough sketches and discussed with the director. In general, the heavier the shoe, the heavier the walk of the character wearing it. Shoes with soft soles create a lighter, more resilient step; hard-soled shoes, especially those with heavy heels, produce a more authoritative walk. High-heeled shoes create a walk with more swing in the hip, and the posture and balance of the figure must be adjusted. The full weight of the body descends on the heel, and the pelvic section is thrust forward as the wearer walks. High heels also alter the shape of the calf muscle and produce a more curvaceous leg. "Common sense" shoes (oxfords with thick heels) produce a "common sense" walk. Sandal and slipper wearers tend to shuffle. Characters that must dance will need shoes appropriate to the type of dance they will do, regardless of period considerations.

Novice designers tend to overlook the importance of shoes. Early decisions about shoe styles are important because the actors should rehearse in the type of shoes they will be wearing in the role and because shoe purchases are a major budget item.

The style and size of handbags and other hand-held props must also be determined early and should be included in the rough sketches. Rehearsal versions of these items will be required so the "stage business" can be developed and so the actor can become familiar with their size, closures, and manipulation.

Hats, too, must be considered for the rough sketches. Until the middle of the twentieth century, headcoverings were an essential part of dress for both men and women, rich and poor alike. The size, scale, and style of a hat are major elements of the complete costume design. In Color plate 7 the exaggerated scale of the bonnet for the First Tart in *On a Clear Day You Can See Forever* is vital to the effect of the total costume. Because the execution of millinery is frequently time-consuming and may become a major budget item, hats should be considered at the same time as other aspects of the costume.

Outerwear (coats, capes) is another aspect of the costume often overlooked by beginning designers. The script may give only scanty references to these items, but they represent major budget and construction considerations and should be included in the rough sketches.

Achieving Balance

As roughs develop for each character, sketches should be compared with one another. Are the costumes different enough? Are they too dissimilar? Are they designed in the same style? Are they done in the same scale? Which characters become most important as groups are combined and recombined? Is the focus in each scene (group of characters) on the important person in that scene? By taking advantage of the advancing and receding effects of the various elements of design, the costume designer can go a long way toward establishing the important character in a scene. Because light or warm colors advance and dark or cool colors recede, characters in light or warm colors usually stand out from those in dark or cool colors. Because shiny, smooth textures advance and dull textures recede, an actress in a satin gown will usually stand out among costumes made of wool. One effect overrides these guidelines, however. The *odd* element in a design will usually attract most attention. One black costume on an all light, bright stage will draw the most attention. One cool-colored costume against all warm colors may draw the eye to itself. And . . . a spotlight overrules everything!

Relationships between characters can be suggested by similarities in their costumes. These similarities can be in color, cut, or texture. The more realistic the style of presentation, the more subtle these relationships need to be. The more stylized or abstract the play, the more obvious the relationships can be. Costumes for comedy, farce, or dance are often very strongly related. Adversaries, particularly opposing armies, must be clearly differentiated for the audiences. Uniforms of different cut and/or colors are the obvious choice. Opposing forces of good and evil should be similarly identified for the audience. In *Romeo and Juliet* the members of the two feuding households, the Montagues and the Capulets, are often designed in complementary colors, each family in its own hue.

PLANNING COLOR

A color layout may be developed before, during, or after the "rough" stage of design work, but it is usually shown to the director when the roughs are discussed. Groups of swatches, chosen to represent types of fabric and colors, are taped or stapled to a sheet of stiff paper as a representation of the colors and textures in the costumes. These may be swatches from the designer's collection or fabrics swatched specifically for the show. Starting with colors dictated by the script or color impressions from the script, an overall color scheme and textural plan is evolved in the swatch layout. This plan may be based on a painting, a print fabric, art objects, or other sources that suggest the mood of the play. Goya's *Blind Man's Bluff*, shown in Color plate 8, inspired the color scheme for a production of *The Marriage of Figaro*; the next step toward developing the color for the production was to organize a swatch board (Color plate 9) to help the designer and the director visualize the show.

When textures are less important, a color plan may be more efficient and can assist the designer with specific character choices. Soft pastels are a quick, useful medium for working out a color plan.

In addition to the actual costume budget, a designer must know what facilities and staff are available for the production. Is costume stock available for use? How extensive and in what condition is the costume stock in the required period? Is rental of costumes possible? How much time is allowed? Are the actors to provide any personal items? The designer should consult with the costume shop manager or costume director to answer these and other budget questions. (Further budget considerations are discussed in Chapter 8.)

BUDGET

At the early stages of design some consideration should be given to budget restrictions. All designers must work within the budget limitations set by the producing organization. No matter how wonderful a set of designs may be, if there is no way to realize them, a designer will need to change the approach. In Figure 5.6 the sketch on the left is the original design for a costume for *Miss USA 1984*. By eliminating costly and time-consuming hand-beading, the designer developed a similar costume (right) which met the limitations of time and budget.

A simple rule of thumb for evaluating costume cost is to divide the total budget by the number of costumes to arrive at an average cost per costume. When the number of costumes is figured, each change and each outer garment must be considered a separate costume. Considering the cost of shoes, hats, and undergarments, is it reasonable to expect to assemble a costume for the amount proposed?

FIGURE 5.6 Left, Susan Hum's original design for a costume for *Miss USA 1984*; a less expensive costume to the right.

Financial restrictions can sometimes stimulate very creative and theatrical solutions to costume problems, but budget limitations should be recognized and faced early in the design process. A simple approach, well executed, will be more effective than an elaborate design uncompleted because it was too expensive, was beyond the skill level of the staff, or was too time-consuming. Remember that the audience sees only what is actually on stage, not the designer's unfulfilled sketches.

SPECIAL CONSIDERATIONS

While the general principles of costume design apply to all situations, each production presents special problems to the designer. The designer is constantly challenged to anticipate and solve the problems unique to each situation.

The Theater Structure

The type of theater in which a production will be seen presents certain considerations in the development of the costumes.

For the costume designer the proscenium stage has both ad-

FIGURE 5.7 *The Marriage of Figaro.* Designed by the author for Brooklyn College.

vantages and disadvantages. A major disadvantage is the psychological barrier produced between the audience and the actors by the proscenium arch. The distance between actor and audience created by the apron (forestage) and orchestra pit becomes difficult to bridge. Much detail is lost if that distance is great. If this detail is desired, the designer must anticipate the problem and enlarge the scale of the detail to read (be seen) from a distance. On the other hand, costumes that are shabby and worn often look wonderful under lights on the proscenium stage. Poor construction and cheap fabrics are less likely to read from this type of stage. Cheap baubles and fake jewelry often give an effect superior to that of the real thing. Fantasy effects and tricks also are easier to achieve behind the proscenium.

The larger the theater regardless of the type of structure, the larger the scale in which the designer must work in order for the costumes to read, but care must be taken to stay within the reasonable limits of the style of the production. Constructing the costume with cording in the seams or trimming the edges of garments with braid or ribbon will help carry the line of the garment over long distances. In Figure 5.7 decorative braid delineates the lines of the costumes for Figaro and Suzanne in *The Marriage of Figaro.* Even when there is little contrast between the braid and garment colors, the added texture creates highlights and shadows which help the costume read throughout the theater.

Making the different pieces in slightly different colors, or shades of the same color, will also help project the costume. Instead of a three-piece suit, for example, a combination of solids, stripes, and textures in the same colors, while appearing the same from a distance, will be read as three pieces instead of a gray or brown blob. Careful shading with an airbrush or spray paint under collars, lapels, pocket flaps, and cuffs can emphasize details and add highlights and shadows to costumes that might otherwise fade over long distances.

Because in thrust and arena theaters actors are seen from all sides, often in close proximity to the audience, special problems arise. Zippers, velcro, and other modern closures used in period clothing are more readily seen and may become distracting. The overscaled trims that would be necessary on the proscenium stage may become comic when used on a small thrust or arena stage. The quality of the fabric, trim, and workmanship is much more obvious to the audience in these theaters. Also the rumpled, soiled costume can be clearly seen. Since the costume is being seen from all sides at once, the back must be as interesting and well thought out as the front. The designer must think specifically of the three-dimensional, sculptural characteristics of the costume. Accessories like shoes and handbags are even more important than in proscenium productions.

In addition to all these problems, arena theaters are often temporary arrangements with limited support spaces (dressing rooms, workshops). Pageants, street theater, and tent theaters for summer stock are often done in the round. There is usually no place for special effects and tricks and no wall against which to disguise a costume change or create an illusion.

The Outdoor Theater

The outdoor theater can be based on any of the above theater types, but the fact that the production is outdoors leads to special problems. Obviously, the weather is the main consideration. The costume designer must understand the variations in temperature to be expected in the particular locale. Extremes of heat and cold as well as excess humidity or rain can adversely affect the actors, costumes, makeup, and wigs. Costume materials should be suitable for the climatic conditions even if these materials are unusual choices for the period or style of production. Easy maintenance of costumes is also important.

In some areas afternoon performers could be cooked with

broiling heat and evening performers could be frozen with a chilling mountain breeze. Costumes designed with removable pieces or layers allow for adjustment to heat or cold. Capes, shawls, robes, or coats can be added or removed. Special undergarments might be needed to adjust for temperature. Thermal underwear for warmth is relatively easy to provide; undergarments with coolants are more difficult and must be specially made.

Almost all outdoor theaters must battle insects. The costume designer may need to limit the exposed areas of the actors' bodies. In addition to stage makeup the costumes must tolerate suntan lotion and insect repellant!

Productions with Music

Music is a major influence on the style of a production. It creates both limitations and possibilities for the costume designer.

Musicals

Much of American theater is dedicated to the production of musicals, and they present the costume designer with a few special problems. Musicals usually have large casts of singers and dancers. While there is generally an element of fantasy present in a musical which allows the designer leeway in interpreting period, finding ways to allow for sufficient movement for dancers and room for singers to breathe and sing may take some ingenuity.

Costumes in musical numbers are under extreme stress and must be well constructed of sturdy fabric and backing. A dancer should never be worried about losing part of the costume on stage. Special stretch fabrics or special construction techniques may be required for long-running productions or energetic dancing.

Trained singers may expand their chest several sizes when singing. Care should be taken to allow for this expansion in the fitting of their costumes. Garments should not restrict the throat.

In many musical numbers all the dancers or singers are costumed alike. Since these parts will generally be cast for voice or dance ability, the shape and size of the individuals may vary considerably. An attempt should be made to choose a style that will flatter as many of the group as possible. If such a style cannot be found, different costumes might be designed for each chorus member, perhaps in related colors and fabrics.

For most musicals the costumes are designed in bright, cheerful colors and in strong, bold shapes. Some exaggeration of scale lifts

FIGURE 5.8 *The All Night Strut.* Musical revue dance costumes designed by Carol Oditz; Ford's Theater, Washington, D.C.

the musical out of the realm of reality. In Figure 5.8 the costumes for *The All Night Strut* make use of bold pattern to express the energy and exuberance of the show. The cut of the garments allows great freedom of movement and emphasizes the legs and feet.

Musicals are often conceived as spectacles with what seems like (and sometimes is) hundreds of costumes. Quick changes are numerous and frantic, so expert organization is essential. Some quick-change problems can be solved with costumes that can be worn over or under other costumes. Breakaway costumes using velcro or large snaps may be necessary. Sometimes complete ensembles must be mounted onto one base garment and treated like a

FIGURE 5.9 *Julius Caesar*. Handel's baroque music influences the ornate quality of these costumes by José Varona. The scale is in keeping with the size of the opera house and the grandeur of the work. Photo © Fred Fehl.

jumpsuit. With this solution, other costumes can be worn underneath and an almost miraculous costume change results.

Opera

Traditionally, operas are not designed in realistic style. Opera, like tragedy, explores emotions, passions, and themes that are often profound and larger than life. Most operas require a sense of grand scale: an exaggerated, highly theatrical, visual approach. The form and feeling of the music are major factors in determining the visual style. Regardless of the period of the story, the period and style in which the music is written should be a major influence. The baroque music of Handel's *Julius Caesar* is the major influence on the costumes in Figure 5.9. These costumes are based on seventeenth-century dress with only touches of Roman and Egyptian detail. In Color plate 10 the humor in Rossini's music is reflected in the color and detail of the costume for *The Barber of Seville*.

Because the music is the primary consideration, the roles in an opera are cast by voice, not by the visual considerations of the character. All the optical tricks of color, line, and form are needed to provide the most becoming and workable costume for the singer who does not physically look the part.

In established opera companies productions are performed in repertory, each opera playing once or twice a week and alternating with several other operas. Costumes for each production are stored together and not used for other operas. This system simplifies maintenance and turnaround time from one production to another.

Costuming large groups of extras and chorus singers is very time-consuming. These costumes should be built to allow for much alteration or designed as "one size fits all" to allow for frequent cast changes.

Dance

Costumes designed for dance must be approached from the choreographer's point of view. In traditional ballets and some other works there is a story line and specific characters to interpret. In other dance forms the dancers may be expressing feelings, interpreting the music, or exploring movement in noncharacter ways. In the former, the designer may have the help of period research and traditional interpretations of the dance piece. In the latter, the designer must become familiar with the choreography, attending rehearsals and discussing the work with the choreographer at all the stages of development. The movements, shapes and forms as well as the relationship of the dancers to the music must be explored for clues to the visual style. What parts of the body are emphasized in the movement? Are the movements circular? Angular? Rhythmical? Do the dancers act in unison or in opposition? Do they express emotions and relationships or abstract movement? What does the music express? What physical attributes of the dancer should be emphasized or modified?

Dancers view their costumes as their "skin." They want to feel the garment as a part of their body, as an extension of the gesture and movement, not an addition to it. Dance costumes should emphasize, complement, and complete the movement. In practical terms the costume must allow the dancer the freedom of movement needed to perform the dance. A formal period dance may require less mobility in the upper torso and may permit the use of a stiff, fitted bodice, whereas a jazz or modern dance piece may need to be done in stretch leotards. Specially cut sleeves, gussets, and stretch fabrics open up possibilities for movement in garments that appear to be close fitting.

Skirt lengths are modified for dance even in period pieces to permit the dancer to move and to allow the audience to appreciate the choreography. In the costume from *Romeo and Juliet* in Figure 5.10 the skirt is shorter than the garments in the historical period and the sleeves have been eliminated to give total freedom of movement.

Designing garments that move well is one of the dance designer's primary responsibilities. Cutting garments on the bias, using variations of the circular skirt, choosing fluid or floating fabrics like tulle, crepe, and chiffon are popular approaches to dance costumes. Generally speaking, dance costumes should be light-weight and fluid, allowing for the full appreciation of the work of the choreographer and dancers.

INSPIRATION

No rules or guidelines produce inspired costumes. Sometimes inspiration defies all guidelines. It cannot be taught. The designer learns with experience when to trust that inspiration. Inspiration, however, rarely flashes like a comet across the sky. More often than not, it is uncovered like a buried treasure after much strenuous effort. The more information (research) assembled, the more likely the rubbing together of ideas that will set off a creative spark. A designer either *is* creative or *isn't*, *has* vision or *doesn't*, but no designer exists or works in a vacuum. Constant stimuli and raw materials for the creative fires are required. The script is the basic source for the designer's inspiration, but seeing plays; reading novels and poetry; visiting art exhibits, museums, and junk yards; studying architecture, decorative objects, and street scenes; travel-ing; and countless other experiences provide raw material for the creative process. The costume designer cannot sit and wait for in-spiration; it must be eagerly sought.

The rough sketch phase should be a period of exploration. The designer should keep an open mind toward all possibilities. Some-times the most unrelated object or experience can stimulate a won-derful idea or approach to a design problem.

FIGURE 5.10 *Romeo and Juliet*. Designed by Natalie Garfinkle. Photo ©Susan Cook.

DIRECTOR/DESIGNER CONFERENCES

A meeting should be scheduled to show the roughs to the director. Pertinent research might also be included. The roughs should be presented with a purpose in mind. Usually, major characters in major scenes are dealt with first and minor characters and chorus

1 *Comedy of Errors.* These identical twin servants are costumed as mirror images. To help the audience identify them, different but related colors (pink and orange) were used for corresponding sections of their costumes. Designed by the author for Brooklyn College. Photo by Richard Grossberg.

2 *Mother Courage.* Changing the period and locale of a play may make it more meaningful to the audience. This production of *Mother Courage*, designed by Carol Helen Beule for the Virginia Museum Theater, was set in the Southern United States during the Civil War. Photo by Carol Helen Beule.

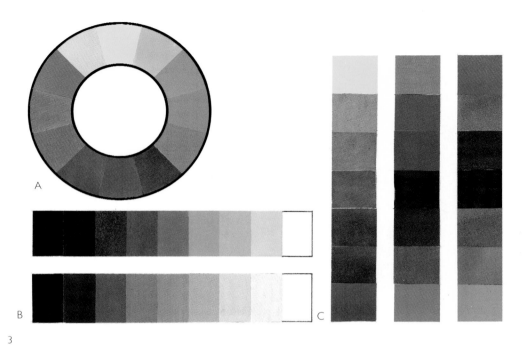

A

B

C

3

3 Color Basics. (a) Basic Color Wheel—
Primary and Secondary colors. (b) Value
chart—adding white to a color raises its
value; adding black to a color lowers its
value. (c) Intensity Chart—adding a color's
complement lowers its intensity.

EVERYMAN

MAIDS

4 Everyman. A chorus of maids shows
how color can provide contrast and
relieve the uniformity of simple costumes.
Designed by the author for Brooklyn
College.

4

5

6

7

5 *The Royal Family*. The design, uses bold areas of color and pattern to contrast with the strong black. Designed by David Murin for The American Stage Festival.

6 *Harlequinade* Multicolored patches emphasize the dancer's movement. Designed by Rouben Ter-Arutunian for The New York City Ballet.

7 *On a Clear Day You Can See Forever*. The exaggerated bonnet completes the amusing costume below by Patton Campbell for the First Tart. Designed for The National Company.

8

8 *Blind Man's Bluff.* This painting by Goya inspired the color scheme for a production of *The Marriage of Figaro.* (See also Figure 5.7.) Prado Museum.

9

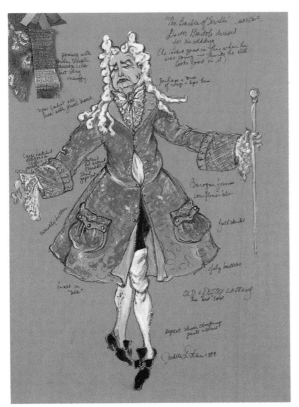

9 Swatch Board. A collection of swatches based on the Goya painting (Color plate 8) helps the designer visualize the show and present ideas to the director.

10 The Barber of Seville. Judith Dolan's sketch for Doctor Bartolo wittily expresses his pomposity and arrogance. The humor in the music is reflected in the color and detail of the costume. Designed for The New York City Opera.

10

11 *Mother Courage.* This costume sketch by Carol Helen Beule for the production shown in Color plate 2 was painted with acrylic paints on beige mat board splattered with colored inks. Note how the rendering style suggests the look of the production.

11

12 *Measure for Measure.* Good sketch presentation helps the designer "sell" the costume to the director. The dramatic use of line and watercolor wash, the placement of the figure, and the artful addition of fabric swatches combine to give this sketch by Michael J. Cesario for *Measure for Measure* great visual impact. Designed for The Louisville Shakespeare Company.

12

13 *Vagabond Stars*. A profusion of printed fabrics in subtle colors are skillfully combined in this costume by Carol Oditz. Designed for the Berkshire Theater Festival.

13

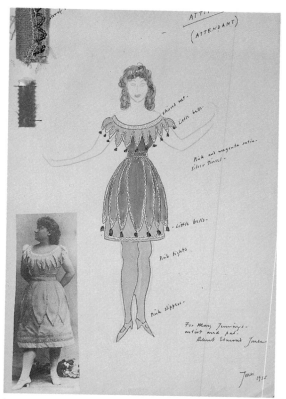

14

14 *Central City Nights*. Including copies of research with the sketch is useful to the pattern maker. This 1930's sketch for "Attitudes" by Robert Edmond Jones includes a photo of the original source (circa 1900). Courtesy of the Theater Department, Brooklyn College.

15 *Molière in Spite of Himself*. This costume for King Louis began with all white fabrics. The variations of color were carefully painted onto the fabric to suggest a watercolor painting come to life. Designed by Hilary Sherred for Colonades Theater Lab. Photo by Diane Gorodnitzki.

15

16

16 *Heartbreak House*. Dyeing techniques can produce interesting costume effects. This costume for Hesione was shaded from blue to burgundy by being dipped in successive dye baths, with areas of each color left undyed by the next solution. Designed by the author for SoHo Repertory Company.

members are considered later. Two approaches are possible. One, the characters can be shown, scene by scene, starting with Act I. The alternative approach is to show all costumes for a character to-gether, then all costumes for the next character, and so on. The choice of approach is a personal one, but the first method seems more appropriate for realistic and ensemble-type plays, and the second approach may work better for plays centering on a few main characters.

Whichever method is used, the designer must be prepared to explain the roughs to the director carefully and completely. The designer should accept graciously, and note in writing, all directorial comment, without becoming defensive or taking criticism person-ally. Collaboration is difficult, and much information must be read between the lines. Often a negative reaction from the director is based on misunderstanding, misinformation, poor sketch presenta-tion, inadequate research, misreading of the sketch, or preconceived ideas which can be discussed and modified. Remember that the director has the final word on how the production is to look. Coor-dination of the scenery, costumes, lighting, and acting style into a unified whole is the director's responsibility.

Asking meaningful questions is the key to communication with the director. The designer should ask for specifics. "She looks too old" is a more meaningful statement from a director than "I don't like it." Always ask, "Do you know why (you don't like it)?" Some-times the reaction is to the posture or figure in the sketch, not the costume itself. Some alterations can be made on pencil sketches during the conference or on tracing paper over the sketch to show possible variations.

This is the time to fill in any blanks from the earlier discussions. Perhaps the sketch does not explain the character because of inade-quate analysis of the script or because the script or the director was unclear. Has the casting of a specific actor clarified the role or changed the director's ideas about the character?

After the conference the designer should analyze the result. Which costumes met with the director's approval? What further work is needed on them? Which costumes were rejected? Why? Is more research needed? Is the concept carried throughout? Will another conference on the roughs be needed? What is happening with the scenery? How does the look of the set affect the direction of the costume design? A checklist for this stage of the work is pro-vided in Box 5.E. This information can be used in making revisions and redesigning. If corrections are relatively minor, the designer may proceed to do finished costume sketches as described in the next chapter.

Box 5.E   Designer Checklist IV: Roughs

1. Does each costume define the character's age, social status, and personality? Does this costume fit within the historical period or concept of this production?
2. Can the actor perform the required actions in each costume?
3. Have the costume accessories been considered? Are they appropriate? Will they help the actor or get in the way?
4. How will this costume look on the actor cast in this role? Is corsetry or padding required? Is this costume becoming to the actor?
5. Is it interesting? Imaginative? Dramatic?
6. Are the proportions pleasing? The scale dramatic?
7. Are the parts logically combined? Do they relate to each other?
8. Do the parts of the costume logically surround the body on all sides? Do they connect in the back or on the other side? What does the back look like?
9. Where is the focus in each sketch? On whom will the focus be in each scene?
10. Is more research needed? Are other accessories needed?
11. Do all costumes appear to be for the same production?
12. Do important characters stand out from the group as a whole?
13. Can we see important relationships among characters?
14. Do the costumes reflect the form and mode of drama of the play?
15. Do the costumes and scenery work together effectively? How will the colors of the costumes work against the colors of the set?
16. Is any character operating on contradictory levels? What aspects of the costume could represent each level?
17. Does the costume reveal *too much* about the character?
18. Do the silhouette (shape), cut and trim (line), fabric (texture or pattern, and hang), and color of this costume reflect important aspects of the visual definition of this character?

Chapter 6
Rendering the Sketch

Of all the skills required of a costume designer, the ability to draw figures and illustrate garments meaningfully is one of the most essential. The designer must be able to work out ideas and convey to the director, the actors, and the costumer the real proportion, emotional content, and construction detail necessary for each to understand the aspects of the costume that most affect them. Designers need to study figure drawing, anatomy, and painting. Such study is a lifelong involvement. This chapter provides some basic drawing and painting instruction for the beginning costume designer.

SETTING UP A WORK AREA

The costume designer needs a reasonable amount of well-organized workspace. A table or desk large enough to spread out palette, paints, water container, drawing board, and other equipment is adequate, but a drawing table set at an appropriate angle and a side table to hold equipment is more desirable. A comfortable chair and a good incandescent light are essential. (Fluorescent light distorts color.) A bulletin board is useful for roughs, swatches, and research material. A large wastebasket should be kept handy for rejects. Right-handed persons should place water and paints on their right side so as not to drip across their work; left-handed persons should set up materials on the left side. Materials should be kept well organized and in good condition. The time spent keeping the work area neat is repaid many times in efficiency and speed.

Art Supplies

The following list of supplies covers the basic techniques used by costume designers as described in this chapter. However, artists are constantly experimenting, and costume designers are no exception. Almost any relatively fast technique can be used for costume designs, provided the resulting sketch is mounted and protected adequately for the extensive handling to which costume sketches are subject. Most designers experiment with many approaches until they find a medium that best suits their own personal style. Versatility is desirable, however, to allow the designer to choose a medium that expresses the concept or mood of the play.

Pencils
Drawing pencils: B (soft) and 2B (softer) are used for sketching. Experiment with 2H (hard) and HB (medium) for different effects. Some designers like mechanical pencils, which can be filled with the desired lead. *Colored pencils* are popular with designers for details or shading, especially in white. Some designers find grease pencils in black and white useful. *Conté crayon* and *charcoal pencils* can be used but require more experience.

Sharpeners
Small metal *pencil sharpeners* with containers for catching shavings are handy. Special sharpeners are required for mechanical pencils. *Sandpaper pads* shape pencils and pastels.

Erasers
Art gum erasers clean up drawings without damaging the surface of the paper. *Kneaded erasers* are used for chalk, charcoal, conté crayon, pastel, and soft pencil and can be formed into shapes to erase small areas. An *ink eraser* can lighten mistakes but may damage the finish of soft papers.

Pens
Drawing pen holders and *nibs* (points), and *felt* and *fiber-tipped pens* can be used by the costume designer. The designer should experiment with a variety of pens to express different types of line. Look for pens that produce lines of varying width and character. Felt-tip and fiber-tip pens should have permanent ink. Metallic felt-tip pens are very useful for decorative detail.

Paints
Watercolors: A designer needs a set of assorted colors or a group of separate tubes. Useful colors are Cadmium Yellow Pale, Naples

Yellow, Yellow Ochre, Raw Sienna, Burnt Sienna, Raw Umber, Van Dyke Brown, Sepia, Cadmium Red Light, Cadmium Red Medium, Scarlet, Alizarin Crimson, Violet, Ultramarine Blue, Cerulean Blue, and Chinese White.

Gouache or *designer colors*: These assorted colors can be used for various opaque effects. White is especially useful for adding detail and for touch-ups.

Metallic paints: Water-base metallic paints add flash and glitz to costumes. Do not use oil-base metallic inks on water color sketches, since oil resists further wash techniques (transparent layers). Wash is discussed later in the chapter under Basic Watercolor Techniques. These inks can also leave an oily "halo" on some papers.

Acrylic paints: A set of assorted colors or individual tubes can be used for wash and opaque techniques.

Pastels

A set of hard or soft pastels (chalk) or pastel pencils offers the designer another useful medium. They can be sharpened with a mat knife and sandpaper block. Paper stumps of various sizes, degrees of hardness, and types of points are used for blending. *Oil pastels* are used for resist techniques and a "crayon look."

Ink

Black waterproof *drawing ink* is used for line and wash. Assorted *colored inks* allow for intense wash techniques.

Papers

Papers are available in pads or loose sheets. Pads of *drawing paper*, *newsprint*, *tracing paper*, or *layout paper* are needed for sketches, roughs, and research. For watercolor, ink, or pen and ink, use *Bristol board* (vellum finish), *Murillo board*, *coquille board*, *illustration board*, or *watercolor papers* with fine finishes. Do not use plate finish papers for wash techniques. *Charcoal paper*, *velour paper*, and *mat boards* come in many colors and can be used for pastels. Mat board can also be used for gouache, acrylic, and watercolor painting. *Rice papers* are suitable for quick, simple sketch style with little correction but are not good for large wash areas.

Papers come in a wide range of weights. For wash techniques, a paper should be at least 80 pounds. If paper is too lightweight, washes will cause them to buckle and crinkle unevenly, distorting the sketch and making painting difficult. Papers with high rag content and of heavier weights make wash techniques and corrections or scrub-outs easier.

The paper surface can be described as hot press, cold press, or rough. *Hot press* papers have a smooth, hard finish and absorb moisture slowly. These papers are used for technical work and illustration. They are good for pen and ink, but washes tend to sit too long on the surface and may run or streak. *Cold press* papers have a slight texture and absorb moisture more quickly. These papers are good for wash techniques. *Rough* papers are usually unsuitable for costume sketches.

Brushes

Only quality brushes should be used for watercolor and ink work. Called pointed rounds, *watercolor brushes* made of red sable or sablene in sizes #1, 4, and 8, are needed for costume sketches. A large brush that makes a good point will serve the designers's needs better than several small brushes. Sizes of various available brands should be compared. Cheap brushes are good only for gluing. Synthetic fiber brushes are satisfactory for acrylics. A small, flat acrylic or oil painting brush is useful for applying rubber cement.

Drafting or Masking Tape

Tapes are used for taping papers to the drawing board and for masking sections of work for sharp-edged shapes.

Fixative

Spray fixatives are used for fixing charcoal, pencil, conté crayon, and pastel sketches to prevent smearing. Spraying should not be done near open flames, nor should spray be inhaled.

Acetate

Acetate (.003 weight) can be cut and taped around sketches to protect them from damage.

Glues

Rubber cement is used for gluing papers together; *white casein glue* is used for gluing heavy boards or attaching swatches to sketches.

Water Containers

Large jars or bowls can be used to hold water. Some designers use two containers, one for washing brushes and one to hold clean water for mixing into paints.

Palette

Mixing trays, small dishes or cups, plastic egg cartons, or plastic ice trays all provide suitable containers for mixing inks and watercolors.

Palettes should be nonabsorbant and white (to prevent visual distortion of paint color during mixing).

Mat Knife

A retractable knife and extra blades are needed for cutting heavy paper and illustration board.

Drawing Board

A drawing board, 20 by 26 inches or larger, is needed to support loose paper during painting. A piece of masonite (with finished edges) or a drawing table can serve as a substitute.

Rulers and T-Square

Metal rulers are needed for measuring and cutting paper for sketches.

Tissues or Clean Rags

Tissues should be kept within easy reach for cleaning brushes and blotting up excess paint.

Wastebasket

Don't let sketches become too precious. If it isn't working, throw it *out* and start over.

Portfolio

The designer will need a string-tied folder for carrying sketches. A presentation portfolio for photos and sketches of shows designed will be needed for job interviews.

Care of Materials

Good art materials are expensive and should be cared for properly. Pens and holders should be wiped clean with a tissue or damp cloth after each use and they should be stored carefully to prevent damage to the points. Caps should always be kept on fiber-tipped and felt-tipped pens.

Good brushes deserve the very best care; poor-quality brushes are not worth having. During painting, brushes should be rinsed often in clean water. They should be washed with cool water and mild soap or commercial brush cleaner occasionally to remove any residue of paint materials. Always dry with a tissue or cloth and shape the tip into a point. Allow it to dry, with brush tip up, in a container. Do not put the brush in the mouth or stroke the tip with fingertips. Never leave a good brush standing, point down, in a water container. When working, rinse the brush and prop the ferrule on a tissue or brush holder when you are not using the brush.

Tube paints should be squeezed from the bottom of the tube. Tops should be kept clean and tightly capped when not in use. Inks and liquid paints may need to be stirred or shook at each use. Check the labels. Clean the rim of the bottles and put the lids on securely when finished.

Palettes and water containers should be cleaned after each use.

The top of the drawing table can be protected with a sheet of mat board or other covering. Always use an extra piece of heavy board under the work when cutting with a mat knife, to prevent scarring the table top.

DRAWING THE FIGURE

To draw, you must close your eyes and sing.
PABLO PICASSO   NBC-TV, September 15, 1957

Proportion

Most costume designers use the "fashion figure" for costume sketches. The average adult body is $7\frac{1}{2}$ times the height of the head, whereas the fashion figure is $8\frac{1}{2}$ times the height of the head. This slight elongation of the figure adds grace to the body and shows the garment to advantage. Further elongation of the figure distorts the body proportions and makes the interpretation of the sketch more difficult. The designer should study the people encountered daily and collect pictures of interesting figures in order to understand the visual effects produced by different body proportions. Deviations from the "ideal" provide needed contrast. Directors often cast actors of various shapes and sizes to create a more interesting stage picture. The designer will want to reflect these differences in the sketches. In Figure 6.1 examples of full-front figures demonstrate the relative proportions of the $8\frac{1}{2}$-head male and female fashion figures.

Female Proportions

The female head is egg-shaped and fills the first head space in Figure 6.1. This shape represents the head before the hair and headdress are added.

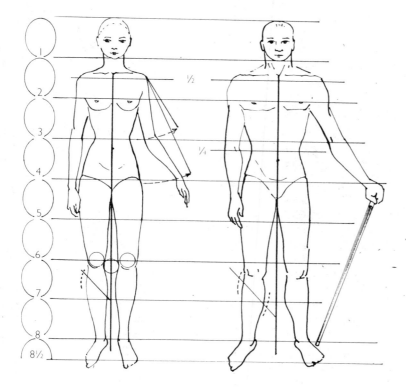

FIGURE 6.1 Basic Fashion Figures. Drawn at 8½ times the head.

The width of female shoulders is 1½ times the height of the head. The shoulders are drawn on a line at the halfway point of the second head space. The nipples are drawn at the second head line, the waist at the third head line. The top of the leg is drawn along the fourth head line. The knee caps are centered on the sixth head line, and the legs begin to taper in just above the seventh head. The ankles are drawn at the eighth head line. The feet take up the last half head or a little more, the actual space depending on the position of the foot.

The arms round off the shoulder points, and the inside of the elbow is even with the waist at the third head line. The outside of the elbow touches the top of the pelvic bone. The wrist lines up with the fourth head line. The hand rests on the thigh down to the fifth head line and is about three-quarters the size of the head.

The upper arm swings from the shoulder in an arc. As long as the arms are in the same plane as the body, the apparent length of the upper arm and lower arm does not change as they swing outward.

The leg curves are higher on the outside and lower on the inside of the leg. The ankle is higher on the inside and lower on the outside.

Male Proportions

Male proportions vary from the female's in several areas. Assuming the two figures are the same height, the following differences exist in the proportions of the male and female fashion figures. The head is wider and more angular. The neck is heavier. The shoulders are the width of two head lengths (Figure 6.1) and are drawn at one-third of the second head. The nipples are on the second head line. The male figure's waist is lowered to a line one-fourth of the fourth head. The top of the legs is at the fourth head. The knees are drawn at the sixth head line and the ankles at the eighth head line. The feet take up the last one-half head.

The arms pivot from the shoulder, and the inside of the elbow is in line with the waist. The outside of the elbow touches the top of the pelvic bone. The pelvic area of the male figure is smaller than that of the female figure. Because the waist of the male is lower, the upper arm is longer. The lower arm is also slightly longer, bringing the hand down just past the fifth head line. The angle of the leg curves and ankles are the same as on the female figure.

The male figure is generally drawn heavier, more muscular and angular, and with larger feet and hands.

Balance

The "balance line," an imaginary line representing the pull of gravity on the body, helps the designer draw a figure that appears to be standing securely on the ground. With the body weight evenly distributed on both feet, the balance line falls from the pit of the neck, perpendicular to the bottom of the paper, and falls *between* the ankles of the figure. When the weight shifts to one leg, the balance line moves toward the supporting foot. When all the weight is supported by one leg, the balance line falls from the pit of the neck to the ankle of the supporting leg. Figure 6.2 shows two full-front action figures. Note the sharp curve of the body and the angles produced by the shift of weight. The hip of the supporting leg is higher than that of the non-supporting leg. The shoulders are tilted in the opposite direction for balance. The breasts are in line with the angle of the shoulders. The part of the body that is most flexible

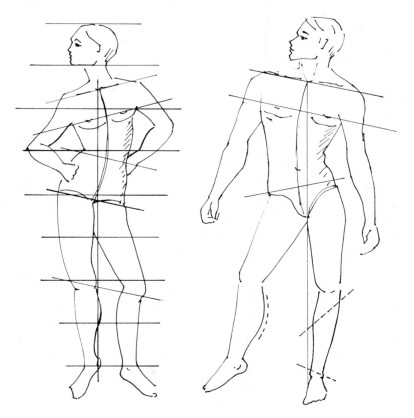

FIGURE 6.2   Full-Front Action Figures. As the weight is shifted from both feet to one foot, the body compensates to maintain its balance, creating a feeling of movement and action in the figures.

is the area between the rib cage and the pelvic bone. This area stretches or contracts for movement.

Eye Level

Most designers sketch costume figures with the viewer's eye level at the chest or waist of the figure. If the eye level is too high, the viewer appears to be looking down from the balcony. If the eye level is too low, the viewer seems to be seeing the figure from below stage level.

With the eye level (horizon line) in the chest area, the viewer can logically see under the hat brim and down onto the skirt. A set of sketches should share the same eye level. A full-front figure is drawn in one-point perspective (the sides, top, and bottom of the figure converge at the same point on the horizon line). Figure 6.3 illustrates the effect of one-point perspective on a figure in costume. Relating parts of the costume to a cube in perspective helps the designer draw them properly.

Varying the Pose

Three-Quarter Views

A set of costume sketches should include a variety of poses. The three-quarter view is a good choice for many sketches because the front and part of the side of the costume are visible. Figure 6.4 shows figures in the three-quarter position. Turning the figure places it into two-point perspective. Visualizing the body as a group of geometrical forms helps the designer place it into perspective. Figure 6.5 illustrates a three-quarter figure in two-point perspective. This figure is standing straight with weight evenly distributed, but at an angle to the viewer.

Although a costume should be illustrated in a simple pose, some action adds interest to the sketch. Keep the action appropriate to the character. Select a moment in the play in which the character makes an important entrance, discovery, decision, or characteristic gesture. Choose a pose and figure type that suggests the age, historical period, and personality of the character. Study research from the period of the play to find the appropriate posture for each character. The posture and fashionable body shape of a period are controlled by the foundation garments worn. A suitable pose will help the director and the actor visualize the costume as it will appear on stage.

Choose a pose that illustrates the costume to advantage. If a long hanging sleeve is a feature of the costume, extend an arm to display the full sweep of the sleeve. The front of a garment is usually the most important view and should be completely explained by the sketch. Profile and rear views limit the information provided by the sketch. If profile or rear views are used, small sketches of the front will also be needed.

Sketches should be large enough for adequate scale and accurate detail. To check the accuracy of the drawing, hold the sketch up to a mirror. If it is drawn on tracing paper, turn the figure over and look at it from the back. Mistakes in drawing are often more obvious when the sketch is reversed.

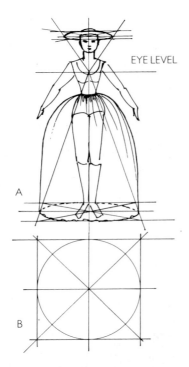

FIGURE 6.3 Figure in One-Point Perspective. The skirt, at its bottom edge, and the brim of the hat form a circle. Relating these circles to a box in one-point perspective (b) helps in drawing them correctly.

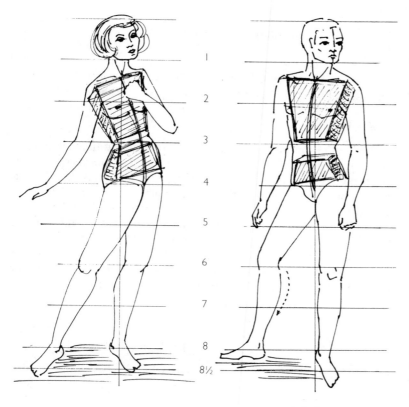

1
2
3
4
5
6
7
8
8½

FIGURE 6.4 Three-Quarter Figures. Costume sketches drawn on three-quarter figures show some of the side of the body as well as the front.

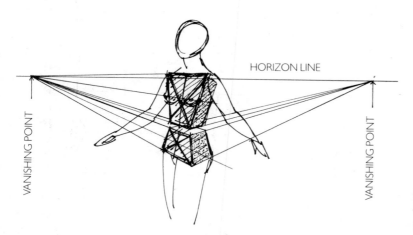

HORIZON LINE

VANISHING POINT

VANISHING POINT

FIGURE 6.5 The body in three-quarter view is seen in two-point perspective.

Rear Views

With the same proportions maintained, the rear view can be drawn simply as in Figure 6.6a. Note that the point of the elbow is below the third head line. The curve of the buttocks is on a line one-quarter head below the fourth head. A figure in three-quarter rear view, as in Figure 6.6b, is more interesting than a straight rear view.

Profile Views

Some feature of the costume may require a profile presentation. In Figure 6.7a a simple profile figure is illustrated. Proportion remains the same as for full-front figure. The head in profile is still egg-shaped but is now tilted so that the face plane is almost perpendicular to the first head line. The arm attaches to the shoulder line at one-half the second head space. The nipples are on the second head line. The top of the leg curves downward in the back, and the fullest part of the buttocks is drawn in the lower half of the fourth head space. The knees are drawn at the sixth head line. The upper leg is almost perpendicular to the balance line in front, but the back

FIGURE 6.6   Rear View. A figure so seen may be needed occasionally to show the back of the costume.

FIGURE 6.7   Profile (Side) View. Some costumes are more effectively drawn on a profile figure.

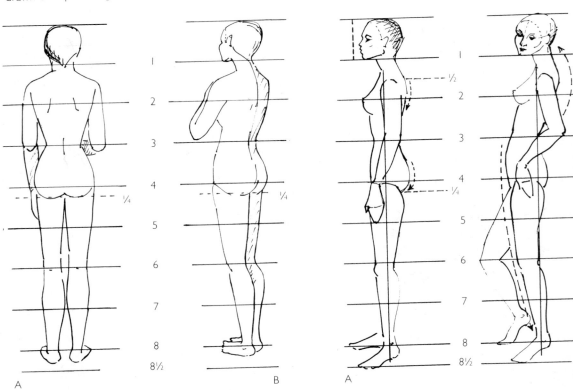

A

B

A

B

of the leg tapers in more sharply. The shin is straight and tapers in to the front of the foot. The calf curves out between the back of the knee and the seventh head line. The back of the leg then curves into the heel. More action can be put into the profile view by thrusting the pelvic section forward as illustrated in Figure 6.7b.

Indicating Age

Proportions vary according to the age of the character. Figure 6.8 shows children of several ages. Babies' heads are much larger in proportion to their bodies than those of adults. As the child grows, the torso, arms, and legs gradually lengthen in relationship to the head until adult proportions are reached. Children tend to be chubby and have prominent tummies, short necks, and no obvious bone structure. Figure 6.9 shows adult clothes scaled down for chil-

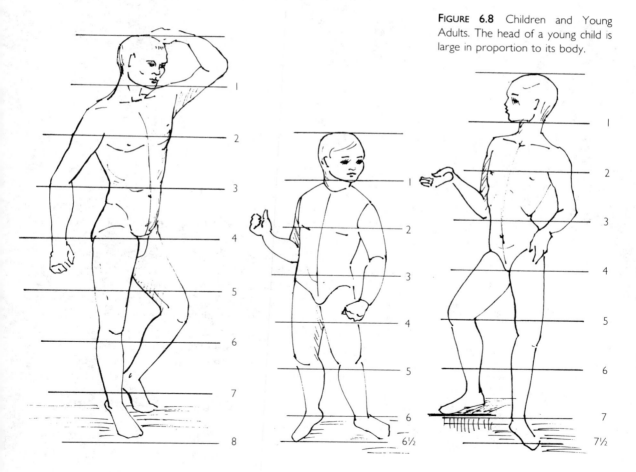

FIGURE 6.8 Children and Young Adults. The head of a young child is large in proportion to its body.

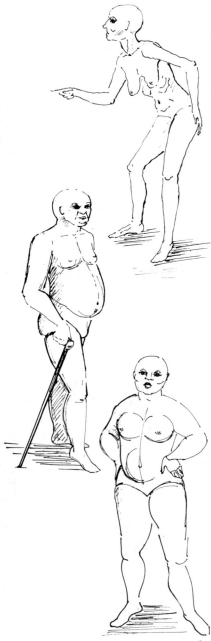

FIGURE 6.9   *The Princess.* These costumes by Carol Helen Beule are for children dressed as adults.

FIGURE 6.10   Aged and Heavy-Set Characters. The costume designer must learn to suggest the age and physique of all types of characters.

dren. An understanding of the differences between the proportions of children and adults was necessary to develop these designs for *The Princess*, a television commercial.

As is illustrated in Figure 6.10, middle-aged characters usually have thicker torsos and less erect posture. Women's breasts begin to sag, and men's muscles become soft and less defined.

Aged characters are drawn at 7 to 7½ heads high. Disease and old age can cause stooping and shrinking of the figure. If the shoulders and back become quite bent, the knees must bend to prevent the figure from falling forward. The head must then be thrust back so the person can see. Extremely old people may be thin and frail with soft muscles and sagging skin. The neck, elbows, knees, and torso, which in youth and middle age have firm muscles and fatty tissue to give them soft round shapes, become bony with age. In women the breasts sag more and the buttocks become flat.

Heavy-set figures can also be drawn 7 to 7½ heads high. Weight settles first in the waist area for most body types. For men

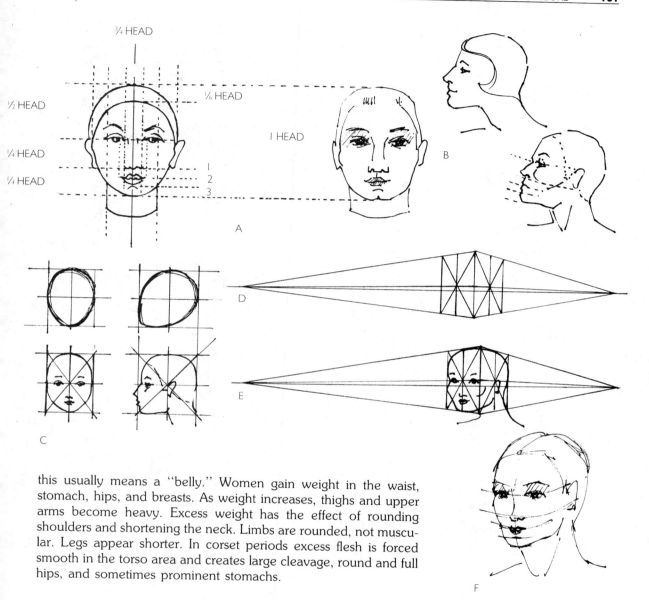

this usually means a "belly." Women gain weight in the waist, stomach, hips, and breasts. As weight increases, thighs and upper arms become heavy. Excess weight has the effect of rounding shoulders and shortening the neck. Limbs are rounded, not muscular. Legs appear shorter. In corset periods excess flesh is forced smooth in the torso area and creates large cleavage, round and full hips, and sometimes prominent stomachs.

Drawing Heads

Figure 6.11 shows the basic proportion of the head in various positions. The eyes are drawn on a line at the one-half point of the head. If the width of the head is divided into five equal parts, the eyes occupy spaces 2 and 4, with the width of an eye between them. The nose is drawn on a line three-quarters of a head from the

FIGURE 6.11 Heads. (a) The ideal proportions of male and female heads. (b) The head in profile (note the position of the ear). (c) The head related to a rectangle (face plane) and a square (side plane). (d) and (e) The head related to a box in perspective. (f) Head in three-quarter view.

FIGURE 6.12   Facial Details.

top and is about the width of the space between the eyes. The last one-quarter of the head is divided into three equal parts. The center of the mouth is drawn on the first line, and the shadow under the bottom lip falls on the second line. The mouth width varies, but it is wider than the nose.

The ears are drawn on the side of the head between the eyes and the nose. Eyes should be drawn with the upper lid covering about one-third of the iris of the eye to avoid a surprised look. The bottom of the iris is just touched by the bottom lid. Do not draw in individual eyelashes.

The female neck lines up with the outside corner of the eye and is a straight-sided cylinder. The hairline is drawn on a line about one-sixth of the head.

The male head is angular and more nearly square with a broader jaw and brow. The male neck is thicker. Other proportions are approximately the same.

The head in profile sits at an angle on the neck which juts out from the shoulders. The vertical divisions of the head are the same as for the full-front view. The nose extends beyond the egg-shape. The jawline curves up to the ear in the center of the egg-shape. The ear fits between the eye line and the bottom of the nose. The eye in profile is half the size of the eye in full face and is drawn closer to the nose than to the ear.

Heads in Perspective

Heads in three-quarter view are the most difficult to draw. It is helpful to visualize the head in a box, with the face and side of the head as the two visible planes. The center line of the face plane and the center line of the side plane can be located in the same way as the center of any rectangle in perspective. (See Figures 6.11c, d, and e.) Remember that the base of the nose is on the centerline, but the nose itself extends beyond the face plane. The ear is drawn from the center line of the side plane toward the back half of the head. The features are widest on the half of each plane nearer the viewer. Less is seen of the features on the half of each plane away from the viewer.

A designer's collection of photos and sketches should include heads in three-quarter view to study and use as models.

Suggesting Age

Some suggestion of wrinkles between the eyebrows and on the forehead, "crows feet" and "laugh lines," dark circles or bags under the eyes, and sagging or double chin will help indicate middle-aged characters. For aged characters, more wrinkles, puffy eyelids, thin lips, drooping mouth, and splotchy skin are characteristic. Prominent bones, hollows in the neck, and an oversized nose are also common characteristics of age. Varying the proportions of different features creates different character faces. (See Figure 6.12.)

Children's faces are more nearly round than those of adults, with larger eyes in proportion to the face. The nose is broader and less defined. Children have small rounded eyebrows, round cheeks, small mouths, and short necks. There is little bone definition. (See Figure 6.13.)

Hair

Since the designer must suggest the hair style of the character, skill in drawing hair is necessary. (See Figure 6.14.) Hair is added beyond the head-sized oval, with the hairline as a guide. For hair styles that cover part of the face, the relationship of the hair to the facial features must be considered. The sketch should suggest the direction in which the hair is combed. Hair should look light and airy, not solid.

FIGURE 6.13   The faces on the costume sketches should reflect the appropriate ages of the characters.

Hands and Feet

Graceful hands add to the beauty of the costume sketch, but details of the hands are less important than correct size. The basic shape of the hand is a truncated diamond about three-quarters of the head length. In costume sketches a suggestion of the hand may be more attractive than an overly detailed hand and fingers. Small hand props or accessories are often indicated in the costume sketch. Understanding the basic shapes and divisions of the hands (Figure 6.15) simplifies drawing them.

Feet are wedge-shaped and must be large enough to appear to support the body. The actual size depends on the position of the feet in the pose. The feet should be positioned to show the style of the shoe and the height of the heel required for the character. If the shoes do not show because of the length of the costume, working drawings or small detail drawings may be included. (See Figure 6.15.)

FIGURE 6.14   Hair should be drawn beyond the head, related to the hairline, and indicating the direction in which the hair is combed.

Once basic proportion is understood, the designer should work for a feeling of movement and style in the figures. A collection of photos and sketches of suitable poses should be assembled to serve the designer as models. Life drawing classes are very valuable for learning about the body structure, but the poses are rarely suitable for costume sketches.

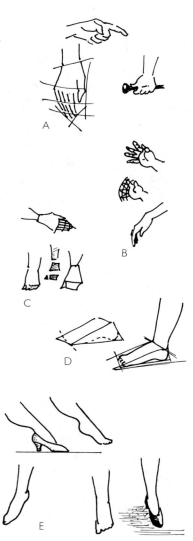

FIGURE 6.15 Hands and Feet. (a) Note the division of the hand at the knuckles. (b) Children's hands are short and round with stubby fingers. (c) Isolate the various shapes in the hand to simplify the drawing. (d) The foot is a wedge shape. (e) The height of the shoe heel affects the shape of the foot and the line of the leg.

Dressing the Figure

Because the body position affects the proportion, hang, and movement of the garment, the designer should not attempt to draw the costume without sketching first the complete figure on which it is worn. To position the garment accurately on the body, the following guidelines should be lightly drawn on the figure: the center of the figure (from the pit of the neck through the navel to the crotch), the base of the neck, the natural waist, the angle of the shoulders and breasts, and the joining of the arm to the torso.

The designer has to analyze the relationship of the period garments to various points of the body. Does the waistline fall at the natural waist? Above or below it? How far from the neck (toward the shoulder) is the neckline? How much chest or bosom shows? What shape does it create? Where on the arm does the sleeve end? Above or below the elbow? At the wrist? How long are pants or skirt? Ankle length? Instep length? Floor length? Does the posture of the period affect the shape of the silhouette? What basic shapes make up the garment? Using the lines blocked out on the figure, the designer draws the garment silhouette and details in correct relationship to specific body points. Figure 6.16 illustrates how the garment relates to the body within it.

If a costume is worn by a corseted figure, the torso is rigid from waist to breast and cannot be twisted or bent except at the exact waist or hip as allowed by the corset. The backbone and rib cage are held together in a solid block so that the whole upper torso must move together as a unit.

Figure 6.17 shows a figure drawn in two-point perspective, showing the position of the center front, side, and center back seams of a large skirt, and how they are established in perspective. The circle that the skirt makes on the floor fits into a square in perspective. The center of the square is formed by the intersection of diagonal lines joining the opposite corners of the square. When this point is connected to each vanishing point, the sides are divided in half. Where these lines touch the outside of the skirt circle, the center front, side seams, and center back can be located. The train is drawn in line with a rectangle extended in perspective, with the center of the train in line with the center back seam.

The designer should study the way garments hang on the body and consider the pull of gravity on different fabrics. Fabric falls from the extended parts of the body or from areas where the fabric has been drawn into the body (points of suspension). Shoulders, breasts, arms, buttocks, waist, and hips can support the fabric. Gravity exerts a downward pull from these points. The density, cut,

FIGURE 6.16 (a) A corseted figure will have a high bosom and the shape of the bosom will change with the shape of the corset. (See also Figure 3.8b.) (b) Establish these important lines on the figure to guide the drawing of the costume. (c–f) The garment must relate to the body within it.

FIGURE 6.17 The Figure in Two-Point Perspective. To draw a garment in three-quarter view correctly, the designer must be able to locate the center front, sides, and center back. These points control costume details and trim placement. Visualizing the skirt in a square or rectangle (a) and placing that shape in perspective (b) will help locate these important points.

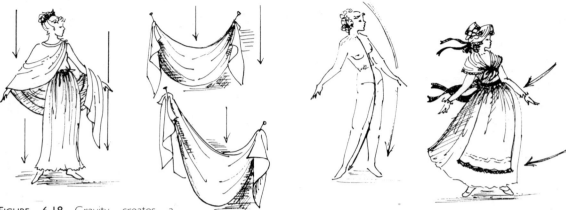

FIGURE 6.18 Gravity creates a downward pull on the fabric from the points of suspension (head, shoulders, elbows, wrists, breasts, waist, hips, and knees). The movement of the body or a slight breeze will alter the hang of the garment temporarily as the flow of air counters the force of gravity.

and hand of the fabric affect its response to the pull of gravity. (See Figure 6.18.)

The gravitational pull on the garment is modified by the movement of the figure. When a figure is standing with its weight evenly distributed on both feet, the pull of gravity causes the garment to hang evenly around the figure. When the weight of the figure is shifted to one leg, the center of the body is no longer perpendicular to the base of the sketch. This shift is expressed in an "action line," an imaginary line that follows the center of the torso from the pit of the neck through the crotch and down the *nonsupporting* leg. The center front line of the garment now relates to the action line of the body. A feeling of motion is also achieved in a sketch if the costume appears to be windblown, and a slight ripple of the fabric toward the back of the figure suggests that the character has been caught in movement.

Drawing Hats

After drawing in the head and hair style, the designer locates the place on the head where the hat actually sits. The crown of the hat usually tilts down in the back, but for some styles it sits flat on the head or forward over the forehead. Enough room should be allowed for the head and hair inside the crown. The brim is added, with its width being judged from the bottom of the crown. Trim is added last. (See Figure 6.19.)

Costume Details

Because the costumer must interpret the sketch, an effort must be made to express details accurately. Figures 6.20 and 6.21 show how to illustrate numerous costume details. Note the differences in shapes produced by gathers, pleats, and flares. Trim that is applied to edges of a garment should be drawn parallel to those edges.

FIGURE 6.19 Proper size of hat.

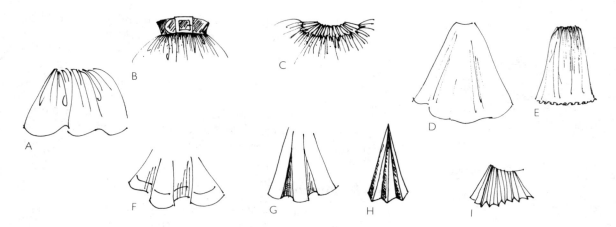

FIGURE 6.20 Costume Details. (a) Gathers in a crisp fabric. (b) Gathered skirt with belt. (c) Cartridge pleats. (d) Flared skirt. (e) Gathered skirt of soft fabric. (f) Circular skirt. (g) Box pleats. (h) Sunburst pleats. (i) Pleated ruffle.

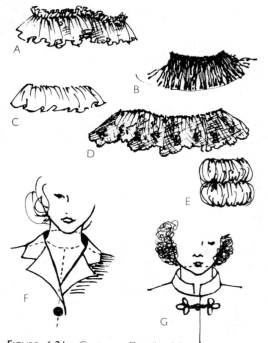

FIGURE 6.21 Costume Details. (a) Gathered ruffle with heading. (b) Fringe. (c) Gathered ruffle set into seam. (d) Gathered lace ruffle. (e) Shirred trim forming puffs. (f) Rolled collar. (g) Mandarin or standing collar.

FIGURE 6.22 Illustrating Patterns. Estimate the number of motifs that would repeat between the neck and the waist of the figure. Maintain that size over the whole garment. Most motifs repeat on fabric in a staggered pattern. Establish a grid on which to space the motifs, with horizontal lines parallel to the hem and vertical lines radiating from the waist.

Aprons and overskirts that are parallel to the underskirt should be drawn to follow its folds and edges. Patterns are illustrated on the basis of a grid as shown in Figure 6.22. The scale of the pattern should usually be the same on the top and bottom of the figure and is determined by how many times the motif could be repeated between neck and waist.

Much about drawing garments can be gleaned from the research of the period in which the costumes are being designed. This information should be carefully noted.

Transfer Methods

Ideally, the designer should be able to copy the costume from the rough sketches directly onto the watercolor paper or board with style and ease, but it may not be possible for the novice designer to do this. Because excessive erasing damages the finish of most paper, designers may wish to trace or transfer the corrected roughs to the paper.

Rubbing the back of the sketch with pencil lead or a graphite stick makes it possible to trace the figure onto the painting surface. If the sketch is on layout or tracing paper, a graphite wash can be used. (After rubbing graphite onto the back of the sketch, the designer paints over it with turpentine. It then has to dry before tracing begins.) A separate graphite tracing sheet can be made by the same method.

Trace the lines and shapes of the figure and garment to get good proportion and correct shape. Take care not to indent the surface of the watercolor paper when tracing, or the wash will puddle in the groove. Redraw details directly on paper, and clean up tracing smudges with art gum or kneaded eraser.

Another method of transfering a sketch is to use a light box or light table. Tape the sketch to the glass of the light box and tape the watercolor paper over it. Redraw the figure, using as a guide the shadow of the sketch produced by the light shining through the paper. If a light box is not available, try taping the rough sketch and paper to a sunny window.

Do not use waxy carbon papers for transferring sketches to be painted in wash techniques, because the carbon resists water. White dressmakers' carbon works on tinted boards if gouache, pastel, or other opaque media will be used. It can be erased with the warmth from an iron (no steam) or hair dryer, but may leave an oily residue. Some designers photocopy or blueprint the pencil drawings and paint the copies with gouache. The paper used for copies is not suitable for wash techniques, but it will accept paints mixed with little water. Many copies can be made for experimenting with various color ideas. The painted copy can be cut out and mounted on colored mat board.

BASIC WATERCOLOR TECHNIQUES FOR THE COSTUME DESIGNER

And never yet did insurrection want
Such water colors to impaint his cause. . . .
HENRY THE IV   William Shakespeare

General Notes

Always mix paints with some water. The beauty of watercolor is strongly related to the transparency of the medium. Always mix more paint in the desired color than seems necessary. (Refer to Chapter 4, Color Theory for Pigments.) A soft matte finish is characteristic of fine watercolor. Work for clean color and flowing line.

Most watercolorists work by painting areas of light color first and adding successive layers of darker color to build up the shadows and darker shapes. They achieve highlights by leaving areas of paper or light wash to show through the darker tones.

To prevent puddling of the paint or visual distortion of the sketch, the drawing board or drawing table should be at about a 30-degree angle. A box, book, or block (1½ to 2 inches high) placed under the board will produce a suitable angle.

Wash

A transparent layer of color on an area of the sketch is a *wash*. Any painting that features large areas of wash must be done on paper or board thick enough not to ripple or swell. Watercolor paper should be taped down to a drawing board first. Washes are done with a mixture of paint and water several shades darker than the desired finished color. Watercolor dries two or three shades lighter than the wet color. The paint must be completely fluid and thoroughly blended with the water. (See Figure 6.23.)

Flat Wash

The area of the wash should be dampened with a brush or sponge dipped in clean water. Water should not pool up on the surface but should leave an even shine over the area to be painted. With a

FIGURE 6.23 Sample Rendering Techniques. (a) Flat wash. (b) Graded wash. (c) Wet-on-wet strokes. (d) Dry brush strokes. (e) Resist techniques: rubber cement, masking liquid, masking tape, and wax. (f) Layered wash, sponge texture, and stippling.

large, fully loaded (but not dripping) brush of paint, strokes are made from left to right (reverse for left-handed persons) across the top of the area. The strokes are repeated down the area, each stroke slightly overlapping. The excess color will collect at the bottom edge of each stroke and be picked up by the next stroke. Excess color at the bottom edge of the last stroke can be picked up with the tip of a clean, barely damp brush. The layer of water on the paper will define the wash area and assist the blending of the strokes. Too much water will cause separation of the pigment, however. Experiment with effects on scrap paper. The layer of water will further dilute the color, so mix a wash tone several shades darker than the desired finished color. (See Figure 6.23a.)

Graded Wash

Starting with an intense mixture of paint, stroke across the sketch. Add water to the brush with each successive stroke, blending the wash evenly to the lightest desired tone. (See Figure 6.23b.)

Wet-on-Wet Technique

Additional paint applied to an already wet, painted surface produces interesting bleeding and fuzzing effects. (See Figure 6.23c.)

Dry Brush

Rough textured effects are produced by using very little water in the paint and removing most of the mixture from the brush. (See Figure 6.23d.)

Resist Techniques

Applying a substance to resist the paint or ink when a wash is applied to the area allows the designer to leave areas with sharp outlines or textures. Masking tape, rubber cement, liquid mask, oil pastels, or paraffin (wax) are common resist devices. (See Figure 6.23e.)

Layered Effects

Numerous layers of watercolor wash, each allowed to dry before the next is painted, achieve a feeling of transparent depth. Layers of paint can be applied with a sponge over wash or stippled with small brush strokes for textures. (See Figure 6.23f.)

PAINTING THE COSTUME SKETCHES

Listed below are the steps to follow in the process of painting the costume sketch.

1. Sketch the costumed figure directly onto a board or paper, or transfer it using one of the methods previously described. Determine the direction of light on the figure.

2. Mask off the areas to remain white, if desired. For smaller shows, work (paint) each step on all the sketches at one time. For large shows, work all the sketches for a scene or an act at one time. If a large group of sketches are painted at once, an overall view is maintained. Sketches progress simultaneously to the same level. This approach avoids overworking one sketch at the expense of others. Sketches that do not work can sometimes be spotted and eliminated before too much time is spent on them.

3. Wash in the backgrounds, if desired. Set them aside to dry. Usually by the time the last one is finished, the first one can be taken to the next step. (See Figure 6.24.) Backgrounds are used to suggest the mood of the play or the color of the set, if it is known. Avoid excess detail in the backgrounds. A suggestion of a shadow cast by a strong light on the figure is effective. Remember the direction of light on the figure. A gradated wash makes an effective background, with the darkest part of the wash being used as the shadow behind the figure. Turn the sketch on its side for left to right gradation. Figures done on tinted papers may not need backgrounds to suggest environment, but since stage costumes are almost never seen against white, a wash to tone down white paper is desirable. Intense background colors tend to detract from costumes; neutral colors enhance costume sketches.

4. Paint the flesh tone areas. A basic paint mix for flesh tones consists of Burnt Sienna or Van Dyke Brown, Yellow Ochre, Chinese White, and a touch of Cadmium Red or Alizarin Crimson. Another flesh tone combination would include Raw Umber, Cobalt Blue, and Cadmium Orange. Varying the amounts of each color produces a variety of skin tones. Keep these flesh tones transparent by limiting the use of white and by adding water. Paint all areas of the skin that will be seen, including parts of the body seen through transparent fabrics. Paint the whole head to prevent a hard hairline. Paint the whole foot and add the

FIGURE 6.24 Steps I Through 3. After transferring or drawing the figure onto watercolor paper or board, mask areas that are to remain white. Wash in backgrounds.

shoes later, unless the skin tone is quite dark. After painting in flesh tones in all the sketches, set them aside to dry.

5. Paint in large areas of costume using the lightest color wash desired. Test the colors on scrap paper before painting the sketch. Leave unpainted paper for the white highlights of fabrics with a hard shine. Leave unpainted paper also for large white details like collars and cuffs. Paint applied to white paper will never be whiter than the paper itself. Leave the paper unpainted for white garments or large white areas of garments and paint in only the shadows using gray, blue-gray, or other pale wash. Strong background tones play up white costumes sketched on white paper. Sketches done on tinted papers or smaller areas of white on colored grounds may be painted in with white gouache.

Mistakes can be blotted up with tissue or a soft, clean cloth. A clean, damp brush can also be used to remove some color. To produce textures, apply heavy color and

FIGURE 6.25 Steps 4 Through 6. Paint in flesh tones and large costume areas using lightest shades of desired colors. When adjacent areas are dry, paint in base tones of all smaller areas and basic shadows.

blot up some of the paint with paper towels or terry cloth. Some color can be scrubbed out of a dry area with a damp brush or cotton-tipped swab. These techniques can be used for corrections or special effects.

6. After the sketches have dried, paint in the smaller areas: hair, shading, features, and accessories. For shading use darker washes of the same color, use lower intensities of the same color (add complement), or use overlay with wash of contrasting color. Shading can also be done with Paynes Gray, Sepia, or Van Dyke Brown. Experiment with unusual colors in the shadows, perhaps indicating the colors of stage lighting reflected off the costume. (See Figure 6.25.)

7. Add details with opaque paint, pencil, pen and ink, or brush and paint. (See Figure 6.26.)

8. Label each sketch with the name of the character, title of the play, act, and scene number. Sign the sketch. Number each sketch consecutively according to the order in which

FIGURE 6.26 Steps 7 and 8. Add details in paint, pen and ink, or pencil. The sketch is then ready for labeling and attaching swatches.

they are seen on stage. Add any details or notes to the costumer. If the sketch is done on lightweight paper, mount it on mat board or other sturdy cardboard. Attach swatches, if they are available. Cover the sketch with acetate to protect it from damage by handling in the conferences and costume shop.

WORKING DRAWINGS

Additional drawings of construction and trim details may be done in pencil or pen and ink on a separate board or on layout paper taped to the sketch. These drawings may be needed to clarify the design for the patternmaker or shopper. Painted or stenciled motifs may require actual size or sample drawings in one-half-inch scale for the painter. Photocopies of pertinent research should accompany the sketches given to the costume shop. Any work the designer must give to someone else to do must be clear and well documented.

OTHER TECHNIQUES

Gouache

Other media can be used for costume sketches, either alone or with watercolor as the base painting. Gouache is a common choice. Because it is opaque, gouache is very useful for adding details over layers of wash, particularly light details over dark colors. Gouache is also good for suggesting heavier fabrics. The colors are slightly duller than watercolor and much less intense than ink colors. Gouache can also be used to paint sketches on colored boards and papers where the transparency of watercolor would allow the paper color to show through and distort the color of the wash. Figure 6.27 is a sketch for *The Ballad of Baby Doe* done with gouache and white pencil on gray board.

FIGURE 6.27 *The Ballad of Baby Doe.* In this sketch by Eldon Elder the gray board is left unpainted for the shadows and flesh tones. Designed for Santa Fe Opera — Tour: Berlin Opera Festival and Belgrade, Yugoslavia, 1961–62.

Acrylic Paints

Acrylic paints can be used as wash or as opaque color. Textures can be built up with acrylics without losing the life of the color. Because acrylics are a form of plastic, some designers find the sheen of the paint harsh. Color plate 11 is a design for *Mother Courage* painted with acrylics on beige board.

Inks and Dyes

Many designers use colored inks or bottled dyes. These can be handled in the same ways as watercolor but require careful mixing and pretesting. Most of the inks and dyes stain the paper immediately. Some correction can be made with bleach, but it must be neutralized with vinegar, and some yellowing of the paper results. Bleach should be applied with an otherwise useless brush or a cotton swab. *Never* use a good sable brush for bleach, since it destroys natural fibers.

Inks provide an intensity of color not available in any other media. Details in ink can brighten delicate watercolor renderings. Permanent inks can be used to ouline figures and costumes before the watercolor is painted in. These lines must be completely dry or else bleeding will occur in the painting process.

Felt-Tip Pens

An extensive range of colors is available to the designer in felt-tip and fiber-tip pens. These colors are also intense and especially good for adding details. Felt-tip pens are good for expressing modern looks and for quick sketches, but subtle effects are hard to achieve and the blending of colors is difficult.

Pastels

Pastels and pastel pencils are used by some designers. They are particularly suitable for ballet tutus or other airy, frothy-looking costumes, but they can also be blended for other effects. Pastels should be used on softer finish papers that absorb the chalk. Paper stumps of various sizes are used to blend the color. For small details rub the pastel onto a sandpaper block, pick up the color on the tip of the stump, and apply the color to the sketch with the stump. Pastels must be sprayed with fixative. In Figure 6.28 gray board forms the background for the pastel sketch from *Twelfth Night*.

FIGURE 6.28 *Twelfth Night.* Sketch for Feste, by the author. Designed for Brooklyn College.

Mixed Media

Designers often experiment with combining media to produce different effects. A collage of various papers used with compatible paints or ink can be very interesting. When combining different

Betty "Star" Prototype

FIGURE **6.29** *Kicks*. William Ivey Long incorporates collage materials in this costume sketch.

color media, keep in mind the type of paper each needs for best results. Figures 6.29 and 6.30 are examples of sketches using a variety of media to produce a desired effect. Figure 6.29 incorporates stars, sequins, and glitter to suggest the dazzle of this costume for Betty in a new Broadway musical called *Kicks*. In Figure 6.30 torn drawing paper in various colors forms the background for a presentation plate for *Waiting for Godot*. Done mostly in pencil, the sketch also incorporates the fabric swatches as an element of the overall composition.

The designer should collect and study examples of various painting and illustration techniques and should adapt them to ex-

FIGURE 6.30   *Waiting for Godot.* Collage materials are used in this presentation sketch by Patricia McGourty, designed for Lehman College.

press the different moods or concepts of plays being designed. In Figure 6.31 the design for Katisha in *The Mikado* is rendered in watercolor, ink, and gouache, effectively suggesting the style of Japanese painting.

PRESENTATION

The completed sketches should again be discussed with the director for final approval. Good sketch presentation helps the designer "sell" the costume to the director. In Color plate 12, a sketch for *Measure for Measure*, the dramatic use of line and watercolor wash, the placement of the figure, and the artful addition of fabric swatches combine to create strong visual impact.

Sketches are important for effective collaboration, whether the show will be built, pulled, or rented. Even with a specialized vocabulary, words are woefully inadequate for describing costumes. Sketches and examples of research make discussions more precise. A clear understanding of the designer's intentions will limit expensive changes later. Careful notes should be made on changes or additions requested by the director.

This is also a good time to discuss and draw up a list of re-

FIGURE 6.31 *The Mikado.* Patton Campbell effectively adapted the style of Japanese painting for this sketch, for The New York City Opera Company.

hearsal costumes with projected dates for introducing them into the rehearsal process. (See Chapter 8.)

Depending on the schedule and type of producing organization, a designer may be asked to present the finished sketches at the first cast meeting or at the first rehearsal. The actors will be anxious to know how they are to look and the types of garments with which they must work. Presentation of completed sketches may be done either by character, in order of appearance, or by scene. A designer should be prepared to explain the concept behind the designs, the effects desired by the director and designer, and special skills required to use the costume effectively. Actors may request rehearsal costumes and assistance with special items.

Several sets of photocopies of the approved sketches can be useful (1) for the actors so they can visualize themselves in the actual costume, (2) for the director and stage manager, so they can answer costume questions that arise during rehearsals, and (3) for the costume shop, in order to reduce handling of the original sketches and allow several people to work on the same costume at once. If the approved costumes differ from the costume plot (see p. 40) it should be revised to reflect the changes. Copies should be made for the director or stage manager and the costume shop. As the work progresses, occasional updates may be needed.

With the sketches complete and approved, the work of assembling the necessary staff, materials, patterns, trims, and accessories can begin in earnest.

Chapter 7
Choosing Fabrics

Another piece of real slop-work. What a selvage! Here it's broad, there it's narrow; here it's drawn in by the wefts goodness knows how tight, and there it's torn out again by the temples. And hardly seventy threads weft to the inch. What's come of the rest? Do you call this honest work? I never saw anything like it.

THE WEAVERS   Gerhart Hauptmann

FABRIC BASICS

Because fabric is the medium through which a designer develops the costume, more than just a casual knowledge of its properties is necessary. The characteristics of fiber, yarn, construction (weave), and finish all contribute qualities to a fabric which produce different effects of texture and movement.

Fiber

A minute, hairlike tissue having a length of at least 100 times its diameter or width is called a *fiber*. Fibers are the basic components of textile fabrics. *Staple fibers* are short lengths measured in inches or fractions of an inch. *Filaments* are long continuous fibers, measured in yards or meters. Fibers fall into two basic categories: *natural fibers* and *synthetic fibers*. Natural fibers are derived from animal and plant sources. All natural fibers, except silk, are staple fibers; silk and synthetic fibers are filaments but can be cut to staple lengths. Each fiber has its own characteristics and care requirements. See Box 7.A.

The shape, length, chemical composition, and performance characteristics of fibers contribute greatly to the final characteristics of the fabrics in which they are used. Natural fibers are irregular and subtle, absorbent and porous. Short staple fibers give rougher, fuzzier, duller qualities to the texture of a fabric, whereas long filament fibers produce fabrics that are shinier, smoother, and cooler feeling. Staple fibers, because they are short, tend to make softer, less smooth yarns which reflect light off more minute surfaces, diffusing that reflection. Synthetics are highly resilient (thus wrinkle resistant) and generally low in porosity and absorbency. Filaments, being long and smooth, tend to make harder surfaced yarns which reflect more light in sharper highlights. The way a fiber reflects light is a factor in our perception of texture in the finished fabric, therefore in the costume. (See Box 4.D Material Responses to Light.)

Fiber *blends* are fabrics combining two or more different fibers. The fiber present in the highest percentage will usually dominate the fabric, but all fibers contribute to the final character of the fabric.

Box 7.A   Natural and Synthetic Fibers

Natural Fibers

FIBER AND SOURCE	CHARACTERISTICS	TYPICAL FABRICS	CARE
Cotton — From seed pod of cotton plant	Strong, absorbent, tends to wrinkle, dyes well, shrinks if not treated	Corduroy, denim, poplin, velveteen, muslin	Most may be washed: colorfast in hot water, warm or cold for others; dryer safe, iron while damp, chlorine bleach safe for white fabrics
Linen — From flax plant	Strong, absorbent, dyeing difficult, wrinkles unless treated, shrinks	Variety of fabrics with coarse texture and natural luster, very delicate to heavy weights	Dry clean to preserve crispness, wash if softness desired, iron while damp
Silk — From cocoons of silkworms	Strong, absorbent, retains body heat, wrinkle resistant, dye may bleed, weakened by sunlight and perspiration	Brocade, chiffon, satin, crepe, jersey, charmeuse	Usually dry cleaned, may be hand washed, no bleach, iron at low temperature

FIBER AND SOURCE	CHARACTERISTICS	TYPICAL FABRICS	CARE

Wool
    From fleece
    of sheep
	Less strong, highly absorbent, holds in body heat, wrinkles fall out, dyes well, needs mothproofing	Crepe, knits, flannel, tweed, gabardine, jersey	Usually dry cleaned, some knits hand washable, do not use chlorine bleach, some wools machine washable — follow instructions of manufacturer

Synthetic Fibers and Sources

FIBER AND TRADEMARKS	CHARACTERISTICS	TYPICAL FABRICS AND USES	CARE

Acetate
    Acele,
    Avicolor,
    Avisco,
    Celanese,
    Celaperm,
    Celara,
    Chromspun,
    Estron
	Relatively weak, moderately absorbent, holds in body heat, tends to wrinkle, dyes well but is subject to atmospheric fading, resists stretching, accumulates static electricity, luxurious and silklike, excellent draping qualities	Brocade, crepe, faille, satin, taffeta, jersey, tricot, lace	Usually dry cleaned, hand washable or gentle cycle, low heat drying cycle, iron at low temperature

Acrylic
    Acrilan,
    Creslan,
    Orlon,
    Zefkrome,
    Zefran
	Strong, low absorbency, resists wrinkles, holds in body heat, accepts dye, accumulates static electricity, often blended with other fibers, heat sensitive, tends to pill	Fake fur, fleece, double knit, knits	Dry clean if recommended, can be machine washed and tumble dried, use fabric softeners for less static electricity, little or no ironing required

Glass
    Beta,
    Fiberglas
	Strong, nonabsorbent, resists wrinkles, resists dyeing	Drapery fabrics from sheer to heavy
		[Should NOT be used for clothing — may irritate skin]
			Hand wash, ironing not usually needed

Metallic	Weak, nonabsorbent, heat sensitive, may tarnish if uncoated	Glitter fabrics, lamé, eyelash cloth	Dry clean or hand launder in warm water, iron at low temperature

Modacrylic
    Dynel,
    Verel
	Low absorbency, holds in body heat, resists wrinkles, very heat sensitive, dries quickly, nonallergenic, flame resistant, resists mildew and moths	Fake fur
		Wigs
			Dry clean
			Hand wash, do not iron fabrics or use curling irons on wigs

FIBER AND SOURCE	CHARACTERISTICS	TYPICAL FABRICS	CARE

Nylon
  Antron,
    Blue C,
    Caprolan,
    Cedilla,
    Celanese,
    Enkalure,
    Qiana,
    Touch
	Strong, low absorbency, holds in body heat, tends to pill; resists wrinkling, moths, mildew, and dirt	Satin, jersey, fake fur, chiffon	Hand wash, gentle machine wash, use fabric softener to reduce static electricity, tumble or drip-dry, iron at low temperature

Olefin
  Durel,
    Herculon,
    Marvess
	Nonabsorbent, holds in body heat, difficult to dye, heat sensitive, nonallergenic	Upholstery, insulating fillers for outer garments	Machine wash in lukewarm water, use fabric softener in final rinse, tumble dry at low setting, iron at lowest temperature

Polyester
  Avlin,
    Dacron,
    Encron,
    Fortrel,
    Kodel,
    Quintess,
    Trevira,
    Vycron
	Strong, low absorbency, holds in body heat, resists wrinkling, accumulates static electricity, retains heat-set pleats and creases, difficult to dye in piece	Crepe, knits, linings, blends	Wash by hand or machine using warm water, tumble or drip-dry, use fabric softener to reduce static electricity, needs little or no ironing, low iron setting for touch-ups

Rayon
  Avril,
    Beaunit,
    Coloray,
    Englo,
    Fibro,
    Zantrel
	Relatively weak, absorbent, holds in body heat, dyes well; wrinkles, shrinks, or stretches unless treated, dye unstable	Butcher linen, crepe, matte jersey	May require dry cleaning, may be washed by hand in warm water, chlorine bleach may be used on white, iron at moderate temperature

Spandex Lycra	Strong, nonabsorbent, great elasticity, lightweight	Knits, blends	Hand wash or gentle cycle, avoid chlorine bleach, drip or tumble dry, iron at low temperature
Triacetate Arnel	Relatively weak, resists wrinkling and shrinking, dyes well, retains heat-set pleats	Sharkskin, tricot	Hand or machine wash in warm water, drip-dry pleated garments, tumble dry, iron at moderate temperature

Yarn

Most fabrics are made of yarns. *Spun yarn* is made by twisting together staple fibers into a continuous piece of the desired length and thickness. *Filament yarn* is the fiber unwound from the cocoon (silk) or extruded from a chemical solution (synthetics). *Ply yarn* is made by twisting two or more single yarns together. The characteristics of the yarn determine many of the characteristics of the fabric in which it is used. In particular the surface texture and the hand (feel) of the fabric are related to the characteristics of the yarn. Yarns with tighter twist are used in smoother, sturdier fabrics; yarns with looser twist are used for rougher, fuzzier fabrics. Some yarns (bouclé, slub) are irregular and create interesting surface textures when woven.

Construction of Fabrics

Fabrics can be made by weaving, braiding, knotting, knitting, crocheting, or felting.

Woven Fabrics

The most common method of making fabrics is *weaving*. Weaving is generally the sturdiest and the most stable type of fabric construction. Lengthwise (warp) yarns are stretched onto a loom in such a way that they can be alternately raised and lowered by movable frames (harnesses). Crosswise (filling or weft) yarns are then inserted at right angles to the lengthwise yarns by the use of shuttles. Weave structures can be varied by the rearrangement of the pattern in which lengthwise and crosswise yarns intersect.

The basic weaves are *plain weave, twill weave,* and *satin weave.* Most other weaves are variations of these three. Figure 7.1A and 7.1B show these basic weaves and some of their variations.

FIGURE 7.1A Samples of the Three Basic Weaves. (a) A plain weave linen fabric. The diagram shows the plain weave structure. (b) A wool twill. The diagram shows the twill weave structure. (c) A silk charmeuse. The diagram shows the long floats of the satin weave.

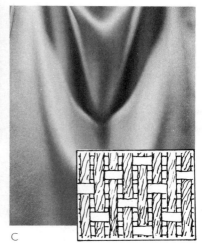

A   B   C

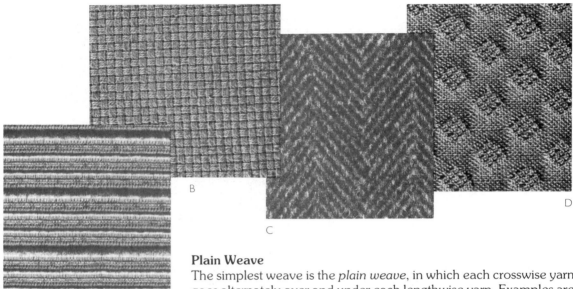

A

B

C

D

Plain Weave

The simplest weave is the *plain weave*, in which each crosswise yarn goes alternately over and under each lengthwise yarn. Examples are muslin, voile, challis, percale, buckrum, crinoline, chintz, chiffon, crepe, georgette, organdy, and shantung.

Twill Weave

The *twill weave* is a basic weave in which crosswise yarns pass over at least two, but not more than four, lengthwise yarns; on each successive line, the crosswise weave moves one step to the right or left, forming a diagonal ridge. Twill weaves are generally sturdier, heavier, closer in texture, and more durable than plain weaves. Examples are cavalry twill, denim, foulard, gabardine, serge, sharkskin, surah, and whipcord.

Satin Weave

The *satin weave* is a basic weave in which a lengthwise yarn passes over four to eight crosswise yarns in staggered pattern similar to the twill weave but spaced so as not to show ridges. The yarns exposed on the surface, called *floats*, contribute substantially to the characteristic sheen of satins. The most reflective types of satin are made of filament yarns. Examples of satin weave are antique satin, crepe-back satin, charmeuse, and slipper satin. The *sateen weave* is a variation in which the floats are formed by the crosswise yarns. Sateen is usually made of cotton.

Variations of Basic Weaves

The interlocking of yarns in various weaves combined with the variety of fibers and types of yarn produce a wide variety of fabrics.

In the *rib weave*, a variation of the plain weave, a rib is pro-

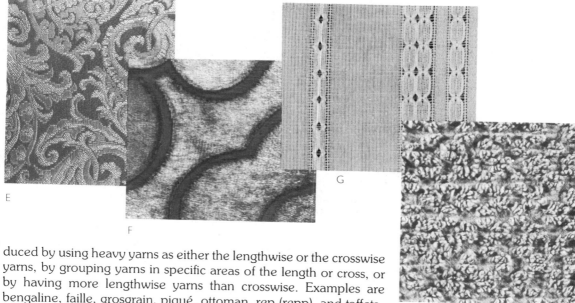

duced by using heavy yarns as either the lengthwise or the crosswise yarns, by grouping yarns in specific areas of the length or cross, or by having more lengthwise yarns than crosswise. Examples are bengaline, faille, grosgrain, piqué, ottoman, rep (repp), and taffeta.

The *basket weave* is a variation of the plain weave in which two or more yarns are used in the alternating pattern. The yarns are not twisted together, but laid side by side in the weave. If the fabric is made of a relatively low number of yarns to an inch, it will tend to stretch, shrink, and fray. Examples are hopsacking, monk's cloth, and oxford shirting.

In a *herringbone weave*, a variation of the twill weave, the ridges reverse directions, forming a zigzag pattern. This pattern is often emphasized by the use of different colored yarns in the cross and length.

Numerous small-patterned weaves are produced by attaching to the plain weave loom a "dobby," which raises and lowers certain sets of lengthwise yarns. The resulting *dobby weave* fabric has small all-over floral or geometric patterns. An example is bird's eye piqué.

When a Jacquard attachment is added to the loom, cross and lengthwise yarns can be controlled individually to create elaborate woven patterns called *jacquards*. Examples are brocade, damask, and tapestry.

In *pile weave* fabrics, extra crosswise or lengthwise yarns are added to a plain or twill weave and are drawn into loops on the surface by thick wires. The loops can be cut, sheared, or left in loops. Examples are corduroy, fake fur, plush, terry cloth, velour, and velveteen.

Velvets are woven on double shuttle looms which weave two layers of fabric at once with the pile yarns stretched between the two

FIGURE 7.1B Variations of the Three Basic Weaves. The illustrated fabrics are a few of the variations on the basic fabric weaves. (a) Ottoman—example of the rib weave. (b) Monk's cloth—example of the basket weave. (c) Herringbone. (d) Bird's eye piqué—an example of a dobby weave. (e) Brocade—an example of a jacquard weave. (f) Cut Panne Velvet—an example of a pile weave. (g) Leno—a decorative leno weave combined with areas of plain weave. (h) Chenille—an example of a swivel weave.

layers. The layers are cut apart through the pile yarns with a blade, leaving half the pile yarn attached to each layer of cloth.

A leno attachment to the loom continually changes the position of the lengthwise yarns to twist them in a figure eight around the crosswise yarns. The *leno weave* is used to produce an open mesh structure. This weave may be combined with other weaves to create patterns. Examples are gauze and marquisette.

In *swivel weave* fabrics, extra crosswise yarns are added to the fabric to form small figures like dots on the surface of a basic weave fabric. Each swivel yarn is carried on the wrong side of the fabric from one design to the next but is usually cut after the fabric is woven. Examples are dotted swiss, coin-dot chenille, and eyelash cloth.

Knitted Fabrics

Knitted fabrics are made by creating a series of interlocking loops with continuous yarns. Knitted fabrics come in a wide range of texture from fine and sheer (tricot), to heavy, bulky, novelty knits. All have some stretch. Some knits stretch in one direction, others in both directions. Generally, knits are not as durable as woven fabrics, but their soft, clinging properties and their interesting textures more than compensate for their weaknesses. Figure 7.2 illustrates knit construction.

The plain *jersey knit* is a single construction in which all loops are pulled to the back of the fabric, leaving the right side smooth. Plain knits stretch more in the width than in the length.

The *purl knit* is a single construction in which loops are pulled in alternating rows to the right and wrong side of the fabric. Purl knits have nearly the same stretch in both lengthwise and crosswise directions.

A *rib knit* is a single construction which arranges rows of purl and plain knit to form ribs on both sides of the fabric. Rib knits have exceptional stretch in the crosswise direction, making them useful for cuffs and waistbands.

Combinations of plain and purl knits can produce complicated patterns in the knitting process.

Double knits are produced with two yarn-and-needle sets working simultaneously. The resulting fabric has two layers of knit fabric which are connected. Double knits have limited stretch and substantial body.

Other Types of Fabric Construction

Braiding, knotting (netting), and *crocheting* all produce decorative fabrics or trim with interesting textures. The strength of these fabrics and trims varies but, in general, is a great deal less than that of

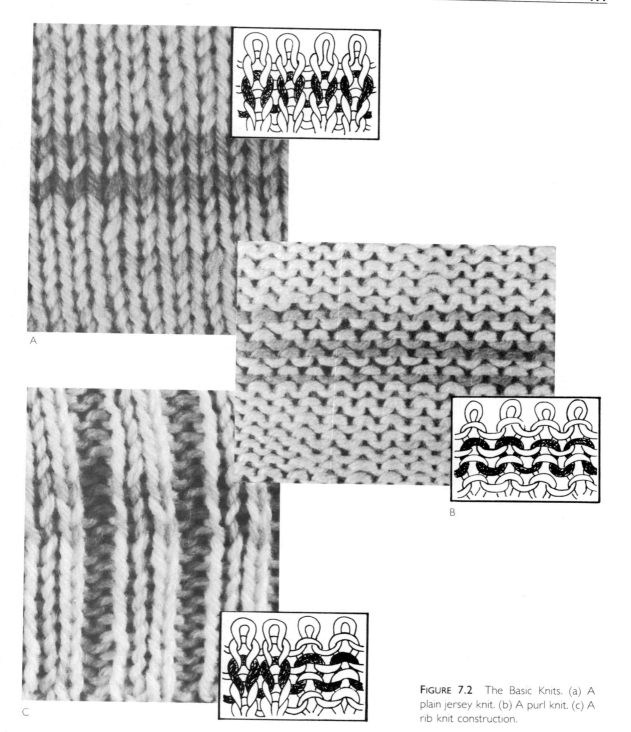

A

B

C

FIGURE 7.2   The Basic Knits. (a) A plain jersey knit. (b) A purl knit. (c) A rib knit construction.

woven fabrics. Figure 7.3 illustrates a few of the possibilities of novelty fabrics and trims.

Lace construction is varied and complex. Most laces have a netted ground with a pattern of other openwork construction. Laces come in all widths, many with borders or edgings.

Felting produces a fabric (felt) which has bulk but not great strength. Moisture, compression, and heat are applied to short fibers, causing them to adhere to one another. The "no-raveling" properties and the soft, light absorbent surface of felt make it a popular appliqué fabric for costume use.

Similar to felting, *fusing* or *bonding* uses an adhesive or bonding agent to cause fibers to adhere to one another. Fabrics made by this process are often used for interfacings.

Finishes

Processes applied to the woven fabric are known as fabric finishes. Most of the finishes are decorative: dyeing, bleaching, glazing, flocking, embossing, moiréing, and printing are examples. Some finishes are functional, such as permanent press finish, mildew resistance, waterproofing, and flameproofing. The type of finish applied to a garment may alter its structural or visual texture.

FABRIC CONSIDERATIONS

> . . . it is useless for a producer to spend hundreds and thousands of francs in purchasing authentic costumes and real jewels, when a great designer will procure a far more sumptuous impression by focussing a ray of light on a doublet of coarse cloth studded with lumps of glass. . . .
>
> REMEMBRANCE OF THINGS PAST   Marcel Proust

Many designers begin to swatch fabrics during the "rough" or "thumbnail" stage. If decisions are made before the sketches are painted, the fabrics can be suggested in the final rendering. If sketches are painted first, the designer or shopper should analyze the hang and look of the fabric suggested by the sketch and choose a suitable fabric for expressing it. Choice of costume fabric is determined by (1) the visual effects desired, (2) appropriate period fabric choices, (3) stress requirements, (4) planned fabric treatments, and (5) budget limitations.

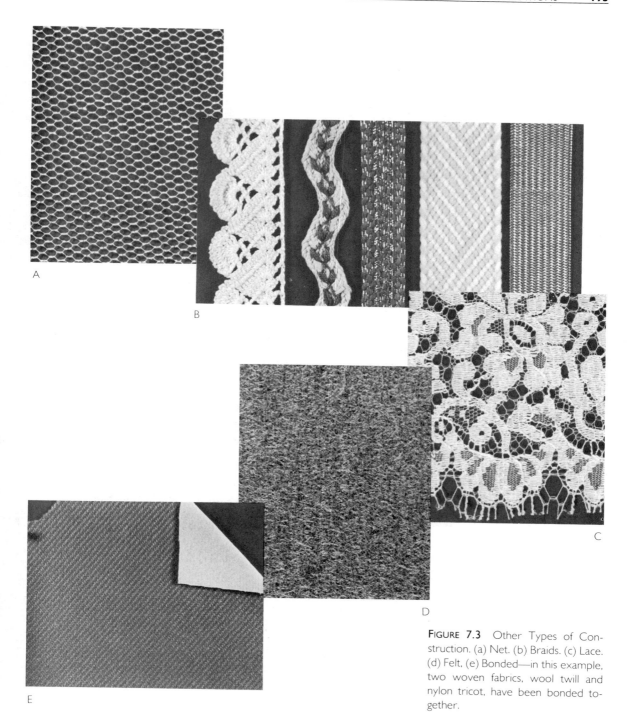

A

B

C

D

E

FIGURE 7.3 Other Types of Construction. (a) Net. (b) Braids. (c) Lace. (d) Felt, (e) Bonded—in this example, two woven fabrics, wool twill and nylon tricot, have been bonded together.

Visual Effects

The designer's first consideration is finding fabrics that will produce the desired visual effects of the costume. Most designers start looking for fabrics in suitable colors, but the way a fabric hangs and moves is often more important than the color, which can usually be modified. The designer may choose a fabric with an airy, floating quality to express the character's personality, even if that fabric is not historically accurate. A heavy fabric might be chosen to express a deep, moody character. If the decorative motif and texture are appropriate but the fabric is too soft to hold the desired line, an appropriate lining may be used to give the correct hang. If the fabric is too stiff, sometimes it can be softened by washing and adding fabric softeners. (Test the process on a small piece of fabric before treating all the fabric.) Cutting the garment on the bias softens the way it hangs, but bias cutting may not be appropriate for the period. In costume designs like the one in Figure 7.4, suitable fabric choices are essential to effective interpretation. Much detail may be lost between the stage and the audience, but the flow and weight of a garment are visible over long distances.

The choice of a suitable fabric texture to express the character may be the next consideration. Even textures that are not clearly seen can add depth and richness to the overall feeling of the costume. The layering of sheer fabric over a base fabric gives variety in texture and a depth of color which is more interesting than a single layer of fabric. Fabrics with the appropriate patterns and qualities of light reflection must be sought for each character. (See Chapter 4, Color and Texture, for other considerations.)

Matching the colors of the sketch with suitable fabrics takes time and patience. Some flexibility may be necessary on the designer's part, but remember that color changes made for one character will surely affect the colors chosen for other characters. Dyeing or dipping to the desired tone may be required.

Choosing the appropriate scale of a desired pattern may be the most difficult problem for the novice designer to solve. The larger the house (theater), the larger the print or pattern must be in order to read, but very large-scale motifs begin to take on a comic or operatic feeling which may not be desirable. Finding a group of prints or brocades in related colors and compatible designs can be very time-consuming, but the effect can be rich and interesting. In Color plate 13, a sketch for *Vagabond Stars*, the combination of the printed fabrics produces a costume of rich visual texture. Sometimes overdyeing or painting can bring a print into the color range needed.

FIGURE 7.4 *Choephoroe.* Effective interpretation of Judith Dolan's costume sketch for Clytemnestra requires silks or extremely soft cottons and linens to create the drapery indicated without excess bulk. Designed for Standford University.

Period Fabrics

The research done for a play should include information on the types of fabrics used within the period or culture. Reproducing in the costumes the same silhouette or feeling as that of the original garments may well depend on choosing the appropriate fabrics. Many older fabrics are no longer made or may now be called by different names. The study of antique garments familiarizes the designer with older fabrics and makes possible effective substitutes.

The more realistic the play, the more necessary the use of historically appropriate fabrics. If a play is stylized, more liberties in the choice of fabric are possible. In a stylized production the designer may decide to select fabrics to carry out a concept rather than reproducing a period look. The smaller the theater, the more obvious the fabric effects are to the audience.

One of the things that dates a costume design is the choice of fabrics. For example, in the 1920's designers used the currently fashionable fabrics to build costumes representing other periods.

A

These costumes have the limpid look of the fashionable 1920's clothes. In Figure 7.5a the lady's gown for *The Three Musketeers* (1920's production) was made of soft panne velvet such as might have been used in a fashionable dress of the 1920's (Figure 7.5b) instead of the heavier, stiffer, crisper fabric typical of the seventeenth

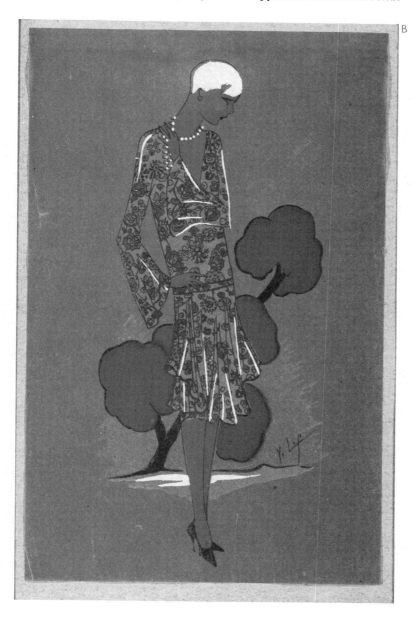

FIGURE 7.5 (a) *The Three Musketeers*, 1920's Production. Billy Rose Theatre Collection, New York Public Library at Lincoln Center; Astor, Lenox and Tilden Foundations. (b) The soft fabric hang preferred in the 1920's is illustrated in this fashion plate. *Tres Parisian*, 1926.

century. The costume designer may however, choose to use fabrics different from those associated with a given period for special effects or when designing "fancy dress" in a production. For example, costumes designed for the Act III masquerade ball in *The Boyfriend* offer the designer an opportunity to create 1920's versions of period or fancy dress.

The use of modern fabrics also dates a contemporary production. The more authentic a designer desires to be, the more carefully the fabrics must be selected. However, in theater, authenticity is not the only consideration. A new interpretation of a period play may require the use of modern materials and effects. A modern fabric may offer desirable characteristics which solve specific problems. For example, few occasions call for authentic cotton muslin petticoats, and their care is a great burden to the wardrobe crew. A permanent press cotton and polyester fabric would be a welcome alternative.

The designer must deal with the difficulties presented by modern synthetic fibers. Until the twentieth century all fabrics were made of natural fibers, which have a mellowness and a light-absorptive quality different from most synthetic fibers. Synthetic fibers often reflect light in a harsh and vibrating manner. Many designers prefer to use only natural fibers on stage because of their subtler qualities of light reflection. Unfortunately, few costume budgets today allow for 100 percent natural fiber fabrics. Blends of synthetic fibers with cotton, wool, or silk are more economical substitutes. Thus some proportion of natural fibers lessens the objectionable traits of the synthetic fibers while retaining the good properties of the natural ones. Unless a deliberate modernization is desired, the designer should attempt to choose synthetics or blends with the same hang and reflective qualities as the fabrics from the play's historical period.

Stress Requirements

If costumes are being built for long-running shows, for traveling productions, or for rental or reusable stock, the choice of a durable fabric is important. If built properly of suitable fabrics, costumes should not need frequent replacement. Costumes to be used for fight scenes, dance sequences, acrobatics, or other vigorous action should be planned to be of durable fabrics and linings. Stretch fabrics resembling suitable period fabrics may be needed to solve serious stress problems.

Other forms of stress to which costumes are subjected may include rough flooring, stage blood, food, makeup, heavy perspiration, frequent cleaning, and quick changes. Fabrics must be chosen that will hold up under these stresses for the run of the show or at least for a reasonable length of time. Some delicate fabrics become satisfactory if suitably lined or backed. Taffeta, washed muslin, cotton twill, or poly/cotton broadcloth are reasonable linings, but others are also used depending on budget, surface fabric, desired effect, and availability. Linings must be laundry compatible with outer fabrics.

Fabric Treatments

Sometimes a choice must be made between buying the wrong fabric in the right color and dyeing an appropriate fabric. Time and budget permitting, dyeing should be the choice.

The fiber content is important when paint, dye, or other such processes are being planned. Household or union dyes work best on natural or cellulosic fibers. Most modern fabrics designed for ready-to-wear or home sewing are made of all or part synthetic fibers; some of these fibers are difficult to dye and may require special types of dyes. If painting or dyeing will be necessary, fabric should be selected very carefully. If the fabric is not labeled, a burn test may help the designer determine the fiber content. Box 7.B describes the result of burn tests on common fibers. Tests can be made on swatches of fabrics under consideration. Burn tests *cannot* be done in the store, however. It may be necessary to buy a yard of fabric for testing before purchasing large quantities to be treated.

Budget

The amount of money allotted to each costume is a major factor in making fabric choices. Designers must usually be reasonable about the price of the large yardages required but may splurge where smaller quantities are needed. A larger share of the fabric budget should be allotted to more important or higher ranking characters. More discussion on budget is found in Chapter 8.

SOURCES AND SWATCHING

The process of swatching for a show can be very time-consuming and tiring. The designer, assistant designer, or shopper may be sent to seek out suitable possibilities. Whoever shops, careful preparation and organization are necessary. Lists of fabrics required (organized by type), approximate yardages, and price range should be prepared before the shopping trip. Photocopies of the sketches are also helpful. Without this information, the shopper may waste

Box 7.B   Fiber Reaction to Burn Tests

FIBERS	APPROACHING FLAME	IN FLAME	AFTER REMOVAL	ODOR	APPEARANCE OF ASH
Natural Fibers					
Cotton	Does not fuse or shrink away from flame	Burns quickly without melting	Continues to burn without melting afterglow	Burning paper	Small, fluffy gray ash
Linen	Does not fuse or shrink away from flame	Burns quickly without melting	Continues to burn without melting afterglow	Burning paper	Small, fluffy gray ash
Natural Silk	Fuses and curls away from flame	Burns slowly with some melting	Burns very slowly; sometimes self-extinguishing	Burning feathers	Round black bead, brittle, pulverizes easily
Wool	Fuses and curls away from flame	Burns slowly with some melting	Burns very slowly; sometimes self-extinguishing	Burning hair	Lumpy, blistered ash, brittle, breaks easily
Synthetic Fibers (Cellulose)					
Acetate	Fuses away from flame	Burns with melting	Continues to burn with melting	Acetic acid or vinegar	Leaves brittle, black, irregular-shaped bead
Rayon	Does not shrink away from flame	Burns very rapidly	Leaves a creeping ember	Burning wood	Small or no ash
Synthetic Fibers (Chemical)					
Acrylic	Fuses away from flame	Burns rapidly with melting	Continues to burn with melting; material shreds	Acrid	Leaves brittle, hard, black, irregular-shaped bead
Nylon	Fuses and shrinks away from flame	Burns slowly with melting	Usually self-extinguishing	Boiling string beans	Leaves hard, gray, tough, round bead
Polyester	Fuses and shrinks away from flame	Burns slowly with melting	Usually self-extinguishing	Chemical	Leaves hard, black, tough, round bead
Spandex	Fuses but does not shrink away from flame	Burns with melting	Continues to burn with melting	Chemical	Leaves soft, fluffy, black ash

time looking at fabrics that are too expensive or at pieces with insufficient yardage.

General fabric categories for groups of characters should be determined. These categories should evolve from the design concept. For example, the women's dresses in a scene might all be planned in taffetas. The similarity of fabric would provide unity as well as simplify the shopping and fabric decisions.

The costume designer must take the time to cultivate local fabric sources. Most fabric stores are not in the habit of giving swatches of fabric. Ask to speak to the manager and explain the necessity for swatching the show. Be prepared to show some proof of the project (sketches). Being on friendly terms with the store owners and personnel can sometimes get the designer big bargains, help in locating difficult items, special orders, and even donations. Buying large amounts at one time in a store can sometimes earn large discounts. Negotiate for the best price.

Swatches should be cut along the cross grain of the fabric and should include three-quarters to one inch of the selvage and a few inches across the width of the fabric. If a swatch has already been taken from a fabric, start at the place where the first swatch was cut and continue across the fabric so that the store does not lose additional yardage. The manager may prefer that the store personnel cut the swatches. Mark each swatch with a tag giving the source, the price per yard, approximate available yardage, and the width of the fabric. Indicate fabric content if the bolt is labeled. Staple swatches to a card labeled with the name of the store, or put the swatches into an envelope marked with the store's name. Unmarked swatches are useless. Do not expect to remember the price or where the fabric came from after shopping several stores. Etiquette demands that the shopper not refer to competitors' fabrics while swatching in a store.

Stores specializing in upholstery and drapery fabrics often have very useful fabrics for period costumes. These stores may also be more agreeable to giving swatches, since their customers are often trying to match fabrics to paint or furniture. The shopper must be creative about sources. Specialty houses (suppliers to specific businesses like tie and hat manufacturers), industrial suppliers, and craft supply houses should all be investigated. If costumes are being designed far enough in advance, fabrics can be ordered from sources specializing in theatrical fabrics.

A costume shop should develop sources and maintain an up-to-date source file for fabrics and other often-used items. Each designer should also develop a personal file that indicates sources' specialties and idiosyncrasies and that help the designer to keep track of vendors for unusual items. Figure 7.6 is a sample Source

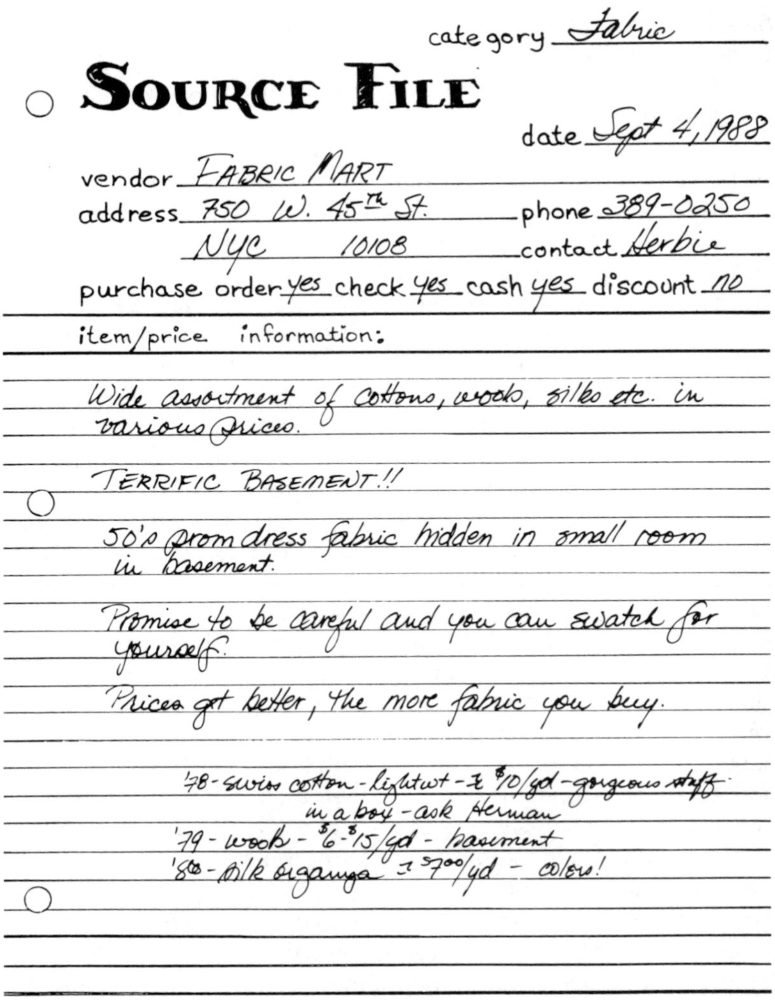

category *Fabric*

SOURCE FILE

date *Sept 4, 1988*

vendor *FABRIC MART*

address *750 W. 45ᵀʰ St.* _____ phone *389-0250*
NYC *10108* _____ contact *Herbie*

purchase order *yes* check *yes* cash *yes* discount *no*

item/price information:

Wide assortment of cottons, wools, silks etc. in various prices.

TERRIFIC BASEMENT!!

50's prom dress fabric hidden in small room in basement.

Promise to be careful and you can swatch for yourself.

Prices get better, the more fabric you buy.

'78 - Swiss cotton - lightwt - $10/yd - gorgeous stuff
  in a box - ask Herman
'79 - wools - $6-$15/yd - basement
'80 - silk organza $700/yd - colors!

FIGURE 7.6   Source File Sheet.

File sheet. This or a similar form reminds the designer what information may be needed for future reference.

The designer will find it helpful to keep a collection of fabric swatches. These are useful when the designer is planning color schemes, deciding on fabrics, and discussing with the shop supervisor and shopper what types of fabrics are needed.

Linings, backings, and fabric trims must also be located and purchased. Some costume shops keep these items in stock and charge them off to the show as they are needed. In other situations all necessary materials will need to be purchased for each garment.

Final fabric decisions should be made on large yardages first. Groups of identical costumes, and costumes that require complex cutting or special fitting, are usually dealt with first in a costume shop. Consult with the costumer about shop priorities and make the relevant fabric selections first.

ADAPTING FABRIC

When the perfect fabric cannot be found, the designer must choose among second choices. Many aspects of a fabric can be changed. Color and pattern can be altered. The hang and reflective quality can sometimes be modified. Weave cannot be changed, but sometimes the wrong side of a fabric has the desired effect.

Dyeing

The most common method of adapting fabric is to alter the color by dyeing. If the appropriate fabric can be dyed and the facilities for dyeing are adequate, dyeing is preferable to using a too stiff or too shiny or otherwise inappropriate fabric even if it is the right color.

Interesting special effects can also be achieved by dyeing. In Color plate 16 Hesione's dress for *Heartbreak House* was *ombréd* by being dipped in successive dye baths. Each time less of the garment was immersed and areas of previous color were left undyed by that solution.

Most costume shops have some dye facilities. The designer should check on the capacity of these facilities before planning dyeing projects. Dyeing should generally be done in the piece (before the garment is cut). Doing this requires extra time at the beginning of the production period: the fabric must be washed, dyed, rinsed, dried, ironed, and rolled before the cutter can begin to cut the garment. This process can add ½ to 1½ days to the production calendar for each large fabric piece. Mixing and matching dyes to paint samples can be quite difficult, unpredictable, and time-consuming. Pieces over 25 yards should be sent out to professional dyers, but this is a costly alternative.

In some shops the designer may be responsible for the dyeing. The guidelines in Boxes 7.C and 7.D will be helpful for the beginning dyer.

Box 7.C Dyeing Guidelines

1. Select fabrics and dyes that are compatible. (See the chart in Box 7.D.) Read the directions carefully. Check for chemical assistants (mordants) required.

2. Wash the fabric to remove sizing and finishes. Permanent press finishes resist dye and are extremely difficult to remove. Fabrics with these finishes should be avoided for dyeing projects.

3. For even color, the fabric must be uniformly damp before entering the dye bath. This process of dampening is called "wet-out."

4. Mix the dye with a small quantity of hot water and stir to dissolve.

5. Stir the dye into the water for a dye bath, straining if any undissolved particles remain.

6. Always close the dye containers immediately and clean any spilled dye before proceeding. Keep damp fabrics out of the way until the area is clean. Dye particles settling on damp fabric will spot instantly.

7. Test a swatch for color accuracy before immersing the whole piece. Keep records of dye swatches and formulas.

8. The color is darker when fabric is wet, so samples should be dried to check the color. Rinse the swatch and iron it dry between paper towels. Do not place an iron directly on the sample, since direct heat may alter the color.

9. Saturation of color is determined by the quantity of dye to the weight of the fabric, fiber content of the fabric, temperature, and length of time in the dye bath, not by the amount of water in the dye bath.

10. Promote even dyeing by (a) allowing sufficient water for the fabric to move freely, (b) keeping the fabric moving at all times, and (c) heating the fabric slowly.

11. Use rubber gloves to protect the skin from chemicals in the dye. Wear a particle mask when mixing and handling large quantities of powdered dyes, to prevent inhaling of chemicals.

12. When the fabric has reached the desired shade (remember it will dry lighter), rinse it completely. Some dyers recommend a cold rinse followed by warm and then hot rinses. Check directions for the dye used. Do not skip or skimp on the rinse process. Dye that is not absorbed during the dyeing process will *not permanently* adhere to the fabric. This excess dye will come off in handling or wearing and can stain the skin of cutters, stitchers, and actors. Additional dye will come off poorly rinsed fabric during future washings and will stain other garments in the same wash.

Hand-dyed fabrics are best washed separately or dry cleaned. A sample of the fabric should be tested to determine the best cleaning procedure.

13. Do not delay the rinse process. Dye will settle in fabric folds and cause streaking.

14. When the fabric is dry, iron and roll it on a cardboard tube. Be careful to maintain proper grain alignment while ironing.

15. Dyeing before cutting is usually preferable to dyeing a completed garment. Careful cutting can avoid unevenly dyed areas. Dyeing after cutting, but before construction, can create some interesting effects but may distort the cut pieces. Garments dyed after construction have less life than garments made from predyed fabrics.

Box 7.D   Fiber – Dye Compatibility

FIBER	DYES
Cotton	Fiber-reactive dye, direct dye, basic (with mordant), union (household) dye, vat dye
Linen	Fiber-reactive dye, direct dye, basic (with mordant), union (household dye), vat dye
Wool	Fiber-reactive dye (less intense color), acid dye, some direct dye, basic dye, union (household) dye, disperse dye
Silk	Fiber-reactive dye (less intense color), acid dye, some direct dye, basic dye, union (household) dye, disperse dye
Rayon	Direct dye, basic (with mordant), vat dyes
Nylon	Some acid dyes, some direct dye, union dyes, disperse dye
Polyester	Sometimes union dye, disperse dye
Acrylic	Sometimes basic dye

Applying Pattern

Painting designs and patterns on fabric is a relatively simple but time-consuming process. Many methods are available to the designer.

FIGURE 7.7 *The Resurrection.* Even modest fabrics can become interesting when painted. Designed by the author for Bethlehem Arts. Photo by Robert Ipcar.

Stencil

This is a useful technique for applying repeat designs on fabrics. The standard technique is to cut the design from stencil paper or thin plastic and spray or paint the motif on the fabric with textile paints, permanent felt-tip markers, dyes, or leather sprays. Figure 7.7 shows a costume for Mary in *The Resurrection* that was made of sheeting, sprayed with dye, and decorated by means of a stencil and permanent felt-tip markers. Variations of this technique use sticky-back shelf paper to make the stencil and adhere it directly to the cloth. "Found" objects like plastic doilies can be used as masking devices or incorporated into a stencil to create interesting effects.

FIGURE 7.8 *Kicks: The Showgirl Musical.* Designed by William Ivey Long.

Silkscreen and Block Printing

These techniques require more equipment and experience and add extra time to the production period. They are, however, useful for reproducing complex patterns. *Block printing* is the printing of a motif by pressing onto the fabric an inked block of wood or linoleum on which the design has been carved. *Silkscreening* is the printing of a motif by forcing thick ink through a piece of silk that is mounted on a frame. The areas through which the ink should *not* pass are blocked by attaching to the silk a lacquer film or paper stencil or by sealing the silk with a blockout liquid designed for this process. Silkscreening can perfectly reproduce a period fabric, creating an authentic note in just the right color combination. The fabric for the costume in Figure 7.8 would be silkscreened to order. The motif was taken from the wallpaper in the Men's Room of Radio City Music Hall.

Free-Hand Painting

Designs that need not repeat precisely can sometimes be sketched on the fabric and painted by hand with textile paints or dyes. Printed

FIGURE 7.9 *You're a Good Man, Charlie Brown.* Fabric was painted with textile paint to produce a suitable plaid for this costume. Designed by the author for Brooklyn College.

fabrics can be enhanced with hand painting to add color or definition to the design.

Many products are available for painting on fabrics — textile
paints, inks, acrylics, leather dyes, and a variety of other media.
Always check labels carefully for instructions, and especially make
sure the fabrics are appropriate for the medium under consideration.

Even apparently simple painting projects can sometimes
become major time-consumers. When a plaid of suitable scale and
color could not be found for Patty's costume in *You're a Good Man,
Charlie Brown* (Figure 7.9), 1½ days of hand painting had to be
squeezed into the production schedule to produce the fabric.

Skillful painting can enhance and add dimension to all stage
costumes. The intensity of stage lighting tends to wash out details
and the contours of the figure unless emphasized with paint. In
Color plate 15 the costume for King Louis in *Molière in Spite of
Himself* was designed in all white fabrics. The dimension and color
variations were carefully painted into the fabric to give the look of a
watercolor painting come to life.

Aging and Distressing

Many plays require the costumes of certain characters to look old,
dirty, or torn. These are referred to as "distressed costumes." The
first step for the designer is to consider the type of fabric that will
distress well yet hold up to stage use.

Aging is accomplished by dyeing, bleaching, painting, scraping
with a grater, wire-brushing, sandpapering, and numerous other
aggressive techniques.

Because dyeing and painting often require special equipment
and skill, the designer must be sure that time, facilities, staff, and
budget permit these processes. On the other hand, skillful use of
these crafts may prove to be an economical substitute or alternative
for expensive trims and fabrics.

Appliqué

Fabric design can also be altered by the use of appliqué. Fabric
choices for appliqué work should be considered carefully. Fabric
too loosely woven may fray and sag when used as an appliqué.
Appliqué work stiffens the effect of the garment and may alter the
hang of the entire garment. Careful consideration should also be
given to the effect of the combination of fabrics. A heavy fabric
appliquéd to a lighter fabric may cause sagging and distortion of the
garment.

Fabric shopping and selection is time-consuming and tiring for the designer, but the final effect of a set of costume designs rests solidly on the fabric decisions made. Little can be done for a costume that does not hang correctly because of a poor choice of fabric. Much time and effort might be needed to overcome the disadvantages of a too-shiny, too-soft, or too-stiff fabric. Box 7.E is a Designer Checklist that will help the designer make appropriate fabric selections.

Box 7.E   Designer Checklist V: Fabrics

1. Do the fabrics chosen help define the character?
2. Do the fabrics support the concept?
3. Are the fabrics suitable for the period and/or the hang of the garment? Will linings or extra stiffeners be required?
4. What fabric treatments will be needed? Is there enough time and labor available to handle the required treatments?
5. Is the scale of each pattern compatible with the character and style of the production?
6. Will this fabric meet stress and maintenance requirements?
7. Does each fabric fit within the budget allotment? Can adjustments be made in other areas to allow for extra expenditures on certain fabrics?
8. Can the extra time and labor required to make a cheaper fabric work be balanced against dollar savings? Will the cost of extra linings, dyes, and paints override the savings?

Chapter 8
Getting the Show Together

. . . a tailor called me in his shop
And showed me silks that he had bought for me,
And therewithal took measure of my body.
THE COMEDY OF ERRORS   William Shakespeare

ORGANIZING THE WORK

Once the sketches are approved, the designer's focus shifts from designing appropriate costumes to supervising and participating in the translation of the sketches to the finished costumes. Efficient organization of this work requires the division of the various costume problems into an endless number of categories. Each designer has a personal approach to this organization, but the forms presented in this chapter are designed to simplify the process for the novice designer.

Costume Lists; Pull/Rent/Buy Lists

Listing all necessary items for each costume for all characters gives the designer an overall view of the total requirements of the play. Determining the probable source of each part of the costume gives an idea of the budget difficulties and the amount of work required. The Costume List in Figure 8.1 is a form which assists in this process.

The designer should assemble all the sketches for each character in the order of appearance in the play. Assuming that the

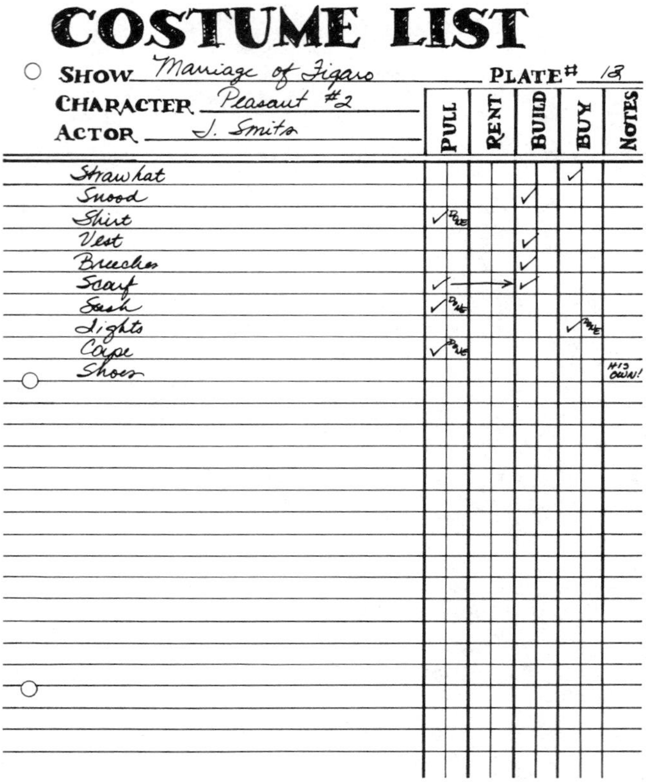

COSTUME LIST

SHOW _Marriage of Figaro_   PLATE # _13_
CHARACTER _Peasant #2_
ACTOR _J. Smith_

	PULL	RENT	BUILD	BUY	NOTES
Straw hat				✓	
Snood		✓			
Shirt	✓ ⁿ⁴⁵				
Vest			✓		
Breeches			✓		
Scarf	✓ →		✓		
Sash	✓ ᴮ⁴⁵				
Tights				✓ ⁿ⁴⁵	
Cape	✓ ᴮ⁴⁵				
Shoes					ⁿ¹³ OWN!

FIGURE 8.1

actor is providing nothing but modern underwear, the designer should list each article of clothing, piece of jewelry, and costume accessory in each sketch (indicating plate number and act and scene numbers). If the character just stepped out of the shower, what would he or she need to wear? Tights? Corset? Dance belt? Petticoats? Each layer of clothing should be considered from the skin out. What is necessary to create the shape of the garment? Are the same undergarments suitable for all the costumes worn by one character? Will the character be seen dressing or undressing on stage? Will the undergarments need to be period designs? How does this list compare with the original costume notes? Are there any additions or eliminations?

When each list is complete, the probable or preferred source of each item should be determined. Will it be bought, built, rented, or pulled from stock? Can it be borrowed or supplied by the actor? This information is then transferred to Pull/Rent/Buy and To Build

☑PULL ☐RENT ☐BUY

○ **SHOW** _Marriage of Figaro_

ITEM _Shirts_   **CREW** _Millie_

✓	actor	character	description	size
	T. Smith	Antonio	peasant - beige	15½ - 34
	M. Romero	Pedrillo	peasant - beige	15 - 33
	K. Leech	Figaro	peasant - off white	15½ - 33
✓	K. Rowikow	Bartholo	18ᵗʰ cent. - white	15 - 32
✓	J. Holland	The Count	18ᵗʰ cent. - white	16 - 34
✓	V. Gladstone	Cherubino	18ᵗʰ cent. - pale rose	14½ - 31
✓	E. Felix	Basil	18ᵗʰ cent. - white	15½ - 34
✓	S. DeMari	Doongirdle	18ᵗʰ cent. - beige	15 - 34
✓	J. Claassen	Bailiff	18ᵗʰ cent. - grey	16 - 32
○✓	M. Campo	Double-deal	18ᵗʰ cent. - beige	15½ - 34
	B. Briggs	Peasant #1	peasant - khaki - Rags	large
	J. Smith	Peasant #2	peasant - Brown	xx large
	R. Len	Peasant #3	peasant - Brown	small
	H. Cunningham	Peasant #4	peasant - grey - Rags	med.
	J. Doe	Peasant #5	peasant - Brown	med.
○				

FIGURE 8.2

forms (see Figures 8.2 and 8.11). All related items from the same source are grouped on the same form and sizes are added from the measurement sheets as soon as measurements are taken.

These lists serve as the basis for organizing and distributing the work of pulling from stock, shopping, and selecting rental costumes. Although this procedure may seem to take up valuable time, its purpose is to ensure that nothing is overlooked. Variations of the system may be developed to meet the requirements of different shows. Reorganizing and grouping the items according to source and kind of garment makes it possible to divide up the work among several assistants. All skirts can be pulled at one time; all shoes, petticoats, and tights can be dealt with as a group rather than each piece individually. Even when only one person is working on a show, good organization ultimately saves time and duplication of effort.

Beginning designers often resist making lists. Confident that they have excellent memories, they insist on keeping all the information in their heads. One problem with this method is that even if they manage not to forget anything important, no one else can be of much help unless gifted in mind reading. Working out ways to make clear notations frees the mind to do more important things and lessens the chances of truly disastrous lapses of memory. One of the most difficult problems for the costume designer is coping with the staggering number of details involved in even the simplest costume project. No aid to easing this burden should be scorned.

Rehearsal Costumes

The need for rehearsal garments varies with each production. Once the final sketches have been approved, the director and designer should draw up a list of rehearsal costumes with projected dates for introducing them into the rehearsal process.

What kind of rehearsal garments will be needed? The designer should look at the costume sketches and analyze the actors' needs. Practice will be needed to handle costumes that are greatly different from currently worn garments. Long skirts, trains, capes, and shoes with appropriate heels are typically provided for period plays. In plays requiring unusual undergarments (bustles, crinolines, farthingales) the actor should be given rehearsal garments that at least suggest the size and movement of the finished costume. The actual undergarments should be put into work in the costume shop first, and as soon as they are no longer needed in the shop, the actors should use them with rehearsal garments. Costume pieces that are frequently handled or needed for special stage business may have to be provided early or "mock-ups" made. Handbags, large hats, fans, and parasols or umbrellas are items that the designer and director may agree to use for rehearsal. Sometimes an actor will request a specific rehearsal costume.

Not all rehearsal items are needed at the same time. Long skirts and shoes should be worn as soon as blocking begins, but items to be hand carried or taken off and on are not useful until the actors are "off book" (no longer carrying the script).

A complete list will be required for whoever is responsible for pulling together the rehearsal items. In some situations actors are asked to provide their own rehearsal garments. Some items may be provided by the properties person. In producing organizations that have stock costumes available, rehearsal garments may be pulled from stock by the shop manager. The designer must be aware that doing this takes time and must be considered in the labor budget. Sometimes pulling rehearsal clothes is the designer's responsibility and must be coordinated with the shop manager. An assistant designer may be assigned to assemble rehearsal costumes from stock or thrift stores.

Although rehearsal items are important to the actors and director, the designer must limit the amount of time spent on these items or the actual costumes may not get finished. For educational theater and repertory theater a collection of items reserved for rehearsals is a practical solution.

The designer should be sure that a responsible person (usually the stage manager) has provided suitable storage and procedures for the use of rehearsal costumes. Keeping in contact with the stage manager concerning changes, new stage business, and problems related to the rehearsal costumes helps the designer make adjustments as costume construction progresses and minimizes the confusion during dress rehearsals.

Assessing Resources

Prepared with sketches, costume plot, and accurate lists, the designer confers with the costume shop manager. Although preliminary discussions may have been held when the designer was developing roughs, complete plans for execution of costumes must now be made. The shop manager is responsible for organizing and guiding the show through the costume shop, ordering supplies, and hiring and supervising costume staff. The shop manager must thoroughly understand the costume designs, budget, and the designer's requirements. A complete discussion of the responsibilities each person will undertake is imperative. In order to divide the work efficiently, the designer and the shop manager must each have a clear picture of the whole project. The designer should not minimize the work or hold back information. While some additions and changes are inevitable, deliberately omitting or minimizing costume requirements is unprofessional and detrimental to the final product.

If the theater maintains a stock of costumes, the shop manager, costume supervisor, or stock person will determine what might be available. Items like tights, petticoats, capes, hats, and men's shirts may be found in stock. If items on the Pull list are not available from the stock, they should be added to the Rent, Buy, or To Build lists.

The designer and shop manager should discuss the stress requirements of costumes used in strenuous action and the durability of fragile garments. Back-up garments may be needed for garments that are at risk. Duplicates are usually required of costumes that are exposed to stage blood or water, particularly if more than one performance a day is scheduled. These duplicates must be figured into the cost and time schedule as separate costumes.

The shop manager will distribute the work among the available personnel according to their skills and positions in the shop. Box 8.A lists the types of positions found in costume shops and provides a general job description of each. The number and types of positions in any given costume shop vary greatly according to the type of shop, the kind of projects usually undertaken, and the labor available. The job descriptions, responsibilities, and skills vary from shop to shop as well.

The designer and the shop manager should have a clear understanding of the timetable for shopping for fabric, taking measurements, pulling from stock, fittings, and the arrival of rental costumes. On the basis of available personnel, the manager will estimate the time required to produce the costumes, the time for fittings, and the time needed for alterations of bought and rented costumes. The designer may need to make adjustments in the planned costumes because of time and personnel limitations. Renting one or two more costumes instead of struggling to build them may make the difference between a good-quality production and an unfinished show with an exhausted, burned-out shop crew.

Copies of the sketches, costume plot, and all the lists should be given to the shop manager for reference.

Box 8.A   Costume Construction Personnel

There is much variation in the use and definition of terms for costume construction personnel. Many theater craftspersons and technicians are skilled in more than one area. The following definitions provide a general guideline.

Costume Designer: Theater artist employed to design, coordinate, and supervise the execution of costumes for stage, television, and film. Hired by the producer and/or director.

Assistant Costume Designer: Assistant hired by the designer to do research, swatch fabrics, shop, organize, take notes, or do any other job required by the designer.

Costume Shop Manager: Highly skilled technician with experience in all areas of costume construction. Responsible for supervision of personnel, maintenance of shop equipment, purchase of supplies, scheduling the work through the shop, and some construction projects. (Also called Costume Shop Foreman.)

Costume Director: Regional (for regional theater) or academic (for educational theater) position incorporating responsibilities of the Costume Designer, Costume Shop Manager, and sometimes teacher. (Also called Costume Supervisor)

Costumer: Person skilled in costume pattern making, construction, and some crafts. Capable of seeing project through from sketch to finished costume. (Also called Costumier.)

Patternmaker: Person skilled in making patterns, usually by flat-pattern or drafting methods. Responsible for making patterns, cutting all parts of the garment, and preparing the garment for stitching.

Draper: Person skilled in making patterns by the draping technique. Responsible for patterns, cutting all parts of the garment, and preparing the garment for stitching.

Cutter: Another term used for the person responsible for cutting garments after the patterns are made by the patternmaker. The term is also used for either the patternmaker or the draper.

First hand: Assistant to the patternmaker, costumer, draper, or cutter. (Also known as Draper's Assistant.)

Tailor: Specialist in men's wear hired by the costume shop for pattern making and construction supervision of men's costumes and special women's costumes.

Project Manager: In large costume shops where several projects are being worked on at the same time, a liaison person is hired by the costume shop to work with the designers and to guide each project through the shop.

Shopper: Person responsible for locating, pricing, and purchasing fabrics, trims, and accessories needed to assemble costumes. May be hired by the shop or directly by the designer.

Stitcher: Sewing machine operators employed by the costume shop to stitch costumes together.

Finisher: Personnel skilled in hand-stitching techniques used to finish costumes — hems, snaps, hooks and eyes, buttons, trim.

Stock Person: Person responsible for organizing, maintaining, pulling, and striking stock costumes in a rental house or educational or regional theater.

Craftsperson: A general term for the technician skilled in one or more of a variety of costume- and prop-related crafts: Celastic construction for masks or armor, latex and foam molding, fiber glass construction, jewelry making, and others.

Milliner: A specialist in hat construction and decoration. Hired by the costume shop or free-lance.

Dyer/Painter: A specialist in fabric dyeing, fabric painting, and aging or breakdown techniques for costumes or fabric.

Wardrobe Crew: Persons responsible for the maintenance of the costumes during the run of the show — laundry, dry cleaning, repairs — pre-show setup, and quick changes. Hired by the producer.

Wardrobe Supervisor: Person responsible for the supervision of the wardrobe crew.

Dresser: A member of the wardrobe crew assigned to assist actors with changing costumes, or a personal valet hired by an actor to assist with dressing and makeup.

SHOP SCHEDULE _Twelfth Night_

SUN	MON	TUES	WED	THURS	FRI	SAT
_15_ OFF	_16_ NYC SHOPPING	_17_ 1ST READ THRU SKETCH PRESENTATION *Measurements	_18_ Full Staff In →	_19_	_20_ 10-4	_21_
_22_ OFF	_23_ NYC SHOPPING ACTORS' DAY OFF	_24_ *ALL FABRIC DUE ← 1ST MUSLIN	_25_ FITTINGS + STOCK →	_26_ DYER IN ←	_27_	_28_ → 10-4
_29_ OFF	_30_ NYC RENTAL ACTORS' DAY OFF	_31_ EXTRA HELP IN → HAIRCUTS	NOVEMBER _1_	_2_ PAINTER IN →	_3_	_4_ → 10-4
_5_ FINAL FITTINGS	_6_ *RENTALS DUE IN ACTORS' DAY OFF	_7_ ← FINAL FITTINGS	_8_ →	_9_ 2:00 DRESS PARADE 8:00 RUN THRU w/COSTUME PIECES	_10_ 2:30 TECH 8:00 TECH	_11_ 2:00 DRESS TECH *8:00 FULL DRESS
2:00 DRESS? _12_ 8:00 FULL DRESS w/ PHOTO CALL *	_13_ ACTORS' DAY OFF	2:00 DRESS? _14_ 8:00 PREVIEW	2:00 RUN THRU _15_ 8:00 PREVIEW	2:30 RUN THRU _16_ 8:30 PREVIEW	2:30 RUN THRU? _17_ 8:00 OPEN!	_18_ COLLAPSE!

FIGURE 8.3 Shop Schedule. Careful organization of the shop production schedule is needed to keep work flowing. (See also Figure 2.10, Designer's Production Schedule.)

Production Calendar

At this point the designer and the shop manager must update and complete the production calendar. Working backwards from the first dress rehearsal, they establish a set of dates and deadlines for the dress parade, final fittings, arrival of rental costumes, first fittings, patterning, arrival of fabrics in the shop, dyeing or painting (including ordering of materials), items required for rehearsal, measurements, and any other important phase of the work.

Priorities should be established. Rehearsal items, garments to be distressed, fabrics or costumes to be painted, and foundation garments to be built should be scheduled into work first. Careful planning of the production schedule reduces traffic jams in the costume shop and helps the designer and shop manager pace the work. Good scheduling also prevents the designer or crew from straying off into trivial work while important priorities remain undone. Figure 8.3 shows a carefully planned work schedule. The designer and the shop manager have coordinated responsibilities, projects, deadlines, and rehearsal requirements.

The designer must be realistic about the time required for various projects. A given project will never take *less* time than anticipated; invariably it will take *more* time than expected. Box 8.B gives an approximation of the amount of time that must be allowed for different types of costume activities. The actual time spent on each costume varies greatly depending on the complexity of the garment, quality of desired workmanship, skill of the crew, and

---

Box 8.B   Estimating Work Hours per Task for Each Costume

Actual time spent on each costume varies greatly. This chart is a guide to evaluating the work load of a production. The designer should confer with the shop manager when considering work time. (Work time does not include interruptions!)

TASK	TIME ALLOTMENT
Measurements (per actor)	15 to 25 minutes
Shopping (per costume)	1 to 8 hours
Pattern making (per costume)	1 to 16 hours
Layout and cutting (per costume)	30 minutes to 16 hours
Pattern grading (per size, per costume)	15 minutes to 5 hours
Fabric preparation (per yardage piece): wash, iron or steam, roll	2 to 6 hours
Dyeing (in addition to above time)	30 minutes to 4 hours
Marking (per costume)	15 minutes to 2 hours
Serging or merrowing-finishing seams with overlock stitch (per costume)	10 minutes to 2 hours
Stitching (per costume)	1 to 24 hours
Finishing (per costume)	15 minutes to 8 hours
Painting (per costume)	1 to 16 hours
Pulling (per costume)	15 minutes to 4 hours
Fitting (per rented or pulled costume)	20 minutes to 1 hour
Fitting (per costume muslin)	30 minutes to 1 hour
Fitting (per constructed costume)	1 to 3 hours

availability of sources. The shop manager, familiar with these variables, should assist in estimating work time. Time studies suggest that the average constructed costume requires between forty and fifty work hours. Forty hours may be a week's work for one person or ten hours each for four people. There is, however, a point at which additional people may not speed the work. At certain stages of construction, shop space and equipment may limit the number of persons that can work at a time.

Projects must also be matched to the qualifications of available personnel. After conferences with the costume shop personnel, necessary revisions should be made in designs, organization, schedules, and budget. If discussions were held with the shop in the early design stages (roughs), major revisions should not be necessary. However, the director must be informed if major changes in approach are required by limited funds or staff. Ideally, these discussions will occur in production meetings in which all concerned parties participate.

Evaluating Budget Allotments

Each costume presents its own costing problems. For regional and educational theaters, the skill level of workers may be a large factor. The less skilled worker will take longer and make more mistakes than the professional costumer. The costume for Olivia in Figure 8.4a was designed for a production of *Twelfth Night* at Brooklyn College using both student and professional labor. Figure 8.4b is an analysis of the factors involved in determining the cost of the garment. Other cost variables include the quality of the fabric and trim chosen and the acceptability of stock petticoats. (See the finished garment in Figure 1.3.)

Once the Pull/Rent/Buy lists are complete, an estimated budget can be worked out. Figure 8.5 shows a sample budget, excluding labor. (Labor costs in many producing organizations are figured as part of the general running expenses. If permanent staff cannot handle the size show planned, extra personnel may be hired and that cost assigned to the show budget.) Shoes, wigs, and hats must be accounted for in the budget; these items can gobble up large portions of time and money if they are not available in stock or owned by the actors. (Equity actors must be paid a rental fee for personal clothing used for costumes.) Some pre-shopping may be necessary to get an idea of the current market value of required items. For producing organizations that maintain a costume stock, the value of an item may depend on its future use. If an item is a desirable addition to stock, buying better quality is more economical

FIGURE 8.4A   *Twelfth Night.*
A costume design by the author for Brooklyn College.

in the long run. The shop manager should assist by advising on stock items and estimating the fabric yardage required for the costumes being built. Dividing this yardage figure into the overall allotment for fabric gives the shopper the approximate price per yard for the fabrics to be purchased. (See also Chapter 7.)

For a large professional production, several costume houses may bid on the job, giving estimates of the cost of building the costumes. The producer may take the lowest bid, or the designer may urge the use of the costume house whose work the designer prefers. The total number of costumes may be divided between more than one costume house.

Although the designer is sometimes asked for budget estimates, the amount of production money allotted to costumes is usually predetermined by the producing organization. This allotment may not be realistic for the style of the production, size of staff available, and the director's requirements. Obviously, adjustments are needed. The options are: request additional funds, consider rented or borrowed items, seek volunteer help, seek sources of free items or items to use in exchange for program credit, simplify designs,

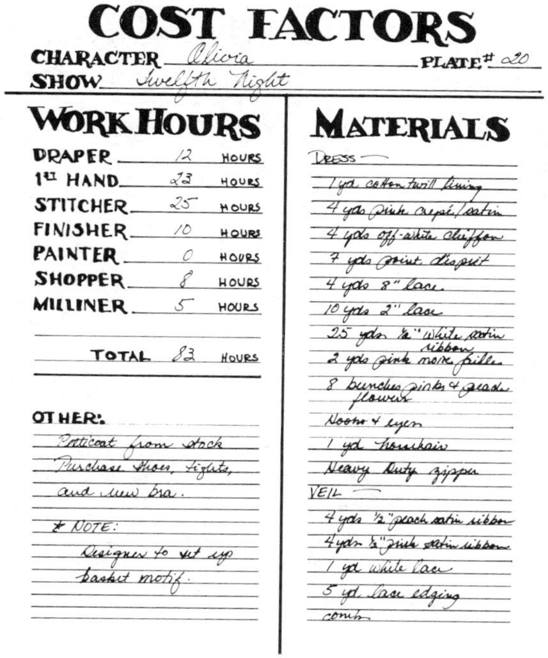

COST FACTORS

CHARACTER _Olivia_   PLATE # _20_
SHOW _Twelfth Night_

WORK HOURS

DRAPER	12	HOURS
1ST HAND	23	HOURS
STITCHER	25	HOURS
FINISHER	10	HOURS
PAINTER	0	HOURS
SHOPPER	8	HOURS
MILLINER	5	HOURS
TOTAL	83	HOURS

OTHER:
Petticoat from stock
Purchase shoes, tights,
and new bra.

* NOTE:
Designer to set up
basket motif.

MATERIALS

DRESS –
1 yd cotton twill lining
4 yds pink crepe/satin
4 yds off-white chiffon
7 yds print dia print
4 yds 8" lace
10 yds 2" lace
25 yds ½" white satin ribbon
2 yds pink moire frill
8 bunches pink & peach flowers
hooks & eyes
1 yd horsehair
heavy duty zipper
VEIL –
4 yds ½" peach satin ribbon
4 yds ½" pink satin ribbon
1 yd white lace
5 yd lace edging
comb

FIGURE 8.4B Cost Factors. The analysis of the labor and materials for this costume took into consideration the fact that both student and professional labor was involved in its production. (See finished costume in Figure 1.3.)

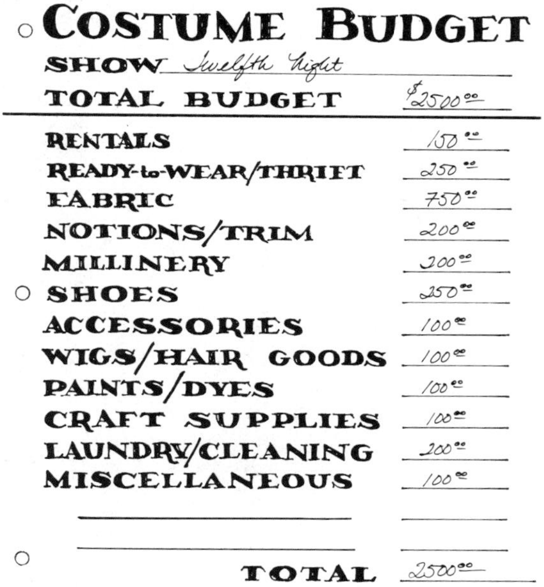

COSTUME BUDGET

SHOW _Twelfth Night_

TOTAL BUDGET	$2500.00
RENTALS	150.00
READY-to-WEAR/THRIFT	250.00
FABRIC	750.00
NOTIONS/TRIM	200.00
MILLINERY	200.00
SHOES	250.00
ACCESSORIES	100.00
WIGS/HAIR GOODS	100.00
PAINTS/DYES	100.00
CRAFT SUPPLIES	100.00
LAUNDRY/CLEANING	200.00
MISCELLANEOUS	100.00
TOTAL	2500.00

FIGURE 8.5 Sample Budget.

develop a new concept, pull additional items from stock, negotiate director requests, compromise in all areas, withdraw from the project. Designers are often asked to work absolute miracles on shoestrings or less. In such a case the designer must decide whether the experience and credit for doing the show warrant the effort to overcome insurmountable odds. There is a tendency to view costumes as "clothes" and to fail to comprehend the complexity and cost of even the simplest costume projects. The designer should have realistic estimates of cost and time and be prepared to discuss these with the director and the producer. The costumes make a major contribution to the success of the production, and the designer should not allow that contribution or the work of the costume staff to be undervalued.

The commercial costume shop determines the cost (the price to the producer) of building a costume by estimating the number of

FIGURE 8.6A *Daughter of the Regiment. Designed by Eduardo Sicongco for Texas Opera Theater.*

work hours required for each phase of the work, then multiplying each by the rate per hour for that type of labor, adding the cost of materials, overhead, and hopefully, profit for the shop. The costume for *The Daughter of the Regiment* in Figure 8.6a was designed to have all buttons, patches, and trims painted onto the garment. It therefore required not only pattern making, cutting, stitching, and finishing, but dyeing, painting, and steam setting. Figure 8.6b is an analysis of the cost factors involved in building the costume in a professional shop. If additional personnel are hired to meet the needs of the show, the cost of such additional labor is figured into the total cost.

Given enough money and personnel, almost anything can be

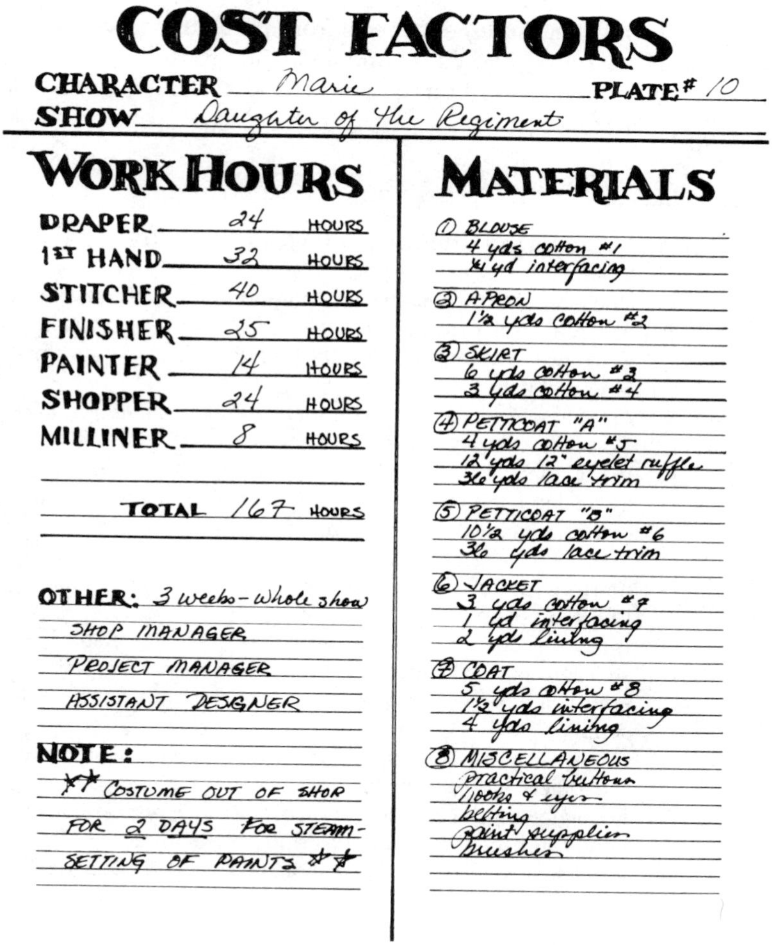

COST FACTORS

CHARACTER _Marie_   **PLATE #** _10_

SHOW _Daughter of the Regiment_

WORK HOURS

DRAPER	24	HOURS
1ST HAND	32	HOURS
STITCHER	40	HOURS
FINISHER	25	HOURS
PAINTER	14	HOURS
SHOPPER	24	HOURS
MILLINER	8	HOURS

      TOTAL 167 HOURS

OTHER: 3 weeks - Whole show

SHOP MANAGER

PROJECT MANAGER

ASSISTANT DESIGNER

NOTE:

** COSTUME OUT OF SHOP

FOR 2 DAYS FOR STEAM-

SETTING OF PAINTS **

MATERIALS

① BLOUSE
  4 yds cotton #1
  ¼ yd interfacing

② APRON
  1½ yds cotton #2

③ SKIRT
  6 yds cotton #3
  3 yds cotton #4

④ PETTICOAT "A"
  4 yds cotton #5
  12 yds 12" eyelet ruffle
  36 yds lace trim

⑤ PETTICOAT "B"
  10½ yds cotton #6
  36 yds lace trim

⑥ JACKET
  3 yds cotton #7
  1 yd interfacing
  2 yds lining

⑦ COAT
  5 yds cotton #8
  1½ yds interfacing
  4 yds lining

⑧ MISCELLANEOUS
  practical buttons
  hooks & eyes
  belting
  paint supplies
  brushes

FIGURE 8.6B Cost Factors. Labor is the major cost factor in a professional shop. The number of work hours are determined and multiplied by the rate per hour for each type of labor; then is added the cost of materials, overhead, and profit for the shop.

done in almost any length of time. However, few productions have the benefit of unlimited resources. Time equals money. If you don't have time, you need more money; if you don't have money, you need time.

Box 8.C gives a Designer Checklist for this stage of the organization of the show.

Taking Measurements

Accurate measurements are crucial to the correct fit of the costume. The designer should know how to take measurements correctly and should be prepared to do so. In professional productions and many educational situations the costume shop staff will take the measurements. Most tailors, pattern makers, and drapers prefer to take the measurements of actors for whom they will make patterns. In repertory companies measurement sheets from previous shows may be kept on file, but they should be updated when reused, since some actors gain and lose weight frequently. Many actors (particularly in

---

Box 8.C   Designer Checklist VI: Organization

1. Does the director understand and approve the sketches?
2. Are rehearsal costumes needed? What kind? By when? Who will be responsible for providing and caring for rehearsal items?
3. Are all pieces of the individual costumes listed on the Costume Lists and the Pull/Rent/Buy Lists?
4. What resources are available to assemble this show? Are they adequate to meet the design needs? What adjustments can be made with the least damage to the visual concept of the production? Hire more staff? More money? Rent or pull more costumes? Are there creative and imaginative solutions to the problems?
5. Is the production calendar complete and reasonable? Is sufficient time allowed for each part of the project? Have arrangements been made for all required personnel and supplies?
6. Are appointments for measurements and fittings properly scheduled and conducted?
7. For what special projects should I assume responsibility? How can I see that work goes smoothly?
8. What staff is available? How should the work be assigned?

very active roles) can fluctuate greatly in size from the beginning of rehearsals to opening night.

Taking measurements should be approached in a very professional manner. Comments or asides about the actor's size are inconsiderate and unprofessional. Appointments with the actor should be made in the costume shop. A complete set of measurements should take 15 to 25 minutes.

Box 8.D   Taking Measurements

(a)	Chest or bust: over nipples, straight across back.
(b)	Above bust: (not needed for men) above breasts, around back.
(c)	Below bust: (not needed for men) under breasts, straight around back.
(d)	Across front: across chest from arm to arm.
(e)	Waist: around waist, level with small of back.
(f)	Hips: around fullest part of buttocks.
(g)	at Bone: around at top of pelvic bone.
(h)	Neck: around at base of neck, form ring with tape measure.
(i)	Front neck to waist: down the front from pit of the neck to the waist.
(j)	Shoulder to apex: from center of shoulder to tip of apex (nipple).
(j/k)	Shoulder to waist: from center of shoulder across apex to waist.
(l/m)	Armpit to side waist: from bottom of armpit to waist at side.
(n)	Across shoulders: across back on the top of the shoulders from bones at shoulder/arm joint.
(o)	Across shoulder blades: across back from arm to arm over largest part of shoulder blades.
(p/q)	Back neck to waist: down center back from top bone of spine to small of back.
(p/r)	Back neck to floor: down back from top bone of spine to floor, skimming body.
(q/s)	Waist to buttocks: down center back from waist to fullest part of buttocks.
(t/u)	Waist to knee: from waist, over buttocks to back of knee.
(t/v)	Waist to calf: from waist, over buttocks to fullest part of calf.
(q/r)	Waist to floor at back: down center back from waist to floor.

(m/w)   Waist to floor at side: down side from waist to floor, not following leg curves.

(x/y)   Waist to floor at front: down center front from waist to floor.

(z/aa)   Under bust to floor: down from under bust at side front to floor, skimming body.

Outsleeve

(ab/ac)   Neck to shoulder: from neck along shoulder ridge to bone at shoulder.

(ac/ad)   Shoulder to elbow: from bone at shoulder around to elbow with arm raised and bent.

(ac/ae)   Shoulder to wrist: with arm raised and bent, from bone at shoulder around to elbow and to wrist bone.

Insleeve

(af/ah)   Armseye to elbow: from where arm joins chest down inside arm to elbow.

(af/ag)   Armseye to wrist: from where arm joins chest down inside arm to wrist.

(ac/l)   Armseye: around armhole from shoulder to bottom of armpit back up to shoulder.

(at)   Upper arm: around the bicep.

(ah)   Wrist: around the wrist at wrist bone.

Outseam

(m/ai)   Outseam to knee: from waist at side to kneecap.

(m/aj)   Outseam to ankle: from waist at side to ankle bone. Outseam to pants length: based on costume sketch or period information.

Inseam

(ak/al)   Inseam to knee: from crotch to knee on inside of leg.

(ak/am)   Inseam to ankle: from crotch to ankle on inside of leg.

(an)   Thigh: around upper leg.

(ao)   Knee: around kneecap.

(ap)   Calf: around fullest part of lower leg.

(am)   Ankle: around ankle at ankle bone.

(al)   Below knee: around knee below kneecap.

(j/ak/j)   Girth: around body from center of shoulder in front, through crotch, up the back to center of shoulder (for unitards/leotards).

(aq)   Height: measured without shoes.

(av)   Head: around head, above ears on forehead and angling down in back.

(as/p)   Forehead to nape: across top of head from hairline in front to nape in back.

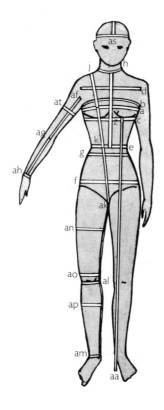
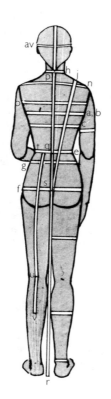
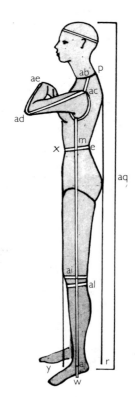

FIGURE 8.7 Taking Measurements. The basic positions for the tape measure on the form.

Measurements must be taken carefully. Tailors and pattern-makers may vary slightly from one another in their methods of measuring, but Figure 8.7 and Box 8.D shows a standard way to take the basic measurements. The actor should provide the shoe size (including width), weight, and other statistics not easily measured.

Figure 8.8 shows an example of a measurement form for use in a costume shop. These measurements provide most of the information needed for building costumes, but additional measurements may be taken for special projects. (Figure 8.9 shows a short measurement form for shopping or renting costumes. Separate sheets should be used for men and women. The second form can be filled out from the first or may be the only form required if the show is completely rented or shopped.)

Photocopies of the measurement sheets may be made for the shopper, patternmakers, and designer.

BROOKLYN COLLEGE COSTUME SHOP

MEASUREMENTS DATE 10/87

ACTOR J. Doe PHONE 555-1214

SHOW Marriage of Figaro CHARACTER Peasant #5

MALE ✓ FEMALE

CHEST/BUST 40

ABOVE 39 BELOW 37

ACROSS FRONT (chest) 15

WAIST 32

HIPS 38 at BONE 36

NECK 15 1/2 FRONT NECK to WAIST 16

SHOULDER to APEX (front) —

to WAIST (front) 18 1/2

ARMPIT to SIDE WAIST 9

ACROSS SHOULDERS (back) 16

ACROSS SHOULDER BLADES 15

BACK NECK to WAIST 17 1/2

to FLOOR 64

WAIST (back) to BUTTOCKS 10

to KNEE 23 to CALF 28

WAIST to FLOOR: at BACK 47

at SIDE 46 at FRONT 45

UNDERBUST to FLOOR —

OUTSLEEVE: NECK to SHOULDER 6

SHOULDER to ELBOW 13 to WRIST 26

INSLEEVE: ARMSEYE to ELBOW 9 to WRIST 26

ARMSEYE 22 1/2 UPPER ARM 13 WRIST 6 1/2

OUTSEAM: to KNEE 22 1/2 to ANKLE 42

to PANTS LENGTH 45

INSEAM: to KNEE 18 to ANKLE 33

to PANTS LENGTH 36

THIGH 22 KNEE 13

CALF 15 ANKLE 10

BELOW KNEE 12 1/2 GIRTH 66

HEIGHT 6'4" WEIGHT 180

HEAD 23 1/2 HAT

FOREHEAD to NAPE (wig) 14

SHOES 12C TIGHTS X Large

DRESS SIZE — BRA SIZE —

SHIRT 16-35 BLOUSE —

SUIT 42XL PANTS 32/36

PIERCED EARS no GLOVE large

EYES Blue HAIR dk brown

COMPLEXION olive

ALLERGIES none

OTHER

ITEMS PROVIDED BY ACTOR
shoes
dance belt

CHARACTER OR FIGURE NOTATIONS
active – gymnast
check for gussets

FIGURE 8.8 Measurement Sheet. This shortened form is more convenient for shopping, renting, or pulling costumes from stock.

BROOKLYN COLLEGE COSTUME SHOP

MEASUREMENTS ☒ MALE ☐ FEMALE

SHOW Marriage of Figaro

ACTOR	NECK	BUST/ CHEST	WAIST	HIPS	ACROSS BACK	HEIGHT	WEIGHT	DRESS	SHIRT/ BLOUSE	PANTS	SUIT	TIGHTS	HEAD	SHOES
T. Smith	15 1/2	40	32	41	15 1/2	5'8"	150	—	15 1/2-32	32-32	40R	Med.	23	10C
M. Romero	15	38	30	39	15	5'10"	135	—	15-33	30-34	40R	Med.	23 1/4	9D
K. Leach	15 1/2	39	31	40	15 1/4	5'11"	143	—	15 1/2-34	32-34	40R	Med.	22 7/8	10D
K. Konikow	15	37	30	38	15 1/2	5'7"	138	—	15-31	30-32	38S	Sm.	23	8D
J. Holland	16	42	34	44	16	6'3"	160	—	16 1/2-35	34-35	42L	Lg.	23 1/2	11D
V. Gladstone	14 1/2	36	29	37	15	5'9"	135	—	15-32	30-32	36R	Sm.	22 5/8	9C
E. Feliz	15 1/2	37	30	38	15	5'8"	140	—	15 1/2-33	30-32	38S	Sm.	22 3/4	9C
D. DeMasi	15	37	31	37	15 1/2	5'9"	132	—	15 1/2-33	31-31	38R	Med.	23	10 1/2 D
J. Claassen	16	44	36	49	16 1/4	5'10"	185	—	16-34	34-34	46L	XLg.	24	11 1/2 C
M. Campo	15 1/2	39	32	40	14 3/4	6'	170	—	15 1/2-34	32-34	40L	Med.	23 1/2	9 1/2 D
B. Briggs	15	38	32	38	15 1/2	5'8"	150	—	15-32	32-32	40S	Med.	23 1/2	10 1/2 D
J. Smith	16 1/2	43	34	42	17	5'11"	170	—	16 1/2-36	34-34	44L	Lg.	23	10C
R. Lee	14 1/2	36	30	37	15	5'7"	149	—	15-32	30-31	38S	Med.	23 1/4	9D
H. Cunningham	15 1/2	38	30	39	15 1/2	5'8"	160	—	15 1/2-33	30-31	38R	Med.	23 5/8	10C
J. Doe	15 1/2	40	32	38	16	6'4"	180	—	16-35	32-36	42 XL	Lg.	23 1/2	12C

FIGURE 8.9 Summary of cast measurements.

The Shop Bible

Most costume shops assemble a book, referred to as *the bible*, one for each show in the shop or a master book of all the work in the shop. All pertinent information (photocopies of the costume sketches, measurement sheets, production schedules, ledgers, rehearsal schedules, Costume Lists, Pull/Rent/Buy Lists, To Build or swatch sheets) is kept in the bible, where it can be found by everyone working on the show. Appointments for measurements, fittings, and conferences are also kept in the bible or an appointment book. The designer will also need to maintain a personal appointment book or calendar containing the same information.

ASSEMBLING THE COSTUMES

> *Good-mornin', ladies and gentlemen! … Has the young mistress anything for me today? I've got beautiful ribbons in my cart, Miss Anna, an' tapes, an' garters, an' hooks an' eyes. An' all in exchange for a few rags.*
>
> THE WEAVERS   Gerhart Hauptmann

The costumes for most productions are assembled by a combination of purchasing, pulling from stock, renting, and building garments. The proportion of costumes from each source depends on the size and quality of the stock, the size of the budget, and the size of the costume crew available.

Shopping

Shopping should be planned like a military offensive. Any expedition should have a clear set of priorities. Which fabrics are needed first? Are shoes more important than underwear? Which items are needed for rehearsal? Which items are needed for the first fittings? Will any items need to be ordered and shipped? Shopping trips should be planned so that vendors in the same area of the city are dealt with at one time, provided the highest priorities can be met with this approach. Basic materials are needed before trims, but if the trim store is in the same block as the fabric store, two trips should be unnecessary.

Thrift store shopping is particularly unpredictable. Items come and go daily, hourly. Thrift shopping requires the designer to make instant decisions, but few low-budget shows could be done without this source of costumes.

Locating Sources

Costume shops develop a Source File or Vendor Book for the items frequently needed for shows. Each designer should likewise develop a file of sources; it saves valuable time locating supplies. A sample page appears in Chapter 7 (Figure 7.6). Pertinent information on the vendor and items available are entered on the form, which is kept in a ring binder, although some designers and costume shops prefer to keep their source information on index cards. The information is dated to indicate how current the prices are. Each time the information is used, corrections should be made. Notes about service and billing procedures are helpful to the next person to use the file. The name of a contact person saves time on return calls and allows the designer to build up an understanding with the vendor about the special needs of the costume shop. The Source File should be organized by category or subject with a table of contents or index listing vendor names. Box 8.E lists some of the categories found in a designer's source file.

Box 8.E   List of Source File Categories

Accessories
    (Ties, suspenders, shirt fronts, collars)
Armor
    (Weapons, military gear, costume armor)
Art Supplies
    (Adhesives, paints)
Books
    (Catalogs, magazines, directories)
Corset Supplies
    (Bones, corset cloth, laces)
Costume and Formal Rental
Craft Supplies
    (Beads, hemp, fabric printing supplies, basket materials)
Dance Wear
    (Leotards, tights, dance shoes)
Dyes
    (Dyes, fabric paints)
Equipment
    (Sewing machines, steam irons, steamers, laundry equipment)
Fabrics
    (Specialty and regular)
Feathers and Flowers

Foam Rubber
Labels
Laundry Supplies
    (Bulk detergent, bleach, fabric softener)
Leather Goods
    (Leather, leather tools, glues, findings)
Makeup
Millinery Supplies
    (Hat supplies and manufacturers)
Notions and Trims
    (Sewing supplies, closures, trims)
Novelties and Magic Tricks
Pattern-Making Supplies
    (Paper, tools)
Plastics
Repair Services
Shoes
    (Special order, special sizes, slippers)
Theatrical Supplies
Wigs and Hair Goods
    (Rental, period, modern)

To develop the source book or to find items not listed in it, the "Yellow Pages" is the obvious choice. Time spent locating supplies by phone is time well spent. Calling ahead to make sure the item is in stock in desired colors and sizes saves time, frustration, money, and energy. The vendor may be asked to deliver or to hold the order for pickup. Of course, only items that can be specifically described over the phone can be dealt with this way. Unfortunately, some vendors will not give prices or other information over the phone. When this method is successful, however, the time saved is worth the effort.

Costumers and other theater technicians often need specialized materials. These materials are advertised in theater publications and listed in theater source directories. Membership in theater associations and subscriptions to theater magazines give the designer access to the directories they publish as well as much other valuable information. (See Periodicals and Newsletters, Costume Societies, and Unions and Guilds at the end of this book.)

Before going shopping, the designer should check that the lists are complete, the priority items are indicated, and suggested sources are listed. Good preplanning makes shopping less strenuous and less time-consuming.

Keeping Track of Expenditures

The designer needs to have a firm understanding with the producer concerning the procedures for purchasing. Some cash is necessary for small items, but the theater may have charge accounts with some merchants or may prefer to issue checks or purchase orders made out to the vendor. Whatever the arrangement, the designer should be extremely cautious about spending personal funds if the producer is slow to advance cash. Many designers have found themselves unwittingly subsidizing a production by purchasing supplies with personal funds for which reimbursement was slow or nonexistent.

Keeping careful records of expenditures is absolutely essential. All receipts should be immediately checked for correct total and clear figures. The designer should initial the back of cash register receipts and write the item purchased, the date, and the store name (if not on the front). Carbon copies of receipts should be checked for legibility. Receipts should be kept separate from the purchases themselves to prevent loss in transit or during unpacking. As soon as possible, purchases should be entered on a ledger sheet to provide a running account of expenditures. Receipts should be kept in a secure place until time to account for cash. A record of purchases made by charge, check, or purchase orders must be kept to provide an overall total of expenditures. Figure 8.10 shows one method of keeping a record of expenditures and receipts. Note that entries are initialed if more than one member of the shop is handling the ledger. (Ledger paper can be purchased at stationery stores.)

Procedures for handling money vary among theater organizations. The designer should be clear about the procedures for each project. He or she should meet with the business manager, bookkeeper, and/or accountant responsible for costume expenditures and follow their guidelines. Be creative with the costumes, but not with the handling of production funds!

When purchasing new articles of clothing, the designer must make sure that store policy allows for return of merchandise for refund if the garments do not fit. In thrift shops and discount houses returns may not be accepted. If the budget allows, several possibilities may be purchased and final decisions left until fittings. If care is taken not to soil the garments during fittings and if the store policy permits, extras may be returned later.

Some garments are best purchased by the actor. Bras and shoes can be special fitting problems. The actor should purchase the correct style and present the receipt for reimbursement.

BROOKLYN COLLEGE COSTUME SHOP

COSTUME RECEIPTS

SHOW _Twelfth Night_   DESIGNER _P. Cunningham_

RECEIPT NUMBER	DATE	VENDOR	ACCOUNT	PAYMENT METHOD	AMOUNT	PETTY CASH BALANCE	SHOW BALANCE 2500 00	
	10/12	Petty Cash Received	—	check		500 00	2000 00	RC
1	10/14	Art Max Fabrics	Fabric	P.O.	200 00	—	1800 00	RC
2	10/16	Beckensteins	Fabric	Cash	129 50	370 50	—	EF
3	10/18	B & J Fabric	Fabric	check	320 00	—	1480 00	AC
4	10/19	Capezio	Shoes	check	200 00	—	1280 00	RC
5	10/19	Selva Shoes	Shoes	cash	15 00	355 50	—	RC
6	10/19	M & J Trim	Trim	cash	30 00	325 50	—	EF
7	10/19	Putnam Dye Co.	Paint/Dye	check	75 00	—	1205 00	MR
8	10/23	Manny's	Millin.	P.O.	225 00	—	980 00	RC
9	10/23	Art Max Fabrics	Fabric	Cash	110 00	215 50	—	MR
10	10/24	Pearl Paint Co.	Paint/Dye	check	50 00	—	930 00	RC
11	10/30	Eaves-Brooks	Rental	P.O.	175 00	—	755 00	RC
12	10/30	Ideal Wig Co.	Wigs	check	100 00	—	655 00	RC
13	10/31	St. Vincent dePaul	thrift	cash	25 00	190 50	—	EF
14	10/31	Steinlauf & Stoller	trim	cash	89 00	101 50	—	EF
15	11/1	Taudy Leather	craft	check	110 00	—	545 00	CR
16	11/2	Alexander's	Ready Wear	check	189 50	—	355 50	CR
17	11/2	Salvation Army	access.	cash	15 00	86 50		
18	11/2	Subway Tokens	misc.	cash	18 00	68 50		

FIGURE 8.10   Costume Receipts. This form simplifies the keeping of basic financial records for the designer or shopper.

Rental Procedures

Ideally the designer should go to the rental house to pick out the costumes. This allows decisions on necessary substitutions to be made more easily. The designer should measure costumes for size, since rental stock is frequently altered and cannot be permanently sized. Waist, across back, chest or bust, waist to floor, or inseam measurements can be measured on the garment. If the designer cannot travel to the rental house, photocopies of the sketches with complete color notations should be sent along with the measurement sheets and order blanks provided by the costume house. Careful note should be made of the time required for delivery and the fees charged for various types of shipping. Shipping costs must be provided for in the budget. The director should be alerted to the deadlines for rental orders to minimize cast changes after costumes are rented.

Some modifications can be made in rented costumes. Some trims may be removed or replaced. Fitting alterations are permitted. Layers of sheer fabric can be added over finished garments to modify color or texture. Anything that can be undone before the costume is returned is permitted. Rental costumes should *never* be cut, painted, or dyed without the written permission of the rental house. The rental contract should be read carefully, and the crew instructed on correct handling of the rented items.

Rental houses usually charge a flat fee per costume. This fee usually covers everything needed for the costume except shoes. This system makes estimating the budget much easier. However, a "miscellaneous" category will still be necessary for additional trim, accessories, and last-minute items, even if *all* the costumes are rented.

Because of the high cost of tailoring, men's costumes are often rented. For period shows it is usually cheaper to rent a costume than to build it. Rental stock may be limited for modern dress, how-

FIGURE 8.11 A stock or thrift shop purchase (A) can be adapted to suggest the period (B). Designed by the author for Brooklyn College. Photo by Hilary Sherred.

A

B

ever. Much more variety is usually available in thrift shops, in department stores, or from personal wardrobes.

Adapting Stock and Thrift Shop Purchases

Whereas restraint is required with rental costumes, designers may be allowed to cut up, take apart, or otherwise change garments purchased or pulled from stock. Clearance for irreversible alterations may be required from the shop manager or costume director.

Permission may not be granted to alter antique garments from stock, since these may be more valuable as study pieces than as costumes. Actual period garments may be too small and too fragile to be of real use as costumes. They may also be too expensive to purchase and maintain for low-budget shows.

When pulling or shopping, the designer should keep in mind the basic construction of the desired garment, the type of fabrics that would be desirable, and the possible alterations that would make a garment over into a useful piece. Reshaping the neck, dyeing the garment, and shortening the sleeves or skirt are all relatively simple alterations to give the garment the right style.

With a complete understanding of the silhouette and fabric requirements of the desired period, a designer can often make "a silk purse from a sow's ear." In Figures 8.11a and 8.11b a 1930's evening gown (a) of suitable fabric (hang) and silhouette has been converted to a 1914 gown (b). The addition of an underbodice with appropriate neckline and sleeves and a cummerbund to give the correct waistline transformed the gown into a 1914 tango dress.

UNDERSTANDING COSTUME CONSTRUCTION

> *Here's snip and nip and cut and slish and slash,*
> *Like to a censer in a barber's shop.*
> *Why, what, a devil's name, tailor, call'st Thou this?*
> > TAMING OF THE SHREW   William Shakespeare

The term *construction* or *building* is used for the cutting, sewing, and assembling of costumes because of the heavy-duty techniques so often required for costumes. Because the garments must withstand vigorous activity, perspiration, body heat, and heat from stage lights, costumes cannot be delicately assembled. Costumes may also include craft items of leather, wire, metal, plastics, and other materials which are not lightweight and may not be sewn.

Pattern making and costume construction is a major area of study, requiring great skill and expertise. A complete study of these fields is beyond the scope of this book. However, this general discussion will help the novice to understand the procedures involved and will give the designer a working vocabulary in these fields. A more thorough study is necessary for the potential designer. The more knowledge a designer has of cut and construction, the better able that designer will be to explain clearly the costume design, to supervise and collaborate with the costumer, and to produce a costume personally when the need arises.

Designer/Costumer Collaboration

The costume designer's sketch is a plan or blueprint for the costume. A good costumer can take a poor sketch and make a wonderful costume; a poor costumer can take a good sketch and interpret it clumsily. Just as the designer strives to interpret the director's concepts of the play into costumes, the costumer must work to interpret the designer's sketch into a finished costume that creates the desired effect, fits the actor playing the role, and meets budget and schedule requirements. The skilled costumer is as much an artist as the designer is. The sensitive and knowledgeable interpretation of a sketch requires an esthetic understanding of clothing, fabric, the human form, and theatrical values. A practical understanding of pattern making, cutting, construction techniques, and historical period is also required.

Translating the sketch into the finished costume is a critical aspect of the designer's work. Close collaboration between the designer and the costumer is required. Building a costume is a constant process of making choices. Many of these decisions can be made on the basis of the designer's or costumer's experience with other garments. Other choices depend on the requirements of the current production or the designer's taste. The designer must be available to make decisions and answer questions during the entire construction process. The wise designer will appreciate the skill and experience the costumer brings to the project and encourage the costumer's creative input. The designer should attempt to make the development of the costumes an exciting and creative process for everyone involved.

In a large costume shop the shop manager will assign or distribute the various costumes among the staff. The designer and/or shop manager will then discuss with each costumer (pattern maker, draper, cutter, or tailor) the garments for which each is responsible, covering the specifics of garment cut (darts or princess seams? gores or half-circle?), fabrics, trims, and closures (front or back? zippers or lacing? velcro?). The designer will need to explain any unusual aspects of stage business to be done in the costume and any special requirements of the director or actor.

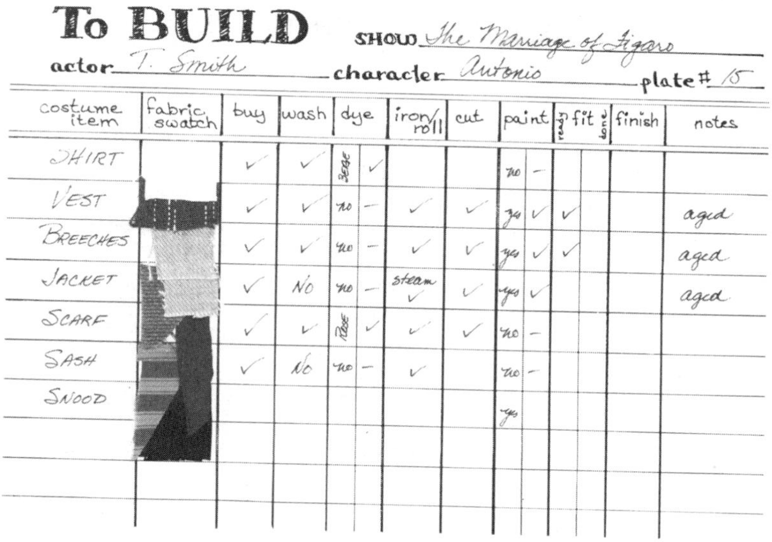

To BUILD

SHOW _The Marriage of Figaro_

actor _T. Smith_ character _Antonio_ plate # _15_

costume item	fabric swatch	buy	wash	dye	iron/roll	cut	paint	fit	finish	notes
SHIRT		✓	✓	no ✓			no —			
VEST		✓	✓	no —	✓	✓	yes ✓	✓		aged
BREECHES		✓	✓	no —	✓	✓	yes ✓	✓		aged
JACKET		✓	No	no —	steam ✓	✓	yes ✓			aged
SCARF		✓	✓	no ✓	✓	✓	no —			
SASH		✓	No	no —	✓		no —			
SNOOD							yes			

FIGURE 8.12

The designer should provide any pertinent technical information or research material that would be helpful to the costumer. In Color plate 14, a sketch by Robert Edmond Jones for _Central City Nights_, the designer has included a photo of the costume on which he based his design. (See also Figure 1.8.)

For large constructed shows, keeping track of all the different stages of the work can be very difficult. Figure 8.12 shows a sample To Build Chart. All costume items to be built and each process or step are listed on the chart. Since many different crew members may be working on the different steps, checking off the various processes as they are done helps the shop manager, costumer, and designer keep track of the progress of each garment piece.

As the work progresses, the designer should be available to approve each stage of the costume's development.

Interpreting the Sketch

How to begin? The designer and/or costumer must first analyze the sketch in terms of the _shapes_ produced by the separate parts. Visualizing the costume without the trim should reveal its basic structure. Once the units are isolated, to what shapes do they relate? What type of pattern or garment cut would best reproduce the desired shapes? Decisions can then be made about the most efficient and appropriate method of patterning each unit. Box 8.F is a De-

**Box 8.F   Designer/Costumer Checklist VII:
Interpreting a Sketch**

1. What are the basic shapes of the garment?
2. Are the different units separate or connected? What patterns are required: Bodice? Skirt? Tunic? Sleeve? Pants?
3. How narrow or full are the different parts? How do the different sections relate to the body: Neckline depth? Sleeve length? Bodice length? Skirt length?
4. How do the different parts of the garment fit: Tight? Easy? Skimming? Loose? Baggy? Voluminous? How are the shape and fit best achieved: Darts? Seams? Pleats? Gores? Insets? Gathers? Tucking?
5. What is the finished length desired: Calf-length? Ankle-length? Floor-length?
6. Are garment sections cut on the straight grain or the bias?
7. What type of pattern or garment cut would create the shapes desired? Is a similar pattern in stock or commercially available? Should this garment be an authentic period cut?
8. What is the best method by which to develop each pattern part: Drafting? Flat-patterning? Draping? Which method is the fastest?
9. Where are the closures? What type is desired? Required?
10. What type of fabric is being used? What inner structure will be required: Inner facings? Flat linings? Wires? Horsehair? Buckram? Other stiffening? What parts require linings?
11. Are any fabric treatments planned: Dyeing? Painting? Aging? At what stage of construction will these treatments be applied? Will the costume leave the shop for treatment?
12. What types of trim are to be used, and how are they to be applied: Mounted on top? Caught in seam? By machine? By hand? Bonded? Glued?
13. Are special undergarments required? Are they in stock? Can they be purchased? Are they to be built? At what stage of the costume development will they be needed?
14. What must the actor do while wearing the costume: Dance? Fence? Fight?
15. Where does this costume stand in order of priority: High priority? Medium priority? Low priority?
16. Is this costume to be built for short use? Prolonged use? Stock?
17. What is the most efficient or economical way to produce this costume without sacrificing the style and quality? Do the cost and level of priority justify the approach? Can any part be purchased or made to order more quickly or at a more reasonable cost than in-shop construction?

signer Checklist for interpreting a sketch for patterning and construction.

Calculations for yardage, lists of materials, and decisions about cutting, stitching, and trim are easily forgotten. Most costumers keep a notebook in which the decisions and information about the garments can be kept. The notebook is a valuable reference when the designer is not available.

Figure 8.13a shows a sketch for Nora's tarantella dress from *A Doll's House*. What must be done in this costume? How must it move? What undergarments are required to hold the shape? Although Nora does not actually dance in this dress, it must appear that she could. A small bustle and a full-bosom corset are needed to suggest the period. How is the dress cut? Of what shapes is it composed? The bodice is princess style and dips to a low U in the front. The neck is low but not revealing. The skirt is assembled of straight panels. The lace trim at the neck appears to be straight and gathered. The skirt ruffle is a straight piece of even width but cut on the bias (see the diagonal stripes). Figure 8.13b shows a more complete analysis and notations on construction decisions for this costume.

Developing Costume Patterns

There are times when the designer is expected to produce a pattern, cut, and sew the costume. To prepare for this possibility, the prospective designer will want to collect useful patterns and study pattern-making techniques.

There are essentially five sources of costume patterns: (1) new or old commercial patterns, (2) enlargements of scale drawings in costume books, (3) drafting patterns from measurements, (4) flat-patterning from slopers, and (5) draping. The choice of pattern source depends on which option is available, the designer's or costumer's training or skill, the equipment and space available, time, the demands of authenticity, and personal preference.

Commercial Patterns

Only a limited number of contemporary commercial patterns are useful for period shows. The majority of commercial patterns for masquerade or costume dress are oversimplified and overinfluenced by contemporary fashion. "Fancy dress" patterns frequently have darts for period styles that had no darts, and they are designed to be worn over currently fashionable underwear. There is rarely adequate fabric in the skirts of "period" styles. Men's costume patterns are cut along modern lines and have simplified patterning and construction. These patterns are rarely appropriate for stage costumes. Of

FIGURE 8.13A Nora, *A Doll's House.* Designed by the author for Brooklyn College.

course, commercial patterns for modern dress costumes might be more useful.

If the designer is careful to analyze shapes, silhouette, and fit, however, some useful basic patterns can be found in the commercial pattern books. Adjustments must be made for period fit and style. Adaptable patterns include pajama patterns, basic fitted bodices and skirts, gored skirts, princess-style dresses, and wedding dress patterns (often loosely based on period garments).

Some authentic patterns for peasant and period dress are available through small specialty shops and mail order sources. These patterns may include transfer designs for embroidery and other special decoration. (See Periodicals and Newsletters in the Bibliography.)

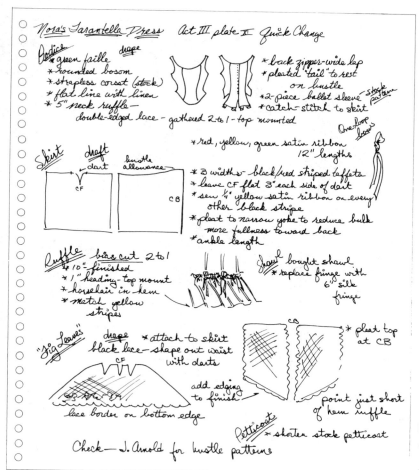

FIGURE **8.13B** Costumer's Notes. Analysis of the costume shapes help determine the type of pattern to be developed.

Authentic period patterns can sometimes be purchased in thrift shops, flea markets, and antique stores. Although these patterns are usually too fragile to use, they can be copied onto heavier paper or muslin.

The advantages of using commerical patterns are (1) they save time, (2) they usually require less knowledge and skill, (3) the cost may be less than the cost of the labor needed to develop a pattern, and (4) they may be available in a large range of sizes. The disadvantages are (1) most are seriously lacking in period feeling and detail, (2) a limited number of appropriate styles are available, (3) they must be located and purchased, and (4) they have contemporary fit and modern consciousness.

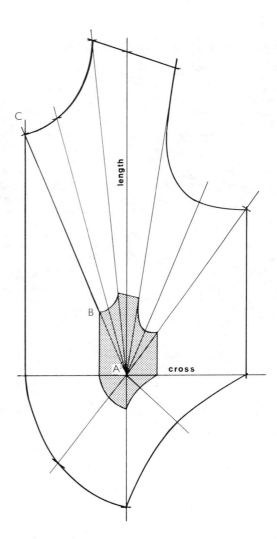

FIGURE **8.14** Enlarging Scale Patterns. After the pattern is copied from the source, lines are extended from one chosen point (a) through all pertinent points of the pattern. The length of the lines depends on the scale of the pattern: for 1/8-inch scale the distance from point (a) to (b) is multiplied by 8 to find point (c). When all lines are extended, the new points are connected for the enlarged pattern.

Reduced Scale Patterns

Many of the books listed in the Bibliography show period patterns in reduced scale. Ladies' magazines of the nineteenth and twentieth centuries often included patterns for ladies' clothes. These can be enlarged to full scale by using the technique illustrated in Figure 8.14. See Box 8.G.

The scale of the published drawing varies depending on the source and must be determined first. The scale should be indicated on the pattern source. The patternmaker must remember that the pattern is not necessarily represented in the size required for the

Box 8.G   Enlarging Scale Patterns

1. Trace the pattern carefully from the source, using tracing paper. Transfer the copy to pattern paper, using carbon paper.
2. Establish a lengthwise line and a crosswise line intersecting at right angles ([a] in Figure 8.14) to each other and relating to the pattern at important points (waist, bottom edge, center front or back).
3. Draw lines from intersection (a) to each point of the pattern that represents a corner or the depth of a curve.
4. Measure the distance from intersection point (a) to the outline of the pattern on each line and multiply that measurement by the scale ratio. The scale is indicated in the pattern diagram source. (For example, if the diagram is marked 1/16 inch scale, each 1/16 inch on the diagram represents 1 inch on the finished pattern, and the scale ratio is 16 to 1, 1/8 inch scale = 8 to 1, 1/4 inch scale = 4 to 1. If scale ratio is 4 to 1, a 1-inch line on the traced pattern will be 4 × 1 inch, or 4 inches on the enlarged pattern.)
5. Measure along the line from intersection (a) the calculated distance, and cross-mark.
6. Using a ruler and French curve, connect the cross marks to produce the pattern in the enlarged size.

costume. In some examples a standard size is printed; in others, the pattern is taken from an authentic garment which was sized for a specific person. After scaling up to full size, the costumer will need to adjust the pattern to fit the actor's measurements and then test it in muslin.

The advantages of using patterns from these diagrams are (1) if they are based on authentic garments, they will represent very accurate period looks, and (2) more variety is available than in commercial patterns. The disadvantages are (1) diagrams in some books do not adequately credit the source of the pattern, (2) some patterns do not fit well and must be extensively reworked, (3) the scale of some patterns is unclear, (4) some diagrams look authentic but are based on reinterpretations of period dress, and (5) authentic patterns may require adjustments to account for differences in modern body development. (The contemporary human form is broader in the shoulders and longer in the arms and legs than previous generations. Women of previous generations began wearing corsets as children, altering the development of the bone structure in the torso.)

Drafting from Measurements

Drafting is a method of creating patterns from measurements using one of the systems developed for this technique. The costumer follows a series of instructions using the measurements of the actor or the standard size desired and creates the pattern shape on paper. The pattern is then cut out of muslin and checked for fit and hang. Many simple garments and garment pieces can be patterned in this way. There are systems for men's tailored patterns, and many women's styles can also be developed by this approach. Figure 8.15 and Box 8.H illustrate a sample project for a drafted pattern.

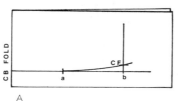

A

FIGURE 8.15   Drafting. The project is a simple drafted collar developed from measurements.

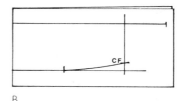

B

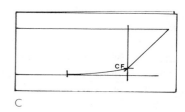

C

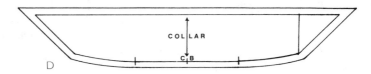

D

The advantages of this method are (1) little special equipment is needed, (2) patterns can be developed to size, and (3) patterns can be crisp, clean, and accurate. The disadvantages of this method are (1) a set of instructions for the pattern project must be available, (2) extensive skill and training are required for complex garments, (3) visualizing the three-dimensional garment on flat paper can be very difficult, and (4) in the hands of a novice, garments made from drafted patterns may look stiff and fail to relate properly to the body.

Box 8.H   Drafted Convertible Shirt Collar

1. Measurements required: (a) neckline from center back (CB) to shoulder. (b) neckline from center back to center front (CF). (See Figure 8.15.)
2. Cut a rectangle of paper 2 × (b) + 6 inches by 2 × desired width of collar.
3. Fold paper as illustrated in (A). Label the fold, "CB fold."
4. Draw a base line the length of the paper and perpendicular to the CB fold.
5. Measure off the distance (a) and cross-mark. This mark becomes the shoulder notch.
6. Measure off measurement (b) and cross-mark. Draw a line perpendicular to the base line at this mark.
7. Measure ½ inch up from the base line on this perpendicular line. Label "CF."
8. Use a metal curve to connect the shoulder notch and CF mark. Measure from CB along the base line and following the curve the distance (b) and adjust the distance if required.
9. Measure along the perpendicular line from the CF mark the desired width of the collar (B). Mark.
10. Draw a line through this mark, perpendicular to the CB fold. This line represents the outside edge of the collar. Extend the line to the desired length of the point.
11. Connect the CF mark to the collar edge to form point (C).
12. With layers of paper pinned together, trace lines and notches to the second layer and add seam allowances.
13. Trim along the seam allowance lines and unfold (D).
14. Establish the CB notch and grain line on the CB fold. (Collars may also be cut on the bias.)
15. Cut the collar out of muslin and test the pattern on the garment.

Flat-Patterning with Slopers

The *flat patterning* technique uses *slopers* to develop a variety of more complicated patterns. Slopers are basic pattern shapes (bodice front, bodice back, sleeve, straight skirt front, etc.) which are cut of oaktag or cardboard and have no seam allowances. Slopers can be developed from commercial patterns, drafted from measurements, or copied from draped garments. The designer/costumer

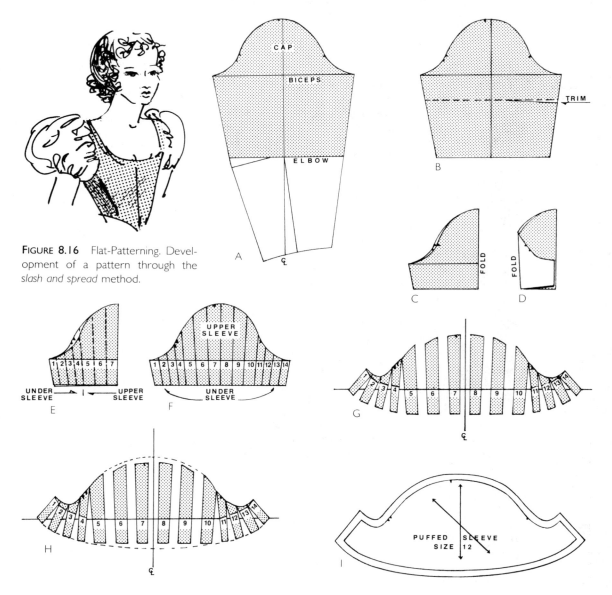

FIGURE 8.16 Flat-Patterning. Development of a pattern through the *slash and spread* method.

will find that a set of basic *slopers* in small, medium, and large sizes is very useful.

The two basic techniques for manipulating slopers are *slash and spread* and *pivot*. Figures 8.16 and 8.17 illustrate the two techniques applied to the development of a sleeve pattern (see Boxes 8.I and 8.J).

Box 8.I   Flat-Patterning Puffed Sleeve by Slash and Spread Method

1. Copy the sleeve sloper from cap to elbow line including biceps line, center line (CL), and notches (A). (See Figure 8.16.)
2. Trim the sloper to the desired length of sleeve (B).
3. Fold on the center line (C). Match the outside edges to the center fold (D), dividing the sleeve into under and upper sections.
4. Divide the folded undersleeve into four sections and the upper sleeve into three sections (E). Unfold the sleeve and number each section *before* cutting them apart (F). Cut.
5. On pattern paper, draw lengthwise and crosswise grain lines intersecting at right angles (G).
6. Matching the biceps line on each pattern piece to the cross grain line on the pattern paper, arrange the upper sleeve sections in numerical order with half of the pieces on each side of the center line. The spaces between the pieces should be equal. (The size of the spaces depends on the size of sleeve desired and the weight of the fabric to be used.)
7. Arrange the undersleeve sections (1–4 and 11–16) on each side of the upper sleeve sections so that the tops (sleeve cap edge) are touching and the bottoms are spread about one-half the space between the upper sleeve sections.
8. Mark the top and bottom edges and underarm seams. Transfer the notches for the shoulder and for front and back of the sleeve cap. Remove the paper pieces.
9. Add ½ inches to the top and bottom at the center line (H).
10. Using a French curve, blend a line along the top and bottom from underarm seam to underarm seam as illustrated.
11. Establish a grain line on CL or at a 45-degree angle for bias (I).
12. Add seam allowances.
13. Cut out the sleeve pattern. Label.
14. Cut a muslin copy to test the pattern.

Books on flat-pattern techniques are also listed in the Bibliography. After learning the basic methods of sloper manipulation, the pattern maker learns to adapt the techniques to the requirement of a specific costume.

The advantages of flat-patterning are (1) precise measurements can be made of parts being manipulated, (2) patterns can be very accurate, (3) it is more economical to use paper than muslin for the early stages of pattern development, and (4) the work can be put

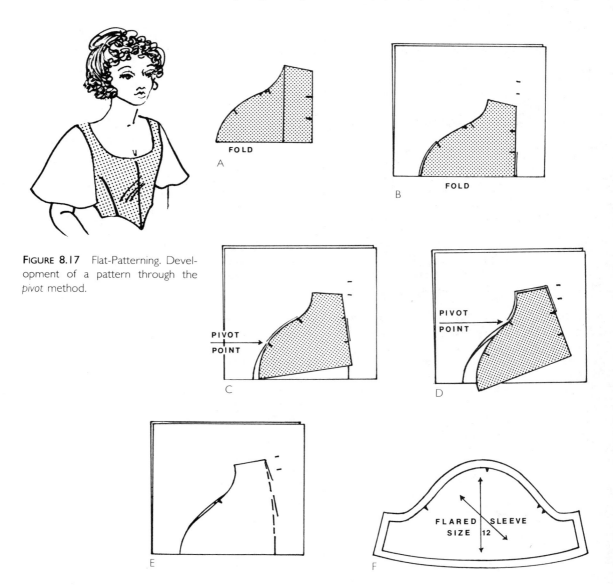

FIGURE 8.17 Flat-Patterning. Development of a pattern through the *pivot* method.

away or transported in an unfinished state with little risk. The dis-advantages are (1) visualizing the three-dimensional garment on flat paper can be difficult, (2) the finished garment has a tendency to look stiff and awkward if it is not properly refined in muslin, (3) it requires skill and training, and (4) instructions are needed for deve-loping many patterns.

Some costumers refer to all forms of pattern making done on paper as "drafting."

Box 8.J   Flat-Patterning Flared Sleeve by the Pivot Method

1. Copy the sleeve sloper and adjust the copy to desired length. (See Figure 8.17.)
2. Fold along the center line and place sleeve front down (A).
3. Divide the cap into three equal sections and mark.
4. Divide the bottom edge into three equal sections and mark.
5. Cut the pattern paper 6 inches longer and 10 inches wider than the sleeve sloper. Fold in half as illustrated. (B).
6. Matching the folded edge of the sloper copy and the folded edge of the paper.
7. Divide the distance between the edge of the sleeve and the desired width of the finished sleeve into two equal parts and mark it on pattern paper.
8. Copy the cap to the first cap mark and the bottom edge to the first bottom mark.
9. Holding the sloper at the first pivot point, pivot the sleeve to the first width mark (C). Copy the second section of the cap to the second cap mark, and the second section of the bottom to the second bottom mark. Fold back the top layer of the sloper copy to draw in the front cap line.
10. Holding the sloper copy at the second pivot point, pivot the sleeve to the second width mark (D). Copy the third section of cap, the third section of the bottom, and the underarm seam. Fold back the top layer of the sloper copy to draw in the front cap line. Copy the notches.
11. Using a French curve or metal curve, draw in the bottom line and true (correct) the cap shape, eliminating small dips (E).
12. Pin the paper together. Trace the bottom line through to the other side of the folded paper.
13. Unfold the paper and correct the front cap line (F). Add seam allowances and indicate the desired grain line. Cut out the pattern.
14. Cut a muslin copy to test the pattern.

Draping

Draping is a method of pattern making in which fabric (usually un-bleached muslin) is smoothed over and pinned to a dressmaker's form in the shape of the desired style. The resulting seams are marked and *trued* (corrected) to produce a pattern. The muslin pieces may then be used for cutting the costume or may be traced to paper for a more stable pattern. Once on paper, they can be manipulated as a drafted pattern would be. Adjustments to the specific measurements of the actor may be made in the muslin or in the paper pattern. The draping technique is used frequently for women's costumes because this approach allows for easier visualization of the garment. Figure 8.18 and Box 8.K show the bodice pattern for Nora's tarantella dress being developed by the draping technique. Note that the bustle has been added and the dress form is padded for period shape.

The advantages of draping a pattern are (1) it is easier for the pattern maker and the designer to visualize the garment, (2) it is possible to experiment with the hang and fall of the fabric, (3) subtle refinements can be built into the pattern as it is being developed, because muslin behaves like fabric whereas paper behaves like paper. The disadvantages of draping are (1) more expensive equipment is required (dress forms), (2) muslin is easily distorted in manipulation and the resulting pattern may be distorted, (3) the piece cannot be removed and transported without risking distortion, (4) many students find the techniques difficult to learn.

The Fitting Muslin

The first fitting for constructed costumes is usually done with a *fitting muslin*. This is a full garment of muslin which is tried on and adjusted to the actor's body. It enables the costumer to check the pattern and adjust the fit, style, and proportion. This garment should be sewn together with large machine stitches for easy adjustment. If there are few alterations or changes in the fitting muslin, it can sometimes be used as a lining for the finished garment. If the pattern has been adjusted to the actor's measurements in the paper stage, the lining or backing fabric may be used for the first fitting.

All fittings should be made over appropriate undergarments. The actor should provide modern underwear, but period or special undergarments must be provided by the designer or costume shop. If body padding is to be used, it must be constructed and fitted first in order to properly fit costumes to be worn over it. Hoops, bustles, paniers, and other special shapers must be constructed before the outer garments can be fitted. Rehearsal items and stock pieces may be fitted either at this time or later, depending on the schedule.

The designer should be present at all fittings to make decisions on such questions as: How short should the skirt be? (Skirts tend to look shorter than they are if the audience is sitting below stage level.) Is it full enough? How low should the neck be? Where should the closure be?

The sketch should always be available for reference. The designer should show the sketch to the actor in order to help the actor visualize the finished costume. The actor should demonstrate any action or stage business that may affect the fit or use of the costumes. Notes should be made on required adjustments (extra ease, lower neckline, reinforcements, double stitching, gussets, stretch fabric, elastic sections).

Careful notes should be made concerning changes in the pattern, and the muslin should be marked clearly. Safety pins should be used where possible for fitting and marking so that the corrections will not be lost. Depending on the complexity of the costume, 30 to 45 minutes should be allowed for a muslin fitting *per costume*. As many of one actor's costumes should be ready for fittings as possible to save the actor trips to the shop and to save shop time for setting up accessories and undergarments.

Fittings should be conducted in a courteous and businesslike manner, efficiently but without rushing. Major problems should not be discussed in front of the actor but rather discussed with the costumer privately. After solutions are found, the fitting should be rescheduled.

Cutting and Stitching

The costumer should make careful, clear corrections of the pattern before cutting the costume, to prevent mistakes in the stitching of the garment. The cutting must be done with great care because mistakes in cutting may be impossible to correct. The pattern maker or cutter lays out the fabric and places the pattern according to the planned use of the fabric. Patterns, stripes, and plaids must be matched or placed strategically on the garment. Costumes made of one-way prints or napped fabrics must be cut with the top of all pattern pieces going in the same direction.

In addition to the main garment pieces, linings, interfacings, ruffles, facings, cording, pockets, and other extra pieces must be planned and cut. Special padding, boning, closures, or quick-change rigging must be worked out before the garment is stitched. All pieces of a costume should be bundled together to prevent lost parts, and the bundle should be labeled with the actor's name and the costume plate number or the act and scene number.

Stitchers then sew the major pieces of the garment together to

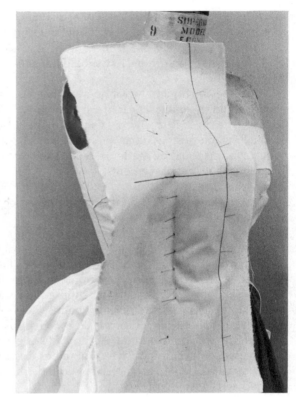

Box 8.K Draping a Bodice

1. The dress form is padded for period shape and dressed with a bustle pad and a petticoat. The new neckline is marked with seam tape. Note the seam lines marked on the padding. (See Figure 8.18.)
2. Muslin is pinned to the dress form along the neck, center front, and princess seams. The cross grain line is centered on the apex.
3. The side front was developed and is pinned to the center front panel. Large seam allowances have been left to permit adjustments.
4. The bodice pattern has been pinned together to check the fit of the seams and the shape of the bodice.
5. The muslin pieces have been pressed and are being transferred to paper.

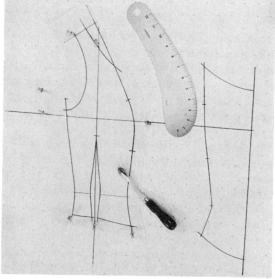

FIGURE 8.18 Draping. The bodice for the costume in Figure 8.13 being draped. Photos by Melissa A. Wentworth.

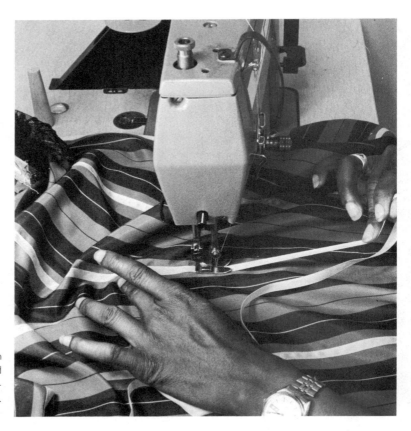

FIGURE 8.19 Stitching. Here ¼-inch satin ribbon is being applied to striped taffeta to add definition to a too-subtle stripe. Photo by Melissa A. Wentworth.

prepare it for the second fitting. This may be done with a large stitch so that it can be easily ripped out for changes.

Trim may be applied by machine or by hand, depending on the skill of the stitcher, the stress on the costume, the effect desired, and the costume's reuse potential for stock. In Figure 8.19 yellow satin ribbon is being applied by machine to enhance the striped taffeta for Nora's skirt.

The basic sewing skills required for sewing costumes are the same as for home sewing, and several good sewing books are available. Special techniques for costumes can be found in *The Costumer's Handbook* by Ingham and Covey, *Designing and Making Stage Costumes* by Motley, and other books listed in the Bibliography (see sections there on Developing the Costume and Getting the Show Together).

The designer should expect, even insist upon, quality construction. Seams should be carefully matched, stitched with firm stitches (8 to 10 stitches to the inch), and pressed smooth and pucker-free. A few extra minutes of care can make a big difference in the finished garment. On the other hand, responsible judgments regarding the amount of time to spend on a particular garment must be made. Is the garment for stock? A long run? A few days? Does it have high stress requirements? Is it on stage for the whole play or only a few moments? Can it be reused? The designer and costumer can easily get sidetracked into construction details and lose sight of the onstage product and the overall production schedule.

Second and Final Fittings

Ideally, all the pieces of the costume should be ready for the second fitting. The undergarments must be complete so the garment can be correctly fitted. The shoes must be available so the hem can be marked. The wig must be available so the hat can be fitted. (Trim may not be important if it is to be applied to the finished garment instead of stitched on before the garment is constructed.) All pieces of the costume should be labeled with the actor's name. In Figure 8.20 a second fitting is in progress. This jacket is being fitted in the

FIGURE 8.20 Fittings. Photo by Hilary Sherred.

actual velvet, which has been hand-basted together so the garment fit can be checked before permanent stitching is done.

If the costume is very complicated, both a second fitting and a final fitting may be required. In whichever is the final fitting, the actor should move around in and get the feel of the costume. The actor should attempt any business he or she feels might be affected by the costume. The designer should suggest or demonstrate ways to use the costume to best advantage.

All aspects of the costume should be checked. Depending on the complexity of the costume, the second fitting may take 45 minutes to an hour or more. Fittings should never be set for more than one actor at a time or scheduled too close together. Also allow time at the end of the fitting to label, mark, and write detailed notes about the work still to be done. Poor notes on a fitting cause confusion about remaining work, result in poor quality finishing, or create the necessity for an extra fitting. Box 8.L is a Designer Checklist for fittings.

Finishing

The term *finishing* refers to the final touches required to complete the costume. Mostly hand work, finishing includes hems, facings, hooks and eyes, snaps, buttons, and trim. The quality of the finishing often makes the difference between a well-made costume and one that lacks finesse and does not hold up well.

Assembling Accessories

In addition to garment construction, a designer needs to know something about millinery, hair styling, and costume crafts. In educational and repertory theaters the costume shop may handle all of these areas. For professional productions different specialists work in each area.

Hats, wigs, shoes, and jewelry can be major time and money consumers. A great deal of shopping time may be required to find appropriate shoes of the correct size, affordable hats, jewelry of the right type, suitable wigs, and hair accessories.

As much time may be required to construct a hat as is needed for a garment. Hat making requires some special supplies and equipment which may not be available in a small shop. A milliner may need to be hired for a show with many important hats. Men's hats and women's hat shapes of the correct type can sometimes be purchased from costume specialty houses and trimmed in the costume shop.

Hats that are not removed on stage should be attached secure-

Box 8.L   Designer Checklist VIII: Fittings

1. Are the chosen undergarments appropriate and well fitted?
2. Does the garment fit neatly across the bust/chest area? Are the darts or princess seams in the correct position? Is there enough room across the back? The front? Do the center front and center back line up properly with the body?
3. Is the waist at the correct place for the period or desired style? Is it snug, yet reasonably comfortable?
4. Are the armholes correctly shaped and low enough? Does the sleeve allow for enough movement to meet the needs of the blocking? How long should the sleeve be?
5. Does the neck fit smoothly across the back, comfortably in the front? Is it the right shape and depth? How much chest/bust is to be shown?
6. Does the skirt hang properly? Is the shape correct? Are the petticoats sufficient to maintain the proper shape? What is the desired length? Should it be even or longer in the back?
7. Are the closures appropriate? Do they work properly? How will the quick change work?
8. Do the accessories work well with the costume?
9. Can the actor perform the action required in the costume? Does the action create undue stress on the costume? Does the action distort the look of the costume in undesirable ways? Is the action appropriate to the character and period? Can the action be performed in other more appropriate ways?
10. What guidance can be given the actor for effective use of the costume?
11. Will another fitting be necessary?

ly to hair or wig. Straps of one-quarter inch elastic for under the chin or the back of the head should be added where needed. (Straps should be dyed to match skin tone or hair color.) Small combs can be sewn into the hat to help secure it. Horsehair loops through which hairpins can be pinned are also helpful. Hat pins can be used on hats that must be removed, provided there is sufficient hair through which to pin.

Some modification of stock shoes (change of color, addition of decoration or gaiters) is possible. The correct style of toe and heel should be sought for the period. The type of shoe required by the character for walk and posture should be found. However, fit is crucial. The actor cannot be expected to hobble around in ill-fitting shoes, no matter how period-perfect they are.

Shoes for dancers should usually be constructed specifically for dancing and purchased through a dance supply house. The addition of heel braces and dance rubber to the heel and/or sole may be required for safety and comfort. Nondancers may also need these modifications if they run or fight on stage or if the stage floor is *raked* (built on a sharp slant).

Wigs can be purchased or rented. Special costume wigs are available through costume supply houses, or some commercial styles can be adapted for period use. A sketch should be provided for the wig rental house, and the wig will be dressed accordingly. For shows using many wigs, a hairdresser should be available for wig maintenance and to assist actors with attaching wigs.

Craft items like masks, armor, and jewelry may require long periods of time for sculpting, mold making, and casting. Large work areas away from garment construction are needed for craft work, which may involve paint, glue, chemical solvents, and other messy materials. Some items can be built on basic shapes purchased from theatrical supply houses, but unusual masks, armor, or jewelry will need to be built. Knowledge of many materials and craft techniques is necessary for the designer to choose the one that will produce the most appropriate effect. Research into new materials and experiments with new techniques are part of the designer experience. Theater publications offer articles on solutions found for specific craft problems, as costumers and designers share discoveries and experiences with new and old materials.

Whatever technique is chosen, accessories should be begun early in the production schedule to ensure their on-time completion. An assistant or crew person assigned specifically to accessory problems helps to keep the work moving.

PREPARING FOR PERFORMANCE

. . . Go, and make thee ready straight, In all thy best attire, thy choicest jewels, Put them all on, and, with them, thy best looks. . . .

VOLPONE   Ben Jonson

Organizing the Costumes

As the pieces of each costume are assembled and finished, they should be labeled and put together on a rack or in a cabinet, where they will not be mixed up with items still "in work." Small articles like tights, handkerchiefs, and gloves can be kept in a drawstring bag on a hanger with the larger costume pieces. Very small items like jewelry and crushable accessories like fans are safer in a small box inside the bag. Rack markers with the actors' names help the wardrobe crew and the actors to locate the correct costumes easily. Traveling companies need large hampers or wardrobes designed to keep the costumes organized.

Wardrobe Crew

The wardrobe crew is the staff responsible for the orderly maintenance and use of the costumes during the run of the show. Often this crew begins a few days or a week before first dress reheasal to help with the organization and finishing of the costumes. The designer and shop manager should discuss the maintenance and special requirements of the costumes with the wardrobe supervisor. The designer should instruct the wardrobe crew on the proper sequence of costumes in the show and give them photocopies of the final costume plot and costume lists. A discussion of quick-change problems and special costume situations will help the wardrobe crew prepare and set up the costumes for the dress parade and the first dress. The wardrobe supervisor should attend several run-throughs (rehearsals of the entire play) before the first dress rehearsal for a clear understanding of the onstage action.

The designer and the wardrobe crew organize the backstage changing areas and work out the logistics with the stage manager and properties crew. Pre-planning for backstage costume changes saves a great deal of time and minimizes confusion when dress rehearsals begin. The wardrobe supervisor should make specific requests for the kind of racks, tables, lights, mirrors, and screens that are needed. The setup and organization of the dressing rooms is also the responsibility of the wardrobe crew.

Once the show opens, the wardrobe crew is responsible for the repair, cleaning, and pressing of the costumes. The designer and shop manager should instruct the crew on any special costume care required. For long-running shows the wardrobe supervisor should notify the stage manager or producer if replacement costumes are needed.

Dress Parade

Many designers and directors like to schedule a *dress parade*, a time set aside for the director and designer to see each actor on stage in costume and to look carefully at the total effect. The costumes should be seen against the set and under appropriate lighting for an accurate picture of their effect to be evaluated. Characters who play together in certain scenes should be studied together so the combined effect can be assessed. While in complete costume, actors should try stairways and doors to check for problems. If the schedule permits, a walk-through in costume with time to work trick costumes and quick changes will alleviate many problems before first dress rehearsal.

Dress Rehearsals

Dress rehearsals are the time to integrate costumes into the performance. The designer must attend the dress rehearsals to evaluate and assist with adjustments to the costumes. Designer assistance may be needed to work out quick changes and the blocking of special costume effects. The visual balance of the costumes in each scene should be analyzed. Costumes that are too bright may need to be sprayed, dipped, or dyed down. Costumes that fade out or seem too dark may need more colorful trim or accessories. Adjustments may need to be made for any unexpected effects of the lighting. Changes in lighting levels or gel colors may be a faster, better solution than changing the costume. The director, lighting designer, and costume designer should discuss the problems and work out the most expedient and esthetically valid solutions.

The designer may need to work with individual actors to solve movement problems presented by the style or fit of the costume. The goal is to make the actor look and feel at home in the costume and to create the desired visual effect. Period costumes are more confining than modern clothes and alter the posture and movement of the actor. The actor will need time to become accustomed to the feel of such costumes. Practice will be required to handle capes and trains. Some actors will have difficulty with high-heeled boots or shoes.

Costume is part of *performance*. The visual effect of the costumes and the drama of the costumes in motion should be a major contribution to the total effect of the play. Actors should be encouraged to use their costume for dramatic effect. Many inexperienced actors are overwhelmed by and resist using their costumes. The designer should point out how the costume was designed to enhance the actor's portrayal of the character and offer whatever assistance the actor may need to use the costume effectively. If time was allowed at the final fitting for the actor to work with the costume, there should be less difficulty at the first dress rehearsal.

Actors should be asked not to smoke, drink, eat, or leave the theater in their costumes. Costume items furnished by the actor are to be considered property of the theater while being used in a production. They should be kept with the other costume items and cared for by the wardrobe crew. Care should be taken that all costume items are kept safe from damage or theft between perfor-

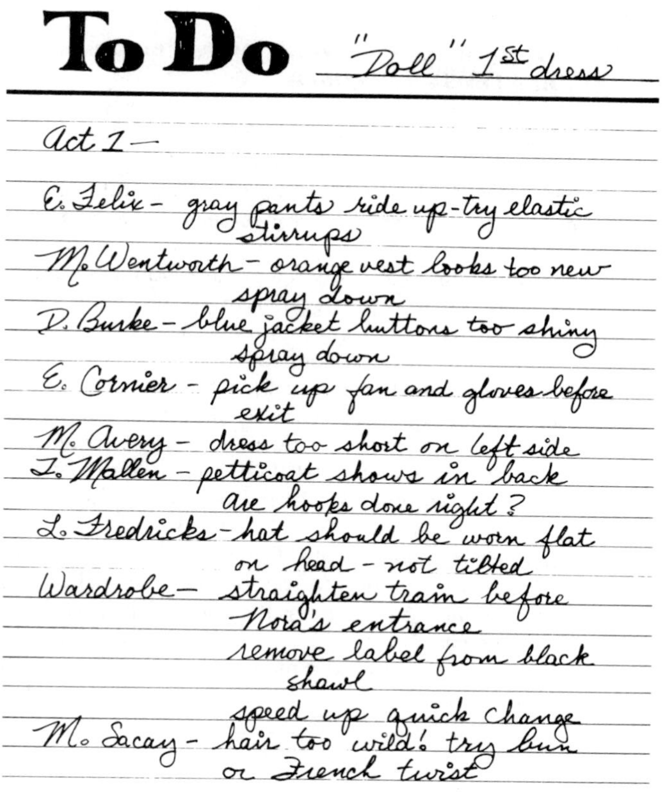

To Do "Doll" 1st dress

Act 1 —

E. Felix — gray pants ride up-try elastic
     stirrups

M. Wentworth — orange vest looks too new
     spray down

D. Burke — blue jacket buttons too shiny
     spray down

E. Cornier — pick up fan and gloves before
     exit

M. Avery — dress too short on left side

I. Mallen — petticoat shows in back
     are hooks done right?

L. Fredricks — hat should be worn flat
     on head — not tilted

Wardrobe — straighten train before
     Nora's entrance
     remove label from black
     shawl
     speed up quick change

M. Sacay — hair too wild: try bun
     or French twist

FIGURE 8.21   Dress Rehearsal Notes.

mances. The wardrobe crew should be given full instructions on the use of back-up garments.

The wardrobe crew and the designer should take clear notes on adjustments, corrections, and misuse of costumes during dress rehearsals. Notes should include the actor's name, specific costume, act and scene, and the specific problem. Figure 8.21 shows some sample notes from a dress rehearsal.

The actor should also be asked to give costume notes to the wardrobe crew in writing whenever possible. In the confusion of the dressing rooms, verbal communications may be forgotten or misunderstood.

Making Adjustments

The dress rehearsal period is a hectic time. Changes are being made each day based on the notes taken at the previous dress rehearsal. The designer must keep the priorities clearly in mind. The first things

---

**Box 8.M   Designer Checklist IX: Dress Parade
and Dress Rehearsals**

1. Is everything organized for orderly distribution to the actors? Is the wardrobe crew well briefed?
2. How does each actor look in his or her costume? Does each costume help the actor project character and presence?
3. Do the costumes look good together? Do the appropriate characters stand out? Are adjustments needed?
4. Are all the costumes in the same scale?
5. Do the costumes look complete?
6. Do all costumes function well for the action?
7. How do the lights affect the costumes? Is any costume "glowing" (reflecting too much light) or vibrating?
8. Are there areas of the set that might catch or snag the costumes? Are there problems with using doorways or stairs?
9. Are quick changes smooth? Can improvements be made?
10. Can actors be assisted to use the costumes better?
11. Are the pants and skirt hems the correct length and even? Do petticoats show?
12. What corrections must be made before the next dress rehearsal?

---

to deal with are fitting corrections and solving problems with items with which the actor needs to work. Trim and visual problems can be solved later. The director's notes to the designer must be given careful consideration. Discussion of the director's priorities and the timetable for dealing with notes should follow each rehearsal.

The designer should supervise revisions or corrections and check that all pieces are in usable condition for the next rehearsal. Box 8.M is a Designer Checklist for dress parades and dress rehearsals.

Opening Night

Brains I have beyond question, with good taste sufficient to pass judgement and give an opinion on everything without need of study, to sit on the stage and play the expert at first nights (occasions I dote on) and give a rousing lead to the audience at all the fine passages that deserve their applause. . . .

THE MISANTHROPE   Molière

FIGURE **8.22** *The Wiz.* There are few experiences to match the excitement of an opening night. Stephanie Mills gives us a sense of that thrill as Dorothy. Designed by Joffrey Holder, photograph © Kenn Duncan.

The excitement of rehearsals and preparations culminate with the performance on opening night (Figure 8.22). The designer must then turn the show over to the wardrobe crew. The running of the show becomes their responsibility when the curtain goes up.

On opening night many designers extend tokens of gratitude to the costume crews and others with whom they have worked on a show. Successful collaboration deserves recognition. This practice helps create good will among all parties but will not erase any serious working problems that may exist between designer and staff.

During long-running shows conscientious designers return periodically to check the overall look of the costumes. If the show has begun to look shabby, duplicates of the costumes may be needed. Sometimes the actors become creative with their costumes and alter the way they are worn. The stage manager and wardrobe supervisor should be consulted and corrections made. Diplomatic negotiations may be necessary.

Strike

In some situations the designer is expected to help with the *strike* (closing and putting away) of the show. In repertory, stock, or educational theater the designer may be responsible for assisting with the final cleaning, storing, return, or disposal of the costumes. Rental costumes should be returned promptly or a late fee may be charged. Delay in striking a show may interfere with the schedule of the next show in the shop.

Avoiding Hysteria

With all the variables involved in assembling the costumes for a production, there are frequent opportunities for hysteria, flaring tempers, and chaos. The primary reasons for confusion and hysteria are:

1. Poor organization of work.
2. Overdesigning of the show resulting from a lack of consideration or understanding of the limitations of the budget, staff, or time.
3. Failure to meet deadlines.
4. Poor communication between costume designer and director, producer, or shop manager.
5. Lack of experience, self-confidence, or decisiveness on the part of the designer or other staff members.

The designer should work to keep the project well organized and the communication open and meaningful. When the designer has a clear vision for the show and has designed the costumes with reasonable consideration of the circumstances of the production, then decisions can be made with relative ease and authority.

PREPARING TO BE A DESIGNER

A vast amount of knowledge and experience must be acquired for one to be a successful costume designer. A prospective designer should study costume history, costume design, theater history, dramatic literature, art theory, art history, social history, drawing, rendering techniques, pattern making, fabric, costume construction, craft techniques, and psychology (to name a few areas). Full expertise in *all* these fields is fortunately not necessary, but a designer should understand and be conversant with all areas and be expert in many.

There is no substitute for actually working in the theater. Prospective designers should have experience on wardrobe and construction crews and as assistant designers before attempting to design. Designing for educational productions, community theaters, charity, and summer theater productions may provide experiences for the beginner.

Portfolio and Resume

The designer must collect material for a portfolio and resume. Professional designers present their sketches and photos of their work to producers and directors to show what they can do. Photos should be taken of the designer's costumes, or arrangements should be made to have copies of show photos. Full-length shots of one or two characters are best, because the costumes can be seen to the best advantage. Photos of costumes or accessories built by the designer are also important.

Some designers assemble their work in portfolios that have large acetate sheets to hold the photos and sketches. Others carry the designs loose and present the photos separately. The designer should remember that (1) the producer and director want to see evidence that the designer can carry the project through from sketch to finished costumes, and (2) they are looking to see if the style of work presented is related to the project they have in mind. Therefore, a variety of styles should be represented where possible.

Generally, only the best work should be shown. As a designer becomes more experienced, new and better work should supplant the older pieces. Too much in a portfolio is not good. Include enough to show variety and the range of skill, but not so much so as to become repetitive or boring. A large group of sketches from two or three shows and smaller groups or individual sketches to illustrate other styles should be adequate. All materials should be neatly presented and labeled. "Paper projects" (unproduced work) can be included to indicate skill and talent in styles not represented by actual productions.

Some designers prepare a portfolio with color photo copies of their sketches. Doing this greatly reduces the weight of the portfolio for mailing or carrying to interviews. However, this process is expensive, it is not readily available in all areas, and the colors are not

**RESUME
COSTUME DESIGNER**   EDMOND FELIX   111-60 128th Street
Queens, N.Y. 11420
(212) 967-3955

DESIGN EXPERIENCES

Theatre for the New City (Off Off Broadway)	
Rosetti's Apologetic	1985
The Dispossessed	1984
The Dog That Talked Too Much	1980
Theatre Works USA (National Tours)	
When The Cooky Crumbles	1986
King	1986
Berkshire Choral Institute (Berkshire Music Festival)	
Iolanthe	1987
The Gondoliers	1985
Eastman Opera (University of Rochester)	
La Colisto	1987
The Bartered Bride	1985
The Bronx Opera	
The Ballad of Baby Doe	1986
New York Gilbert and Sullivan Players	
The Yeoman of the Guard	1985
The Gondoliers	1985

Kingsborough Community College - Resident Designer 1983-1985

The Philadelphia Story	*Dracula*
Trojan Women	*I Am a Camera*
Bedroom Farce	*Babes in Arms*
A Flea in Her Ear	*The Imaginary Invalid*
Jacques Brell is Alive and Well and Living in Paris	

St. John's University (1984-1986)

The Scarecrow	*Victoria's House*
Barnum	*Camelot*
You're a Good Man, Charlie Brown	

Hofstra University - Summer Theatre

Peter Pan	1987
My Fair Lady	1984

Brooklyn College

Cabaret	*The Miracle Worker*
The Taming of the Shrew	*A Raisin in the Sun*
The Fifth of July	*Vanities*
The Playboy of the Western World	

EDUCATION

Queens College	BA	American History
Brooklyn College	MFA in progress	Costume Design

FIGURE **8.23** Resume. A designer keeps an updated resume to send to producers and directors when applying for design positions.

perfectly true. Other designers take slides of their sketches and the costumes. A set of slides can be copied and mailed for job consideration at reasonable cost. However, not everyone is prepared to project slides, and viewing them without enlargement does not show the designer's work to advantage.

A resume must accompany the portfolio. Figure 8.23 shows a sample resumé for a professional costume designer. Many designers revise the resumé to put the information most pertinent for the current position in a prominant position. Some designers put the most impressive credit first; others list credits chronologically with the last credit first. Some designers also indicate the director of the productions for which they designed.

The art of the costume designer lies in the ability to create costumes that engage the audience and serve the actor and the production. Beginning with the research and planning the designer does before the sketch, through the supervision and collaboration with the costume construction crew and the adjustments deemed necessary in rehearsals, the designer's ability is challenged at each stage. These enormous challenges make costume design an exciting, stimulating, ever-changing, never-boring, rewarding artistic endeavor.

Appendix I
Historical Research Sources

The following chronological list of suggested research topics for the costume designer includes sources for costume detail and visual style. Though it is by no means exhaustive, a wide variety of references has been included. Note there will be some overlap between periods, with a particular artist appearing more than once (second listing followed by an asterisk).

EGYPTIAN,   4000 B.C.–30 B.C.

Statues
Architecture
Wall Paintings
Mummy Cases

GREEK,   600 B.C.–100 B.C.

Sculpture
Vase Painting
Architecture

ROMAN,   753 B.C.–330 A.D.

Sculpture
Coins
Wall Painting
Architecture
Mosaics

BYZANTINE, 400–1100 A.D.
ROMANESQUE, 900–1200 A.D.

Mosaics
Tapestries
Sculpture
Frescos
Manuscript Illumination
Architecture (churches)

GOTHIC: EARLY GOTHIC, 1200–1350 A.D.
LATE GOTHIC, 1350–1450 A.D.

Sculpture
Manuscript Illumination
Brasses
Paintings
Stained Glass
Tapestries

Artists

Italian

Cimabue   1240–c. 1302
Ducchio   c. 1255–1318
Giotto   c. 1266–1337
Simone Martini   1284–1344
Andrea Orcagna   1308–1368
Pietro Lorenzetti   active 1320–1345
Ambrogio Lorenzetti   active 1319–1347
Francesco Traini   c. 1321–mid 1300s
Fra Angelico   1387–1455
Antonio Pisanello   c. 1395–1455
Paolo Uccello   c. 1396–1475
Massaccio   1401–1428
Fra Filippo Lippi   c. 1406–1469

Flemish

Roger van der Weyden   c. 1400–1464
Dirck Bouts   c. 1415–1475
Jan van Eyck   active 1422–1441

EARLY RENAISSANCE, 1450–1550

Wood Cuts
Manuscript Illuminations
Sculpture
Engravings
Tapestries
Brasses

Artists

Italian

Piero della Francesco   c. 1410/20–1492
Benozzo Gozzoli   1421–1497
Alesso Baldovinetti   1426–1499
Gentile Bellini   1429–1507
Cosimo Tura   c. 1430–1495
Andrea Mantegna   1431–1506
Giovanni Bellini   1431–1516
Andrea Verrochio   1435–1488
Antonio Pollaiuoli   1432–1498
Cosimo Rosselli   1437–1507
Piero Pollaiuoli   1441–1496
Luca Signorelli   c. 1445–1523
Perugino   c. 1445–1523
Sandro Botticelli   1447–1510
Domenico Ghirlandaio   1449–1494
Ercoli Roberti   c. 1450–1496
Leonardo da Vinci   1452–1519
Bernardino Pinturicchio   c. 1454–1513
Filippino Lippi   1457–1504
Lorenzo di Credi   c. 1458–1537
Michelangelo Buonarroti   1475–c. 1564
Giorgione   1476–1510
Raphael   1483–1520
Sebastiano del Piombo   1485–1547
Andrea del Sarto   1486–1531
Titian   1487–c. 1576
Vittore Carpaccio   active 1490–c. 1526
Giovanni Baptista Rosso   1494–1540

Jacopo Pontormo   1494–1556
Paris Bordone   1500–1571
Francesco Parmigianino   1503–1540
Agnolo Bronzino   1503–1572
Francesco Primiticcio   c. 1504–1570
Georgio Vasari   1511–1574

French

Jean Fouquet   c. 1420–1480
Jean Clouet   c. 1485–1540
François Clouet   c. 1510–1572

Flemish/Dutch

Hans Memling   c. 1430–1495
Hieronymus Bosch   1450–1516
Quentin Matsys   c. 1464–1530
Gerard David   d. 1523
Anthonis Mor   c. 1517–1576
Pieter Brueghel   c. 1525–1569
Guillim Stretes   active 1530's to 1550's

German

Matthias Grünewald   c. 1470/80–1528
Albrecht Dürer   1471–1528
Lucas Cranach   1472–1553
Hans Baldung   c. 1484–1545
Barthel Bruyn   c. 1492–1555
Hans Holbein the Younger (worked in England)
     c. 1497–1543
Christoph Amberger   c. 1500–1561

LATE RENAISSANCE (ELIZABETHAN), 1550–1625

Portraits
Authentic Garments
Engravings
Miniatures
Tapestries
Sculpture

Artists

Italian

Francesco Primiticcio*   d. 1570
Paris Bordone*   d. 1571
Agnolo Bronzino*   d. 1572
Georgio Vasari*   d. 1574
Titian*   d. 1576
Jacopo Tintoretto   1518–1594
Giovanni Battista Moroni   1525–1578
Paolo Veronese   1528–1588
Michelangelo Merise de Caravaggio   1573–1610
Guido Reni   1575–1642

English

Federigo Zuccari   c. 1540–1609
Hans Eworth   active c. 1545–1574
Nicholas Hilliard   1547–1619
Marcus Gheeraerts   1561–1636
Inigo Jones   1573–1652
Isaac Oliver   active 1590–1617

Flemish

Pieter Pourbus   1523–1584
Peter Paul Rubens   1577–1640

Spanish

Alonzo Sanches-Coello   c. 1531–1588
El Greco (born Greek)   1548–1614

French

François Clouet*   d. 1572

SEVENTEENTH CENTURY: CAVALIER, 1625–1660 RESTORATION, 1660–1715

Authentic Garments
Engravings
Wood Cuts
Paintings

Artists

Italian

Guido Reni*   d. 1642
Carlo Dolci   1616–1686

Flemish/Dutch

Rubens*   d. 1640
Franz Hals   1580–1666
David Teniers, Elder   1582–1649
David Teniers, Younger   1610–1690
Cornelis de Vos   1584–1651
Nicholaes Elias   c. 1590–1654
Jacob Jordaens   1593–1678
Anthony van Dyck   1599–1641
Adriaen Brouwer   c. 1605–1638
Rembrandt van Rijn   1606–1669
Jan Miensz Molenaer   c. 1609–1668
Adriaen Ostade   1610–1684
Bartholomeus van der Helst   1613–1670
Gerard Terborch   1617–1681
Jan Steen   1626–1679
Gabriel Metsu   1629–1667
Pieter de Hooch   1630–1677
Jan Vermeer   1632–1674

French

Antoine Le Nain   1588–1648
Jacques Callot   c. 1592–1635
Louis Le Nain   1593–1648
Simon Vouet   1590–1649
George de La Tour   1593–1652
Philippe de Champaigne   1602–1674
Abraham Bosse   1602–1676
Mathiew Le Nain   1607–1677
Pierre Mignard   1612–1695
Charles le Brun   1619–1690
Nicolas de Largillière   1656–1746
Hyacinthe Rigaud   1659–1743
Nicholas Lancret   1660–1743
Antoine Coypel   1661–1722
Jean François de Troy   1679–1752

Antoine Watteau   1684–1721
Jean Baptiste van Loo   1684–1745
John Baptiste Joseph Pater   1695–1736

English

Inigo Jones*   d. 1652
Daniel Mytens   c. 1590–c. 1647
Gerard S. van Honthorst   1590–1656
Cornelius Johnson   1593–1661
Wenceslaus Hollar   1607–1677
Sir Peter Lely   1618–1680
Jacob Huysmans   1633–1696
Sir Godfrey Kneller   c. 1646–1723

Spanish

Jusepe de Ribera   1588–1652
Franciso Zurbarán   1598–1664
Diego Velázquez   1599–1660
Bartolome Esteban Murillo   1617–1682

EIGHTEENTH CENTURY:
EARLY GEORGIAN,   1715–1750
LATE GEORGIAN,   1750–1790
DIRECTOIRE AND FIRST EMPIRE (REGENCY),
1790–1815

Antique Garments
Paintings
Fashion Plates (end of century)
Engravings
Book Illustrations

Artists

Italian

Giovanni Battisti Tiepolo   1696–1770
Antonio Canaletto   1697–1768
Pietro Longhi   1702–1785
Francesco Guardi   1712–1793

French

Antoine Watteau*   d. 1721
Antoine Coypel*   d. 1722
John Baptiste Joseph Pater*   d. 1736
Nicholas Lancret*   d. 1743
Hyacinthe Rigaud*   d. 1743
Jean van Loo   d. 1745
Nicholas de Largillière*   d. 1746
Jean Baptiste van Loo*   d. 1745
Jean-Marc Nattier   1685–1766
Louis Toque   1696–1772
Jean Baptiste Simeon Chardin   1699–1779
J. E. Liotard   1702–1789
François Boucher   1703–1770
Quentin La Tour   1704–1788
Carle van Loo   1705–1765
Louis-Michel van Loo   1707–1771
Jean-Baptiste Perroneau   c. 1715–1783
Jean Baptiste Greuze   1725–1805
Francois Hubert Drouais   1727–1775
Jean Honoré Fragonard   1732–1806
Antoine Vestier   1740–1824
Jean Michel Moreau (le jeune)   1741–1814
Jacques-Louis David   1748–1825
Louise Elizabeth Vigée-Lebrun   1755–1842
Paul-Pierre Prud'hon   1758–1823
Louis Boilly   1761–c. 1830
J. B. Isabey   1767–1855
François Gerard   1770–1837
Antoine Jean Gros   1771–1835
Jean-Auguste-Dominique Ingres   1780–1867
Theodore Géricault   1791–1824

Spanish

Francisco de Goya   1746–1828

English

Sir Godfrey Kneller*   d. 1723
Joseph Highmore   1692–1780
William Hogarth   1697–1764
Arthur Devis   c. 1711–1787
Allan Ramsey   1713–1784

Joshua Reynolds   1723–1792
Francis Cotes   1725–1770
Thomas Gainsborough   1727–1788
Johann Zoffany   1733–1810
George Romney   1734–1802
Samuel Cotes   1734–1818
Francis Wheatley   1747–1801
Joseph R. Smith   1752–1812
Robert Dighton   1752–1812
William Beechey   1753–1839
W. R. Bigg   1755–1828
Thomas Rowlandson   1756–1827
Isaac Cruikshank   c. 1756–c. 1811
James Gilray   1757–1815
John Hoppner   1758–1810
Adam Buck (Irish)   1759–1833
John Opie   1761–1807
George Morland   1764–1804
Thomas Lawrence   1769–1830

American

Joseph Blackburn   1700–1765
Robert Feke   1705–1750
Joseph Badger   1708–1765
John Hesslius   1728–1778
John Singleton Copley   1737–1815
Benjamin West   1738–1820
Charles W. Peale   1741–1827
Ralph Earle   1751–1801
Gilbert Stuart   1755–1828
John Trumbull   1756–1843
Edward Savage   1761–1817

Scottish

Henry Raeburn   1756–1823

NINETEENTH CENTURY:
ROMANTIC, 1815–1830
CRINOLINE, 1840–1865
BUSTLE, 1865–1890
THE GAY NINETIES, 1890–1900

Authetic Garments
Engravings
Fashion Plates
Daguerreotypes (1839–1851)
Book Illustrations
Paintings
Illustrated Magazines
Photographs (after 1850)

Artists

French

Antoine Jean Gros*   d. 1835
François Gerard*   d. 1837
Louise Elizabeth Vigée-Lebrun*   d. 1842
J. B. Isabey*   d. 1855
Jean Auguste-Dominique Ingres*   d. 1867
Horace Vernet   1789–1863
Eugène Delacroix   1798–1863
Garvarni   1804–1866
Constantin Guys   1805–1883
Honoré Daumier   1808–1879
Jean-François Millet   1814–1875
Theodore Chassériau   1819–1856
Gustave Courbet   1819–1877
Edouard Manet   1832–1883
Edgar Degas   1834–1917
James Tissot   1836–1902
      (worked in England after 1870)
Claude Monet   1840–1926
Berthe Morisot   1841–1895
Pierre-Auguste Renoir   1841–1919
Henri Rousseau   1844–1910
Paul Gauguin   1848–1903
Jean Béraud   1849–1935
Vincent van Gogh   1853–1890
Georges Seurat   1859–1891

Henri-Marie-Raymond de Toulouse Lautrec   1864–1901
Pierre Bonnard   1867–1947
Joseph Marius Avy   1871–c. 1941

Italian

Pier Celestino Gilardi   1837–1905
Mariano Fortuny y de Mandraso   1871–1949
Amedeo Modigliani   1884–1920

Prussian

Franz Winterhalter   1806–1873
     (Court painter in England and France)

Belgian

Alfred Stevens   1828–1906

Swedish

Carl Larsson   1853–1919

English

W. R. Bigg*   d. 1828
Adam Buck*   d. 1833
Henry Alken   1784–1851
Robert Cruikshank   1789–1856
George Cruikshank   1792–1878
H. K. Browne (Phiz)   1815–1882
John Leech   1817–1864
Ford Madox Brown   1821–1893
Holman Hunt   1827–1910
Dante Gabriel Rossetti   1828–1882
John Millais   1829–1896
Edward Burne-Jones   1833–1898
William Morris   1834–1896
Aubrey Beardsley   1872–1898

American

Samuel Waldo   1783–1861
Thomas Sully   1783–1872
Samuel Morse   1791–1872
William Jewett   1795–1873
Winslow Homer   1836–1910

Thomas Nast   1840–1902
Thomas Eakins   1844–1916
Mary Cassatt   1845–1926
William Merritt Chase   1849–1916
Howard Pyle   1853–1911
James McNeil Whistler   1854–1903
Edwin Austin Abbey   1852–1911
John Singer Sargent   1856–1925
Joseph Pennell   1860–1926
Charles Dana Gibson   1867–1944

TWENTIETH CENTURY

Authentic Garments
Paintings
Photographs
Fashion Magazines
Ladies' Magazines
Book Illustrations
College Yearbooks
Mail Order Catalogs
Men's Magazines
Newspapers
Movies
Photo Journals

Artists

French

Alphonse Mucha   1860–1939
Henri Matisse   1869–1954
Raoul Dufy   1877–1953
Fernand Léger   1881–1955
Erté   1893–

Norwegian

Edvard Munch   1863–1944

Belgian

James Ensor   1860–1949

Russian

> Marc Chagall   1887–1985

Italian

> Giorgio de Chirico   1888–1978

Spanish

> Pablo Picasso   1881–1973
> Joan Miró   1893–1983
> Salvador Dali   1904–1987

German

> Max Ernst   1891–1976

Belgian

> Rene Magritte   1898–1967

Swiss

> Paul Klee   1879–1940

American

> Maxfield Parrish   1870–1966
> Edward Hopper   1882–1967
> Thomas Hart Benton   1889–1975
> Grant Wood   1892–1942
> Norman Rockwell   1894–1980
> Reginald Marsh   1898–1954
> Ben Shahn   1898–1969
> Jackson Pollock   1912–1958
> Andrew Wyeth   1917–
> Frank Frazetta   1928–

Appendix II
Historical Costume Outline

The following historical outline is designed to give the student an overview of the history of occidental dress. The periods and cultures discussed are those most commonly required in Western European and American drama.

Fashion is evolutionary; major changes occur slowly. In every period there are holdover fashions. New features appear before major silhouette changes are made. The older, the conservative, and the poor retain familiar or simpler styles; the young, the elite and wealthy, and the counterculture groups seek new, different, and sometimes shocking fashions. The costume periods represented here fall into generally accepted divisions. The fashion emphasis can be seen to shift from vertical to horizontal, stiff to soft, and "natural" to "contrived" silhouettes.

Wars, powerful figures, exploration, new sources of trade, revolution, political viewpoints, economics, sexual mores, and archaeological discoveries have long been major influences on dress. More recently improved communication, popular music and dance, discovery of new synthetic materials, and space exploration have all had their impact. This outline represents only major trends and influences. Idiosyncratic fashions are not generally addressed. Since the history of costume is not as episodic as such an outline suggests, it is offered only as a springboard for further study and diligent research.

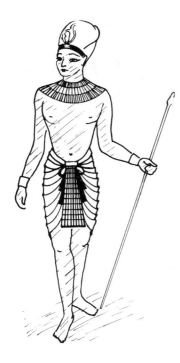

EGYPTIAN 4000 B.C.—30 B.C.

General Characteristics

Egyptian dress was simple in construction and depended on the graceful arrangement of fabric into folds and pleats for its effect. The silhouette for both men and women was essentially vertical and placed emphasis on the head by the use of wigs, makeup, and elaborate collars. Garments were made of linen in fabrics ranging from very fine to coarse.

Dress For Men

Egyptian men wore a simple loincloth (*schenti*), alone or topped by a wrapped skirt or a T-shaped tunic (*kalisiris*). The men's tunic or skirt length might be above the knees, calf length, or ankle length. Some men's skirts were stiffly starched, while others were softly ·draped. The tunic was often of sheer fabric and could be either very close-fitting or full and flowing. The excess fullness in all these garments was concentrated in the front with drapery or pleats held by a girdle or belt. The cloth or leather girdle could have a decorated tab.

A variety of shawls were draped to please the wearer. The *royal haik*, worn by Pharaohs and their queens, was a large, sheer, shawl-type garment which, when wrapped and tied around the figure, gave the impression of a skirt, a tunic with capelike sleeves, and sometimes a cloak.

Hair for men might be long or cut in a round bob or in "shingled" layers. Hair could be dressed in corkscrew curls or braids and was often arranged to expose the ears. The hair was usually parted in the middle and held by a *fillet* of leather, ribbon, or metal. The Egyptians' natural hair was black and abundant, but during some periods of Egyptian history heads were shaved and elaborate wigs were worn. Some wigs were dyed in fantastic colors such as red or blue. The hair or wig was sometimes covered with a cloth of plain or striped fabric. The characteristic shape of the Egyptian head and hair was broad at the temples and somewhat large in relationship to the body.

Very elaborate headdresses or crowns were worn by the pharaoh, his queen, and other members of the royal family. These headdresses incorporated the symbols of the *uraeus* (hooded cobra), the solar disk (symbol of eternity), the vulture, and the royal feather or plumes. Upper Egypt and Lower Egypt each had a characteristic crown. When the two portions of the country were united under the same ruler (around 1450 B.C.), the two crowns were combined into one.

The most recognizable Egyptian accessory is the collar. Made of enameled shapes or colorful beads strung together in rows both horizontally and vertically, the collar was worn by both sexes. Other jewelry included wide bracelets, arm bands and anklets, simple necklaces, rings, and the decorated girdle. The *pectoral*, a semi-official ornament worn by members of court, was a necklace consisting of a large gold and enamel medallion hanging from a chain and resting on the chest below the collar.

Men were generally clean-shaven and used *kohl*, a black makeup, to create a black line around their eyes and extending outward toward the hairline. The *postiche*, the only beard represented in Egyptian art, appears to be false and ceremonial in nature.

Simple sandals consisted of a pointed sole of leather or woven grass with a decorated strap through the toes and across the instep.

Dress for Women

The three basic garments for women were a skirt, a T-shaped tunic, and a shawl. The high-waisted skirt, supported by one or two straps, was wrapped or gathered on a string under the breasts, leaving them exposed. Covering some of these garments was a mesh of beads or cut leather worked in petal or feather motifs. The straps and girdles were often embroidered with geometric or organic designs.

Two versions of the tunic were worn by women: (1) a full tunic or robe of pleated or draped fabric, and (2) a plain, close-fitting version of the T-shape tunic, loose or girded. Shawls were used by women to protect themselves from cool, evening air and hot sun. Royal women might also wear the royal haik. A woman's garments might be draped in a wide variety of ways. Belts of leather, cord, and woven ribbons were used to hold them in place. Garments are represented in most Egyptian art as tight-fitting, but many were actually loose and flowing.

Collars, necklaces, arm bands, and anklets were all worn.

Women also wore wigs, but in most periods they were worn over their own hair. Most styles for women were long, but there are examples of the short, shingled style for women. Women's wigs were dressed with fillets, diadems, cloth coverings, and crowns for queens. A cone-shaped ornament containing scented ointment was sometimes worn on the top of the head.

Women wore kohl eyeliner and eyeshadow and painted their lips, fingertips, and toenails with henna.

GREEK   600 B.C. – 100 B.C.

General Characteristics

Greek dress was the result of the artful draping of rectangular pieces of soft, wool cloth. Fabrics were woven to size for their intended use and were edged with borders. Small, all-over designs were embroidered, woven, worked like tapestry, or painted. Fabrics were dyed in bright colors, and some were pleated.

The silhouette was vertical with a natural relationship between the head and body.

Dress for Men

Dress for Greek men consisted of a *chiton* and a *himation* or a *chlamys*.

There were basically two types of chitons: the *Doric* and the *Ionic*. The older Doric chiton (also called *peplos*) consisted of a large rectangle of cloth (usually wool) measuring the wearer's height plus one foot by twice the width from either fingertip to fingertip or elbow to elbow. The top edge was folded down, and the whole piece was wrapped end to end around the body leaving the right side open. With the back pulled over the front, the garment was pinned together on each shoulder with *fibulae* (decorative pins). The fabric was drawn taut across the back of the neck with a drape formed in the front by allowing extra fabric between the pins. A thin girdle was tied at the waist, and the excess fabric was bloused up over it.

The Ionic chiton was similar to the Doric but did not have an overfold. The Ionic was usually fuller and more often of cotton or linen. The ends of the rectangle might be sewn together. The garment was then pinned at the shoulders and girded in the same manner as the Doric. A distinguishing characteristic of the Ionic chiton was sleeves, created by pinning the top edges of the rectangle together with fibulae.

The himation, a large rectangular cloak, was usually worn like a shawl. First draped over the left arm and shoulder, it was then pulled across the back, under or over the right arm and shoulder, then again thrown over the left arm. The edge of the himation that rested across the back could be drawn up over the head for protection from the weather. Many variations of this arrangement were possible. The himation was often the only garment worn by men.

The chlamys was a smaller rectangle of cloth used as a cape by soldiers, horsemen, travelers, and sometimes women. It too might

be worn by men as their only garment. The chlamys was wrapped around the neck and tied or pinned with a fibula.

Old men wore their garments to the floor, while young men often wore their chitons well above the knees. Occasional examples of the Asiatic tunic are found represented in Greek dress, usually as an undergarment for a chiton.

The Greek men wore rings but did not wear arm bands or anklets. For festivals wreaths of leaves were worn, and kings might wear a gold diadem.

From the fifth century most Greek men wore their hair short and curly, held in place with a fillet. Older men wore short beards and moustaches.

The *petasus*, a large brim hat of felt or straw, was worn by the Greeks when traveling. Other small caps were sometimes used.

Although men frequently went barefoot, sandals or soft, calf-length boots of leather were also worn.

Dress for Women

Greek women wore both the Doric and the Ionic chiton, often together. A wide variety of girding was used by women, creating high-waisted, natural-waisted, and low-waisted effects. The Doric overfold varied in length from just below the bosom to about knee-length. The side of the chiton might be open or stitched, and some were stitched across the shoulders.

Women wore both the himation and the chlamys, draped in a variety of ways. A fold might be brought over the head, or a separate veil might be worn.

Women's hair was dressed in a knot at the back of the head on a line designed to balance the nose. A variety of diadems, fillets, bag caps, and scarves were used around the head to hold the hair. Women also wore the petasus.

Women were often barefoot but also wore sandals similar to those worn by men.

ROMAN   753 B.C.–330 A.D.

General Characteristics

The Romans were influenced by the Greeks in art, culture, and dress. Roman dress tended to have more bulk than Greek dress. This was achieved by layering several garments or by wrapping the voluminous *toga* many times around the body. Roman art and dress expressed a taste for solid forms, bold colors, and strong contrasts.

In Republican and Imperial Rome the primary fabrics were linen and wool. Later, silk was imported from China. Fabrics were used in the natural off-white or were bleached for men's togas and other garments. Women's fabrics were dyed with borders embroidered or woven at the edges. In Imperial Rome increasing use was made of gold embroidery.

Dress for Men

The basic dress for Roman men consisted of a loincloth, tunic (*tunica*), and a large, wrapped *toga* or a cloak. Workmen wore a tunic and loincloth; upper-class men might wear a tunic and toga or a toga alone.

The Roman tunica consisted of two rectangles of cloth sewn together at the top and sides to form a knee-length shirt. The openings for the arms were allowed along the sides of the rectangle, rather than from the top as in the Greek chiton. Most tunics had sleeves to the elbow or just covering the upper shoulder. The long-sleeved tunic (*manicata*) was common by the time of the Empire. The long tunic with long sleeves (*talaris*) was worn by older men and dignitaries. A fuller, T-shaped tunic with wide sleeves (*dalmatica*) was developed about the second century. More than one tunic might be worn at a time. The tunic was often white or off-white wool and could be decorated with bands of embroidery or woven stripes at the neck, sleeves, and hem. The *clavi* (decorative bands about 1½ inches wide) were placed down each side of the tunica, front and back. Until the third century these decorations carried class distinctions.

For centuries the toga was the garment that distinguished Roman citizens from "foreigners." The earliest distinct version was a piece of woolen cloth shaped like a segment of a circle, approximately 16 feet along the straight edge by 6 feet at the widest point. The toga was sometimes trimmed along one edge with a colored band. The wrapping and arranging of the toga was varied and complex. A simple wrapping started with one point at the left foot, the fabric over the left shoulder with the straight edge along the neck and down the back, under or over the right arm, one or more wraps around the body, and up over the left shoulder or draped across the left arm.

The color and decoration of the toga identified its wearer by class and occasion. The *toga pura* or *virilis*, an untrimmed cream-white wool, was the ordinary dress of the Roman citizen. The *toga praetexta* was a toga trimmed with purple bands and reserved for public officials, priests, magistrates, consuls, and others. Candidates for public office donned a bleached white toga called the *toga candida*. For mourning, the *toga pulla*, a dark gray, brown, or black toga, was worn. The triumphal *toga picta* was worn by victorious generals and was the official dress of emperors. It is believed to have been of purple fabric embroidered with gold thread.

When not wearing the toga, the Roman men wore cloaks and capes. The *paenula*, a semicircular cloak with or without a hood, was made of heavy cloth or leather and was used as outerwear by poorer folk, travelers, and sometimes soldiers. Similar to the Greek himation, the *pallium* was associated with philosophers and teachers. The *palludamentum* was a square of fine wool, white, scarlet, or purple, which was worn by Roman officers.

Men's hair was cut short, curled, and dressed forward over the forehead. Most men were clean-shaven, except while in mourning. In about 50 A.D. neatly clipped beards and mustaches came into vogue.

Few hats were worn, but the petasus was used for traveling, and small caps were worn by workers. The back fold of the toga was pulled up over the head for warmth or protection. Wreaths of laurel leaves were given as prizes, to celebrate victories, and, reproduced in gold, to denote divinity. Later emperors, declaring their divinity, claimed the gold wreath as their crown.

The *femoralia*, a kind of short pants, were sometimes worn under the toga; they were adopted from the barbarians by soldiers. Otherwise, the legs were bare. The feet were shod in sandals, soft leather shoes, or calf-high boots.

Men wore fibulae and signet rings that were used as seals. Young boys wore an amulet called the *bulla*.

Dress for Women

Roman women wore a variety of tunics, chitons, and shawls. They tended to wear more layers than the Greek women.

A loincloth and a snug band which supported the breasts were worn as undergarments. The *tunica intima*, a version of the Greek chiton in fine linen, was worn as an undergarment and as a house-dress. The *stola* was sometimes a version of the Ionic chiton, other times a tunica talaris. A variety of girdings were possible. The Roman woman wore her stola instep-length and sometimes added a train by inserting a piece of fabric (*institia*) into the back of the girdle.

Over the stola was worn a shawl, a draped palla, or, for travel, the paenula. An ungirded dalmatica gradually took the place of the palla in the later part of the period. Frequently trimmed with clavi, this garment is prominent among the representations of the early Christian saints.

Greek hair styles were also worn by Roman women, but in the later periods hairdressing became much more elaborate. False hairpieces were used. Roman styles featured height in front achieved by frizzing or curling the hair or wearing a coronet or false hairpiece. Back hair was arranged either high or low on the head in braids, buns, or curls. Women sometimes covered their head with a veil or a fold of the palla.

Sandals and soft leather shoes for women could be brightly colored — red, green, pale yellow, or white.

The Roman woman had bracelets, earrings, rings, fibulae, hairpins, and coronets. Jewelry was worked in gold, inlaid with colors, or set with uncut stones or *cameos* (profiles carved in relief into precious or semiprecious stones).

BYZANTINE 400–1100
ROMANESQUE 900–1200

General Characteristics

Garments in both the Eastern and Western Roman Empires were developments of the garments of Imperial Rome. In Byzantium, dress reflected the oriental influence of the countries to the east and the wealth of the Eastern Empire. Garments in the Western Empire began to incorporate influences from the barbarians. Modesty in dress was required of both men and women: no bare arms or legs for persons of status.

Byzantine fabrics were extraordinarily rich. Linen, wool, cotton, and silk were used. Borders and medallions of embroidery were enriched with gold, gems, and pearls. Western European fabrics were coarse, heavy, and usually unadorned. Wool was woven into stripes, plaids, and simple patterns. Various weights of linen and cotton were also available in solids, plaids, and stripes and were sometimes creped or pleated. Silk was rare and expensive in the countries farthest from the East. Velvet was also available by the end of this period.

Dress for Men

For undergarments men wore a *chemise* (loose-fitting tunic with long sleeves) and *braccae* or *braies* (loose-fitting breeches). Hose cut of woven cloth were gartered or tied to the breeches. A tunic cut like the tunica manicata or talaris was then added. The neckline was high and round with a small slit to admit the head. The neck, wrists, and hem might be trimmed with a band of embroidery or braid. The length varied from slightly below the knee to the floor. A loose-sleeved over-tunic (dalmatica) might be worn. This combination became associated with liturgical dress and royalty.

The Romanesque tunic (*bliaut* or *bliaud*) was a semifitted garment with sleeves; it was laced or sewn up under the arms each time it was worn. The sleeves of the bliaut were either close fitting or wide at the wrist. Tunic lengths varied from above the knee to calf or floor. Slits in the front and back or sides allowed for freedom of movement. Gores were sometimes added from the hip down for extra fullness. A girdle of leather or fabric might be worn at the waist or hip.

A rectangular or semicircular cape or cloak was then added for both indoor and outdoor wear. The *cope* was a half-circular cape that was worn draped over the left shoulder and fastened on the right shoulder with a large brooch. A distinctly Byzantine decoration consisted of a large square or diamond-shaped patch, the *tablion*, positioned to rest on the breast of the wearer. The *chausable* was a large circle or oval with a hole for the head. This garment later became part of church vestments.

The toga was reduced to a stiff and elaborately embroidered band used as a symbol of official office and became part of the church vestments of the Eastern Orthodox church.

Hair for men could be a short (ear length) or a long (chin length) bob or "page boy" style. Men either were clean-shaven or had small pointed beards and thin mustaches.

Byzantine men wore few headcoverings, but Western European men wore a small skullcap, a *coif* (a cloth cap which tied under the chin), or a hood. Fillets (bands of material) were still common, and chaplets or wreaths of flowers were worn for festivals and celebrations. Soft, felt caps and the Greek petasus were worn. The Byzantine emperor's crown was a wide, gold band flaring outward and was set with jewels and strings of hanging pearls. Western European kings wore a variety of crowns, many of them with foliated tops.

Jewelry for men included collars, rings, brooches, elaborate girdles, and belts set with pearls and uncut stones. Byzantine jewels were more elaborate than those of Western Europe and boasted a profusion of pearls.

Men's shoes were slightly pointed and made of cloth or soft leather elaborately decorated.

Dress for Women

Women wore an ankle-length chemise of off-white linen with long sleeves and high neck as an undergarment. A T-shaped tunic was worn over the chemise, usually covering it completely. A shorter tunic (dalmatica) might be worn on top. Byzantine and early Romanesque tunics were still decorated with the Roman clavi. The neck of the upper tunics might be high with a slash opening or a shallow scoop revealing the chemise or undertunic. The edges of sleeves, necklines, and hems were often trimmed with bands of embroidery or woven stripes. The position of the girdle varied from high to natural waist to hipbone level.

The women's bliaut was the formal court costume in Western Europe during the eleventh and twelfth centuries. A gown with a tight-fitting torso, the bliaut was very full in the skirt and had hanging sleeves.

Romanesque women also wore the *cote*, another version of a T-shaped tunic. The cote was fitted in the body, usually had fitted sleeves, and flared from the hip to a very full hem. The neckline sometimes dipped in a low shallow curve. The sleeves and the body were laced up or stitched with each wearing. For ladies of status the length of gaments began to exceed the wearer's height and dribbled luxuriously on the floor. The *surcote* was a loose, sleeveless overgown with large armholes.

A variety of rectangular and semicircular cloaks or mantles were worn over the other garments, both indoors and out. Byzantine women wore a chausable or cope clasped with a brooch on the left shoulder (the empress on the right). Romanesque women wore a chausable or fur-lined mantle that opened in the front.

Byzantine women dressed their hair in the fashion of Imperial Rome. The empress added an elaborate crown set with uncut stones and decorated with hanging pearls. Other women wore turbans or veils. Byzantine hair fashions persisted in Western Europe until about 1000 A.D. Romanesque women parted their hair in the center and dressed it in long braids worn down the back. A fillet, a small crown, or a *chaplet* of flowers (real or of metal) might be worn around the head. Braids were sometimes pinned up and the veil wrapped around or draped over the head and pinned to the braids.

Jewelry for women included rings, belt buckles, brooches, and crowns, made of gold and uncut stones. Byzantine women wore large earrings and elaborate collars of jewels and gold which covered the neckline of the garment underneath. Pearls were particularly abundant in Byzantine jewelry.

Shoes for women were embroidered cloth or soft leather and shaped to the foot. Knee-length stockings, cut of woven cloth, were worn.

EARLY GOTHIC   1200–1350

General Characteristics

A silhouette resembling a narrow-based triangle evolved. Garments were generally long, and finer fabrics made garments more fluid and graceful. Though not revealing bare arms, legs, or chest, clothing began to express a less serious nature through a variety of whimsical touches. *Parti-coloring*, the practice of making garments half one color and half another, was popular. Heraldry developed from the identification worn by the Crusaders.

Wool, linen, and cotton in various weights were used for garments and veils. Silk was more common than in previous periods and was woven into brocades, satins, velvets, and thin tissues for veils. Furs were used to line cloaks for sumptuousness and extra warmth.

Dress for Men

The man's chemise was shortened to midthigh and slit up front and back to facilitate movement. The cote might be knee, calf, ankle, or instep length. The sleeves of the cote were wide at the shoulder and narrow at the wrist. Buttons, a recent innovation, fastened the sleeve from the elbow down. Below the hip belt the cote flared slightly for easy movement.

The sleeveless surcote was added over the cote. The length of the surcote was also varied. Slits in the front and back of the skirt section were needed for horsemen. The surcote might be parti-colored and elaborately decorated around the neck. Many displayed heraldic designs. Later surcotes began to have sleeves or decorative hanging pieces at the armhole.

A new garment (about 1300) was the *cotehardie*. A tailored garment with a fitted body and slightly flared skirt, the cotehardie was often buttoned down the front. The length varied from the upper leg to the floor and it, too, might be parti-colored. The sleeves might end above the elbow with a *tippet* (narrow hanging strip of fabric) or be long and fitted (also buttoned from elbow down). For extra warmth a quilted or furlined *doublet* or *jupe* might be worn between the chemise and the cotehardie.

With the exposure of the legs, hose became better fitting and perhaps were made of knitted cloth. The wool hose were separate (not tights) and tied to a belt at the waist or to the underpants. As tunic skirts grew shorter, underpants grew shorter and hose became longer. Hose were often parti-colored.

Hair was cut jaw-length or a little longer, often with bangs, and set in waves. After 1300, small neatly clipped beards and mustaches appeared.

Jeweled circlets of metal continued in fashion. Felt caps, some with brims, were worn, but the most common headcovering after 1300 was the *coif*. A small, close-fitting cloth bonnet, the coif had strings that tied under the chin. Made of white linen or black silk, the coif was used for centuries, both alone and under other hats.

The *chaperon*, a hood with a shoulder-length cape attached, was a very popular headcovering. Usually seen with the cotehardie, it was also worn with other tunics or robes. Combined with a long, loose-fitting tunic, it became part of the monks' habit. The point on the back of the hood was called the *liripipe* and grew to exaggerated lengths. The hood was often worn off the head, hanging down the back. The cape was frequently trimmed along the bottom edge with *dagging* (scallops or other shapes cut along garment edges).

Other capes and mantles also had an attached hood or shoulder-length cape (*pelerine*). The circular or semicircular cape or mantle continued to be worn both indoors and out.

Brooches were used as clasps on tunics and cloaks and to decorate hats. Elaborate belts were sometimes worn, either set the full length with jewels or adorned with decorative buckles and tips. Rings and ornate jeweled "collars" (c. 1350) might incorporate the insignia of a man's house or overlord.

Shoes of soft leather, slippers, and close-fitting boots were worn by men. Sometimes decorated, they were often black and had a more exaggerated point that those of the previous period.

Dress for Women

The women's cote (also called *kirtle*) was a simple, round neck tunic with a slit down the front. The tight sleeves might now be fastened with buttons from elbow to wrist. Some versions had long hanging sleeves or tippets. The torso of the cote was snuggly fitted to the hip where the skirt began to flare to a wide hem which dribbled several inches on the ground. Worn at the hip, the belt was tied or buckled, allowing a length of belt to hang to the knees. After 1300, cotes began to have lower necklines, scooped out in a wide shallow curve or square (particularly popular in Italy).

The woman's surcote might have large or small armholes and might even have sleeves tied into the openings. About 1300 a fashion for scooping out the garment under the arms, providing a glimpse of the tight-fitting cote underneath, earned it the name "windows of Hell." The surcote provided women with a way of displaying armorial bearings. It might be parti-colored and highly decorated with embroidery. A mantle lined in fur completed the costume of a lady.

The hair of married women was braided, wrapped into a bun, and covered with a veil or headdress. Gold nets were sometimes used to hold the hair. Free-flowing locks were reserved for queens and unmarried girls.

Headdresses might incorporate a chin strap, stiffened band or small hat, a *gorget* (a draped neck covering), and a *wimple* (veil). The wimple and gorget were worn primarily by widows, older women, and the pious recluse. Later this combination was adopted as part of the nuns' habit. Many of the brimmed hats were also worn by women, over either a coif or chaperon.

Jewelry for women consisted of brooches, crowns, hair ornaments, rings, elaborate belts, and decorative collars or necklaces. Few bracelets or earrings date from this period. Shoes were the same as in the Romanesque period.

Men and women hung purses from the belt of the cote (often concealed under the surcote). Other useful objects (shears, knife, keys) might also be hung from a hip belt or a *bandolier* (belt worn diagonally across the chest from one shoulder to the opposite hip). Gloves were more common than previous in periods.

LATE GOTHIC   1350–1450

General Characteristics

Between 1350 and 1400 many earlier styles continued and a feeling of soft, flowing draperies prevailed; after 1400 the fashionable silhouette became stiffer and more restrictive. Many silhouettes suggested a wide-base triangle as hanging sleeves added to the width of the lower torso and tall headdresses extended the silhouette upward. Other styles featured width at the shoulders, foreshadowing the square silhouette of the Renaissance. Whimsical and charming details were added to dress and accessories.

Silk, linen, cotton, and wool were used to produce a wide variety of fabrics, including rich brocades and taffetas, many domestically reproduced from oriental samples. Velvet became increasingly available and popular. Furs were highly prized.

Dress for Men

Over the thigh-length chemise was worn the short garment developed from the cotehardie and known as the *jupe, pourpoint, corset,* or *doublet.* The doublet was tight fitting, buttoned or laced up the front or back, with or without sleeves. A second doublet with long, tight sleeves might be worn over the sleeveless one. While the inner doublet might be waist-length, the outer one had a short skirt. After 1400 this garment might be padded.

After 1400 a full gown or robe (knee, calf, or full length) with moderate sleeves might be worn over the doublet. The fullness in this gown was arranged in pleats and was held into the body with a belt at or below the waist. This garment became associated with more sober and intellectual persons and eventually scholars.

A robe called the *houppelande* was developed near the end of the fourteenth century. The distinct characteristics of this robe include (1) a high standing collar, (2) long, wide hanging sleeves, and (3) a long, full skirt. This garment was used as an outdoor wrap, but it was also worn indoors. The top fitted the body neatly, and the full skirt section was usually held to the body at the waist or slightly above with an ornate belt. The stiffened collar of the houppelande might be a high, closed neckband or a flared collar, open at the front to reveal the neck. Collars soon began to appear on doublets and other garments.

Sleeves of earlier doublets were usually tight fitting, but the fuller sleeves of the houppelande and gown were added to later doublets. These sleeves include a *leg-o'-mutton* (large at the shoulder and tapered from elbow to wrist) and a *bag* sleeve (a full sleeve caught into a wrist-size cuff, usually with a long vertical slit).

Hose were long and tied to the doublet, the waistband of underpants, or the bottom edge of the underpants with *points* (strings tipped in metal). For wearing with shorter garments, hose were made with a crotch like modern tights. Although they were primarily tailored of woven cloth, some may have been knitted. Some hose were made with feet, others with stirrups, still others with soles to be worn without shoes.

The bobbed hair style of the Early Gothic period continued to be worn, but some men cut their hair in a short, close-cropped style. Also common was the *bowl cut* (shaved part-way up the back and cut straight around the head). Beards were more common than in the previous period.

The fillet might still be found in this period, but more and more hats and headdresses are found, many of them elaborate and whimsical. The coif in white linen or black velvet continued to be worn alone or under other hats. The chaperon was still found in its previous form. The liripipe grew to such length that it had to be tucked in the belt, draped over the shoulder, or wrapped around the neck. Toward the end of the fourteenth century the face opening of the chaperon was set on the head or over the crown of a hat, the cape section was arranged to the side, and the liripipe was wrapped around the head to keep the whole concoction on the head. Eventually, this arrangement was imitated in constructed headdresses of separate pieces sewn together for a turban-like appearance. A large variety of brimmed felt hats and soft caps were also worn by men.

Jewelry for men included rings, belts, crowns, S-chain collars or necklaces, jeweled daggers, pendants, buttons, and brooches, now set with faceted stones. A *baldric* or bandolier decorated with a foliated edge, jewels, or gold bells was worn as an accessory. Gloves of varying quality were worn by both elegant men and laborers.

Poulaines, shoes with long pointed toes, were worn by fashionable gentlemen. Some extreme examples had points so long that they had to be tied up to the knee. Soft calf-length and knee-length boots were worn for hunting and riding. The *patten* (a slip-on shoe with thick wooden soles) was worn by peasants and gentry to protect shoes from the mud. Shoes might have thick soles, but no heels.

Dress for Women

Women wore one or more gowns layered over a chemise. The *corset* was a "princess-line" gown essentially the same as the cote and kirtle, which was snug fitting in the torso and flared at the hip to a wide skirt. The corset laced up the back or the front. In Italy it was worn alone, but in northern countries it was usually covered by a surcote, gown, or houppelande.

The "Windows of Hell" surcote continued into the second half of the fifteenth century. Extra length was a prominent feature of all overgowns, many of them extending into a train.

The woman's houppelande was similar to the man's: close fitting in the shoulders, flaring to a full skirt, arranged in pleats held with a belt at the waist or just under the breast. The sleeves flared into long trumpet shapes and were lined in fur or contrasting fabric. The collar might be the flared or standing style, a round turndown, or a large "sailor collar." The houppelande was often trimmed or lined in fur.

After 1400 the most fashionable gown had a high-waisted,

snuggly fitted bodice with a long, extremely full skirt set to the bodice in pleats. The excessive length required the lady to lift or tuck up the skirt when walking. A wide belt emphasized the high waistline. This gown had long, fitted sleeves with cuffs that could be worn over the hands or turned back to reveal a contrasting lining. The neckline was a deep V, plunging to the belt and revealing the corset underneath. A shawl collar of fur or contrasting fabric was added to the neckline.

Women wore hose to the knee and shoes similar to those of men, but with less exaggerated toes.

Unmarried girls still wore their hair loose, controlled by a chaplet or circlet (fillet), or topped by a turban or headdress. Unmarried older women wore gorgets and wimples. A variety of fanciful headdresses appeared in this period. In Italy a large headdress resembling a smocked cushion was worn on the back of the head, either enclosing the hair or on top of flowing locks. Turbans and *rondels* (a large stuffed ring worn around the head) were combined with veils and coifs.

After 1400 exaggerated headdresses began to sweep back and up from milady's face. The *hennin* was a conical-shaped hat with a veil of sheer fabric floating from the point. Variations of the hennin had two or three points or were cut off several inches short of the point. The veil could be supported by wires out from the hennin which made it appear to float. Women plucked their eyebrows and hairlines to create a high forehead. The *frontlet* (a black velvet strip across the front of the headdress) hung to the shoulders on each side of the face. Chaperons were worn combined with rondels and brimmed hats.

Jewelry consisted of crowns, jeweled collars or necklaces, pendants, buttons, and rings, sometimes set with faceted stones.

Outerwear continued to be a mantle or cloak.

RENAISSANCE   1450–1550

General Characteristics

National differences in dress became stronger. A broadening at the shoulders suggested either a square or wide trapezoidal silhouette. Padding and stiffening added bulk to the figure. Parti-coloring continued, but dagging was replaced by *slashing* (incisions which allowed a lining or undergarment to be seen).

Elegant garments were made of silk brocades, velvets, satins, taffetas, and metallic cloths. Silk mesh, gauze, crepe, and chiffon were used for hair nets, veilings, and scarves. Woolens were available in many qualities. Linen and cotton were less common and used for chemises and headcoverings. Furs were used for collars and cuffs.

Dress for Men

The chemise developed into a shirt with full sleeves. The full body was gathered into a neckband or ruffle. The wrist and neck were often decorated with embroidery of black, red, and gold.

A *doublet*, with or without sleeves, was worn over the shirt. This garment had either a high, square neck or a deep V-neck and was laced or buttoned in the front or back. *Slashes* in the doublet allowed the shirt or doublet lining to be pulled through to create a "puff." The doublet was not usually worn alone.

The *jerkin* was worn over the doublet. The body of the jerkin was fitted to the waist, and a flared or pleated skirt was added. Its skirt varied from hip length to knee length. The square or V-shaped neckline sometimes cut away most of the jerkin front, revealing the doublet or shirt underneath.

Jerkin sleeves were often made of sections tied together and tied into the jerkin with strings. The shirt was pulled through the spaces and arranged in puffs at the shoulder and elbow. While the doublet sleeve was close fitting, the jerkin sleeve was large at the shoulder, full and stiff to the elbow or wrist. The armseye might be concealed at the shoulder by a *wing*, a crescent shape stitched to the shoulder of the doublet.

The legs were covered with hose to the waist or with *upper* and *nether stocks*. *Upper stocks* were either close-fitting trunks or full, bloomer-like pants. The *nether stocks* covered the lower part of the legs and were usually knitted. The *codpiece*, a triangle or pouch of cloth, was laced or buckled to the front of the hose to cover the opening.

Over the jerkin was worn a full, loose gown. Younger men preferred a short version; older men wore a longer style, the forerunner of the modern academic gown. A wide collar of fur or brocade decorated the front opening. A circular cape or other cloak might be added for outer wear.

Hair was worn "bobbed" at almost any length. Young Italian men wore long, loose styles; northern men wore shorter styles. Beards and mustaches, when worn, were neatly clipped.

The coif was still worn, often of black velvet and topped with a brimmed hat or soft cap. The cap and coif combination became associated with scholars. Brimmed hats might be decorated with

slashes, feathers, or jeweled pins. Hats were worn flat on the head or tilted to the side with feathers drooping downward.

Jeweled brooches were used on hats, on sleeves, and as pendants. S-chains, belts, swords, sheaths, and dagger hilts were all jeweled. Men wore earrings and many finger rings.

Shoes widened at the toe to a broad duck-foot shape. Shoes were flat and many had ankle straps. Embroidery, slashes and puffs, jeweled ornaments, and buckles decorated the tops.

Dress for Women

The V-neck gown of the late Gothic period continued into the early part of the Renaissance. A number of new gowns appeared as transitional garments. The bodices were stiffened and pressed the bosom flat. Most of them featured a wide, square neckline (open, or filled with the chemise), sleeves tied into the armhole revealing puffs of chemise, and voluminous skirts attached at the natural waist or above. Later gowns were open down the center front of the skirt to reveal the undergown. The characteristic square neckline developed a definite upward bow in the center.

After 1510, wider, fuller sleeves appeared on women's dress, especially in Italy. The northern gowns had a natural shoulder with the sleeves widening at the elbow into a large fur or brocade cuff, or a balloon or hanging sleeve. Some gowns had short sleeves below which the sleeves of the chemise or undergown were seen. No bare arms were yet revealed by women of status. Skirts were always long, sometimes with trains. The full silhouette was achieved by the layering of voluminous skirts one upon another.

Hair dressing and headdresses varied according to locale. Italian women displayed more hair than northern women. Small caps, hairnets, or large turbans might be worn. German women developed elaborate headdresses of starched white linen.

Popular headdresses included the *gable* headdress (also called *kennel* or *pedimental*). The jeweled front of this headdress resembled the roof of a house and the back of the head was covered with a velvet veil or a bag-like cap. The *crescent* or *horseshoe* headdress was a stiffened curve of velvet or brocade, adorned with jewels and attached to a cap or veil. The crescent sat back from the forehead and revealed the hair, parted in the center and pulled down smoothly to the ears. The back hair was dressed in the cap or hidden by the veil. Another headdress, associated with Mary of Scotland, consisted of a heart-shaped brim attached to a bag or veil.

Women wore earrings, rings, pendants on hats or necklaces, jeweled belts or girdles, and jeweled headdresses. Pearls were increasingly popular. Small objects like scissors, rosaries, or keys were hung from milady's girdle.

Women wore soft slippers. Cloaks with hoods were used for outerwear.

LATE RENAISSANCE (ELIZABETHAN) 1550–1625

General Characteristics

National preferences were evident in dress of both men and women. Northern and Spanish styles were generally stiff, dark, and extremely artificial in silhouette; Italian styles were softer and more graceful. The silhouette for men was somewhat narrower than the previous styles. For women a square, rectangular, or trapezoidal silhouette created the feeling of great bulk. The torso gradually lengthened to a long point in the front, creating the illusion of a figure with a long torso and short legs.

Jewels, embroidery, slashes, and puffs decorated clothing in abundance. Lace appeared on ruffs, coifs, and cuffs. Padding and hoops were required to create the artificial silhouette. Bare arms were not seen, but decolletage was sometimes extravagant, and some dresses were shortened for dancing or walking.

Elaborate fabrics like brocade, taffeta, metallic cloth, satin, and velvet were used in court dress. More modest garments were made of wool, linen, and cotton. Embroidery was used on caps, jackets, aprons, stomachers, and shoes.

Dress for Men

The full, soft shirt of linen or silk was finished with a plain neckband or turndown collar. Over the shirt was worn the *waistcoat*, an unstiffened jacket with or without sleeves. This garment was not visible when the gentleman was fully dressed.

Over the waistcoat a doublet with a standing collar was worn. The waist of the doublet dropped to a point in the front. A peplum or skirt was usually attached at the waistline. A wing or roll of cloth was attached at the shoulder to hide the armhole. Matching or contrasting sleeves were sewn in or tied in with *points*. Italian doublets were less stiff and followed the body shape. Northern and Spanish styles were often heavily padded with *bombast* (wool or cotton fibers). The doublet with the *peascod belly* was an extreme example of the padded doublet: in profile the shape of the doublet swooped

out from the chest, expanded the belly, and hooked downward, sometimes to the crotch. Doublets usually opened in the front but might lace up the back.

Tied around the neck of the fashionable gentleman was the stiffly starched *ruff* (a plain or lace-edged ruffle mounted on a band). Ruffs varied in width and depth according to the taste and status of the wearer. An *underpropper* (wire structure) was used to support the back of the ruff and tilt it upward to frame the face. The *whisk* collar was a fan-shaped collar wired to stand up and away from the neck.

Sleeves varied from a moderate shape to an exaggerated *leg-o'-mutton* shape (large at shoulder, tapering to wrist). Long vertical slashes were found on some sleeves; others were decorated with braid, a series of short slashes, or fabric puffs.

Upper stocks developed into a wide variety of "breeches" ranging from very short to below the knee. *Pumpkin* or *melon hose* were short, round, usually padded breeches. They were worn over long hose or over a pair of *canions* (tight-fitting, knee-length breeches). Pumpkin hose might have *panes*, a layer of narrow panels caught at the waist and at the bottom of the hose, through which the lining might be seen. Sometimes the soft, full lining was pulled out between the panes and hung in soft puffs. *Venetians* were padded or unpadded breeches, full at the top and tapering to below the knee. *Galligaskins*, a favorite with sailors, were wide, calf-length breeches unbanded at the bottom. These and other full, unpadded breeches were also called *slops*.

Over the doublet and hose was worn a jerkin, gown, or cape as outerwear. These garments were fastened under the ruff or collar. The popular *Spanish cape* was hip length and very stiff.

Hair was cut short and brushed off the forehead. Small, pointed beards and mustaches were popular, but some men preferred to be clean-shaven.

Earlier, caps and coifs were worn by merchants, scholars, and clergy. The fashionable gentleman wore a hat with a narrow brim and tall crown with a jeweled band and feather. As the period progressed, larger brims were increasingly popular. Hats were made of leather, beaver, felt, velvet, or other fabric. The hat was worn indoors.

Men wore rings, earrings (usually only one), chains, brooches, and pendants.

After 1600 heels (sometimes red) were added to men's shoes. The sole was thick and the shoe was slightly tapered with a squared-off toe. The ankle strap was decorated with a rosette. Boots were of soft leather and were tight fitting, often pulled high over the knee.

Dress for Women

The white chemise, sometimes with a low neck, was still worn as an undergarment. The *farthingale* was any one of a number of structures used to support the skirt in exaggerated shapes. The *Spanish farthingale* was a petticoat with graduated hoops (smaller at the top and larger at the bottom) which created a smooth bell shape. The *French farthingale* was wider on the hips and somewhat narrower in the back and front. The *cartwheel hoop*, popular in England, created a drum-shape skirt which was often ankle or instep length. The *bolster*, a stuffed roll that could be tied just below the waist, was also used. Some skirts were open down the front, revealing an undergown.

The sleeves of the undergown might extend below the sleeves of the *bodice* (a close-fitting garment covering the upper torso). The bodice developed a long point in the front. *Stays* (flat strips of metal, bone, or wood) were used to stiffen the bodice, which was flat across the breasts and laced very tightly to produce a small waist. The long bodice point was often accented by a *stomacher* (a triangle of cloth, elaborately decorated with embroidery and jewels). Later in the period, the undergown was less often worn, and the skirt and bodice became more elaborate. A round or square-shaped neckline was popular, but modest gowns had a high neck finished with a collar or ruff.

Ruffs were worn by women, as was the fan-shaped whisk collar set around the back and sides of the bodice neckline. An open-neck gown might be filled in with a *guimpe* (a shaped cloth placed around the neck and under the bodice).

Sleeves could be (1) large at the shoulder and tapering to the wrist, or (2) short puffs worn over tighter undersleeves or combined with hanging sleeves. Sleeves were often finished with lace-trimmed cuffs.

A short, loosely fitted jacket or loose uppergown was sometimes worn, either open or closed.

Hair was combed off the forehead and dressed over rolls to create a halo or heart-shaped effect, then adorned with pearls or feathers. A lace-trimmed cap or coif might be worn. Women wore mannish styles for riding and hunting.

Shoes for women were made of brocade or leather and often had high heels.

Ropes of pearls, chains, earrings, pendants, brooches, and rings were worn in abundance. Small rigid fans became a popular accessory for ladies. Makeup was used at court.

CAVALIER 1625–1660

General Characteristics

Padding and starch disappeared from dress. Waistlines rose, and artificial skirt supports disappeared. Excess ornamentation was reduced. Women's sleeves for the first time in centuries revealed part of the lower arm. Rounded shoulders combined with full, soft skirts created a bell-shaped silhouette for women. The silhouette for men resembled an inverted triangle. Garments were trimmed with lace, ribbon and braid.

Patterned brocades and cut velvets were still used, but plain satins and velvets were more prevalent. Lace and linen continued to be important for caps, collars, and cuffs. Wool, cotton, and linen in solid colors were used for modest dress.

Dress for Men

The full, white shirt had large sleeves and either a neckband or turndown collar. The doublet was no longer padded but might be stiffened. The high waistline was often decorated with a row of *points* (metal-tipped ribbons that held the breeches to the doublet). The hip-length skirt or peplum of the doublet was cut into tabs. The body and skirt of some doublets were cut together with long vertical seams for shaping. Long vertical slashes decorated the doublet front and back.

The sleeves of the doublet were moderate shapes, fuller at the armhole than at the wrist. Long, vertical slashes revealed the shirt or lining. The wrist was finished with linen or lace cuffs.

Older folk still wore the stiff ruff of the previous period, but the unstarched *falling ruff* was more fashionable. A square lace or linen collar appeared as a new accessory.

The new tubular-shaped pants were upper-calf length and loose at the bottom. Unpadded knee breeches and slops were still worn. Most breeches were fuller at the top and tapered toward the bottom.

Men grew their hair long and wore it loose and wavy. Small, neatly trimmed mustaches and beards ("Van Dykes") were popular. Mustaches could be worn alone or with a small beard tuft in the center of the chin.

The fashionable hat was a large-brimmed, low-crowned felt trimmed with a jeweled band and ostrich plumes.

Certain religious and political groups chose shorter hair styles and more austere garments to express their religious beliefs or in opposition to the extravagance of the fashionable court practices.

Ankle-strap shoes with square or round toes and long vamps were trimmed with buckles or rosettes. The moderate heels (two inches) were often red. Boots were frequently substituted for shoes, and spurs were worn even when one was not riding. The tops of the boots could be extended over the knees but were usually worn turned down and back up to form a cup-shaped cuff. Inside the cuff could be seen the lace top of the *boot hose*. Shorter boots were turned down once to form a cuff.

The jerkin became a kind of jacket, frequently of leather, popular with soldiers, sailors, and hunters. Semicircular capes of varied lengths were the usual outerwear for men. The unstiffened cape was draped around the body in a variety of ways. The collar or ruff was always worn on the outside of the cape or jerkin. Long gowns were still worn by scholars, some clergy, and statesmen.

Gloves with large embroidered *gauntlets* (wide cuffs) were worn. A purse was tucked into the belt under the doublet or jerkin.

Dress for Women

The chemise was rarely visible. Except in Spain, petticoats replaced the farthingale structures that were previously used to support the skirt.

The boned bodice became shorter and was often finished with a set of tabs like a man's doublet. The stomacher was worn with its point resting on the skirt, and the overgown was laced over it. A split-front skirt might reveal an elaborate undergown or petticoat. Skirts were extremely long and were often held up or bunched through a belt for walking.

The square neckline shared popularity with a wide, slightly scooped neckline finished with a *Bertha collar*, a wide, round collar covering the shoulders. A variety of lace and linen collars were used on women's dress.

Three-quarter-length sleeves revealed the lower arm. Sleeves were one large puff or were divided into two or three puffs with ribbons and finished with a lace or linen turned-back cuff. Long gloves were worn with the shorter sleeves.

Widows, peasants, and older women continued to wear caps. Fashionable ladies dressed their hair with a center part, curled or frizzed the sides, and dressed the back in a high knot or bun. A fringe of curls or frizz was arranged across the forehead. Loops of pearls, feathers, and ribbons were used to adorn the head. Hoods or men's hats were worn outdoors.

Cloaks with sleeves or large circular capes were worn for outerwear. Hoods might be attached or separate.

Modest women wore long-sleeved, simple garments of current cut. A folded kerchief, pinned at the neck, might take the place of a collar. A white linen apron was a common accessory.

Bracelets, chokers, long strings of pearls, and small drop pearl earrings were popular. Jeweled rings, buttons, pendants, and hair ornaments were worn.

Ladies' shoes were similar to men's styles and often had high, red heels. Other accessories for women included a muff, fan (rigid or folding), purse, and mask (in public).

RESTORATION   1660–1715

General Characteristics

A frivolous abundance of ribbons, curls, and exposed shirt or chemise was popular. The waistline returned first to the natural position and later to a lower line. Small shoulders, narrow torsos, coats, and skirts widening at the bottom created a narrow, triangular silhouette. The early frivolity gradually stiffened into a rigid, ornate, and dignified style.

In addition to the brocades, velvets, satins, and wools previously available, linen and cotton prints began to be domestically produced. Lace was used for trimming sleeves, collars, caps, aprons, cravats, stomachers, petticoats, and handkerchiefs.

Dress for Men

The white shirt was made of fine fabric and was extremely full in body and sleeves. The neck was finished with a drawstring or collar. Over the shirt was sometimes worn a waistcoat.

Two types of coat were popular. One was very short (ribcage length) and allowed the shirt to show around the waist. The second, the *cassock* coat, was fitted in the body, above-the-knee length, and flared from the hip to the hem. This coat was collarless and buttoned down the front from neck to hem. It was often worn open from the chest down to reveal a puff of shirt and a bunch of ribbons at the waist. Both coats had short sleeves which exposed the shirt. The sleeves of the shirt might be caught into puffs with ribbons. Later coats had three-quarter-length sleeves with large turned-back cuffs. As the period progressed, waistcoats became more important. Cut along the lines of the coat, the waistcoat also had buttons from neck to hem, often had long fitted sleeves, and could match or contrast with the coat.

With the short jacket were worn either the tubular pants of the

Cavalier period or the new *petticoat breeches* (a full, open-bottomed pant like modern culottes). The latter was often profusely decorated with ribbon loops at the bottom edge and on the sides. With the longer coat, full knee breeches were more common. By the end of the period, breeches were closer fitting and buttoned or buckled neatly below the knee.

Hose (above-the-knee length) were worn under or over the breeches. Although boots were no longer worn for dress occasions, boot hose were sometimes still worn, gartered to allow the lace ruffle to flutter at the knee. Shoes continued to have high heels, often red.

A lace collar with a front pleat might be tied at the neck. A pair of plain tabs set on a band might be substituted by conservative folk. As the period progressed, the *cravat* came into fashion. A long strip of fine white cloth with lace ends, the cravat was wrapped around the neck (over the shirt collar) and tied in the front with a bow or half-knot. A ribbon tied in a bow was sometimes added under the cravat.

Long wigs of luxurious curls were fashionable for men. Parted in the middle, the hair was dressed to rest on the chest and down the back. The gentleman's own hair was clipped short. A cap was worn for warmth when the wig was removed at home.

Steeple-crown hats developed with high crowns and stiff, narrow bands. By 1690 men were wearing wider hats, turning up the brims on three sides, and the resulting *tricorn* hat became the most popular style for the next century. The brim edges were trimmed with braid or ostrich.

Capes were still worn as outerwear.

Dress for Women

The bodice might have short sleeves or be sleeveless. The puffed chemise sleeves tied with ribbons showed below the bodice sleeves. Later, bodice sleeves were close fitting to just below the elbow and finished with a flounce of lace or a puff of chemise. The waist of the bodice dropped to the natural waist or lower. The long, stiffened point in front was sometimes duplicated in the back. The neckline might have the wide Bertha collar of the previous period. The combining of an underbodice and an overgown created a square neckline. A kerchief or scarf was sometimes draped to fill the neckline, or the chemise might be visible. A wide, deep collar was worn by many modest women.

The overgown revealed part of the bodice front and the decorated petticoat. It might have a train and was often draped back, revealing the lining and creating a back drape. Horizontal trim emphasized the hem.

The *Dutch jacket* was a short, loose garment lined or trimmed in fur and worn indoors. The *night-rail* was a muslin and lace cape, originally a boudoir jacket and later worn as a light wrap over a gown.

Decorative aprons of lace or linen were worn by women of all classes. Knee-length hose gartered at the knee and shoes much like those of the men were worn.

Hair was dressed with a center part or combed straight back from the forehead with loose curls around the face. Toward the end of the period a more formal style developed in which the hair was dressed in high mounds on the top of the head. The *fontage*, a cap featuring a tall arrangement of lace ruffles and ribbons, brought caps back into fashion for aristocratic ladies.

Drop earrings, rings, brooches, watches on chains, and necklaces of pearls or other stones were popular, as were fans and muffs as accessories.

EIGHTEENTH CENTURY: EARLY GEORGIAN   1715–1750

General Characteristics

A shift to lighter, more delicate fabrics and colors began with the reign of Louis XIV in 1715. Powdered wigs, delicate trim, and a more feminine silhouette (soft shoulders, small waists, and full skirts on gown or coat) developed for both men and women. Decoration was applied to garments with embroidery, quilting, appliqués, ruching, ruffles, ribbons, and festoons.

Brocades, damasks, satins, taffetas, and printed cottons in pastels and floral tones were popular. Black velvet was much used for men's breeches. Wools were used for modest dress and outerwear. Silk gauze was used for scarves and fichus. Linen, lace, and cotton lawn were used for trim, caps, aprons, and undergarments.

Dress for Men

The full shirt was finished at the neck with a band or turndown collar. A *jabot* (ruffle) trimmed the front opening. The sleeves were finished in a ruffle of plain fabric or lace. Around the neck was worn the *cravat* (neck cloth) or the newer *stock* (a strip of crushed muslin tied or buckled in the back).

The waistcoat or vest reached just above the knee and buttoned from neck to hem. Some vests had sleeves. The vest might match or contrast with the rest of the ensemble. Many vests were elaborately trimmed with braid or embroidery.

The coat developed from the previous style. The skirts were flared and stiffened. The pockets moved up from the hemline. The collarless coat retained the row of buttons from neck to hem but was rarely worn completely closed. The coat sleeve was just short of the wrist (allowing the shirt ruffle to show) and was trimmed with a wide cuff buttoned back to the sleeve. The coat might be ornately trimmed with braid or embroidery.

Knee breeches were full at the top, neat fitting, and buttoned or buckled at the knee. Frequently of black velvet, breeches could also be of light-colored satin, in matching or contrasting colors to the coat or vest. Knee-length hose were worn over or under the breeches. Dress hose were of silk, everyday hose of wool.

Shoes had heels, tongues, and buckles. For riding, men wore gaiters or boots fitted over the knee in front and cut out in back.

Although retained by judges and older men, by 1730 the full-bottom wigs of the previous period were generally replaced with tied-back wigs. The front of the wig was combed away from the face and dressed in rolls over the ears. The back hair was tied into a queue with a ribbon or caught in a black silk bag. Since most wigs were powdered to look white or gray, the silk bag protected the back of the coat. Conservative or unpretentious men wore their own hair tied back with the sides rolled or frizzed.

The tricorn was the most commonly worn hat. Quakers, clergymen, and country folk might still wear the steeple-crown hat from earlier periods. Tricorns were decorated with braid, ostrich, ribbons, cockades, and lace. Caps were worn at home after the wig was removed.

Jewelry for men was reduced to rings, fancy buttons, decorated swords, and watches on chains. Watches were worn under the vest and were not often visible when the gentleman was fully dressed.

Dress for Women

The bodices of the eighteenth century were slim, tight, flat-front, heavily boned, and long-waisted. The bodice usually dipped to a center front point which was emphasized by trimming, often a series of graduated ribbon bows. A square neck formed by the combination of corset or bodice and overgown was frequently seen, but a low, round neck was also popular. The neckline might be trimmed with a

lace ruffle or collar, or filled with a fichu. Most bodices were laced up the back. A corsage of real or artificial flowers might be worn on the bodice. A small ruff of lace or ribbon was sometimes tied around the neck.

A slim, elbow-length sleeve finished with a lace flounce became popular, though modest women wore long, fitted sleeves.

The skirt could be trimmed in the front or split to reveal a decorative petticoat. Quilted petticoats were popular among middle-class women. Most skirts were floor length or instep length, some with trains. However, dance dresses and street frocks were sometimes shortened almost to ankle length. Early in the period, hoops returned to fashion. Although many women relied on stiffened petticoats to extend their skirts, whalebone hoops created the bell shape under the more fashionable gowns. Toward the middle of the century the *panier* (a series of hoops, wider on the sides than in front and back) was developed. As the panier became wider (some over three feet), the skirt was constructed with a seam along the top of the panier which allowed the skirt to fall evenly at the bottom.

The *sack-back gown*, an overgown with a loose back, was worn over a corset and petticoat. This gown was also known as the *robe à la française* in England, and later as the *Watteau-back* gown because it appeared frequently in Watteau's paintings. The variations of this garment included a loose, sleeveless gown, and a sleeved gown with tight-fitting front (which could be worn without an undergown). The full back was pleated into a narrow yoke and fell freely from neck to floor. Garments in this style were worn as dressing gowns, for day wear, and as formal wear.

Hair was dressed away from the face in the style now known as *pompadour* after Madame de Pompadour, mistress to Louis XV. The back was arranged in twists or curls, and loose tendrils or long ringlets were often allowed to hang down the back or over the shoulder. Frequently powdered, the hair was also decorated with delicate ornaments of ribbon, flowers, lace, and pearls.

Caps were not worn for formal wear but were popular for day. The *mob cap*, the most popular style for peasant and gentry alike, was a circle of fine cloth gathered to fit the head and trimmed around the edge with a plain or lace ruffle. The *shepherdess hat* (a large brimmed straw hat tied on with a wide ribbon) was often worn over the mob cap. A hood might be worn for warmth, either separate or attached to a cloak.

The tricorn hat was worn by women mainly as part of the riding habit, except in Venice, where it was combined with a black lace mantilla and accompanied by a half mask to disguise the wearer.

Jewelry was simple and used with restraint. Pearl drop earrings,

rings, jeweled buttons and hair ornaments, watches worn at the waist on chains, and small chokers or necklaces were among the possibilities.

Shoes had high, *spool* heels (wide top, narrow middle, wide base) and pointed toes. *Mules* (backless shoes with heels) were also worn.

Gloves and mitts were worn with the shorter-sleeve gowns. Muffs were used for warmth. Folding fans made of silk were a necessary accessory for formal wear. Women carried parasols when walking outdoors.

EIGHTEENTH CENTURY: LATE GEORGIAN 1750–1790

General Characteristics

Fashion made a quick change of silhouette toward the end of this period. The first thirty years (1750 to 1780) saw two movements in women's dress. The first, an exaggeration of early eighteenth-century styles, included paniers of incredible widths and coiffures of incredible heights. The second trend was a romantic adaptation of peasant dress. Clothing for men gradually and steadily became slimmer and neater.

Between 1780 and 1790 new styles rapidly appeared. For women the further development of peasant styles created elegant yet simple garments which omitted the artificial shape of the panier. For men a slim, vertical silhouette was developed with tight-fitting knee breeches, short vest, and coat whose skirt was reduced to slim tails. Extremes of ornament disappeared after 1780.

Before 1780 elaborate brocades, damasks, satins, taffetas, embroideries, wools, plaids, stripes, and printed cottons were fashionable. After 1780 simple fabrics were more frequently used. Except for court dress, woolen broadcloth took the place of satins and brocades in men's wear, and cotton muslin was extensively used in women's dress. Velvet returned to favor for overgowns and turbans. Before 1780 light colors continued to be fashionable. After 1780 muslin in white or light tones was often teamed with heavier fabrics in dark, rich colors.

Dress for Men

The full shirt was rarely worn open at the neck. The stock and jabot (ruffle) were the usual neckwear, although cravats (neck cloths) were still worn for more casual dress.

Vests gradually became shorter until they reached the waist. They were usually single-breasted and cut straight or with two points at the bottom. Late in the period double-breasted vests with lapels and standing collars appeared.

Men's coats began to lose skirt fullness, and by 1770 the *cutaway* style was predominant. This coat retained the vent in the back but sloped away sharply from the center front waist to the back hem. The front edge was decorated with buttons, buttonholes, braid, and embroidery. The sleeves were wrist length, slim, and finished with cuffs, embroidery, or a buttoned slit on the outside of the arm. The shirt ruffle of lace or linen was seen at the wrist. Pocket flaps moved up toward the waist and farther to the back. After 1780 there appeared a short-waisted coat with high collar and sloping tails that started from the side front and dropped to knee or calf length. Workmen and country folk wore a short, informal coat called the *bob-tail*.

As coats and waistcoats shortened, knee breeches became more neatly fitted. A buckled band finished the breeches just below the knee, and a row of buttons up the outside of the leg held the opening closed. Breeches were made of black velvet, light colored satins, wools, and doeskin.

Pale knitted stockings of heavy silk, sometimes *clocked* (decorated with designs on the ankle), were worn by elegant gentlemen. Others made do with wool.

Shoes had low heels and medium-high tongues and were closed with buckles or strings. Top boots and gaiters were worn by civilians and military men.

Powdered wigs were dressed away from the face with a queue or pigtail down the back. Exaggerated versions had a very high roll in the front. After 1780 a fuller, bushy style of wig came into fashion, and more men began to wear their own hair, powdered or unpowdered. At home turbans were worn to cover shaven or clipped heads. Almost all men were clean-shaven.

The tricorn hat remained fashionable, but after 1780 three new hats appeared: (1) a low-crowned beaver hat with medium brim, (2) a hat cocked in two places (*bicorne*), and (3) a steeple-crown hat with a stiff brim and tall, tapering crown similar to the older "Pilgrim" style.

Men's jewelry consisted of rings, watches, fancy shoe buckles, knee buckles, and snuff boxes.

For outerwear men wore capes and the *great coat*, a large overcoat shaped like the dress coat.

Dress for Women

Bodices continued to be tight, flat-front, and heavily boned. The earlier garments still featured the elbow-length sleeve with flounce popular in the first part of the century; later gowns often had wrist-length sleeves. The square neck was still predominant. Until 1780 bodices continued to be long-waisted with a long front point.

Formal gowns were extended to amazing widths with paniers, but day dresses were less extreme. The sack-back overgown continued to be worn, sometimes with the skirts draped up in the back in the style known as *polonaise*. A short version of the sack-back gown was called the *sacque*. Petticoats and skirts were often elaborately decorated with quilting, ruffles, ruching, flowers, festoons, lace, or other trims. Overgowns matched or contrasted with petticoats and underbodices. Simple gowns with plain, fitted bodices and full skirts were also common. Dresses for walking or dancing were sometimes shortened to the ankle.

Coiffures for formal occasions were elaborately constructed of false hair, rose high on the head, and were decorated with flowers, birds, jewels, plumes, birds in cages, miniature ships in full sail, and countless other novelties. Even a fairly modest style was swept up over a roll, with the back dressed in curls, held in place with pomade, and powdered.

Caps also returned to fashion, and their size increased with the increased size of the coiffure. Turbans and mob caps were common. The *shepherdess* hat (large-brim straw) was still popular. Other hats were devised to wear on the large hair styles, usually perched at a slant on the front of the head. The *calash*, a large hood held away from the hair by hoops, was devised to wear over the large hair styles.

After 1780 many gowns had round, sashed waists and round necklines, sometimes filled with a fichu or scarf. By that time paniers were definitely out of fashion, and skirts were supported by heavy petticoats with extra fullness at the back. The *levite*, an undraped overgown with fitted back, became popular. After 1780 the height of hair styles decreased, and their width increased. This style was less often powdered, and natural colored hair gradually returned to fashion. Low-crowned, wide-brimmed hats and a feminine version of the steeple-crown hat were worn.

Cloaks and capes, sometimes with hoods or sleeves, were the usual outerwear. A shaped shawl called a *mantelette* was sometimes worn when only a light wrap was needed. A caped overcoat called the *redingote* was developed from the riding habit and was worn over a shirt, waistcoat, and skirt.

Rings, brooches, watches, bracelets, shoe buckles, jeweled drop earrings, necklaces, and hair ornaments were among the jeweled treasures of the eighteenth-century woman. Cameos, necklaces of gold beads, and diamonds were popular. Even a modest housewife might have a silver *chatelaine*, a hook to be attached to the bodice or waistband from which to suspend a key chain or other useful items.

Women carried parasols, fans, gloves, muffs, and walking sticks.

DIRECTOIRE AND FIRST EMPIRE (REGENCY) 1790–1815

General Characteristics

A slim, vertical, high-waisted silhouette dominated the fashion scene for both men and women in this period. Simple fabrics, especially wool and cotton muslin, were extremely popular for most of the period. Later more lavish fabric and trim began to return to fashion. Women's fashion featured "classical" drapery. Emphasis in men's fashion shifted from the use of elaborate trim and ornate fabrics to fine tailoring, sober colors, and impeccable grooming.

Dress for Men

A white shirt with jabot and standing collar was typical for the gentleman of the period. A black or white cravat wound around the collar or a white stock with a black ribbon over it finished the neck. The shirt sleeve was finished with a narrow ruffle or cuff.

Vests were waist length or a little longer, square or cut with two points in the front. Often double-breasted, the vest was worn with the top buttons left undone and the lapels turned back. Stripes were popular for vests, and embroidery was used on formal wear.

Coats had high, standing collars, lapels, and tails. The front might be cut away starting just above the waist and sloping down to the knee in the back. A square-cut front with the tail starting over the hipbone was especially popular. Both styles revealed the vest at the front.

Knee breeches continued to be worn by older men, by peasant folk, and for formal or court dress. The newer look was a *pantaloon* like those worn by boys and sailors. The fashionable version was tight fitting and was often made of knitted cloth. Originally calf length, pantaloons by 1800 became ankle length and a little looser.

White or neutral hose were worn with knee breeches and pantaloons. "Dandies" were fond of striped hose in bright color combinations. Flat pumps were worn for dress, and boots ranged from calf to knee height.

Hair at the beginning of the period was full on the top and sides with the back caught in a queue. Soon the hair was cut to the shape of the head with the top curled in imitation of Roman styles. Sideburns began to reappear. Powdered hair disappeared among fashionable men.

The bicorne and the *top hat* (stiff, tall-crowned hat with narrow brim) were the two types of hat for fashionable men.

Several short capes were added to the greatcoat in the style now known as the *coachman's* coat. Capes were still worn by men as outerwear.

Dress for Women

Simple, high-waisted, muslin frocks became the fashionable dress in the years following the French Revolution. Inspired by classical garments, early dresses of this period were often made of sheer fabrics trimmed with Greek and Roman motifs. Some ladies wore their dresses over pink tights without petticoats, and some went as far as wearing them wet to imitate the look of classical statuary.

For a time corsets (stays) were abandoned. Within a few years, however, tight bodices with corsets returned. However, because the waistline remained high under the bosom, corsets did not pinch in the waist.

Sleeves were either short and puffed, long and fitted, or a combination of a long sleeve with small puff at the top. The neckline was often square and quite low. A fishu might be tied around the shoulders. A muslin gown with a *surplice* neck (diagonally wrapped) was also popular. High-necked gowns were often finished with a ruffle at the neck.

Over the dress a knee-length tunic might be worn "in the Greek manner." A very short, fitted jacket called the *spencer* was worn for warmth. Long, rectangular shawls were extremely fashionable.

As the period progressed, heavier fabrics were used. To accommodate these fabrics, skirts were cut with a slight flare and less fullness at the waist. The flared hem was accentuated by horizontal trim near the bottom edge. Court dresses were furnished with the *court mantle*, an elaborate train of contrasting fabric falling from the high waistline and supported by straps over the shoulders.

Greek hair styles were revived. Bonnets, turbans, and plumed headdresses added a modern note.

Shoes were flat and tied on with ribbons. Ladies carried small purses, muffs, parasols, and fans. Gloves were very important. With the short puffed sleeves, very long gloves were worn.

For outerwear women wore a *pelisse*, a coat-type garment open down the front and cut with similar lines to the dress. The *redingote*, a caped coat, was still popular. A *pelerine* was a small, shoulder-length cape.

Jewelry for women included bracelets, earrings, tiaras, brooches, necklaces, and hair ornaments. Often three or more of these were of a matching set.

ROMANTIC   1815–1830

General Characteristics

The silhouette for women widened at top and bottom until it resembled two triangles balancing point to point. Frivolous bonnets and trims, enormous sleeves and tiny waists, ankle-length skirts, and flat slippers combined to give the fashionable woman a doll-like look. The silhouette for men echoed the wide, sloping shoulders, narrow waists, and full hips of the women's silhouette.

Men's wear favored sturdy fabrics of wool or cotton. White linen or cotton was used for warm climates. Women's day wear was made of lightweight cottons, such as chintz, muslin, and calico, or lightweight wool or cashmere. Evening gowns were made of taffeta, gauze, satin, silks, or velvet.

Dress for Men

The white shirt had a tall, stiff collar whose points sometimes rose high onto the cheek. Wrapped around the collar was a neck cloth. A bit of pleated shirt front or ruffle might be visible above the vest. Artistic types wore their collars unstarched and open or held together with a loosely tied scarf in the manner of Lord Byron. A great variety of shapes and arrangements of cravat or neck cloth was available to a fashionable gent.

Vests had collars and were cut to the natural waist. To help produce the small-waisted look, many men's vests were boned and laced in the back, much like women's corsets. Waistcoats were no longer visible at the waist when the tail or frock coat was buttoned, but a sliver of color could be seen at the neck, and men often left their coats partially open to reveal more.

The *frock coat* was worn for morning occasions and for sportswear. The *tail coat* took over for formal occasions. The *bobtail coat* was worn by boys, men of low status, and occasionally by gentlemen for country or sportswear. Coat collars stood high on the back of the neck, and the shoulders sloped downward to a modified leg-o'-mutton sleeve.

The fashionable gent reserved knee britches for court dress, although these continued to be worn by country folk and older men. *Riding smalls*, britches made of doeskin, drill, or finely napped fabric, were full at the top and tapered to meet the calf-high riding boots.

Fine hose in neutral tones were worn. Black evening pumps were finished with a small bow or buckle. For day the gentleman were short boots with blunt toes, narrow vamps, and a moderate heel.

Hair was full and brushed forward or back according to taste. Sideburns began to extend downward and slightly forward onto the check. The back of the hair was trimmed to the shape of the head. Small mustaches began to appear toward the end of the period.

Top hats, the most popular headwear, were made of beaver in gray, black, white, and fawn. A flat-crowned, broad-brimmed hat was favored for sportswear, by country folk, and in the American South and West. Caps were worn by boys and by men for sportswear or traveling.

A fitted overcoat was worn for day, and capes with contrasting linings and velvet collars were worn with evening dress. The caped coat worn by travelers and coachmen eventually became known as the *coachman's coat*.

Accessories for men included gloves, rings, watches, and canes.

Dress for Women

Corsets with small waists returned by 1825. The bodice worn over the corset had dropped shoulders and a slightly high waist. A wide-open neck, either round, square, or slightly V-shaped, was favored for evening and sometimes for day wear. The low day dress might be filled in by a *tucker* or *guimpe*. The wide V-neck was often trimmed with a fabric drape, a feature fashionable through much of the nineteenth century.

By 1825 most bodices featured exaggerated sleeves. Extreme fullness was introduced into the sleeve at the dropped shoulder line or at the elbow. The sleeve then tapered to the wrist, where a snug fit was favored. Some sleeves extended to the knuckles.

Skirts expanded to about 2½ yards, and extra fullness at the waist was concentrated largely in the back. Almost all skirts were instep or ankle length, a few calf length. The court mantle was added for court presentations. Skirt trim in horizontal bands was placed near the lower edge to accent the width.

Slippers with flat heels and ankle ribbons or small, dainty ankle boots were worn by ladies. Stockings were white or light colors.

For outdoors a lady added a spencer jacket, a *pelerine* (short cape), *mantelette* (shaped stole), or *pelisse* (long cloth coat cut and fitted like a dress).

Sets of elaborate jewelry were worn by women of means. Cameos cut of shell were set into brooches, producing an inexpensive ornament. Chains and ropes of beads circled the neck, and drop earrings were popular. Bracelets, rings, and hair ornaments were frequently worn.

Hair was arranged smoothly over the brow with a center part. Side hair was dressed in ringlets or loops, and the back hair was drawn up to a knot high on the head. Large bonnets with wide flaring brims were worn, and a variety of caps returned to fashion. Ribbons, plumes, and flowers adorned hats and bonnets.

A fan and gloves were necessary parts of a lady's wardrobe. Muffs, parasols, and *reticules* (small hanging purses) were also much evident.

CRINOLINE 1840–1865

General Characteristics

Though this style was less restrictive than the previous one, the male silhouette continued to be somewhat feminine, with sloping shoulders, padded chest, small waist, and full hips. A variety of garments were developed for special occasions. In women's dress, a small head, sloping shoulders, and small, natural waist were poised over an ever-widening bell-shaped skirt. As skirts increased in width at the hem, hoops returned to fashion.

Wool, cotton, silk, and taffeta in solids and stripes were popular for women's dress. Except for the bold plaids that were popular for trousers, most fabrics for men's wear were sturdy, plain, and subdued in color.

Dress for Men

The white shirt had either a stiffened or pleated front. The starched stand-up collar was more formal, but the turndown style was worn in both starched and unstarched versions. A wrapped neckcloth, stock, bow tie, or string tie was worn over the collar. Day vests were cut high at the neck and included single- and double-breasted styles. Vest necklines varied from high (with and without collars) to a deep U-shape for evening.

The *sack coat*, which had been primarily a jacket for boys and men of low station, developed into a garment for sportswear, informal occasions, and sometimes business. The *tail coat* and *frock coat* were the more fashionable styles, and variations suitable for many occasions were available. Evening wear generally included a black tail coat and a black or white vest. Frequently part of the wardrobe of the upper classes, the black frock coat was also an important part of the average man's wardrobe, worn for special occasions from marriages to funerals. The *cutaway coat* was deemed suitable for daytime visits and gradually became known as a "morning coat." All styles of coat gradually became less fitted in the waist, and collars gradually decreased in height. Sleeves were straight and set in without extra top fullness.

Most trousers were tubular and had stirrups to keep them neat. Pants were worn without cuffs or creases. Plaid and striped pants were popular. In general, men's wear became more sober.

Men's hair styles were full, but shaped to the head. Whether brushed straight back, or parted on the side or in the center, men's hair was generously slathered with macassar oil to hold it in place. Long, full sideburns blossomed on cheeks and beards on chins, though not always accompanied by mustaches.

The top hat in one of its many variations was the appropriate hat for most occasions. A number of wide-brimmed straw or felt hats with low crowns were worn for the country, and the *bowler* (also called *derby*) appeared.

Men wore short elastic-sided boots under their trousers and pumps or thin shoes for evening. Shoes with canvas tops buttoned up over the ankle were also worn.

Capes with velvet collars were worn with evening clothes. Topcoats and the plaid *Inverness cape* (coat with a shoulder cape added) were popular for outerwear.

Dress for Women

A lady's bodice was tight fitting and allowed for a rounded bosom shape. The front waist frequently dipped to a point, and the neckline and armhole contrived to create a drooping shoulder line. The wide V-shape was popular for evening. A small collar of lace or embroidery was often added to a high-neck day bodice; a lace *tucker* might fill in a low-neck gown. Bell-shaped sleeves were set into the

dropped armhole. A sheer undersleeve was gathered into a band at the wrist or midarm.

Skirts were instep or floor length and gathered or pleated into the small waist. The bottom edge of skirts from the 1850's and 1860's measured from 10 to 25 yards depending on the thickness of the fabric. Horizontal rows of trim, particularly ruffles, accented the width of the hem. The voluminous *crinoline* (petticoat of horsehair or starched cotton) was replaced after 1855 by a hoop petticoat consisting of a series of graduated steel rings hung from the waist by tapes. This lightweight structure encouraged even further exaggeration of the skirt size. Toward the 1860's the skirt shape became elongated toward the back.

Hair was parted in the center with soft ringlets or braids arranged over the ears. The back hair was curled or braided and arranged in a bun on the back of the head. Caps were worn for day by widows and many modest women. Older women might wear them with evening dress. Younger women adorned their evening coiffures with feathers, lace, flowers, and pearls. Large- and small-brimmed hats or bonnnets were worn for day.

Flat-soled, tight-fitting boots of soft leather were worn outdoors, and heelless slippers were worn indoors. Small parasols, folding fans, *reticules* (drawstring purses), and gloves or mitts were frequent accessories. Large aprons were added by the working woman.

Sets of matched jewelry were much prized. Small dangling earrings, necklaces, brooches, bracelets, rings, and hair ornaments were made of gold or silver and set with precious or semiprecious stones, pearls, and cameos. Black jet jewelry was considered appropriate for mourning; coral, turquoise, and garnets were popular.

Shawls, mantelettes (semi-fitted, triangular shawls), and capes (with and without armholes) were used for outerwear.

BUSTLE   1865–1890

General Characteristics

Men's dress developed soberly along previously established lines. The cutaway, frock, and sack coats varied little from previous styles. A slim, vertical silhouette with less padding in the chest and a natural fit in the waist was fashionable. An ever-increasing interest in sports required development of specific new garments for both participants and spectators.

The backward thrust of the women's skirts in the late Crinoline period led into the development of the bustle skirt. When viewed from the front, the silhouette was narrow and vertical. In profile, however, the lower half of the figure extended backward dramatically. Heavy drapery and carefully controlled ruffles adorned most versions of the bustle dress, and trains were common. Eighteenth-century costume details enjoyed a revival.

Wool fabrics dominated men's wear, although cotton, linen, and some silk were also used. Women's fashions took advantage of a wide variety of fabrics, most of them with substantial body.

Dress for Men

The all-important white shirt was usually furnished with a starched front. The stiff collar and cuffs were often detachable and might be made of celluloid, white rubber, or heavy paper. Collars were of medium height and might be *wing-tip*, straight band, or turndown style with points or rounded front edges. Separate collars were attached with collar buttons. A string tie, *Windsor* tie (soft silk), *ascot* tie, or *four-in-hand* tie provided a flash of color at the neck.

Vests were cut rather high with a collar and might match or contrast with the coat and pants. A knitted cardigan appeared in the 1880's and was sometimes worn in place of a vest.

Tail coats were gradually relegated to evening dress, and their cut was changed little for decades. The frock coat and cutaway were equally popular for formal daytime functions —social, political, and business. The sack coat gradually began to appear in more situations. Striped *blazers* and *Norfolk* jackets (jackets with pleated body held in with a belt) appeared for sports and casual wear. Except for the tail coat, most coats were cut high at the neck revealing a minimum of shirt and vest. All types of coats and vests might be trimmed in braid.

Pants might still be of plaid or stripes worn with plain coats. Suits consisting of matching sack coat, vest, and pants were popular, but combining contrasting pieces was also acceptable. Pants were long and uncreased. Casual pants might have cuffs, and *knickers* (full knee breeches) were revived for a variety of sporting activities.

Hair styles for men were close to the head and featured a center or side part held in place with macassar oil. A wide variety of sideburns, beards, mustaches, and combinations were worn.

The top hat was still favored for most formal occasions, but the derby became increasingly popular. The *straw boater* was a popular summer hat, and a variety of other hats and caps appeared for sportswear.

Shoes with elastic insets on the sides, and high-buttoned shoes

with canvas or kid tops became popular in the 1880's. Low-cut oxfords appeared for summer, and a canvas and rubber shoe was developed for tennis.

A variety of overcoats and top coats were worn including the Inverness cape of plaid wool. A knitted cardigan sweater appeared in the 1880's.

Dress for Women

The bodice was smooth and tightly fitted, allowing for rounded bosoms. There were three variations of silhouette. The first bodice shape retained the sloping shoulders and the natural or slightly shortened waistline of the crinoline period. A round or slightly pointed waistline, a narrow V-neck, and three-quarter-length sleeves were typical of this bodice. The *basque* waist appeared in about 1874. This bodice was fitted in a smooth, tight line from shoulder to hip or below. (The basque was later extended into a *princesse dress*, whose skirt fullness began at the knee.) The third bustle bodice extended just to the hip with its waist somewhat low. The shoulders were less sloping, the sleeves were full length, and in most day versions the neck was finished with a high-standing collar. Necklines in this period included a narrow square and a heart-shape neckline. Evening bodices were often extremely décolleté, with small sleeves or bands across the shoulders. The back of most bodices was elongated and furnished with pleats that spread out over the bustle.

To create the bustle silhouette, a crescent-shaped pad was added at the back waist, or a half hoop structure was worn, extending from the back waist to the floor. The early bustle dresses echoed the eighteenth-century polonaise dress, flat in front, with overdrapes and swags accenting the bustle. The skirt accompanying the basque waist was extremely tight and furnished with a flounce and train at the bottom. Toward the end of the period, when the bodice shortened again, the fuller skirt returned and garment trimming was reduced and simplified.

Skirts were usually floor or instep length, but some garments for walking or sports were shortened two or three inches from the ground. Floor-length gowns often had trains.

Hair was dressed high and to the back in braids, buns, and curls. A fringe of curls might soften the forehead. The early look echoed the eighteenth century, but as the period progressed, many women chose simpler styles, and the back hair was often worn low on the neck. Toward the end of the period the hair was once again drawn upward, this time to the top of the head. Hats were worn at a tilt over the forehead at the beginning of the period, and later they were placed more squarely on the head. Some bonnets were worn on the back of the head. Caps were worn indoors by older women, and evening coiffures were elaborately trimmed with ribbons, flowers, feathers, and jewels.

High-top shoes, buttoned or laced up the front, were popular. High-cut pumps were also worn. Both types of shoe had *French* (spool) heels.

Earrings and brooches continued in popularity; bracelets, lockets, and hair ornaments were also common.

Shaped capes and mantles, coats cut to fit over the bustle, and simple jackets were worn as outerwear.

THE GAY NINETIES   1890–1900

General Characteristics

Men's clothing developed gradually along previously established lines. The silhouette was somewhat straighter with square shoulders and less fitted waists. Sack suits continued to take over the places formerly held by frock coats and cutaways. The latter were primarily found on professional men and at very formal daytime occasions. Wool flannels and tweeds became increasingly popular along with traditional broadcloths. Linen, cotton duck, and seersucker were used for summer wear.

Once again the fashionable silhouette for women resembled two triangles balanced point-to-point. Enormous sleeves created width at the shoulders, corsets reduced the waist to the smallest possible size, and gored skirts skimmed the hips and swept to a wide hem. Tailored combinations of jacket, *shirtwaist*, and skirt were worn by women for sport, work, and travel.

Stiff or sturdy fabrics were required for most women's dress, and solids, plaids, and stripes were prominent. Horsehair was used to support the sleeves and the bottom of the skirt.

Dress for Men

The stiff-front, neckband shirt (with back opening) was still predominant for formal day and evening wear. The detachable collars worn on these shirts were stiff and extremely high, whether standing band, wing-tip, or rounded turndown style. The *shirtwaist*, a front-buttoned shirt, was popular for casual and sportswear. Farmers and workmen wore unstarched shirtwaists with attached collars, or collarless neckband shirts.

White bow ties accompanied evening dress; black bow ties were appropriate with tuxedos. Ascots, four-in-hand ties, or bow ties were worn with the sack suit, frock coat, and cutaway. Soft silk ties were worn for casual or sportswear and by men of "artistic" tastes.

Vests were high cut with collars. Conservative men wore plain vests, matching or contrasting with coat and trousers. More adventurous dressers might wear bright-colored vests. A watch chain was frequently draped across the vest front between the pockets. The vest was omitted from many summer and sports costumes. Pullover and cardigan sweaters worn under the jacket became a permanent part of the male wardrobe.

Sack suits were high cut and had straight fronts, squared at the bottom edge. The *tuxedo*, a dinner jacket based on the sack coat, was introduced for all-male evening functions and informal dinners at home. Frock, cutaway, and tail coats had a less fitted look than in previous periods. Coat sleeves were straight and neatly fitted at the shoulder.

Dress pants were straight and narrow; casual pants were somewhat fuller. Informal suits might have cuffs and creases in the pants. Cuffed trousers were shorter and revealed a bit of hose. Knickers continued to be worn for active sports. Belts were sometimes substituted for suspenders on knickers.

Hair was close to the head and parted in the center or slightly to the side. Beards and extravagant sideburns were found only on older men; mustaches were cultivated in a variety of styles.

The top hat was still the appropriate headwear for important occasions, but the *boater* (stiff, flat-crown, medium-brim straw hat), *bowler* (hard, round-crown, medium-brim felt hat), *fedora* (creased-crown, medium-brim felt hat), and *slouch hat* (made of soft felt) were all popular. Caps were worn for many sporting occasions.

High-top shoes in black or brown were worn in winter. Low-cut, string-tied shoes (sometimes white) were worn in summer. Patent leather shoes and spats were appropriate for formal dress.

Overcoats of dark wool were worn in winter; gray or tan topcoats were worn in spring and summer. Overcoats varied from knee to calf length.

Dress for Women

The firm corset produced the fashionable S-curve figure which had a high, full, *mono-bosom* (no definition between breasts), a *wasp waist* (extremely small), sway back, and full hips. Padding to improve bosoms and hips was commonly used. The bodices of the period often incorporated fabric fullness in the front and sometimes blousing all around. The bodice was finished at the waist with a crushed band, belt, or peplum. Bodices for day wear all featured a high-standing collar, some of which flared out to frame the head. Necklines for evening might be a narrow square, heart-, or U-shape. The depth of the decolletage varied and the off-the-shoulder line disappeared.

Enormous leg-o'-mutton sleeves ballooned out from the shoulder and tapered dramatically from the elbow to the wrist. The shape was maintained with crinoline linings, pleated ruffles inside the sleeves, small pads worn at the shoulder, or whalebone hoops. Ruffles, lapels, and other trims accented the shoulder width and the narrow waist.

Skirts were cut in *gores* (triangular-shaped panels) to produce width at the hem without excess fullness at the waist and hip. Skirts were not excessively decorated and were worn over two or three starched petticoats. Some skirts had extra fullness pleated into the center back. In about 1898 an unstiffened skirt appeared and gradually began to dominate dressy day and evening occasions. The stiffer skirt continued for tailored wear.

Bloomers appeared for women cyclists, although most women rode in skirts.

Hair was usually drawn up on top of the head in a bun or twist. A large, full style was created by adding false hair or pads over which the hair was dressed with a bun on the crown of the head in the style now called the *Gibson girl*.

Hats began fairly small and were seated squarely on the top of the head, attached securely to the bun with a long hat pin. As hair styles grew larger, so did hats. Some styles reached quite extravagant proportions and were profusely trimmed with flowers, feathers, ribbons, lace, and veilings.

Earrings were out of fashion, but jeweled hairpins and combs were worn for evening. Wide, dog-collar necklaces of pearls, diamonds, or other precious stones were also popular for evening. Daytime jewelry was often limited to a cameo or other brooch centered on the front of the high collar. Lockets and chains were worn around the neck, and watches hanging from a small pin were worn on the left shoulder.

High-buttoned or laced shoes had pointed toes and spool heels. Low-heeled, laced boots were worn for sports, and evening shoes had spool heels and pointed toes with straps, bows, or buckles. *Lisle* (fine cotton) or wool stockings were commonly worn; silk stockings were a rare luxury for most women.

A variety of princess-style coats were worn by women. Shoul-

der-length and knee-length capes were worn over many day and evening ensembles. Linen dusters with large veiled hats were worn for traveling in open cars.

EDWARDIAN 1900–1915

General Characteristics

Men's clothes differed little from those of the preceding period, although a general trend to less formal dressing continued. A square silhouette (broad, padded shoulders and straight body) was typical for men. New inventions like the zipper (used for shoes) and "man-made silk" (rayon, used for hose) began to find their way into fashion.

Women's clothes softened, sleeves became modest, and a soft, triangular silhouette developed. Later in the period the triangular-shaped skirt was reduced to a cylinder, producing a narrow, rectangular silhouette. Bodices and skirts were more often combined into dresses, and lighter construction techniques were employed. Tailored looks became more popular as women began to fight for the vote and World War I loomed on the horizon. Top fashion designers experimented with unusual silhouettes.

Soft fabrics like crepe, charmeuse, chiffon, and batiste were popular for tea dresses and evening gowns. Dresses of all lace, or embroidered cotton combined with lace, were extremely fashionable for summer. Firmer fabrics were used for tailored wear.

Dress for Men

The stiff-front shirt was worn primarily with formal dress. Pleated-front shirts were worn with tuxedos, and soft shirts were appropriate with all other types of dress. Striped and colored shirts with white collars and cuffs were worn for less formal occasions. Detachable collars (the wing-tip, neckband, and rounded turndown) were still high and stiff. Attached turndown collars (with medium points) increased in popularity.

Although ascots and string ties were still worn, four-in-hand and bow ties were the most popular.

Collared vests matched business suits and were cut a bit lower. Vests of faille, brocade, or satin were worn with evening wear — black with tuxedos, white with tails. Matching or contrasting vests were worn with the cutaway and frock coats. V-neck sweaters were sometimes substituted for vests, and cardigan sweaters for jackets, in casual dress. Turtleneck sweaters and jerseys appeared in sports-wear.

The square, loose sack coat influenced the shape and fit of the frock, cutaway, and tail coats. Younger men neglected the frock coat and wore the cutaway for formal day occasions. The tuxedo was accepted for all but the most formal evening occasions. Blazers and Norfolk jackets were worn with matching or contrasting trousers for casual wear. Although frocks and cutaways might still be high cut, sack coats began to button lower.

Pegged trousers with pleats at the waist appeared on younger men. Most pants were creased, and some were cuffed. Belts began to replace suspenders except for formal wear.

Men's hair was close-cut and the center part went out of fashion about 1910. Side parts and *pompadour* styles (brushed straight back with lift in the front) were popular. Except for some small mustaches, young men were clean-shaven (thanks to the invention of the safety razor). Older gents retained the sideburns, mustaches, and clipped beards of their youth.

The gentleman wore a fedora or felt slouch hat with his business suit in winter and in summer he donned a straw boater or *Panama* straw (a high-crown, medium-brim hat of fine straw). The bowler or derby was also a popular hat, worn for a wide variety of occasions. Top hats were reserved for formal occasions.

High-top shoes were worn in winter, but *oxford* (low-cut, front-tied shoes) were worn in summer. With cuffed pants some men chose colorful, patterned socks. Men's hose were made of wool, cotton, silk, and the new synthetic fiber, rayon.

Outerwear featured simple, long overcoats with velvet collars as well as shorter, lightweight topcoats. The *polo* coat developed from the "wait coat" worn by polo players.

Dress for Women

A wasp-waist corset was worn into the new century. The bust was lower than in previous periods; the abdomen, hips, and buttocks were flattened.

A variety of undergarments were available to meet the needs of season and fashion. Among them were union suits, camisoles, pantaloons, corset covers, short petticoats, chemises, and *combina-tions* (one-piece garments which combined corset cover or camisole and pantaloons). Silk undergarments gradually replaced cotton for fashionable ladies.

Bodices featured the *pouter pigeon* front, a soft blousing that puffed over the top of the belt and accented the full, low, mono-

bosom look. Short, straight sleeves were acceptable for day wear. Shirtwaist and skirt combinations, tailored suits with matching or contrasting blouses, and a variety of day gowns were worn. Skirt lengths varied from long and trailing to ankle or calf length for sports.

Day wear might still have a high-standing collar, although it was not as tall and stiff as in the previous period. Afternoon and evening dresses might have simple square or round necklines. *Surplice* (wrapped look creating a V-neckline) necklines were revived. Neckties and stocks were adopted from men's styles to wear with shirtwaists.

Hair in the beginning of the period continued to be done in the pompadour style of the Gibson girl. Hair ornaments, combs, hairpins, barettes, bows, flowers, and headbands were popular.

After 1910 a straighter silhouette developed and a high-waisted look became fashionable. The corset was more relaxed in the waist and aimed for a smooth cylindrical figure. The *dolman* or *kimono* sleeve (sleeve cut in one with the body of the garment) appeared on some garments. Soft, sheer overskirts and tunics returned to fashion.

Skirts were narrow and straight, sometimes with a slit up the front, back, or side to allow for walking. The *hobble skirt*, a pegged skirt — narrow at the bottom and full at the top — enjoyed a brief period of fashion. Wrapped skirts appeared. By the end of the period most garments were instep or ankle length. Many garments had long trailing panels, even if they were fairly short in the front. Designers experimented with new and unusual shapes, but most women settled into the more practical styles.

By 1910 many women parted their hair in the center and dressed the sides in poufs. The back hair was curled or braided and twisted into a bun. False hair was added in the form of braids or curl clusters. Hair styles diminished in size and height. Fashionable hair was often "*Marcelled*" (set in tightly controlled waves) before being dressed into the prevailing style.

A wide variety of hats, many with elaborate trimming, were seen in this period. Early hats were of reasonable size and sat squarely on top of the head. In the middle of the period, hats grew larger and often tilted forward. A number of tall toques and large "lampshade" hats could be found among fashionable headwear. Large hats were held to the head with long ornate hat pins. Toward the end of the period, hats were generally smaller, often with tall, vertical feathers. Brims began to turn down over the face and many hats were worn at a dashing angle.

Jewelry included lockets, bracelets, rings, and watches worn pinned at the shoulder or on a fob at the waist. Toward the end of the period, the first wristwatches were designed.

High-top shoes with French heels were still worn. Pumps were worn in summer with day and evening dress, and oxfords were worn for most sportswear. Shoes had pointed toes and long vamps. Stockings were black, white, or matched to the dress.

Coats and jackets of various lengths were worn. Early coats were high-waisted and fitted; later styles were full and sometimes based on oriental garments. Evening wraps were made of luxurious fabrics and trimmed in fur. Dusters or driving coats were still worn in open cars. Women wore cardigan and pullover sweaters for casual wear.

WORLD WAR I AND THE ROARING TWENTIES 1915–1929

General Characteristics

The war brought about many military influences in civilian dress. Young men sought more comfortable clothing, better suited to the faster pace of modern life. Coats had "natural" shoulders and high, nipped-in waists; pants were pencil slim. Military colors became popular in civilian dress.

To facilitate their participation in the war effort, women turned to practical, functional clothes. Corsets were made less restrictive or were abandoned; skirts were shortened; excess ornament and frivolous decoration were eliminated. Experiencing the freedom of these simpler garments produced a profound change in the attitude of women toward dress. Clothing henceforth would be required to permit women to work, dance, and participate in a wide range of activities in relative comfort.

The slightly high waistline of the war years dropped first to the natural (although not cinched) waist, then to the lower hip. The silhouette of the early years was slightly wider at the bottom, but by the middle Twenties most dresses were rectangular, very little wider at the bottom than at the shoulders. A drooping, downward effect was produced in the look of the clothes by the cut of the garment and the use of soft, lightweight fabrics.

Dress for Men

Men wore a one-piece cotton undergarment or knitted union suit.

Except for formal wear, most shirts were soft and buttoned

down the front. White was still the only proper color for business or formal wear, but colored and striped shirts were worn for casual and sportswear. Influenced by military styles, more shirts had attached, turndown collars that were lower and soft. Four-in-hand and bow ties predominated.

Formal evening dress changed little, but by the Twenties tuxedos were acceptable for most evening occasions. Single-breasted sack suits were worn with matching vests, but the double-breasted coat was rarely seen with a vest. In summer the double-breasted coat or the suit coat and vest were often teamed with white flannel pants. Most coats were buttoned lower than before the war. Early coats had medium-width lapels, but by the end of the Twenties, lapels were wide. A sport coat with pleats and a half-belt in the back joined the blazer and Norfolk jacket for casual wear. In the 1910's many coats were almost fingertip length, but in the early 1920's the coats began to shorten.

Pants were either pencil slim or full straight leg shapes. "*Oxford bags*" worn by college men were extremely wide. Many trousers had cuffs and all were creased. Depending on the season, white linen or tweed *plus fours* (long, full knickers) were worn for golf.

Most men were clean-shaven. Their close-cropped hair was worn slicked to the head, with a side or center part and very short sideburns.

The most popular hats for men were the felt fedora, slouch hat, and the *homburg*, a felt hat with a stiff curled brim and high creased crown. The derby decreased in popularity. Panama straws and the boater (also call the *sennit straw*) were summer favorites. Caps and canvas hats were worn for sports.

Spectator shoes, lowcut, string-tied shoes in black or brown and white, were very popular for summer and resort wear. Fashionable gents wore spats. High-top shoes were worn by older men.

Outerwear included the *Chesterfield* (tailored coat with velvet collar), the covert coat, the camel hair polo coat, and various topcoats. Outerwear was heavily influenced by military dress. A leather version of the officer's coat and jackets based on aviators' gear appeared. Every college man wanted a raccoon coat to wear when cheering his team on.

Dress for Women

The new elasticized foundation garment called the *girdle* was designed to streamline the abdomen, hips, and buttocks without cinching in the waist. A *brassiere* or a snug "bust suppressor" was worn to minimize the shape of the bosom. The two together produced the boyish figure deemed desirable. A sliver of silk slip covered the "foundations."

During the war simple suits with ample, though not full skirts were common. Jackets were first high waisted and slightly fitted, then loose and unfitted or "boxy." Dresses were slightly high waisted with easy skirts during the war. After the war the waistline began to drop until in the early Twenties, the waist appeared to be very low on the hip. The whole silhouette was a narrow rectangle. The length of skirt hems started just above the ankle during the war and gradually rose to the calf and finally hovered around the knees. Short skirts were fashionable for both day and evening wear, although many women never wore the shortest skirt lengths. Layers of fringe and all-beaded dresses were popular. By 1929 longer skirts created by the addition of hanging panels or uneven *handkerchief* hems were introduced for evening wear.

Blouses were long and worn over the skirts to create the low waist look of the late Twenties.

Day necklines were simple shapes, usually cut away from the neck. Many featured flat collars. Evening dresses were often sleeveless with scooped out V- or U-shaped necklines which left only thin straps across the shoulders.

Sleeves were slim and neatly fitted at the shoulder and many dresses were sleeveless with matching or coordinating jackets.

For the first time respectable women could cut their hair. Short, "bobbed" styles were the rage. Those women who were unwilling to cut their hair dressed it close to the head with the back hair arranged in a small neat bun on the nape of the neck. Both long and short styles featured side parts and Marcel waves.

Rouged cheeks, red "cupid's bow" lips, pale-powdered skin, and smokey-shadowed eyelids were fashionable in the later Twenties.

Hats began the period as tall, "pot" shapes. As they decreased in height, they began to fit closely the shape of the head. The resulting helmet-like *cloche* sat far down on the head and had a small, asymmetrical brim. Large-brim hats also sat deeply on the head with the brim turned down.

Earrings, when worn, tended to be long and dangling, since the hair covered the ears. Long ropes of pearls or other beads were the most popular type of jewelry, and long scarves wrapped around the neck sometimes took the place of jewels. Wristwatches were more frequently seen.

Shoes with pointed toes, "French" heels, and laces or interesting strap arrangements were fashionable. Pumps, plain or with large buckles, were also worn. Spats, gaiters, and a few shoes

that buttoned over the ankle remained. In the beginning of the period hose were still colored silk — black for day, pale colors for evening. By the end of the period, transparent flesh-tone stockings in real or artificial silk were fashionable.

Coats were straight, loose-fitting, and slightly longer than the dress. Many coats "wrapped" and were held shut or had one button at the hip. Some were trimmed with fur cuffs and large, standing fur collars.

THE THIRTIES   1930–1939

General Characteristics

For many the Depression put a damper on fashion. For those who could still afford to dress in style, men's clothes featured broad shoulders, a nipped-in natural waist, narrow hips, and straight, full, pleated trousers. The introduction of the forty-hour work week gave the working man more leisure time and increased the demand for casual and sport dress. As each new sports craze developed, a new type of garment was developed to allow full participation in the sport. The increased development of sportswear in turn began to influence acceptable dress in the work place, a trend that continues to the present day.

A silhouette with a natural waistline returned to fashion. Smooth, flat hips and a soft, low-bosomed bodice also developed. Soft, draping fabrics were preferred. Dresses were usually cut on the *bias* (a diagonal to the straight grain of the fabric) to produce the desired clinging effect.

Zippers, previously used only on shoes or work clothes, now began to appear in fashionable clothing.

Dress for Men

Shirt collars were elongated, and four-in-hand ties were of medium width. Short-sleeved shirts of knitted or woven cotton appeared for summer casual wear.

Vests were still worn with single-breasted suits but were usually omitted with the more popular double-breasted suit.

The *English drape* suit was a major fashion development of the Thirties. The ventless jacket was buttoned low, with wide shoulders, nipped-in waist, and wide, peaked lapels. The pants were pleated at the waist and tapered slightly to the cuffs. Many of the double-breasted examples were made up in pinstripe fabrics of black/gray or blue/gray combinations.

Linen and seersucker suits were popular for summer and resort wear. Corduroy pants and suits were popular on the college campus. Sweaters were worn for a wide variety of casual occasions. The white dinner jacket with shawl collar took the place of the tuxedo for resort and summer wear.

Hair continued to be close-cut and parted on the side, but many men now wore their hair in the pompadour style. Sideburns continued to be short. Most men were clean-shaven, but a few sported short, neat mustaches.

California life inspired a range of casual garments, such as the *cardigan suit* (collarless jacket), two-tone shirts, and Hawaiian print shirts and shorts. Ski wear allowing freedom of movement and warmth was developed as more and more people headed for the slopes.

The most popular hat was a felt *snap brim* with pinched front and top crease. Most hat brims were wide and worn turned up in the back and down in the front. Homburgs, Panamas, *sennits* (boaters), and bowlers (derbys) were still worn. A new coconut straw hat with ridged crown and medium brim was introduced.

Shoes were natural or slightly tapered shapes with rounded toes. Most shoes were cut to just below the ankle and laced up the front. A slip-on moccasin or *loafer* was introduced in the late Thirties. The saddle oxford was popular with younger men.

Outerwear included reversible coats (wool and waterproof duck), Chesterfields, leather jackets, and the trench coat.

Dress for Women

Undergarments were little changed. Slips became longer as skirts lengthened; many had bra-shaped tops.

Dresses were designed with shirring or pleats in the bodice to create a soft bosom effect. At the beginning of the period shoulders were small and natural. Necklines were simple and featured drapes, cowls, and soft collars. Sleeves sometimes had a bit of extra fullness at the top of the cap. Natural waistlines returned. A self-fabric belt was the usual waist finish.

Skirts dropped to calf length for day, and once again evening gowns were floor length, although many were shorter in the front. Most skirts flared either from the hip or just above the knee. Bias-cut skirts clung to the hips.

Suits were popular for day wear. Suit jackets fit snuggly in the

hips and bloused above the waist. Blouses with soft collars, jabots, or bows were visible at the neck of the jacket. Suit skirts were cut in gores or with pleats.

Long pants were worn by a some women for sports or casual wear. *Lounging pajamas* were luxurious "at home" attire.

Many evening gowns showed "classical" influence. Gowns were often simple in the front with a plunging back neckline, criss-crossed with straps. Simple and dramatic elegance was prized.

Hair was a bit longer than in the Twenties, worn parted on the side and waved around the face. The ends of the hair were dressed in rolls or curls.

Hats continued for a time to fit closely to the head, but they grew more shallow. Toward the end of the period hats sat up on the head and were usually worn at an angle over the forehead. Hat veiling, spider-web fine, adorned many hats.

Many women copied the high, thin, arched eyebrows and dark red lips of the Hollywood movie queens. Even conservative women used face powder and lipstick.

Shoes had pointed toes and higher heels than in the Twenties. Sandals were worn for casual wear, and high-heeled sandals in gold and silver kid were introduced for evening wear. Natural-color "nylons" with seams began to overtake silk stockings.

Coats were long or three-quarter length, often with fur collars. *Boas* (long, narrow scarves) of fox or mink were worn draped around the necks of suits, coats, and evening wear.

THE FORTIES   1940–1949

General Characteristics

World War II dominated the decade of the Forties. As the conflict spread, all resources were conserved and given defense priority. Fashion excesses were out; rationing in. Two-pants suits, vests, trouser cuffs, and long skirts were deemed wasteful. New synthetic fibers were developed that would soon enter the world of fashion. The broad-shouldered, "drape" suit continued in style but gradually became less fitted in the waist and hips.

Military dress again influenced fashion styling for both men and women. As in World War I, women entered the work force in large numbers. Women's clothes took on a crisp, businesslike look. Shoulders broadened, defined waists returned, and skirts were shortened until they just covered the knees.

Dress for Men

Dress shirts had wide-spread, long pointed collars. Toward the end of the war, shirts were made of parachute nylon. Sport shirts (often short sleeved) were made in plaids, large prints, and solid color gabardines. Factory workers often wore sport shirts and slacks instead of work clothes.

The popular four-in-hand tie was wide and was tied in a bulky "Windsor knot." Bold print ties were worn, some with hand-painted designs.

Two-piece, single-breasted suits without vests or cuffs were made during the war years. Lapels, while still wide, had less exaggerated points. Vents appeared in the center back or side back seams of jackets. Suits were made in a wide variety of plaids, stripes, tweeds, and flannels. The *Eisenhower* or *Ike* jacket was a waist-length jacket with shirt-type sleeves, button front, and patch pockets modeled after the military uniform worn by General Eisenhower. Separate sport coats appeared that could be combined with dress slacks or casual wear.

Pants were cut fairly full, pleated in front, creased, and cuffless.

Hair continued close-cut with short sideburns. Most men were still clean-shaven.

Sportswear continued to flourish. Among the new garments to appear were Bermuda shorts, polo shirts, and zipper-front jackets.

Panama and coconut straws, homburgs, and Tyrolean hats were all worn, but the wide-brim, felt slouch hat was the most popular.

For outerwear "fingertip" coats (a short top coat) were introduced. Trench coats remained popular.

Dress for Women

Shirtwaist dresses and "uniform" styles were popular. Large shoulder pads produced broad, square shoulders in dresses, suits, and coats. Skirts and blouses paired with sweaters became a practical way for many women to dress. During the war, skirts fit smoothly over the hips and flared to just below the knee. Garments were cut on the straight grain to conserve fabric. Asymmetrical garments enjoyed new popularity. Popular necklines included the sweetheart, V-neck, and shirt collar styles.

"Teenagers," a new entity, wore blouses, sweaters, skirts, bobby sox, and saddle oxfords. Weekends were spent in blue jeans and dad's oversized shirt. Female defense workers wore uniforms,

many of them coveralls. Some long, full pants and above-the-knee shorts were found in women's sportswear.

Hair was often shoulder-length. In one popular style the front and side hair was dressed in rolls away from the face and the back hair was rolled under and caught in a *snood* (a large hairnet). Other styles swept the hair up to a crown of curls on the top and forehead or let the hair hang loose from a side part to wave and curl about the face and shoulders.

Hats included turbans, toques, adaptations of men's styles, and whimsical concoctions of felt, veiling, and decorations. Hats were worn at an angle over the forehead.

Eyebrows were fuller and more natural in the Forties, but powder and bright lipstick were still used.

Shoes were no longer pointed but followed the natural foot shape. Heels were thick and some were extremely high. Some shoes were built on thick soles called *platforms*. Strap sandals were sometimes worn for day as well as evening. The open-toe *sling-back* pump (open heel with strap) was a popular shoe. Oxfords with stout heels were worn by more practical women.

Nylon stockings were extremely difficult to get during the war years. Cotton anklets and leg makeup were substituted.

Women wore the trench coat and polo coat as well as full-back, unfitted styles in long or short lengths (*toppers*).

After the war Dior introduced (in 1947) the "New Look." An attempt to return to more feminine fashions, the "New Look" featured natural shoulders, a pinched waist, and a long skirt. The skirt silhouette was either full and stiffened or the pencil-slim "straight skirt." In the next few years women all over the world dropped their hems and cinched their waists.

THE FIFTIES   1950–1959

General Characteristics

The Ivy League, natural-shoulder style challenged the heavy padding and square shoulders of previous men's fashions and a slim, straight silhouette took over.

Dior's "New Look" (1947) was a major influence on the women's styles of the Fifties. Women's clothes had either pencil-slim or full, *bouffant skirts* (full at the bottom supported by stiff, ruffled petticoats called *crinolines*). Firm, structured undergarments were again required to produce the high, shaped bosom, small waist, and flat abdomen and buttocks in fashion.

New fibers (polyesters and acrylics) made big news in clothes for both men and women. Fashionable color schemes included neutral colors (gray, charcoal, black, navy) spiced with bright accents (red, lemon, pumpkin) and large areas of white.

Dress for Men

Dress shirts had narrow collars with small pointed or rounded ends. Button-down collars found their way from the college campus to business wear. Collar bars and tabs were devised to keep the collar neatly in place around the tie. Small patterns and pale pastel colors were fashionable in shirts. A wide variety of sport shirts were worn.

Ties decreased in width until some were barely 1½ inches wide. Bow ties were worn primarily for formal wear. Solids, stripes, and small patterns were popular.

The "natural-shoulder," unpadded coat made its appearance. After initial resistance, even older men accepted it in a modified version. Lapels narrowed to fine slivers on some jackets. Most coats had three buttons, although the top and bottom buttons were often left open. Coats were cut straight with little indentation at the waist. Sport coats were popular; "wash and wear" models appeared for summer. The *Continental* suit was more fitted, with a deeply rounded front opening and a high, two-button closure. Three-piece suits were rare, but plaid and fancy vests were occasionally worn.

After formal day wear (cutaway) was rejected as inaugural attire by the new President, Eisenhower, its use rapidly declined. Jackets made of Madras (bright-colored plaid cotton originally from India), batik, or other fancy fabric joined the white dinner jacket and tuxedo for dress occasions. Waist-length, zipper-front jackets of leather or fabric were popular for casual and sportswear.

Pants were cut straight and less full at the beginning of the period. Most trousers had pleats, creases, and cuffs. In the mid-Fifties pants began to taper at the bottom and some uncuffed, flat front pants appeared. Bermuda shorts, *deck pants* (calf-length sailing pants), jeans, and sport slacks were worn for casual wear. New active sportswear included stretch ski pants.

Hair was very close-cut with short sideburns, then combed away from the face with a side part. Some men retained the pompadour style of the Forties, while others favored the short, military-type crew cut. Hair tonic was used to hold the style in place and give

the hair a sheen. Young men began to grow the side and top hair long and used hair oil to comb it to the back of the head in a style known as a "duck's ass."

Hats had narrow brims and lower, slightly tapered crowns. Many sported feathers or other small decorations. A plaid wool hat shaped like the snap brim was popular for sportswear.

Car coats and other short overcoats were popular as more men drove their cars to and from the suburbs. Straight-cut raincoats of black or tan, some with zip-out pile linings, were versatile and practical. Trench coats were still popular. Dressy Chesterfields and simple wool topcoats were also worn.

Dress for Women

Brassieres were heavily structured and held the bosom in firm, high cones. Padding was added when needed. The *"Merry Widow"* was a lightweight corset with elastic insets and boning. Mid-hip length, this "long-line" bra could be worn with or without straps. Separate waist cinchers were also used to create the small, fashionable waist. Girdles were a necessity under straight skirts. Petticoats returned to fashion to support the full silhouette. Stiff horsehair, crisp taffeta, nylon net, or starched ruffles created the lower edge of these petticoats and sometimes three or four were worn together. Skirts were lower calf-length but began to shorten in the late Fifties.

Shirtwaist (open down the front with shirt-style collars) and other simple dresses with fitted bodices and set-in, raglan, or dolman sleeves were popular for day wear. Collars were often large and stood away from the neck. Skirts were either bouffant or straight with *kick pleats* (a box pleat from knee to hem to allow for mobility). Bouffant skirts could be gathered, pleated, gored, or circular. Princess dresses, fitting tightly at the waist and sweeping to wide hems, returned to fashion. Starting from below the calf, skirts were shortened to just below the knee by the end of the decade.

Wide, stiff belts — matching or contrasting — were worn tightly buckled around the waist.

Suits followed similar lines: straight or circular skirts with hip-length fitted jackets or short "bolero" jackets. Suit jackets did not always match the skirt but were sometimes in a bright contrasting color. Coordinated separates (blouse, skirt, sweater, jacket, pants) became established as a classic way of dressing and increased in popularity throughout the twentieth century.

A brief fashion for the *trapeze* dress (a loose triangular-shape dress) and the *sacque-back chemise* dress (straight sheath with

bloused back) foreshadowed less-fitted fashions to come.

Pants of all types were worn for casual wear: shorts (upper thigh), Bermuda shorts (just above the knee), pedal-pushers (upper calf), Capri or toreador (lower calf), and ankle-length.

Evening gowns were frequently strapless or furnished with small *spaghetti* straps. Draped bodices were fashionable and the bouffant skirt was often tulle or sheer organza. *Ballerina length* (ankle or lower calf) was popular. Some evening wear required petticoats with lightweight hoops in the bottom.

Many women wore their hair short and close to the head. Straight-cut bangs were a popular feature. Young women wore the *pony tail*, all hair drawn high up on the back of the head and caught with an elastic band. Longer hair was worn waved and curled about the shoulders or sleeked back into a "French twist."

Hats were small and fit close to the head at the beginning of the period. Hats completely covered with flowers were popular.

Makeup base, powder, lipstick, eyeshadow, eyeliner, and mascara were commonly used. Emphasis was still placed on the mouth with the use of brightly colored lipstick. Dark lines were drawn around the eyes, and eyebrows were plucked to give a high arch.

Pumps were the most popular style of shoe. Pointed toes returned, and heels grew tall and very small at the bottom (*stilletto* or *spike* heels). Sandals, moccasins, oxfords, and "flats" were also available. Seamless nylon hose in black, taupe, navy, and flesh tones were worn.

Coats were either straight or full with "swingy" backs. The *topper*, a short wool coat, was worn for spring or fall. Car coats in corduroy, wool, or suede were available for women.

THE SIXTIES   1960–1969

General Characteristics

Simple, clean lines in easy-care fabrics dominated the clothes of the Sixties. Clothing for both men and women skimmed the body. New plastics and synthetic fabrics were incorporated into all types of clothing. Solid colors dominated the early part of the period.

The late Sixties saw a revolution in men's clothing. Formality in dress was all but abandoned. Men began to wear bright colors for work as well as play. The "Mod" style, "psychedelic" colors, and fantastic prints appeared as the "Hippie" counterculture, rock music, and space exploration all had an influence on fashion.

Dress for Men

Men's shirts had moderate-length, pointed collars in the early Sixties. Small stripes were popular. "No-iron" shirts of polyester and cotton or of cotton with a resin finish swept the market. Wider collars with long points came into fashion later in the decade. By the end of the Sixties brightly colored shirts with French cuffs and large cuff links were worn. Shirts with stand-up collars and ties of matching fabric were also worn. Sweaters, turtlenecks, and knit shirts of all types were popular for a wide variety of occasions.

Ties began the decade as narrow, conservative neckwear and ended the Sixties as wide (three to four inches), bold, brightly colored accents. Silk ties and matching handkerchiefs were worn even by conservative men. Some men substituted a silk scarf tied casually around the neck under an open shirt collar. Necklaces of beads or heavy chains with pendants were sometimes worn instead of traditional ties.

Traditional suits were lightly padded, single-breasted with medium-width lapels, straight and boxy in the body. Pants were slender with flat fronts and straight or tapering legs.

In the late Sixties an array of new styles were created for men. Collarless, zipper-front suits; *Edwardian* suits (high-buttoned, pinched-waist, double-breasted suits); *Safari* jackets (belted jacket based on jungle gear); and new versions of the Norfolk jacket — all appeared along with traditional sport coats in bright colors and plaids. The *Nehru* suit featured a jacket with a standing collar that buttoned to the neck without lapels.

Formal wear reflected the new freedom. Dinner jackets were styled in the Nehru or Edwardian styles, in brighter colors and varied fabrics (brocades, velvets). Shirts with ruffled fronts and cuffs were worn with lapel jackets.

Hair in the beginning of the Sixties was neat and close-cut with short sideburns. By the mid-Sixties sideburns began to lengthen and the "dry look" was in fashion. By the end of the period most men wore their hair over the ears and over the collar in the back in a loose, wind-blown look. Many young men wore their hair shoulder length or longer and held it in place with a headband or tied it back in a queue. Full, bushy beards and mustaches were also common among the "Hip Generation."

Men's hats at the beginning of the Sixties continued the small- and medium-brim styles of the Fifties. Wider brims began to appear in the late Sixties.

Late in the Sixties short, square-toed boots and loafers with tassels or buckled straps became fashionable.

Topcoats and overcoats were short, between hip and knee. Early versions were mostly single-breasted; later ones were double-breasted with "Edwardian" shaping in the waist and chest. Zip-front reversible jackets were popular for casual wear.

Dress for Women

The early Sixties saw a simplification of the silhouette for women's dress. Boxy suits with straight skirts, sleeveless dresses with coats or jackets, A-line skirts, and shifts were popular. The waistline became less important and skirts began to climb. Brightly colored, plain and textured wools were popular. The *mini-skirt* was first shown in the early Sixties. Skirts so named were a minimum of two inches above the knee, and many exposed most of the thigh. By the end of the Sixties, short skirts dominated the fashion scene.

As an alternative to the "mini," many women turned to pants. Pants suits were designed to be worn for work, play, and formal occasions. Jumpsuits and hostess pajamas were again in fashion. After some initial resistance, pants were accepted everywhere and became a staple wardrobe item even among conservative women.

Formal wear was styled along similar lines in fancy fabrics, often beaded. Cut-outs and see-through sections revealed the body underneath.

Toward the end of the Sixties, psychedelic colors and prints were used for dresses, hostess gowns, evening wear, and accessories. Styles based on ethnic dress (gypsy, peasant, Mexican, American Indian, African, Russian) began to appear.

Denim began to dominate casual wear. Jeans were the full-time uniform of the young. Tight-fitting, worn, torn, and sometimes patched, jeans represented the anti-fashion, anti-establishment feelings of the Hippie. The shape of jeans changed to a hip-hugging waist with bell-bottom legs.

Bouffant hair styles of teased or back-combed hair were worn at the beginning of the period. Hair was shoulder or chin length. Headbands or large bows were worn across the top of the head, sometimes to disguise the addition of a "fall" of false hair. In the later Sixties bouffant hairdos were replaced by short geometrical cuts. Hippie women wore their hair long and straight.

Fashionable hats were of solid-color, matching fabrics in small *pillbox*, cap, or helmet shapes. However, because they tended to depress the bouffant hair style, hats were no longer considered a necessity to a fashionable ensemble. Scarves tied simply around the head were frequently substituted. Hats never regained their former status as a required accessory.

The emphasis in makeup switched from the lips to the eyes. Lipstick colors were pale and often pearlized. False eyelashes were common, and eyes were heavily lined top and bottom.

Tights or pantyhose reaching from waist to toe were worn with the mini-dress. Solid colors (often matching the dress), fishnets, ribbed, and other decorative knits were used in legwear.

Shoes had low to medium, chunky heels, and they gradually developed from pointed toes to broad, square toes. Knee-high boots of vinyl or leather were added for winter. Boots were tight fitting and zipped up the inside of the leg.

Cloth coats to match dresses were fashionable in the early Sixties. Toward the end of the decade longer coats — *maxi* (ankle length) and *midi* (calf length) — inspired by the nineteenth-century Russian styles became popular.

THE SEVENTIES   1970–1979

General Characteristics

The counterculture influences of the late Sixties became mainstream fashion in the Seventies. Romantic, "costume" looks inspired by many sources were popular. Blue denim was the most commonly seen fabric on both men and women. Casual styles invaded all occasions. Longer skirts returned, and a general softening occurred in women's clothes. A resurgence of interest in arts and crafts influenced the design of clothing that featured quilting, patchwork, and hand-woven effects. Clothes worn for active sports began to influence fashion. Although the great variety of clothing allowed for individualization of the wardrobe, most garments had natural shoulders and body-conscious lines.

Dress for Men

Undershirts were abandoned by many men. The athletic shirt and the T-shirt were worn alone as casual wear. T-shirts were printed with designs and slogans. Turtleneck sweaters were worn for almost any occasion. Dress shirts were bright, solid colors or bold stripes. Shiny, synthetic knit shirts were tapered for better fit and printed in bold, colorful designs. Collars were wide with long points.

Ties were very wide. Wide stripes and large floral and geometric prints were popular. Large bow ties were also worn. More and more men, however, abandoned ties for the open shirt and gold chain necklaces.

Jackets were cut with wide lapels, two buttons, and nipped-in waist. Even business suits were made of polyester knits or denim and featured *saddle stitching* (decorative stitching). The Western influence could be seen in many garments. *Leisure suits* of polyester knits were popular. The jackets of these casual suits had "shirt" styling — tab fronts, wide collars set on a neckband, and shirt sleeves with cuffs. Patch pockets and yokes were usually top-stitched with heavy, contrasting thread. *Safari* jackets were shirt-styled jackets with patch pockets and short or long sleeves.

Dress pants were cut slightly below the natural waist and had cuffs and creases. Casual, low-waist pants known as *hip-huggers* were worn with wide belts. Pants were tight fitting in the waist, hips, and thighs, then flared to a wide bell at the bottom. Denim and bright-colored knits were popular in pants. Jumpsuits based on workman's coveralls enjoyed a period of popularity.

Toward the end of the Seventies interest in more traditional men's styling revived. Vests and pleated front pants were more often seen. Neutral colors, narrow lapels, thin ties, and suits with soft shaping began to reappear.

Traditional men's tailoring featured two basic styles: the *American cut* and the *European cut*. The American cut featured soft-shoulder jacket with slight waist suppression, notched lapels (4½ inches wide), flap pockets, and vents at the sides or center back. The pants were straight. The European cut featured a close-fitting jacket with high armholes, nipped waist, flaring bottom, padded shoulders, wide lapels (five inches wide), and deep vents at the side or back. The pants were flared, and the suit often had a vest.

At the end of the period formal wear began to be less extravagant and more elegant.

Hair was frequently full and "dry" with long sideburns. Some men retained the very long styles of the late Sixties. Mustaches and beards continued to be popular although they were sometimes neatly trimmed. By the late Seventies neater, shorter hair styles appeared, and sideburns began to shorten.

Boots and blunt-toed, heavy shoes were popular in the Seventies. Shoes had thick soles, and some had platform soles an inch or more high. Some shoes were brightly colored and were decorated with metallic leathers. By 1979 thin soles and tapered toes began to return. Sneakers were widely worn for casual wear.

Longer overcoats also returned — knee to upper calf.

Dress for Women

As a symbol of feminist independence, some women abandoned the wearing of a bra. Others switched to soft, molded bras which provided only minimum support and allowed a lower, less-defined bosom.

Close-fitting sweaters and tops were popular. High waists, low waists, and natural waists were all possible. Most styles were soft, body-conscious shapes. Jackets had wide lapels and long, pointed collars. Romantic styles were based on the gypsy look, ethnic styles, and Victorian lingerie. Wraparound dresses in bright, printed knits and loose "tent" dresses were popular in the early and mid-Seventies. Caftans were worn for hostess and beach wear.

Although the mini-skirt and the new *hot pants* (short shorts) remained fashionable, skirts began to lengthen, and some long skirts were worn. By the late Seventies the majority of skirts dipped below the knee.

Hip-hugger or natural-waist pants with bell bottoms were everywhere. Knickers, gauchos, and all styles of jeans were also worn. Straight, full legs with cuffs appeared in the late Seventies. With the hip-hugger jeans and skirts, belts of leather or chain were worn.

Scarves tied around the head replaced hats for many occasions. Berets, caps, and some mannish hats were worn. The "gaucho" hat and Russian-style fur hats were also fashionable.

Natural hair styles were in fashion. Blow-dry styles, short curly styles, blunt cuts, frizzed hair, Gibson girl, and French braids were all worn. Wigs were considered a fashion accessory and were very popular.

Dark, low-intensity lipstick colors were used with smoke-toned eyeshadow. Many women abandoned makeup in the early Seventies.

Platform shoes with blunt toes and wedge-heel shoes were popular. In the mid-Seventies heels went up, platforms decreased, and a more natural toe returned. Tall boots were worn with coats and short pants.

Midi-length "Russian" coats and tailored capes were popular at the beginning of the period. Full-length, quilted down coats for sport and dress were worn.

THE EIGHTIES   1980–1987

General Characteristics

The Eighties brought revived interest in traditional men's tailoring and styles. The more flamboyant styles of the Seventies disappeared.

A variety of international influences began to make an impact on women's fashion. Early romantic looks began to give way to cleaner, bolder shapes and oversized, draped silhouettes. The fashions of the Thirties, Forties, Fifties, and Sixties each took a turn influencing current styles.

Neutrals and rich, jewel-like tones were favored and natural fibers returned to popularity.

Dress for Men

Dress shirts returned to medium- or narrow-width collars. Colored dress shirts in solids, stripes, and plaids were still popular, although colors were more subtle.

Medium- to narrow-width ties in pastels and medium intensities were worn. Plain or striped red ties and yellow ties with small dots were very popular.

Typical suit coats were less fitted, softer, less padded, and lower in the armholes. Lapels were medium to wide widths at the beginning of the period with some narrow lapels appearing later. A fashion for loose, unlined jackets with large shoulder pads appeared for fashionable young men in the mid-Eighties.

Straight-leg, medium-width pants were worn by conservative men. *Baggies*, a loose trouser tapered toward the bottom, were popular with younger men. A preference for Fifties-style tapered and tight-fitting pants was evident among the counterculture "Punk" groups and spread to fashion in the mid-Eighties.

Casual wear included loose-fitting sweaters, velour running suits, and sweat suits.

Many men returned to wearing classical black tuxedos, with color and pattern introduced in the cummerbund and tie.

Hair styles became shorter and more neatly groomed. Many men returned to a close-cropped nape and cheekbone-length sideburns. Crew cuts, flat-tops, *spiked* hair (hair stiffened into points on the top of the head), and shaved heads were popular among those young people who were influenced by the "Punk" movement. Some men wore long *shag* cuts in imitation of certain rock stars.

Large- and medium-brim hats returned to fashion but were infrequently worn.

Shoes tapered to natural shapes. Thin soles returned.

Dress for Women

Most women favored practical combinations of dress, jacket, skirt, pants, sweater, or blouse. Wider, padded shoulders returned to fashion. Clean, simple shapes evolved.

Fashion influences were more international. Italian designers contributed interesting knit fashions and tailoring. Japanese designers created unusual, loose, oversized, wrapped shapes. American designers developed practical and smart garments based on American classic looks. English designers contributed both traditional styles and eccentric dress. French designers continued to design high-fashion, body-revealing garments.

Skirt lengths varied but many were calf length or lower. Prairie skirts, layered with petticoats, *dirndl* (straight-cut, and gathered or pleated) skirts, and flared calf-length skirts were among the longer styles. Late in the Eighties mini-skirts again appeared. Short, straight skirts were worn with fitted, broad-shouldered tops sometimes with a peplum.

Pants went from straight cut to baggies to tapered leg. The calf-length, fitted styles from the Fifties returned. Tight-knit leggings or pants worn with oversized man-tailored shirts were popular. Loose-fitting sweaters were worn with skirts and pants.

Many women maintained a full mane of shoulder-length hair. Layered hair styles were popular, and in the mid-Eighties short, asymmetrical, or spiked styles were fashionable.

Small hats were worn at an angle over the forehead.

Large chunky necklaces, large dangling or button earrings, and bangle bracelets were fashionable.

In the early Eighties makeup created the "natural look." Bright, clear lipstick colors returned in the mid-Eighties.

Fashionable pointed-toe shoes ranged from flats to high, thin heels. *Sneakers* or *running shoes* were worn for sports, casual wear, travel, and sometimes business.

Quilted down coats in all lengths were popular. By the middle of the decade straight-cut wool coats with large shoulders were more fashionable. Large shawls and scarves were wrapped around the neck and shoulders.

Appendix III
Play Synopses

The following synopses, compiled by Melissa J. Wentworth, include information on the plays referred to in this text.

***Adding Machine, The.* (1923)** Drama. Elmer Rice. Mr. Zero, a clerk for 25 years, is to be replaced by an adding machine. In the single rebellion of his life, he kills his boss. He is tried and sentenced to death for the murder. After death, he arrives at Elysian Fields. Though quite uncomfortable with the unlimited freedom there, he finds a job in a repair shop operating an adding machine. Soon he is seduced by a blonde, called Hope, and convinced to return to Earth. There he gets a job operating . . . an adding machine. Theme of individual versus the modern world.

***All Night Strut — Open Through Harlem.* (1976)** Musical Revue. Conceived and directed by Fran Charnis. A song and dance review featuring music from the 1930's and 1940's.

***Annie.* (1973)** Musical. Book by Thomas Meehan. Music by Charles Strouse. Lyrics by Martin Charnin. Based on the Harold Gray comic strip, "Little Orphan Annie." Annie, age 11, has spent most of her life in the orphanage. Despite her drab existence, the New York City winter, and the Depression, Annie keeps her zest for life, much to the dismay of Miss Hannigan, the sour housemother. Indeed, when Annie is chosen to spend Christmas holidays with Oliver Warbucks, billionaire, Miss Hannigan is quite spiteful. During the visit

Warbucks grows fond of Annie and decides to adopt her. But Annie feels she must first resolve the mystery of her parents' whereabouts. After a series of events — funny, suspenseful, and musical — Annie, her dog Sandy, and Warbucks become a happy family in time for Christmas morning.

Antigone. **(c. 441 B.C.)** Tragedy. Sophocles. Following a civil war in Thebes, King Creon rules that Eteocles, his slain nephew and defender of the city, will be buried with full honor. His other nephew, the traitor Polynices, will be left unburied. Claiming a greater obligation to the divine law of the gods, Antigone defies her uncle and buries her brother. She is sentenced to death. Creon's son, Haemon, in love with Antigone, kills himself. The Queen, too, dies before Creon is convinced of his tragic error by the blind seer, Teiresias.

As You Like It. **(c. 1599)** Comedy. William Shakespeare. Duke Frederick steals the dukedom from Duke Senior and banishes him. Duke Senior takes refuge in the Forest of Arden. His daughter Rosalind, also banished, flees to the forest disguised as a boy. Her friend, Celia, daughter to Duke Frederick, accompanies her dressed as a country girl. Orlando, in love with Rosalind, follows. He fails to recognize Rosalind in her disguise and so, unwittingly, receives from her "lessons in love." Duke Frederick finally repents, and all return to court to celebrate three weddings.

Bald Soprano, The. **(1950)** Comedy. Eugene Ionesco. On an English evening in a middle-class English living room, Mr. and Mrs. Smith — both English — are sitting. They are visited by Mr. and Mrs. Martin and the fire chief. An absurdist view of the human condition.

Ballad of Baby Doe. **(1956)** Opera. Douglas Moore. Libretto by John La Touche. Based on characters and events in American history. Elizabeth Doe, known as Baby, deserts her husband and leaves the mining town of Central City. She meets Horace Tabor in Leadville. Despite his being 30 years her senior, they fall in love. They divorce their respective spouses and marry. Baby is never accepted by society but is content to be with Tabor. When the silver standard collapses, and with it Tabor's wealth, she remains with him. When he dies, Baby honors his last wish that she never sell the Matchless Mine.

Barber of Seville, The. **(1816)** Opera. Gioacchino Antonio Rossini. Libretto by Cesare Sterbini. Based on the comedy by Pierre de Beaumarchais. In eighteenth-century Spain Count

Almaviva falls madly in love with Rosina, but his plans to marry her are thwarted by her guardian, Dr. Bartolo, who plans to marry her himself. Through a series of disguises — the serenader Lindoro, a drunken soldier, and a music professor — Count Almaviva is able to court Rosina and win her love. A compromise is finally reached wherein Bartolo gets the dowry and the Count gets the bride.

Black Elk Lives. **(1981)**   Drama. Christopher Sergel. Based on the book *Black Elk Speaks* by John G. Neihardt. Black Elk had a vision. A litany about the settling of North America through the eyes of the American Plains Indians.

Blue Bird, The. **(1908)**   Fantasy. Maurice Maeterlinck. Two peasant children, accompanied by Bread, Milk, and other allegorical characters, seek the Blue Bird of Happiness only to find it back in their own home.

Boyfriend, The. **(1955)**   Musical. Sandy Wilson. Madame Dubonnet's finishing school near Nice teaches girls to be "perfect young ladies." But with the Carnival Ball this very evening there is no stopping the romancing of Dulcie, Fay, Maisie, and Nancy by four young men. Only Polly does not have a date; her wealthy father has discouraged suitors. When a handsome messenger arrives with her costume, Polly takes fate into her own hands and asks *him* to the Ball. When his true identity becomes known, all obstacles to romance disappear.

Broadway Rhythm. **(1984)**   Musical Review. Produced by Bruce Lucker for the New York State Department of Commerce. A salute to black stars and their Broadway shows.

Cat on a Hot Tin Roof. **(1955)**   Drama. Tennessee Williams. On a hot, summer evening on the Mississippi Delta, Big Daddy's family is gathered on the family plantation to celebrate his sixty-fifth birthday. The undercurrent of greed, loneliness, and past sins is soon apparent. The eruption of the stifling weather into a storm parallels the explosion of suppressed emotions.

Cats. **(1981)**   Musical. Music by Andrew Lloyd Webber. Musical rendition of poems by T. S. Eliot; mainly drawn from *Old Possum's Book of Practical Cats.*

Caucasian Chalk Circle, The. **(1944–1945)**   Drama. Bertolt Brecht. Play within a play, the major portion occurring in an Oriental land in the Middle Ages. Grusha, servant girl at the governor's palace, saves the governor's son during a military coup. Left with the child after the battle, she travels to the mountains to escape the Ironshirts. Grusha makes many sacrifices but manages to keep them both alive. Years later the governor's widow has had the child traced, and Grusha brought to court. The drunken once-a-clerk-now-a-judge Azdak must decide who has acted as a true mother and thus deserves the child and the inheritance.

Central City Nights. **(1935)** Musical Review. Conceived, written, and produced by Robert Edmond Jones. Music by Frank St. Leger. Excerpts from the great plays and operas produced for the Central City Opera during the great boom days of the Gold Rush.

Choephoroe, **or** ***The Libation Bearers.*** **(458** B.C.**)** Tragedy. Aeschylus. Second play from the trilogy *Oresteia*. Agamemnon, King of Argos, has been murdered by his wife. Clytemnestra is now married to Aegisthus, Agamemnon's brother. Orestes returns to avenge his father's death. He and his sister, Electra, are united in revenge. Clytemnestra and Aegisthus are killed. Despite the law which allows families to avenge murders, the Furies gather to chase and torment Orestes because he has killed his own mother.

Comedy of Errors, The. **(c. 1591)** Comedy. William Shakespeare. Aegeon, a Syracusan merchant, was shipwrecked with his wife, his twin baby sons — both named Antipholus — and twin slaves — both called Dromio. His wife, one twin, and one slave reached Ephesus; Aegeon and the others got back to Syracuse. Neither group knows the other has survived. Now, years later, Aegeon, one son, and one slave arrive coincidentally in Ephesus. This comedy of mistaken identities is furthered by a jealous wife, her sister, a courtesan, and a quack doctor.

Country Girl, The. **(1949)** Drama. Clifford Odets. Frank Elgin, an alcoholic has-been actor, lies to himself and others. His wife, Georgie, covers for him and manages to keep them both on their feet. A young director, Bernie, decides to bring Frank back into the spotlight. A disastrous episode the night before opening forces Bernie to see the truth about Frank. The backstage atmosphere is enhanced by several character roles: an ingenue, a young playwright, and a worried producer.

Country Wife, The. **(1675)** Comedy of Manners. William Wycherley. Horner, infamous for his amorous past, spreads the rumor that he is now impotent. The unsuspecting men of London send their wives to Horner to be entertained, assuming there is no risk of being cuckolded. Enter Margery Pinchwife, innocent country girl recently married to the aging, jealous Pinchwife. Too late to hear the rumors, Pinchwife correctly suspects Horner of having designs on Margery. Numerous bawdy situations lead to the conclusion that the pretence of morality is much more fun than true moral behavior.

***Crucible, The.* (1952)**   Drama. Arthur Miller. Dramatization of the Salem witch hunt and trial. A few young women, their story of being possessed by the devil based on lies and hysteria, are able to send 19 men and women to their deaths as witches. Miller writes with parallels to his own time.

***Cyrano de Bergerac.* (1897)**   Drama. Edmond Rostand. In the mid-seventeenth century Cyrano is everything a hero ought to be: a swashbuckling fighter, true friend, poet, and a romantic. But when Cyrano falls in love with Roxane, he does not court her because of his large, unsightly nose. Roxane is attracted to Christian, a handsome, young guard under Cyrano. With Cyrano's coaching, Christian charms Roxane with his words. They marry, but Christian and Cyrano depart immediately for battle. While there, Cyrano writes love letters to Roxane in Christian's name. Christian dies in battle, and Cyrano swears never to reveal their secret. Roxane retreats to a nunnery, where Cyrano visits her weekly for fifteen years. One day he is ambushed by enemies and mortally wounded. He struggles to the convent, dying. At the last moment Roxane realizes that his is the soul that she has always loved.

***Daughter of the Regiment, The.* (1840)**   Comic Opera. Gaetano Donizetti. Libretto by Jules-Henri Vernoy de Saint-Georges and Jean-François Alfred Bayard. Marie was left on a battlefield as a baby and adopted by the Grenadiers who found her. Now she loves Tonio, who once saved her from danger. Tonio, though not sure of her love, joins the Grenadiers because no one outside the regiment may marry her. Meanwhile, the Marquise of Birkenfeld claims Marie as a niece, moves her to a fine house, and arranges marriage to the son of a duke. Maria convinces the Marquise that as she is a daughter of love, she must be allowed to marry for love.

***Day in the Death of Joe Egg, A.* (1967)**   Black Comedy. Peter Nichols. A schoolteacher and his wife share the care of their totally dependent, spastic ten-year-old daughter, Joe. The wife views the child's condition as her punishment for premarital sex. The husband feels he is the brunt of a black joke. Finally, he can no longer seek comfort in his black humor and flees his home.

***Death of a Salesman.* (1949)** Tragedy. Arthur Miller. Willy Loman is 63 years old and does not understand why his life expectations have not been fulfilled. In a series of memories and hallucinations intertwined with the present, Loman searches for the moment when his American dream — contented family and business success — went sour.

***Die Fledermaus.* (1874)** Operetta. Johann Strauss. Libretto by Carl Haffner and Richard Genée. Gabriel von Eisenstein must spend eight days in jail. As his young wife, Rosalinda, packs his belongings, her work is interrupted by Alfred, an old lover. She agrees to meet him once her husband is securely in jail. Dr. Falke, friend to Gabriel, arrived to take him to a festive party before he goes to prison. After they leave, Alfred returns, but the rendezvous is interrupted by the prison warden seeking her husband. To protect her honor, Alfred is identified as her husband and goes off to prison. Later everyone (except Alfred) arrives at the party. Rosalinda, in disguise, flirts with Gabriel and steals his watch. After the party Gabriel goes to the prison to turn himself in, only to find Alfred there in his place. He accuses his wife of infidelity, only to have her display his watch, proving flirtation is a pastime they share. All is forgiven and everyone sings a song in praise of champagne.

***Doll's House, A.* (1879)** Drama. Henrik Ibsen. Nora Helmer excitedly prepares for the Norwegian Christmas. Pampered and frivolous, she plays with the children just as her husband, Torvald, plays with her. Although married eight years, Torvald has sheltered Nora from financial and practical concerns. But unknown to Torvald, Nora once borrowed money to provide him with special care when he was ill. To do so she forged her dying father's name. Now one of her husband's employees threatens to expose her. Torvald's selfish reaction to the threat opens her eyes to the deceit of their marriage. Nora decides she must leave her "doll house" if she is to grow as an individual.

Everyman (c. 1500) Morality Play. Allegory. Seeking companionship on his journey to death, Everyman turns to Strength, Fellowship, Confession, Beauty, and other former friends. All refuse to accompany him except Good Deeds, who follows him into the grave.

Fantasticks, The. **(1960)** Musical. Book and lyrics by Tom Jones. Music by Harvey Schmidt. If you want your children to do something, tell them not to, and they definitely will. At least that is what fathers Bellamy and Hucklebee decide as they plot to unite their offspring (Luisa and Matt). When the elaborate plot goes haywire, it takes the dashing El Gallo, a beautiful moon, a bit of fantasy, and a lot of growing up before Matt and Luisa find each other's love.

Fifth of July. **(1977)** Tragicomedy. Lanford Wilson. The family farm in rural Missouri is now only a house to Ken, a legless veteran of Vietnam, and his lover, Jed. Ken's decision to sell the farm is questioned when his sister, June, and her teenage daughter visit. Add former college buddies and student activists Gwen and John, plus Aunt Sally and her desire to spread her late husband's ashes on the farm, and the play explodes with vivid colors.

Glass Menagerie, The. **(1945)** Drama. Tennessee Williams. Tom tells the story as it took place in a dingy St. Louis apartment in the 1930's. Amanda Wingfield, a faded Southern belle, vainly tries to create a life based on past standards and lost wealth. Her daughter Laura is painfully shy, caused more by her mother's anxious, continuous attention than by her crippled leg. Tom, distracted only by alcohol or movies, is oppressed by Amanda's meddling ways and by the monotony of his warehouse job. Their fragile world is finally tipped out of balance when Tom invites Jim, an ordinary young man, to dinner.

Hamlet, Prince of Denmark. **(c. 1600)** Tragedy. William Shakespeare. Hamlet's father, King of Denmark, has recently died. Queen Gertrude has married Claudius, the King's brother, and they now reign together. The dead king's ghost appears to Hamlet, accuses Claudius of being his murderer, and instructs Hamlet to avenge his death. But with the disintegration of the once honest court, Hamlet is unable to trust even the vision of his father. He is suspicious of Polonius, the Lord Chamberlain, and rejects Ophelia, whom he had loved. Hoping to expose Claudius' guilt, Hamlet arranges for a traveling troupe to perform a play imitating the killing of the king. Claudius reveals his guilt, but Hamlet is still unable to act. When Polonius is accidentally killed by Hamlet, Claudius sets Laertes, Polonius' son, against Hamlet. The conclusion can only be the complete destruction of the court.

***Harlequinade.* (1965)** Ballet. Music by Riccardo Drigo (*Les Millions d'Arlequin.* 1900). Choreography by George Balanchine. A ballet in two acts featuring the characters of Italian commedia dell'arte. Colombine's father tries to separate her from Harlequin and marry her off to a rich, old suitor. (Earlier Balanchine version, 1952.)

***Heartbreak House.* (1916)** Comedy. George Bernard Shaw. Ellie Dunn, a poor but proper young lady, visits Hesione (Hessy) Hushabye at her country house. Ellie is a bit shocked by the lack of conventions in this fashionable world. Hessy's father, an inventor, does not want to invent the objects of destruction which are in demand. Hessy's husband sees himself as a romantic hero and likes to chase young girls. Ellie appears to be his next target. To gain a foothold in her slippery world, she decides to marry Boss Mangan, another guest. She is soon disillusioned with him, too. Finally, Ellie and the starry-eyed father find common interests and romance with each other.

***Henry IV.* Parts 1 and 2. (c. 1597)** Historic Drama. William Shakespeare. Traces the turbulent thirteen years' reign of Henry IV as ruler of England: his fight against Henry Percy, son of the Earl of Northumberland; the civil war following Percy's defeat; and his own son's coming of age and acceptance of responsibility as a ruler. Comic subplot with the elder knight Falstaff and his band of "soldiers" from the Boar's Head Tavern.

***Italian Straw Hat, The.* (1851)** Farce. Eugène Labiche and Marc-Michel. Fadinard, about to be married, is stopped by a strange woman and her lover. His horse has just eaten her exotic Italian straw hat, and they refuse to leave until Fadinard replaces it. Fadinard goes in search of a replacement followed by the future bride, an irate father-in-law, and the wedding guests, who mistake the chase for an innovative wedding ceremony.

***Julius Caesar.* (1724)** Opera. George Frederick Handel. Libretto by Nicola Francesco Haym. Julius Caesar victoriously enters Alexandria in 48 B.C. Cornelia, wife to former ruler Pompey, and her son Sextus greet him and agree to a peaceful transition. Ptolemy, a rival for the Egyptian throne, sends Achillas with a gift for Caesar, the severed head of Pompey. All are shocked by the brutality. Also vying for the throne is Cleopatra, sister to Ptolemy. She dresses as a handmaiden and wins Caesar's heart. Eventually, Caesar wins control of Alexandria and the love of Cleopatra. Caesar crowns Cleopatra the Queen of Egypt.

Kicks, the Show Girl Musical. **(Work-in-progress)** Musical. Music by Alan Menken. Book and lyrics by Tom Eyen. Recounts the lives of four showgirls from just after World War II to the early 1960's.

La Belle Hélène. **(1864)** Operetta. Jacques Offenbach. Libretto by Henri Meilhac and Ludovic Halévy. In a competition among the goddesses, Paris, a mortal, upholds Venus as most beautiful. His reward from Venus is Helen, the most beautiful woman on earth. Unfortunately, Helen is already married to Menelaus, King of Sparta. Paris travels to see her, and they fall in love. With the help of Venus and Paris, Helen escapes and returns with Paris to Troy. Thus begins the Trojan War.

La Bohème. **(1896)** Opera. Giacomo Puccini. Libretto by Giuseppe Giacosa and Luigi Illica. Rodolfo, a poet, and Marcello, an artist, are poor but carefree Bohemians living in an attic room in Paris in the 1830's. They have no fuel, so burn instead Rodolfo's recently written five-act play. Colline and Schaunard, fellow Bohemians, persuade Marcello to go with them to the Café Momus. Rodolfo stays home to write, but there is a knock at the door. Mimi, a new neighbor, asks for a light for her candle. It is love at first sight. They decide to join the others at the cafe. Musetta, an old flame of Marcello joins them. Rodolfo's jealousy soon drives Mimi out, and Marcello and his love separate once more. The two men, mourning the loss of their loves in the cold February weather, are interrupted by a knock on the door. Musetta and a gravely ill Mimi enter. The lovers share a tearful goodbye before Mimi dies.

Lady Windermere's Fan. **(1892)** Comedy of Manners. Oscar Wilde. Late nineteenth-century England. Lady Windermere is the epitome of moral behavior and refuses to be seen with anyone of lower standards. When she discovers Lord Windermere's association with Mrs. Erlynne, a woman of questionable reputation, she decides to run away with Lord Darlington. Mrs. Erlynne learns of the plans and hurries to Darlington's apartment to stop the impetuous action. She reveals herself to be Lady Windermere's mother, who long ago made a similar rash decision. The women leave before Lord Darlington arrives, but Lady Windermere forgets her fan. The men arrive and find the fan. The innocent Lady Windermere is faced with a scandal. Mrs. Erlynne steps in to deflect the scandal, and Lady Windermere gains new understanding of "moral appearances."

Les Bouffons. **(1907)**   Comedy. Miguel Zamacoïs. To live in a castle in France in 1557 implies affluence, but the Château de Mautpré is suffering from the loss of the family fortune. The servants go unpaid, the stones fall from the walls, and the daughter of the house, Solange, never goes to social events. Two young hunters see Solange and seek to court her. The Baron de Mautpré refuses for fear they will discover the poverty of the castle. Oliver, a family friend, arranges to introduce them, along with three others, to the court as jesters. He proposes that they stay for a month; whichever one pleases Solange the most is to stay as the Court Jester. The baron agrees, and Solange finds her prince among the clowns.

Little Foxes, The. **(1939)**   Drama. Lillian Hellman. At the turn of the century in a small southern town, Benjamin and Oscar Hubbard and their sister Regina Gibbons plan to build a cotton mill. The three will do anything to satisfy their greed, including plot against Regina's husband and, finally, against each other. Set against their cruelty is Birdie, Oscar's gentle but intimidated wife, and Regina's daughter, Alexandra, who at 17 can see the greed and selfishness of her family.

Little Mary Sunshine. **(1960)**   Musical. Rick Besoyan. Spoof of the highly melodramatic old musicals and operettas. Characters include Indians, Colorado Rangers (among them a handsome captain), a bevy of silly schoolgirls, a villain, and a beautiful but in-need-of-help heroine, Mary.

Living Newspaper, The. **(1936–1939)**   Part of the Federal Theatre Project begun in 1935 to provide jobs for theater artists. Scripts centered around specific current issues, usually political in tone. Dialogue developed mainly from newspapers and speeches.

Lower Depths, The. **(1902)**   Drama. Maxim Gorki. In a dark, sordid, tenement basement a group of outcasts limp through life. There is a baron turned pimp, a prostitute, an alcoholic has-been actor, a thief, and others. Into their grim existence comes Luka, perhaps a visionary, perhaps just a glib talker. A glimmer of hope grows in the grim room before Luka disappears, as suddenly as he appeared. An argument breaks out over the truth of Luka's vision. A brawl ensues during which the landlord is killed, and the actor commits suicide.

Macbeth (c. 1606)   Tragedy. William Shakespeare. In twelfth-century Scotland Macbeth and Banquo, generals to King Duncan, are returning from battle. They meet three witches who proclaim Macbeth as "King here after" and Banquo as "begetter of kings." The lust for power, seeded by the witches and fed by Lady Macbeth, leads Macbeth to murder the king. The resulting disintegration of order and escalation of violence lead to other murders, the suicide of Lady Macbeth, and finally Macbeth's own death.

Magistrate, The. (1885)   Farce. Arthur Wing Pinero. When the Magistrate married a widow, he did not know she had conveniently subtracted five years from her age. So . . . when his new stepson at the supposed age of 14 begins to chase women, grow a mustache, and bet on horses, the father *is* a bit mystified. All is resolved — comically and quite happily.

Major Barbara. (1905)   Comedy. George Bernard Shaw. Barbara, from a wealthy and fashionable family, becomes a major in the Salvation Army. Her father, a munitions maker, feels that being poor is the greatest evil. Though they are apparently on opposite sides, the father convinces Barbara that true faith cannot be bought with bread. Between the father and daughter are her siblings, a suitor, and the mother, whose lack of understanding of the issues borders on comic.

Marriage of Figaro, The. (1784)   Comedy. Jean-Pierre de Beaumarchais. In eighteenth-century Spain Figaro and Suzanne, both servants to Count Almaviva, happily anticipate their marriage. On the eve of the wedding Figaro discovers Almaviva's plan to spend the night with an unwilling Suzanne. Figaro, Suzanne, and the Countess join forces to match wits against the powerful noble to prevent his invoking the ancient feudal privilege. Woven into the plot are a doctor, a music teacher, peasants, servants, and the flirtatious young Cherubino.

Measure for Measure. (c. 1604)   Comedy. William Shakespeare. The Duke of Vienna pretends to leave on a journey and gives orders for Angelo to act as his deputy. He actually disguises himself as a friar and stays to observe. Quick to administer the laws of morality, Angelo condemns Claudio to death for seducing a woman. He also attempts to clear the city of brothels, causing the comic appearance of Mistress Overdone, Pompey, and Lucio in protest. Isabella, a beautiful novice, pleads with Angelo for her brother's life. Angelo reveals his hypocrisy when he offers to exchange Claudio's life for her virtue. Isabella is further shocked by her brother's hints that the price is not too high for his life. The disguised duke offers a solution, and the announcement of three marriages concludes the play.

***Medea* (431 B.C.)** Tragedy. Euripides. Medea, out of love for Jason, betrays her homeland and helps him win the Golden Fleece. She returns with him to his country, where she is considered a barbarian. Jason, greedy for wealth and power, deserts Medea to marry the daughter of Creon, King of Corinth. Medea is exiled by Creon. To avenge Jason's betrayal, Medea sends poisoned gifts to the king and his daughter, killing both. In her passion for revenge she kills her own two children by Jason. In their final confrontation, Medea escapes in a dragon-drawn chariot.

***Midsummer Night's Dream, A.* (c. 1595)** Comedy. William Shakespeare. On a midsummer's night, the young lovers Lysander and Hermia escape to the enchanted woods near Athens in defiance of Hermia's father, who has declared they shall not wed. Following them is Demetrius, in love with Hermia, and Helena, in love with Demetrius. Meanwhile, Bottom and other mechanicals arrive in the woods to rehearse a play to be performed at the marriage celebration of King Theseus. In the woods, fairy king Oberon and fairy queen Titania have quarreled. For revenge, Oberon squeezes a magic juice in Titania's eyes, causing her to fall in love with the first creature she sees. This is Bottom, turned into an ass by the mischievous fairy, Puck. The magic juice is also applied to Lysander, but it is Helena, not Hermia, whom he sees first. The confusion is sorted out at dawn, and a triple marriage takes place.

***Mikado, The.* (1885)** Operetta. Gilbert and Sullivan. A love story set in the court of the Mikado of Japan. Prince Nanki-Poo flees the court to avoid marriage to the older Katisha. He loves Yum-Yum, but she is engaged to her guardian, Ko-Ko. After several crises, Nanki-Poo and Yum-Yum are united, and Ko-Ko and Katisha find love with each other.

***Misanthrope, The.* (1666)** Comedy. Molière. Alceste is fanatically against the hypocrisy of fashionable society, including gossips, fops, would-be poets, and false manners. Unfortunately, the woman he loves is a leading member of this society and most enjoys seeing men compete over her. When Célimène's hypocrisy to her lovers is exposed, Alceste is still willing to marry her, but only if she forgoes fashionable society. Célimène declines. Alceste, completely frustrated, swears by the love of solitude and departs.

Molière in Spite of Himself. **(1978)**   Drama. Michael Lessac. Adapted from *Molière* or *A Cabal of Hypocrites* by Mikhail Bulgakov. A backstage look at Molière and his company in residence at Versailles. The off-stage intrigues of the decadent court stimulate Molière to produce brilliant but dangerous on-stage masterpieces. A study of the relationship between art and power.

Mother Courage [and Her Children]. **(1939)**   Tragicomedy. Bertolt Brecht. Making a living during the Thirty Years' War is not easy for a woman. Mother Courage survives as a traveling merchant, selling to whichever side is winning. For twelve years she pushes her wagon of goods through Bavaria, Finland, Italy, Poland, and Sweden. She survives the war and the brief peace, but loses all three of her children, each dying in a heroic action. The war then begins anew, and the unsentimental, practical Mother Courage is back in business, never considering the connection between her wagon, the war, and the death of her children.

My One and Only. **(1983)**   Musical. Book by Peter Stone and Timothy S. Mayer. Music by George Gershwin. Lyrics by Ira Gershwin. (Music from *Funny Face* and other Gershwin shows.) In 1927 Captain Billy Buck Chandler's biggest dream is to be the first pilot to fly nonstop between New York and Paris — that is, until he meets Edith Herbert, star of an aquacade touring from England. The romance between the two is briefly thwarted by Edith's Russian manager, but true love prevails in the end.

Noises Off. **(1982)**   Farce. Michael Frayn. In Act I of the play within a play, the actors are rehearsing for *Noises On*, a comedy scheduled to tour the English provinces. The suffering director has all he can do to hold the actors' personalities in check while vainly trying to piece together the play. Act II shows a performance of the play — from backstage. In Act III the scene is the stage of the play, but the play's characters are soon submerged by the boiling personalities of the actors, and true chaos results.

Oedipus the King. **(430 B.C.)**   Tragedy. Sophocles. The power of fate leads Oedipus to the city of Thebes. Finding a leaderless city, he marries the widowed queen and rules. After years of plague in Thebes, Oedipus sends his messenger to the oracle, requesting a cure. The remedy is the discovery of the murderer of the late King Laius. While unraveling the mystery, Oedipus slowly realizes his identity. As a baby, he had been left to die because a prophet foretold he would one day kill his father and marry his mother. Seeing that the terrible prophecy has now been fulfilled, the queen kills herself, and Oedipus puts out his eyes.

Of Mice and Men. **(1937)** Drama. John Steinbeck. Migrant farmhands, George and Lenny, find work in California. They are an unlikely pair: George, intelligent and social, and Lenny, a giant with a child's mind and a love for stroking soft things. Their friendship is cemented by a dream of one day owning their own farm. Candy, an old farmhand, offers to pitch in his savings. The dream may soon come true, if only George and Lenny can survive this job. The boss's son, Curley, doesn't like either one of them. Lenny is provoked by Curley's wife to touch her soft hair; but when she panics, Lenny accidentally breaks her neck. In a tragic ending, George shoots Lenny to save him from a worse fate at Curley's hands.

On a Clear Day You Can See Forever. **(1965)** Musical. Book and lyrics by Alan Jay Lerner. Music by Burton Lane. A young psychiatrist treats a dizzy young woman and finds his Freudian training turned upside down. Under hypnosis his patient not only shows extraordinary powers of ESP but claims quite convincingly to have had a past life as a beautiful, willful woman in the eighteenth century. Trouble develops when the psychiatrist finds himself more attracted, and not just professionally, to "the other woman."

Othello. **(c. 1604)** Tragedy. William Shakespeare. In sixteenth-century Venice, Desdemona, daughter of a Venetian senator, falls in love with Othello the Moor. They marry against her father's wishes. Othello is called upon to defend Cyprus, and he and his bride sail immediately. Iago, ensign to Othello and recently passed over for promotion in favor of Cassio, sees the hasty marriage as an avenue for revenge. Led by a series of Iago's evil lies, Othello's jealousy soon rules his reason, and he smothers his innocent wife. Iago is finally discovered, but not in time to prevent further tragedy.

Peer Gynt. **(1867)** Epic Drama. Henrik Ibsen. After being jilted by Solveig, Peer Gynt, a rollicking rogue, carries another man's bride off into the mountains. The vengeful villagers take all his mother's belongings except her bed. Solveig travels to the mountains to tell him. Peer returns in time to see his mother briefly before she dies. He flees Norway and grows wealthy from slave trading in Morocco, but he is tricked out of his wealth by a dancing girl and her partners. Peer lands in an asylum, the result of one too many tall tales, and rules there as king. He finally returns to Norway, years later, where Solveig still waits for him.

Peter Pan. **(1954)** Music by Jule Styne and Moose Charlap. Lyrics by Carolyn Leigh. Lyrics to Styne songs by Betty Comden and Adolph Green. Based on the play by James M. Barrie. Peter Pan magically takes Wendy and her brothers to Never Never Land, where children never grow old and can eat only what they want. There they meet the Lost Boys, the fairy Tinkerbell, and the evil Captain Hook and his pirates.

Petrified Forest, The. **(1935)** Melodrama. Robert E. Sherwood. Alan Squier — disillusioned young writer, hitchhiker, and philosopher — is ready to call it quits with life. On the way to the "Petrified Forest" he stops at a diner in the Arizona desert. There he meets Gaby Maple, waitress and daughter of the owner. Gaby, restricted by her environment, wants to follow her mother, who fled to Europe long ago. Gangsters take over the outpost. In a moment of twisted heroism, Alan makes Gaby the beneficiary of his life insurance. When he is killed by the gangsters, she at last has the means to follow her dream.

Phaedra. **(1677)** Tragedy. Jean Racine. Based on Euripides' *Hippolytus.* In ancient Greece Phaedra, wife to Theseus, is cursed by the goddess Aphrodite to fall passionately in love with her stepson, Hippolytus. When the false rumor of Theseus' death reaches Phaedra, she is convinced by her old nurse, Oenone, to confess her love to Hippolytus. She does so, only to discover his revulsion of her and his love for the captive princess Aricia. Theseus returns. To cover her guilt, Phaedra is convinced again by Oenone to accuse Hippolytus of her very crimes. Theseus believes her and calls on Poseidon to kill his son. With Hippolytus' death, Phaedra is overcome with guilt. She takes poison, confesses, and dies at Theseus' feet.

Polyeucte. **(1642)** Tragedy. Pierre Corneille. In Armenia, third century A.D., Roman governor Felix of Meletena bids his daughter Pauline to marry local nobleman Polyeucte. Despite her love for the Roman soldier Severus, she complies. When Severus returns to the city, Pauline is torn between her love for him and her duty to her husband. Polyeucte decides to embrace martyrdom for his Christian beliefs and suggests that she marry Severus after his death. Pauline realizes Polyeucte's true nobility as he dies. She becomes a Christian so that, in death, they will be reunited.

Private Lives. **(1930)**   Comedy. Noel Coward. Elyot and Amanda, once married, are both honeymooning with their new spouses. Accidentally arriving at the same hotel and sharing the same balcony, they meet and the old passion flares. Elyot and Amanda desert their new spouses and run off to Paris. Soon the romance wears off and a wild fight ensues. Sybil and Victor, the jilted spouses, arrive. First the women unite against the men, but soon Sybil and Victor are so interested in fighting each other that they forget Elyot and Amanda. The latter recognize this as a sign of true love and, leaving Victor and Sybil to discover this for themselves, run off together once again.

Pygmalion. **(1912)**   Comedy. George Bernard Shaw. Professor Henry Higgins boasts he can train even an ignorant Cockney flower girl in speech and successfully present her to high society. He is successful indeed, as Eliza Doolittle is acclaimed as a duchess, but Higgins has yet his own lesson to learn about human potential and sensitivity.

Resistible Rise of Arturo Ui, The. **(1941)**   Drama. Bertolt Brecht. Draws a humorous but frightening parallel between the rise and reign of Hitler in Germany and the crime lords of Chicago.

Resurrection, The. **(15th century)**   Mystery Play. Episode from the *Towneley Cycle* of English mystery plays. The three Marys journey to the tomb of Jesus on Easter Morning and are greeted by angels and the risen Christ.

Romeo and Juliet. **(c. 1595)**   Tragedy. William Shakespeare. The love between Romeo and Juliet is as youthful and innocent as it is passionate. Shakespeare's well-known "star-cross'd" lovers are sacrificed by the senseless feuding of their own families and by a series of devastating coincidences and impetuous decisions. Set in fifteenth-century Italy, the tragedy is spiced with comic scenes featuring the foolish nurse and the witty Mercutio.

Romeo and Juliet.   Ballet. Popular versions by Sergei Prokofiev (c. 1940) and Tchaikovsky (1893). Based on the play by Shakespeare.

***Room for One Woman.* (1978)**   One-act drama. Samuel Shem. Three women, age 75, 60, and 40, in a seemingly casual conversation, reveal major issues of growing old and fulfilling obligations to husbands and children.

***Ross.* (1960)**   Drama. Terence Rattigan. Lawrence of Arabia, as Aircraftman Ross, seeks anonymity in the R.A.F. Threatened with exposure, Ross falls ill with a malaria fever. He relives in delirium his experiences in the 1916–1918 desert campaigns, seeking the truth about himself—legend, hero, or charlatan?

***Royal Family, The.* (1927)**   Comedy. George S. Kaufman and Edna Ferber. Fanny Cavendish, at 70, is planning her acting tour for the next season. She also reigns over the three generations of the theatrical Cavendish family. There is brother Herbert Dean, past his prime but not willing to admit it; Julie, Fannie's daughter, in the prime of her Broadway career; Tony, the grandson, whose magnetic charm forces him to spend most of his time dodging women. Last, there is granddaughter Gwen, who is just beginning a promising ingenue career when she goes against the family tradition, marries a nonactor, and quits the stage.

***School for Scandal, The.* (1777)**   Comedy. Richard Sheridan. Charles Surface and his brother Joseph both want to marry Maria, ward of Sir Peter Teazle — the former for love and the latter for money. Next door Lady Sneerwell and her school of gossips will do their best to ruin anyone's happiness. Since Sneerwell desires Charles for herself, she attempts to ruin his reputation and improve Joseph's so that Sir Teazle will choose Joseph for Maria. Maria, however, loves Charles. In the meanwhile, Lady Teazle has begun lessons at the school for scandal, making Sir Teazle's life quite difficult. In the end, goodness and true love prevail.

***She Stoops to Conquer.* (1773)**   Comedy of Manners. Oliver Goldsmith. Young Marlow and Kate Hardcastle, although they have never met, have been matched by their parents. Directed to Kate's house by her prankster stepbrother, Young Marlow is under the impression he is entering an inn. This mistake is soon discovered by Kate, but she uses it to her advantage. Mistaken identities and disguises lead to numerous comic scenes. All is resolved happily at the end.

***Skin of Our Teeth, The.* (1942)**   Comic Fantasy. Thornton Wilder. With obvious liberties taken in time and meaning, Wilder creates the Stone Age Antrobus family. Mr. Antrobus' claims to fame include the invention of the wheel and his position as judge for a beauty contest. The comedy takes a serious turn as the elder Antrobus attempts to teach the youngsters the accumulated knowledge of the world before the Ice Age descends.

***Streets of New York, The.* (1857)** Melodrama. Dion Boucicault. The greedy Gideon Bloodgood stole the family fortune from a sea captain's widow and children. Now, 20 years later, the captain's family is having harder times than ever. Badger, clerk to Bloodgood, knows of the crime and first attempts blackmail but later reveals all to the family. Eventually, the daughter is united with her love, the family fortune is returned, and Bloodgood is punished.

***Sugar Babies.* (1979)** Musical. Ralph G. Allen. Conceived by Ralph G. Allen and Harry Rigby. Music by Jimmy McHugh. Lyrics by Dorothy Fields and Al Dubin. Modern musical and comic skits based on the traditional vaudeville and burlesque.

***Summer and Smoke.* (1948)** Drama. Tennessee Williams. It is 1916 in the small town of Glorious Hill, Mississippi. Alma is the puritanical daughter of the town minister; John, the *un*puritanical town doctor. The two love each other, but that love is tested and ultimately defeated by their divergent attitudes toward life.

***Taming of the Shrew, The.* (c. 1594)** Comedy. William Shakespeare. A play within a play: the prologue concerns a drunken tinker named Christopher Sly and a mischievous Lord. The main action: Baptista of Padua refuses to allow his younger daughter, Bianca, to marry until the elder, Katherine the Shrew, has wed. While Bianca has many suitors, none dare approach Kate — until Petruchio of Verona arrives. Their tumultuous courtship is offset by the flowery courting of Bianca by her suitors. The romantic Lucentio, disguised as a schoolmaster, wins Bianca. But in the end, Petruchio proves to have the most devoted and loving wife.

***Tannhäuser.* (1845)** Opera. Richard Wagner. In the thirteenth century at the court of Venus, Heinrich Tannhäuser, German knight, celebrates the pleasures of love with the goddess Venus. He tires of the pagan rites and returns to the court of Landgrave Hermann, ruler of Thuringia, at whose court he once stayed. Hermann persuades him to return. There Hermann's daughter Elizabeth reveals her love for Heinrich. In a rash moment, however, Heinrich dishonors himself by advocating carnal love. He is forced to make a pilgrimage to Rome for absolution before he can marry Elizabeth. Brokenhearted, Elizabeth awaits his return. When the pilgrims return without Heinrich, she dies. He returns soon after, unpardoned. Upon learning of Elizabeth's death, he is completely broken. At that moment news arrives that the Pope's staff has burst into bloom, a sign that God has forgiven Heinrich.

***Tempest.* (c. 1611)**   Comedy. William Shakespeare. Prospero, more interested in magic than in his dukedom, was banished from Milan by his brother, Antonio. Prospero and his daughter, Miranda, found a new home on an enchanted island. There they are served by the spirit Ariel, and Caliban, the half-human son of the witch Sycorax. Now, twelve years later, Prospero creates a tempest to shipwreck his brother and other enemies onto his island. But his desire for revenge is softened, and instead he finds a match for his daughter and secures a promise of the return of his dukedom. He renounces magic, and they all return to Italy.

***Three Musketeers, The.* (1921)**   Drama. Adapted by Charles Rice from the novel by Alexandre Dumas. One of several versions by different playwrights chronicling the romantic, daring, swashbuckling adventures of D'Artagnan, Athos, Porthos, and Aramis as they fight for king and country.

***Threepenny Opera, The.* (1928)**   Comic Opera. Music by Kurt Weill. Bertolt Brecht. Polly Peachum falls in love with Macheath, the notorious gang leader known as Mack the Knife. They secretly wed, but when Polly's parents learn of it, they insist on a divorce. Divorce rejected, the Peachums decide to turn Mack in to the police. Polly warns him, and he escapes in time to hide at Jenny's brothel. But Mrs. Peachum has paid Jenny to inform, so Mack is caught. Polly and Lucy, also married to Mack, visit him in jail. The two women fight and, after Mrs. Peachum takes Polly away, Mack declares his true love for Lucy. The end looks near for Mack, but just before his hanging, the Queen makes Mack a nobleman and gives him a castle.

***Twelfth Night.* (c. 1600)**   Comedy. William Shakespeare. In a series of misadventures, Viola and twin brother Sebastian are shipwrecked. Thinking her brother dead, young Viola disguises herself as a man and, as Cesario, becomes page to Orsino, Duke of Illyria. She falls in love with the duke, but he is in love with his neighbor, Olivia. The duke engages Cesario to intercede in his behalf, but Olivia falls in love with the disguised Viola. Meanwhile, Sebastian appears, and Olivia, thinking he is Cesario, proposes marriage. Sebastian accepts, and the duke discovers his love for the revealed Viola. Subplot allows for several farcical characters: the drunken Sir Toby Belch, Sir Andrew Aguecheck, Feste the Fool, and foolish Malvolio.

Uncle Tom's Cabin. **(1852)** Melodrama. George L. Aiken. Adapted from the novel by Harriet Beecher Stowe. Sympathetic exposure of the conditions suffered by pre-Civil War black slaves. Main characters include the kindly but abused Uncle Tom, and Eliza and George, who flee to Canada with their child. The structure is episodic, traveling from a fashionable plantation, to Ohio, Vermont, St. Claire, and New Orleans with considerable emphasis on spectacle.

Vagabond Stars. **(1978)** Musical. Adapted by Nahma Sandrow. A series of musical vignettes about Jewish immigrants to America based on authentic material of the Yiddish Theater.

Volpone. **(1605)** Comedy. Ben Jonson. The lush Venetian atmosphere is tarnished by greed. Volpone, citizen of Venice, pretends to be mortally ill. He tricks his friends into pledging their wealth to him in the hope of inheriting his estate — one even throws his wife into the bargain! In the end Volpone's greed is his undoing.

Waiting for Godot. **(1952)** Tragicomedy. Samuel Beckett. In a bleak, isolated spot, Vladimir and Estragon wait for Godot. The two have never met Godot, nor do they know what will happen once they do. To pass the time they fight, make up, recite poetry, complain, sleep, do exercises, play-act, and wonder who Godot is. They are visited by the pompous Pozzo and his slave Lucky, who has been reduced to a mechanical doll. A messenger finally comes to tell them that Godot will not be coming today, but surely tomorrow.

Weavers, The. **(1893)** Drama. Gerhart Hauptmann. A group of impoverished Silesian (Eastern European) weavers revolt against their oppressors. Led by Becker, a young weaver, and Jaegar, a reserve officer, they riot and terrorize the manufacturers in an attempt to win fair wages.

Wiz, The. **(1975)** Musical. Book by William F. Brown. Music and lyrics by Charlie Smalls. Based on the *The Wonderful Wizard of Oz* by L. Frank Baum. A lively rendition of Dorothy's adventures in Oz, combining a mixture of rock, gospel, and soul music.

Women, The. **(1936)** Drama. Clare Boothe Luce. Mrs. Mary Haines is a member of fashionable society. Of her peers, she seems the most content and least artificial. When she learns that her husband is having an affair with a "blonde floosie," her world is turned upside down. Her mother suggests that she should ignore the affair and take a long vacation. Her friends are more interested in spreading malicious gossip than in extending true concern. So . . . Mary Haines does the unthinkable. She insists on divorce, and her journey to self-discovery begins.

Woyzeck. **(1836)** Tragedy. Georg Büchner. Leipzig, Germany, in 1834. Woyzeck is a fusilier, used and abused as an orderly by his captain and as a guinea pig by a doctor and his medical students. He loves Maria, mother to his child, but she is seduced by a major and deserts him. Unable to rise above his low station and overwhelmed with pain and passion, he kills Maria and then himself.

You Can't Take It with You. **(1936)** Comedy. George S. Kaufman and Moss Hart. The Vanderhof-Sycamores are quite content. They have just enough money to get by on and can easily entertain themselves. Grandpa collects live snakes and stamps, and argues with the tax collector. Father Paul manufactures fireworks. Mother Penny writes plays because a guest once left a typewriter behind. Essie dances and makes candy; her husband, Ed, plays the xylophone and runs a printing press. The conflict arises when Alice, the second daughter, falls in love with Tony Kirby. Mr. Kirby, business tycoon and millionaire, and Mrs. Kirby visit the Sycamore residence and can't quite believe their eyes. Lots of farcical scenes before the conversion of Mr. Kirby unites Alice and Tony in a marriage promise.

You're a Good Man, Charlie Brown. **(1967)** Musical. Book by John Gordon. Music, lyrics, and adaptation by Clark Gesner. Based on the comic strip by Charles Schulz. Vignettes from the life of Charlie Brown. Poor Charlie Brown is painted by his friends and dog, Snoopy, as simple, dull, clumsy, and sure to fail. But Lucy, Linus, Patty, Schroeder, and even Snoopy have to admit life wouldn't be the same without him.

Bibliography

UNDERSTANDING DRAMA

Corrigan, Robert W., ed. *The Forms of Drama*. Boston: Houghton Mifflin, 1972.

Hodge, Francis. *Play Directing Analysis Communication and Style*. Englewood Cliffs, N.J.: Prentice-Hall, 1971.

Laver, James. *Costume in the Theatre*. New York: Hill and Wang, 1964.

Molinari, Cesare. *Theatre Through the Ages*. New York: McGraw-Hill, 1975.

Nicoll, Allardyce. *Masks, Mimes and Miracles*. New York: Harcourt, Brace, 1931.

Russell, Douglas A. *Period Style for the Theatre*. Boston: Allyn & Bacon, 1980.

RESEARCH

Anthony, Pegaret, and Arnold, Janet. *Costume: A General Bibliography*. London: Costume Society, Victoria and Albert Museum; 1977.

Arnold, Janet. *A Handbook of Costume*. New York: S. G. Phillips, 1974.

Baines, Barbara Burman. *Fashion Revivals from the Elizabethan Age to the Present Day*. London: B.T. Batsford, Ltd., 1981.

Barton, Lucy. *Historic Costume for the Stage*, new ed. Boston: Walter H. Baker Co., 1961.

Batterberry, Michael, and Batterberry, Ariane. *Mirror, Mirror: A Social History of Fashion*. New York: Holt, Rinehart and Winston, 1977.

Blum, Stella, ed. *Ackermann's Costume Plates: Women's Fashions in England, 1818–1828*, New York: Dover, 1978.

Blum, Stella, ed. *Victorian Fashions and Costumes from Harpers Bazaar, 1867–1898*. New York: Dover, 1974.

Boehn, Max von. *Modes and Manners*, 4 vols. 1932. Translated by Joan Josua, Reprint (4 vols. in 2). New York: Benjamin Blom, Inc., 1971.

Boehn, Max von. *Ornaments*. New York: Benjamin Blom, Inc., 1970.

Boucher, Francois. *20,000 Years of Fashion*. New York: Harry N. Abrams, 1967.

Braum and Schneider Publishers. *Historic Costume in Pictures*. Reprint New York: Dover, 1975.

Brooke, Iris. *Costume in Greek Classic Drama*. New York: Theatre Arts Books, 1962.

Bruhn, Wolfgang, and Tilke, Max. *Pictorial History of Costume*. New York: Hastings House Publishers, 1973.

Buck, Anne M. *Victorian Costume and Costume Accessories*. New York: Universe Books, 1970.

Cobban, Alfred, et al. *The Eighteenth Century: Europe in the Age of Enlightenment*. New York: McGraw-Hill, 1969.

Colle, Doriece. *Collars Stocks Cravats: A History and Costume Dating Guide to Civilian Men's Neckpieces 1655–1900*. Emmaus, Pa.: Rodale Press, 1972.

Contini, Mila. *Fashion: From Ancient Egypt to the Present Day*. New York: Odyssey Press, 1965.

Cumming, Valerie. *Gloves: The Costume Accessories Series*. London: The Anchor Press Ltd., 1982.

Cunnington, C.W.; Cunnington, P.E.; and Beard, Charles. *A Dictionary of English Costume*. London: Adam & Charles Black, 1960.

Cunnington, C.W., and Cunnington, Phillis E. *Handbook of English Costume in the 16th Century*. 2nd ed. Boston: Plays, Inc., 1970.

Cunnington, C.W., and Cunnington, Phillis E. *The History of Underclothes*. London: Michael Joseph, 1951.

Cunnington, Phillis, and Lucas, Catherine. *Occupational Costume in England*. London: Adams & Charles Black, 1976.

Davenport, Milia. *The Book of Costume*. New York: Crown, 1948.

Delord, Robert. *Life in the Middle Ages*, Louson, France: translated by Robert Allen. New York: Crown Publishers, 1973.

Ducharte, Pierre Louis. *The Italian Comedy*. New York: Dover, 1966.

Earle, Alice Morse. *Two Centuries of Costume in America 1620–1820*. 2 vols. Rutland, Vt.: Charles E. Tuttle Co., 1971.

Ewing, Elizabeth. *History of 20th Century Fashion*. New York: Scribner, 1975.

Gernsheim, Alison. *Victorian and Edwardian Fashion*. New York: Dover, 1981.

Ghorsline, Douglas. *What People Wore*. New York: Viking Press, 1952.

Gibbs-Smith, Charles H. *The Fashionable Lady in the 19th Century*. London: Victoria and Albert Museum, Her Majesty's Stationery Office, 1960.

Gowing, Sir Lawrence, gen. ed. *Encyclopedia of Visual Art Vol. Two: A Biographical Dictionary of Artists*. Englewood Cliffs, N.J.: Prentice-Hall, 1983, reprint 1985.

Grun, Bernard. *The Timetables of History: A Horizontal Linkage of People and Events*. New York: Simon and Schuster, Touchstone Edition, 1982.

Hall, Maggie. *Smocks*. Aylesbury, England: Shire Publications Ltd., 1979.

Hansen, Henny Harald. *Costumes and Style*. New York: Dutton, 1956.

Hope, Thomas. *Costumes of the Greeks and Romans*. New York: Dover, 1962.

Jones, Edgar R. *Those Were the Good Old Days*. New York: Simon and Schuster, Fireside Book, 1959.

Kemper, Rachel H. *A History of Costume*. New York: Newsweek Books, 1979.

Kesler, Jackson. *Theatrical Costume: A Guide to Information Sources*. Detroit: Gale Research Co., 1979.

Kidwell, Claudia B., and Christman, Margaret C. *Suiting Everyone: The Democratization of Clothing in America*. Washington, D.C.: Smithsonian Institution Press, The National Museum of History and Technology, 1974.

Klaus, Carl H.; Gilbert, Miriam; and Field, Bradford S., Jr. *Stages of Drama: Classical to Contemporary Masterpieces of the Theatre*. New York: Wiley, 1981.

Kohler, Carl. *A History of Costume*. New York: Dover, 1963.

Kybalova, Ludmila; Herbenova, Olga; and Lamarova, Milena. *The Pictorial Encyclopedia of Fashion*. Translated by Claudia Rosoux. London: Paul Hamlyn Publishing Co., 1970.

Lansdell, Avil. *Occupational Costume*. Aylesbury, England: Shire Publications Ltd., 1977.

Larkin, David, ed. *The Paintings of Carl Larsson*. London and New York: Peacock Press/Bantam Books, 1976.

Laver, James. *A Concise History of Costume and Fashion*. New York; Scribner, 1974.

Laver, James. *17th and 18th Century Costume*. London: His Majesty's Stationery Office, 1951.

Laver, James. *Costume Through the Ages*. Illustrated by Erhard Klepper. New York: Simon and Schuster, 1963.

Levitt, Sarah. *Victorians Unbuttoned*. Winchester, Mass.: Allen & Unwin, 1986.

Lucy-Smith, Edward, and Dars, Celestine. *How the Rich Lived: The Painter as Witness*. New York and London: The Paddington Press, Ltd., 1976.

Mackie, Bob, and Gerry Bremer. *Dressing for Glamour*. New York: A & W Publishers, Inc., 1979.

Meredith, Ray. *Mr. Lincoln's Camera Man: Matthew B. Brady*. New York: Dover, 1974.

Metropolitan Museum of Art. *The Imperial Style: Fashions of the Hapsburg Era*. New York: Metropolitan Museum of Art, 1980.

Meyer, Franz Sales. *Handbook of Ornament*. New York: Dover, 1956.

Mirken, Alen, ed. *The 1927 Edition of the Sears, Roebuck Catalogue*. New York: Crown, Bounty Books, 1970.

Oakes, Alma, and Hill, Margot Hamilton. *Rural Costume: Its Origin and Development in Western Europe and the British Isles*. New York: Van Nostrand Reinhold, 1970.

Pakula, Marvin H., and Ogden, Henry Alexander. *Uniforms of the United States Army*. New York: A.S. Barnes & Co., Inc., 1960.

Payne, Blanche. *History of Costume*. New York: Harper & Row, 1965.

Pistolese, Rosana, and Horsting, Ruth. History of Fashions. New York: Wiley, 1970.

Russell, Douglas A. *Costume History and Style*. Englewood Cliffs, N.J.: Prentice-Hall, 1983.

Schroeder, Joseph J., Jr., ed. *1880–1920, The Wonderful World of Ladies Fashion*. Northfield, Ill.: Digest Books, Inc., 1971.

Speltz, Alexander. *Styles of Ornament*. (Translated and revised by David O'Connor. New York: Grosset and Dunlap, n.d.

Swann, June. *Shores: The Costume Accessories Series*. London: B.T. Batsford Ltd., 1982.

Taylor, Lou. *Mourning Dress: A Costume and Social History*. London: Allen & Unwin, 1983.

Tilke, Max. *Costume Patterns and Designs: A Survey of Costume Patterns and Designs of all Periods and Nations from Antiquity to Modern Times*. New York: Hastings House, 1974.

Tozer, Jane, and Levitt, Sarah. *Fabric of Society: A Century of People and Their Clothes*. Manchester, England: Laura Ashley Limited, 1983.

Vreeland, Diana, ed. *The Imperial Style: Fashions of the Hapsburg Era*. New York: The Metropolitan Museum of Art, 1980.

Waller, Jane, ed. *A Man's Book: Fashion in the Man's World in the 20's and 30's*. London: Gerald Duckworth & Co. Ltd., 1977.

Warwick, Edward; Pitz, Henry C.; and Wyckoff, Alexander. *Early American Dress*. New York: Benjamin Blom, Inc., 1965.

Waugh, Norah. *Corsets and Crinolines*. New York: Theatre Art Books, 1970.

Wilcox, R. Turner. *The Mode in Footwear*. New York: Scribner, 1984.

Wilcox, R. Turner. *The Mode in Hats and Headdress*. New York: Scribner, 1959.

Willett, C., and Cunnington, Phillis. *The History of Underclothes*. London: Faber and Faber Limited, 1951.

Wilson, Eunice, *A History of Shoe Fashion*. New York: Theatre Art Books, 1974.

ELEMENTS OF DESIGN

Bell, Ione; Hess, Haren M.; and Matison, Jim R. *Art As You See It: A Self-Teaching Guide*. New York: Wiley, 1979.

Birren, Faber. *Creative Color: A Dynamic Approach for Artists and Designers*. New York: Van Nostrand Reinhold, 1961.

David, Merian L. *Visual Design in Dress*. Englewood Cliffs, N.J.: Prentice-Hall, 1980.

Itten, Johannes. *The Art of Color*. New York: Reinhold Publishing Corp., 1961.

DEVELOPING THE COSTUME

Binder, Pearl. *Dressing Up, Dressing Down*. Winchester, Mass.: Allen & Unwin, 1986.

Ingham, Rosemary, and Covey, Liz. *The Costume Designer's Handbook: A Complete Guide for Amateur and Professional Costume Designers*. Englewood Cliffs, N.J.: Prentice-Hall, 1983.

Lurie, Alison. *The Language of Clothes*. New York: Random House, 1981.

Motley. *Designing and Making Stage Costumes*. New York: Watson-Guptill, 1974.

Russell, Douglas A. *Stage Costume Design: Theory, Techniques and Style.* Englewood Cliffs, N.J.: Prentice-Hall, 1973.

Strong, Roy et al. *Designing for the Dancer.* London: Elron Press, 1981.

DRAWING AND RENDERING

Edwards, Betty. *Drawing on the Right Side of the Brain.* Los Angeles: J.P. Tarcher, Inc., 1979.

Ireland, Patrick John. *Fashion Design Drawing.* New York: Wiley, Halsted Press, 1970.

Nicolaides, Kimon. *The Natural Way to Draw.* Boston: Houghton Mifflin, 1941.

Ruby, Erik A. *The Human Figure: A Photographic Reference for Artists.* New York: Van Nostrand Reinhold, 1974.

Sloane, Eunice. *Illustrating Fashion*, rev. ed. New York: Harper & Row, 1977.

FABRICS

Dryden, Deborah M. *Fabric Painting and Dyeing for the Theatre.* New York: Drama Book Publishers, 1982.

Kafka, Francis, J. *The Hand Decoration of Fabrics: Batik, Stenciling, Silk Screen, Block Printing, Tie Dyeing.* New York: Dover, 1959.

Lyle, Dorothy Siegert. *Modern Textiles*, 2nd ed. New York: Wiley, 1976.

Wingate, Dr. Isabel B. *Fairchild's Dictionary of Textiles*, 6th ed. New York: Scribner, 1975.

GETTING THE SHOW TOGETHER

Arnold, Janet. *Patterns of Fashion 1 c. 1600–1860, English Women's Dresses and Their Construction.* New York: Drama Book Specialists, 1977.

Arnold, Janet. *Patterns of Fashion 2 c. 1860–1940, English Women's Dresses and Their Construction.* New York: Drama Book Specialists, 1977.

Association of Theatrical Artists and Craftspeople. *The New York Theatrical Sourcebook.* New York: Broadway Press, 1986.

Croonborg, Frederick T. *The Blue Book of Men's Tailoring.* New York: Van Nostrand Reinhold, 1977.

Dreher, Denise. *From the Neck Up, An Illustrated Guide to Hatmaking*. Minneapolis: Madhatter Press, 1981.

Edson, Doris, and Barton, Lucy. *Period Patterns*. Boston: Walter H. Baker Co., 1942.

G.P. & J. Baker, Ltd. *From East to West: Textiles from G.P. & J. Baker*, London, 1984.

Folke, Ann, and Harden, Richard. *Theatrical Design and Production*. Lincolnwood, Ill.: National Textbook Company, VGM Career Horizons Division 1984.

Hill, Margot Hamilton, and Bucknell, Peter A. *The Evolution of Fashion: Pattern and Cut from 1066–1930*. New York: Drama Book Specialists, 1968.

Ingham, Rosemary, and Covey, Elizabeth. *The Costumer's Handbook*. Englewood Cliffs, N.J.: Prentice-Hall, 1980.

Jaffe, Hilde, and Relis, Nurie. *Draping for Fashion Design*. Reston: Reston Publishing 1973.

Kopp, Ernestine; Rolfo, Victoria; and Zelin, Beatrice. *Designing Apparel Through the Flat Pattern*. New York: Fairchild Publications, Inc., 1971.

Lawson, Joan, and Revitt, Peter. *Dressing for the Ballet*. London: Adam & Charles Black, 1958.

Motley. *Designing and Making Stage Costumes*. London: Studio Vista, 1965.

Moulton, Bertha. *Garment Cutting and Tailoring for Students*, rev. ed. New York: Theatre Arts Books, 1968.

Reader's Digest. *Complete Guide to Sewing*. Pleasantville, N.Y.: The Reader's Digest Association, 1976.

Tilke, Max. *Costume Patterns and Designs*. New York: Praeger, 1967.

Vogue, *The Vogue Sewing Book*. New York: Vogue Patterns, 1981.

Waugh, Norah. *The Cut of Men's Clothes 1600–1900*. New York: Theatre Arts Books, 1964.

Waugh, Norah. *The Cut of Women's Clothes 1600–1930*. New York: Theatre Arts Books, 1968.

PERIODICALS AND NEWSLETTERS

Bias Line/CosTume Tech
      Bobby Ann Loper, Editor
      115 South Manhattan
      Tampa, FL 33609

Flat Pattern Newsletter
    Mari Decuir, Editor
    902 Tyson Street
    Knoxville, TN 37917
Theater Crafts
    P.O. Box 630
    Holmes, PA 19043–0630.

COSTUME SOCIETIES

Societies interested in the study of costume and its preservation.

The Costume Society
    Mrs. T.A. Heathcote, Membership Secretary
    Cheyne Cottage
    Birch Drive
    Hawley
    Camberley, Surrey, England
The Costume Society of America
    330 West 42nd Street, Suite 1702
    New York, NY 110036
The Costume Society of Ontario
    P.O. Box 2044
    Bramalea, Ontario, Canada L6T 353
The Costume Society of Scotland
    Mrs. E.S. Melville, Hon. Treasurer
    24 Esplanade Terrace
    Edinburgh, Scotland EH15 2ES
United States Institute for Theatre Technology (USITT)
    1501 Broadway, Suite 1408
    New York, NY 10036
    A professional society of scenographers, designers, and tech-
        nicians for theater, opera, dance, television, movies, edu-
        cators, manufacturers.

UNIONS AND GUILDS

Actors' Equity Association
    165 West 46th Street
    New York, NY 10036
    The union for actors and stage managers in legitimate theater.

Association of Theatrical Artists and Craftspeople (ATAC)
    1742 Second Avenue, Suite 3102
    New York, NY 10128
    A professional trade association for craftspeople in theatrical
        production fields.
Theatrical Wardrobe Attendants Union Local 764
    1501 Broadway
    New York, NY 10036
United Scenic Artists (USA) Local 829
    575 Eighth Avenue, Third floor
    New York, NY 10018
    The union representing set, costume, and lighting designers,
        scenic artists, craftspeople, mural artists, diorama, model
        and display makers. Entrance by examination.

Index

*Entries and pages in boldface type indicate definition of the term.